Anglo-Saxon England 18

Her mon mæg giet gesion hiora swæð

ANGLO-SAXON ENGLAND

18

Edited by
PETER CLEMOES
University of Cambridge

SIMON KEYNES
University of Cambridge

MICHAEL LAPIDGE
University of Cambridge

PETER BAKER
Emory University

MARTIN BIDDLE
University of Oxford

DANIEL CALDER
University of California, Los Angeles

ROBERT DESHMAN
University of Toronto

KLAUS DIETZ
Freie Universität Berlin

ROBERTA FRANK
University of Toronto

HELMUT GNEUSS
Universität München

MALCOLM GODDEN
University of Oxford

FRED ROBINSON
Yale University

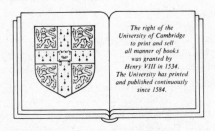

*The right of the
University of Cambridge
to print and sell
all manner of books
was granted by
Henry VIII in 1534.
The University has printed
and published continuously
since 1584.*

CAMBRIDGE UNIVERSITY PRESS
Cambridge
New York   Port Chester   Melbourne   Sydney

Published by the Press Syndicate of the University of Cambridge
The Pitt Building, Trumpington Street, Cambridge CB2 1RP
40 West 20th Street, New York, NY 10011, USA
10 Stamford Road, Oakleigh, Melbourne 3166, Australia

First published 1989

Typeset by
Servis Filmsetting Ltd
Manchester

Printed in Great Britain by
The Camelot Press
Southampton

British Library Cataloguing in Publication Data
Anglo-Saxon England
1972–
1. England to 1066
942.01
ISBN 0 521 38881 3
ISSN 0263-6751

COPYING

SUBSCRIPTIONS: Anglo-Saxon England (ISSN 0263-6751) is an annual journal. The subscription price (including postage) of volume 18 is £41 for UK institutions and £44 elsewhere (US$79 in USA and Canada), £31 (US$50 in USA and Canada) for individuals ordering direct from the Press and certifying that the annual is for their personal use. Copies may be sent airmail where applicable for £7 extra (orders to Cambridge only - dollar subscription price *includes* air delivery to North America) Orders, which must be accompanied by payment, may be sent to a bookseller, subscription agent, or direct to the publishers: Cambridge University Press, The Edinburgh Building, Shaftesbury Road, Cambridge CB2 2RU. Orders from the USA or Canada should be sent to Cambridge University Press, 40 West 20th Street, New York, NY 10011, USA.

Back volumes. Volumes 1–16 £32.00 (US$81.00 US and Canada) each available from Cambridge or the American Branch of Cambridge University Press.

Contents

*Abbreviations listed before the bibliography (pp. 245–7) are used throughout the volume
without other explanation*

Illustrations

ACKNOWLEDGEMENTS

By permission of the Trustees of the British Museum the design on the cover is taken from the obverse of a silver penny issued to celebrate King Alfred's occupation and fortification of London in 886

Permission to publish photographs has been granted by Professor T. Takamiya (pls. I and II), and the Trustees of the British Library (pls. III and IV)

Material should be submitted to the editor most convenient regionally, with these exceptions: an article should be sent to Martin Biddle if concerned with archaeology, to Robert Deshman if concerned with art history, to Simon Keynes if concerned with history, numismatics or onomastics, and to Michael Lapidge if concerned with Anglo-Latin or palaeography. Whenever a contribution is sent from abroad it should be accompanied by international coupons to cover the cost of return postage. A potential contributor is asked to get in touch with the editor concerned as early as possible to obtain a copy of the style sheet and to have any necessary discussion. Articles must be in English.

The editors' addresses are:

Professor P. S. Baker, Department of English, Emory University, Atlanta, Georgia 30322 (USA)

Mr M. Biddle, Christ Church, Oxford OX1 1DP (England)

Professor D. G. Calder, Department of English, University of California Los Angeles, Los Angeles, California 90024 (USA)

Professor R. Deshman, Graduate Department of History of Art, University of Toronto, Toronto, Ontario M5S 1A1 (Canada)

Professor K. Dietz, Institut für Englische Philologie, Freie Universität Berlin, Gosslerstrasse 2–4, 1000 Berlin 33 (Germany)

Professor R. Frank, Centre for Medieval Studies, University of Toronto, Toronto, Ontario M5S 1A1 (Canada)

Professor H. Gneuss, Institut für Englische Philologie, Universität München, 8000 München 40, Schellingstrasse 3 (Germany)

Dr M. R. Godden, Exeter College, Oxford OX1 3DP (England)

Dr S. D. Keynes, Trinity College, Cambridge CB2 1TQ (England)

Dr M. Lapidge, Department of Anglo-Saxon, Norse and Celtic, Faculty of English, University of Cambridge, 9 West Rd, Cambridge CB3 9DP (England)

Professor F. C. Robinson, Department of English, Yale University, New Haven, Connecticut 06520 (USA)

Lincoln and the Anglo-Saxon see of Lindsey

STEVEN BASSETT

It is by no means universally agreed that Lindsey was ever a kingdom or had kings. Stenton, in what is still the most thorough discussion of Lindsey, expressed his doubts on the matter but then dismissed them; there are other scholars who retain theirs.[1] Of those listed, for example, in the supposedly royal genealogy (*not* a regnal list) of Lindsey,[2] none apart from the last named, Aldfrith, is known to have been a king; some of them may indeed have ruled, but Lindsey would be unique if power had always been transmitted by direct royal primogeniture. Certainly our almost total ignorance of Lindsey's history is a considerable obstacle to viewing it as a fully developed kingdom; but that absence of evidence is no doubt largely due to its early subordination to Northumbria and Mercia by turns. Bede's description of it, whatever else he neglected to tell us, as a *prouincia* and its meriting a bishop both point to the conclusion that Lindsey was indeed a kingdom,[3] but one of those which succumbed early on to aggrandizing neighbours.[4]

THE KINGDOM AND BISHOPS OF LINDSEY

How the kingdom of Lindsey came into existence, and what (if anything) it owed to late Roman administrative geography and military dispositions in its area,[5] is unknown. Something useful can, however, be said about its extent. The later medieval and modern administrative region of Lindsey with its three

---

[1] F.M. Stenton, 'Lindsey and its Kings', *Preparatory to Anglo-Saxon England*, ed. D.M. Stenton (Oxford, 1970), pp. 127–35, at 127. Several colleagues have expressed their doubts to me about Lindsey's ever having had the status of a kingdom.

[2] D. Dumville, 'The Anglian Collection of Royal Genealogies and Regnal Lists', *ASE* 5 (1976), 23–50, at 31, 33 and 37.

[3] Bede's *Historia Ecclesiastica* [hereafter *HE*]; see below, n. 45. This source will be quoted subsequently (with page refs.) from *Bede's Ecclesiastical History of the English People*, ed. B. Colgrave and R.A.B. Mynors (Oxford, 1969). The see existed from 678 to *c.* 1011: *Handbook of British Chronology*, 3rd ed., ed. E.B. Fryde, D.E. Greenway, S. Porter and I. Roy (London, 1986), p. 219.

[4] For further discussion see my recent paper 'In Search of the Origins of Anglo-Saxon Kingdoms' in *The Origins of Anglo-Saxon Kingdoms*, ed. S.R. Bassett (Leicester, 1989), pp. 3–27.

[5] B. Eagles, 'Lindsey' in *Origins of Anglo-Saxon Kingdoms*, ed. Bassett, pp. 202–12, at 205–6.

ridings, which can be mapped first in the early twelfth century, had its southern limit on Fossdyke and the River Witham. It looks to be an anciently established territory, probably of pre-Danish origin.[6] For that reason it is normally thought to have been of the same extent as the pre-existing kingdom and diocese of Lindsey. But this notion runs contrary to both archaeological and other evidence of Lincoln's continuing importance in the post-Roman period,[7] and so ignores the strong likelihood that the town (which lies on the Witham at its confluence with Fossdyke) retained control of a substantial region to the south of itself – at a minimum, perhaps, the area between the Trent and the Slea as far south as Ancaster and its hinterland.[8]

The nearest fifth-century Anglo-Saxon sites known to the south of Lincoln are the cemeteries at Newark and Loveden Hill,[9] both about 25 km. from Lincoln. No sixth-century sites are known any closer to the town. Even the communities which used those cemeteries may have been in Lincoln's area of control. Whether many Anglo-Saxons did live within that southern part of the kingdom is not known; but sites to the north of Lincoln have shown evidence suggesting peaceful interaction between Britons and Anglo-Saxons in the migration period,[10] so that co-existence is possible in the southern area too.

If the kingdom of Lindsey extended well to the south of Lincoln, it would have divided readily, along the line of Fossdyke and the Witham below Lincoln, into a northern and a southern half. Whether or not these effectively natural subdivisions were utilized while the kingdom remained autonomous, there is no reason why they should not have become units of local administration by the time the Danes took the area out of Mercian control in the 870s.

Lincolnshire proper, however, composed of the three parts of Lindsey, Kesteven and Holland, was an English creation after the reconquest of the Danelaw in the earlier tenth century. It must have been larger than the area controlled by the Danes of Lincoln, since it also included a considerable portion of Stamford (another Danish borough) and its hinterland.[11] It was also larger than the kingdom of Lindsey, since at least one area within the shire is

[6] *The Lincolnshire Domesday and the Lindsey Survey*, ed. C.W. Foster and T. Longley, Lincoln Record Soc. (Lincoln, 1924), pp. 237–60; Stenton, 'Lindsey and its Kings', pp. 133–4.
[7] See below, pp. 10–11.
[8] The western border of this area may have been not the Trent but the Idle, which Bede identifies as the (north-eastern) boundary of Mercia: *HE* II.12.
[9] B.N. Eagles, *The Anglo-Saxon Settlement of Humberside*, BAR Brit. ser. 68 (Oxford, 1979), 411–12; K.R. Fennell, 'The Anglo-Saxon Cemetery at Loveden Hill . . . and its Significance in relation to the Dark Age Settlement of the East Midlands' (unpubl. PhD dissertation, Nottingham Univ., 1964).
[10] Eagles, 'Lindsey', *Origins of Anglo-Saxon Kingdoms*, ed. Bassett, pp. 208–9 and refs. cited.
[11] F.M. Stenton, *Anglo-Saxon England*, 3rd ed. (Oxford, 1971), p. 338.

shown by the 'Tribal Hidage' to have been a separate territory.[12] The names
Kesteven and Holland, therefore, cannot have referred to the areas of the two
southern parts of Lincolnshire before the middle years of the tenth century,
even though they may have existed earlier as the names of smaller areas.[13]
Accordingly the name Lindsey also may not have been used exclusively of the
area north of Fossdyke and the Witham until the same time.

The Anglo-Saxon bishops of Lindsey

The first bishop of Lindsey was consecrated in 678, the last one to be heard of
in the pre-Viking period disappears after 875, and one or more of the
intervening ones may be unrecorded.[14] As yet the location of their see has not
been identified. The chief purpose of this paper is to show that it was at Lincoln
– more precisely, in the southern suburb of Lincoln known as Wigford.

Pre-Conquest citations (which are few in number and of very different
quality) on first sight seem unhelpful in this respect, mainly describing the
bishops as *Lindissi episcopus*, *Lindissi ecclesiae episcopus*, *Lindensis Faronensis
episcopus*, *Lindisfarorum antistes* and (in later Anglo-Saxon episcopal lists)
Lindisfar[n]orum episcopi.[15] One of them, however – Eadwulf, bishop from 796

---

12 The group called *Bilmiga* probably occupied part of modern SE Lincs.: W. Davies and H.
    Vierk, 'The Contexts of Tribal Hidage: Social Aggregates and Settlement Patterns', *FS* 8
    (1974), 223–93, at 233–4 and 236. Spalding, also in SE Lincs., may not represent the
    settlement areas of the *Spalda* but of an off-shoot group: *ibid.* pp. 232 and 234.

13 Kesteven may mean 'administrative district named *Ched* (forest)': M. Gelling, *Place-Names in
    the Landscape* (London, 1984), p. 292; Holland may mean 'district characterized by hill-
    spurs': *ibid.* p. 289. The late-tenth-century chronicler Æthelweard locates a battle fought in
    894 'on the western side of the place called Stamford. This is to say, between the streams of
    the river Welland and the thickets of the wood called Kesteven (*Ceostefne*) by the common
    people': *The Chronicle of Æthelweard*, ed. A. Campbell (London, 1962), p. 51.

14 *HE* IV.12; *Handbook of British Chronology*, ed. Fryde, *et al.*, p. 219. The see lasted until *c.* 1011,
    after one or more lengthy interruptions in the late ninth and earlier tenth centuries; thereafter
    Lindsey went back to the control of the bishops of Dorchester: D.P. Kirby, 'The Saxon
    Bishops of Leicester, Lindsey (*Syddensis*), and Dorchester', *Leicestershire Arch. and Hist. Soc.
    Trans.* 41 (1965–6), 1–8.

15 Respectively, S (= P.H. Sawyer, *Anglo-Saxon Charters: an Annotated List and Bibliography*, R.
    Hist. Soc. Guides and Handbooks 8 (London, 1968)) 66; ptd W. de G. Birch, *Cartularium
    Saxonicum*, 3 vols. (London, 1885–93) [hereafter BCS], 66 (a forgery, based on *HE* IV.28); S
    891 and 899 (charters of Æthelred II); *Alcuini epistolae*, ed. E. Dümmler, MGH Epist. 4
    (Berlin, 1895), no. 3 (report of the Legates in 786; it is incompletely printed as BCS 250,
    where *Ceoluulfus* (bishop of Lindsey from 767 to 796) is wrongly rendered *Edeulfus*); BCS 425
    (an episcopal profession); and R.I. Page, 'Anglo-Saxon Episcopal Lists, Part III',
    Nottingham Med. Stud. 10 (1966), 2–24, at 5, 6, 10, 11, 15, 16 and 21. The two instances of
    Lindisfarnorum in these episcopal lists (in London, British Library, Cotton Vespasian B. vi (s.
    ix[in]; later corrected), 108r, col. 3 – 109r, col. 2, at 108v, col. 2; and in Cambridge, Corpus
    Christi College 140 (Bath Abbey, *c.* 1100), 115r, col. 2 – 115v, at 115r, col. 7) are obvious
    slips, since both head lists of bishops of Lindsey.

to 836 × 839[16] – is described as *syddensis ciuitatis episcopus* in a Canterbury document of 803 which survives in its original form.[17] *Syddensis* is rendered *siddensis* in an eleventh-century copy of the same text,[18] and, in a spurious document based very largely on it, Eadwulf is entitled *siddensis episcopus*.[19]

Syddensis ciuitas

Syddensis ciuitas has usually been taken as a latinized adjectival form of an unrecorded Old English place-name *Sidnace[a]ster*. This owes not a little to William of Malmesbury who, in rehearsing the chief witnesses of the Canterbury charter of 803, gives 'Edulfus *Sidnacestrensis*'.[20] Most recently James Campbell has argued that the place would have been a former Roman site of some importance, but opinions have varied widely on its probable identification, most scholars favouring Caistor, Horncastle, or Stow-in-Lindsey.[21] Only the case for Caistor, however, has any force at all, since the place is a former Roman walled town of modest size and has a place-name which (it has been suggested) could represent the shortening of a name such as *Sidnaceaster*.[22] But this form is hypothetical. As Caistor is also known as *Thwan[g]castr[e]* from 1190 on to the sixteenth century at least,[23] the case for identifying it as *Sidnaceaster* is very weak indeed.

A little more might be learnt about *syddensis ciuitas* from an examination of the charter of 803 in which this name occurs.[24] The charter is written in what is certainly a contemporary hand, and a clear if not particularly beautiful one. It is largely free of detectable errors. One word, omitted by oversight, has been interlined in a hand which seems to be the scribe's own. Otherwise there are three emendations. An *unquam* has been corrected to *nunquam* by the addition of

---

[16] *Handbook of British Chronology*, ed. Fryde, *et al.*, p. 219.

[17] BCS 312; W.B. Sanders, *Facsimiles of Anglo-Saxon Manuscripts* [hereafter *OSFacs.*], 3 vols. (Ordnance Survey, Southampton, 1878–84) I, no. 4; N.P. Brooks, *The Early History of the Church of Canterbury* (Leicester, 1984), p. 363, n. 16.

[18] *OSFacs.* I, no. 5. [19] BCS 290.

[20] *Willelmi Malmesbiriensis monachi de gestis pontificum Anglorum libri quinque*, ed. N.E.S.A. Hamilton, RS (London, 1870), p. 16.

[21] J. Campbell, 'Bede's Words for Places', *Names, Words and Graves: Early Medieval Settlement*, ed. P.H. Sawyer (Leeds, 1979), pp. 34–54, at 42; A.W. Clapham, 'Introduction', *in* D.S. Davies, 'Pre-Conquest Carved Stones in Lincolnshire', *ArchJ* 83 (1926), 1–20, at 1–2; J.W.F. Hill, *Medieval Lincoln* (Cambridge, 1948), pp. 377–8 and refs. cited. A case has also been made for Louth: A.E.B. Owen, 'Herefrith of Louth, Saint and Bishop: a Problem of Identities', *Lincolnshire Hist. and Arch.* 15 (1980), 15–19.

[22] Clapham, 'Introduction', p. 2, n. 2; C.A.R. Radford, 'A Lost Inscription of Pre-Danish Age from Caistor', *ArchJ* 103 (1946), 95–9.

[23] Kenneth Cameron (pers. comm.). The instance of 1190 is in an early-thirteenth-century hand.

[24] BCS 312 (*OS Facs.* I, no. 4). I am most grateful to Nicholas Brooks and Simon Keynes for discussing this charter with me.

4

a superscript *n* in what is probably a later hand. The scribe has, moreover, written *dorobernis* for *dorobernensis* in both references which the charter makes to the archbishop of Canterbury, with no sign of an abbreviation mark. This seems a curious mistake for a Canterbury scribe to make in so important a document: a single example (due, for example, to omission of a suspension mark) could easily be dismissed as carelessness; but for both instances of the word to be incorrect hints at ignorance of the Latin forms of the names of Anglo-Saxon sees. The errors remained until both were corrected with superscript *-ens-* in a tenth- or more probably eleventh-century hand.

This raises the albeit slight possibility that *syddensis* represents a scribal misreading of *lindensis* or *lyndensis*,[25] and that, whether noticed or not, it too remained uncorrected. (It is worth noting that Eadwulf's immediate predecessor and his immediate successor were both styled 'bishop of [the men of] Lindsey'.)[26] The scribe who eventually rectified *dorobernis* would presumably have been no more aware that *syddensis* was a nonsense than would the charter's eleventh-century copyist. William of Malmesbury, therefore, and later chroniclers would have got their versions of *Sidnaceaster* by extrapolation from the charter's form of the name or (more likely) from the eleventh-century copyist's *siddensis*. However, *dorobernensis* is a word which occurs in many different forms, which suggests that even Canterbury scribes were never quite sure what they were supposed to write.[27] So, although ninth-century scribes are known to have been careless, the notion that *syddensis* is a misreading has little to recommend it.

But *syddensis ciuitas* may indeed represent a latinized form of a lost Old English place-name. Though it is impossible now to determine the exact form of such a name, let alone its meaning, it may have been **sȳðnaceaster*, 'Roman town of the south people'.[28] That form could perfectly well turn up as *Sidnaceaster* in later sources. However, such an explanation would require the scribe of the charter of 803 to have mistaken *ð* for *d* in whatever it was he was working from, whereas he uses *ð* consistently throughout the charter in Old English personal names (none of its place-names needs the letter), even when latinizing one (*Æðelheardus*). He would also need to have rendered *-ð-* as *-dd-*. On the face of it this seems no likelier an explanation than that the scribe simply

---

25 As first suggested in E.M. Sympson, 'Where was Sidnacester?', *Associated Archit. Socs. Reports and Papers* 28 (1905–6), 87–94, at 94.

26 Respectively, *Alcuini epistolae*, ed. Dümmler, no. 3 (*Ceoluulfus, Lindensis Faronensis episcopus*) and BCS 425 (*Berhtredus . . . Lindisfarorum antistes*). There is an episcopal profession for Eadwulf himself, but it is of no help since he is erroneously styled archbishop of York: *Canterbury Professions*, ed. M. Richter, Canterbury and York Soc. 67 (Torquay, 1973), no. 1.

27 Simon Keynes (pers. comm.).

28 **Sȳðe*, 'south people', would be analogous to *Mierce* as a tribe-name derived from OE *mearc*.

misread *lyndensis* (or some other latinized form of the name now represented by Lindsey).[29]

It is clear, then, that there is no easy answer to the problem of *syddensis ciuitatis*. None of the possible solutions mentioned here has any obvious merit. On balance it must be recognized as one of those names whose etymology ought to be left open.[30]

The place-name Lindsey

It can, however, be shown that a place-name **syðnaceaster* would be appropriate, both topographically and etymologically, for the site of the see of Lindsey. The case is based on a proper understanding of the name Lindsey itself.

It has been usual to translate Lindsey as 'island of the people of Lincoln',[31] but its etymology proves to be much more difficult than that translation alone would suggest. The etymology which Margaret Gelling now proposes[32] requires that *two* names should be recognized as the basis of the name Lindsey. One of them is represented by the forms *Lindissi* and *Lindesse*, to be found in Bede's *Ecclesiastical History*, the *Anglo-Saxon Chronicle* (*s.a.* 838 and 873) and other eighth- and ninth-century contexts. Its first element is **Lindēs*, 'people of Lincoln or *Lindum*', but its final element is unexplained.

The other name is *Lindesig*, meaning 'island of the **Lindēs*'; from it the eventual form, Lindsey, is derived. It is found in the D-version of the *Anglo-Saxon Chronicle*,[33] and in Asser's *Life of King Alfred*, both transmitted in eleventh-century manuscripts; but Margaret Gelling believes[34] that it too was current in earlier centuries. The name Lindsey has usually been taken to refer to an extensive area north and east of Lincoln (the whole kingdom in fact) which was effectively surrounded by water in the earlier medieval period.[35] However, not one of the many other known place-names in *ēg* seems to have originated as a regional or provincial name. Instead they all describe true

---

[29] William of Malmesbury's own manuscript reads *Sidna-*. The several known copies of it have various forms, one of which (of the first recension) is *Suthna-* (*De gestis pontificum*, ed. Hamilton, pp. xx and 16, n. 2).

[30] Simon Keynes suggests (pers. comm.) that it meant something to the scribe of the early-ninth-century Canterbury document, and meant little or nothing to anyone thereafter (i.e. that later forms are probably worthless).

[31] Gelling, *Place-Names in the Landscape*, p. 39.

[32] See appendix below, pp. 31–2. I am very grateful to Dr Gelling for her most helpful comments on this and the other place-names discussed here.

[33] 838 D (= 841): *An Anglo-Saxon Chronicle from British Museum, Cotton MS., Tiberius B.IV*, ed. E. Classen and F.E. Harmer (Manchester, 1926), p. 24.

[34] See below, pp. 31–2, and pers. comm.

[35] E. Ekwall, *The Concise Oxford Dictionary of English Place-Names*, 4th ed. (Oxford, 1960), p. 299; Stenton, 'Lindsey and its Kings', pp. 132–4.

islands or else relatively limited areas of low-lying land partly surrounded by water, most of the latter becoming settlement names.[36] The name *Lindesig* too, therefore, should have been coined for an area of limited extent. Moreover, neither *Lindissi* nor *Lindesig* is at all likely to have been used as the name of a whole kingdom until the latter had come to be dominated by people associated with the unknown feature and 'island' of the **Lindēs* which respectively gave rise to those names.[37]

Asser (loosely copying from the *Chronicle*) took *Lindesig* to be the name of a region (*in paga, quae dicitur Lindesig*), not a place,[38] which suggests that it and *Lindissi/Lindesse* (the name of the kingdom in earlier sources) were effectively synonymous by his day. That is not hard to envisage: whatever the literal meaning of *Lindissi/Lindesse*, people were doubtless customarily referring to a settlement when they used the name. If that settlement was on *Lindesig*, then the two names (*Lindissi/Lindesse* and *Lindesig*), which must have sounded very similar in speech, would easily have become conflated. It is not surprising, therefore, that it was *Lindesig*, rather than *Lindissi/Lindesse*, which gave rise to the eventual form of the name Lindsey.

*Lindēs, the first element of both *Lindissi/Lindesse* and *Lindesig*, is derived from British Latin **Lindenses* which itself comes from the stem of British *lindon*, 'pool', with the suffix *-enses* added.[39] **Lindenses* was, therefore, the Latin name of a group of people who lived either in the Roman city of *Lindum* (*colonia*) or at the pool called *Lindum*. From this it appears that when Anglo-Saxons came to settle at Lincoln, they found people living there who were by then called **Lindēs* but who had been at the place since the Roman period. In adding *ēg* to the people's name the Anglo-Saxons may well have been describing an 'island' which was adjacent to these Britons' main area of settlement and intimately associated with it – 'the island of the people of Lincoln'. However, the Britons could equally well have been living on the 'island' itself, in which case 'the island of the people of *Lindum* [i.e. the pool]' would be appropriate.

In either case it is clear that the 'island of the **Lindēs*' was of considerable importance both before and after the Anglo-Saxons arrived at Lincoln. They may well have settled there (though as yet there is no archaeological evidence at all of their presence in any part of the town). Whatever their initial status in

---

36 Gelling, *Place-Names in the Landscape*, pp. 34–40.

37 This is broadly analogous to the extension of the topographical name *hwicce* to cover an entire kingdom: M. Gelling, 'The Place-Name Volumes for Worcestershire and Warwickshire: A New Look', *Field and Forest. An Historical Geography of Warwickshire and Worcestershire*, ed. T.R. Slater and P.J. Jarvis (Norwich, 1982), p. 69.

38 *Asser's Life of Alfred*, ed. W.H. Stevenson (Oxford, 1904), p. 34; but see below, p. 9, for the chronicler Æthelweard's different reading of it.

39 K.H. Jackson, *Language and History in Early Britain* (Edinburgh, 1953), pp. 332 and 543; K. Cameron, *The Place-Names of Lincolnshire*, EPNS 58.1 (Cambridge, 1985), 2–3.

relation to Lincoln's British population,[40] the subsequent extension of the names *Lindissi/Lindesse* and *Lindesig* to a kingdom, a see and (later on) a major administrative region shows the great significance which attached to Lincoln – and to a settlement on its 'island' – once the Anglo-Saxons had taken control of the place.

This prompts two further comments. The first concerns the etymology of Lincoln's own name, which is derived from British *lindon*, 'pool' and the British form of Latin *colonia* (an officially established, walled, settlement of time-expired legionaries).[41] It is notable that OE *ceaster*, 'Roman walled town', is absent from most forms of the name, 'suggesting perhaps that the significance of the second element of Lincoln was understood by the early Anglo-Saxon settlers'.[42] This may mean that for a long while a clear distinction existed between the walled town itself and the presumed settlement on the 'island' called Lindsey.

The second comment concerns the entry for the kingdom of Lindsey in the 'Tribal Hidage' – *Lindesfarona (landes)*, the genitive of the folk-name *Lindesfara*,[43] of which latinized versions appear in other early sources. Dr Gelling suggests[44] that it can only mean 'people who resort to a place called *Lindesse/Lindesig*' (as also must the name of the inhabitants of the Northumbrian island now called Lindisfarne). If so, that strongly reinforces the notion that *Lindesse/Lindesig* was originally a specific settlement, not a region – and a settlement, moreover, with a central role in the kingdom's life, perhaps not least as a major trading centre.

Use of the name 'Lindissi/Lindesse' by Bede and Æthelweard

Two Anglo-Saxon writers, widely separated in time and space, appear to use the name *Lindissi/Lindesse* to denote a specific settlement. Bede refers eight times in his *Historia ecclesiastica* to the *prouincia Lindissi*, and once to *Lindissae prouinciae*.[45] Both can be translated 'the kingdom of Lindsey'; on other occasions he speaks of the *prouincia Lindisfarorum*, 'the kingdom of the men of Lindsey'.[46] The three variants are far better taken to mean a kingdom dependent on a particular centre, or on its inhabitants, than – as, for instance,

---

[40] Conceivably that of mercenaries, as elsewhere: M. Biddle, 'Towns', *The Archaeology of Anglo-Saxon England*, ed. D.M. Wilson (London, 1976), pp. 99–150, at 104–5, and 112 and refs. cited there in n. 104. On the problems of identifying Germanic mercenaries, see C. Hills, 'The Archaeology of Anglo-Saxon England in the Pagan Period: a Review', *ASE* 8 (1979), 297–329, at 297–307. [41] Cameron, *Place-Names of Lincolnshire*, pp. 2–3.

[42] *Ibid.* p. 3. [43] BCS 297. [44] See below, p. 32.

[45] *HE* Preface (p. 6); ch. headings to II (p. 120); II.16 (p. 190); III.11 (*bis*) (p. 246); III.27 (p. 312); IV.3 (*bis*) (pp. 336 and 344); and III.11 (p. 246) respectively.

[46] *HE* III.24 and IV.12 (pp. 292 and 370). For convenience of reference I shall continue in most contexts to use Lindsey as the name of the kingdom and the see.

in the modern usage 'the kingdom of England' – a kingdom *called* Lindsey. This is in keeping with the general tendency of sources of the middle Saxon period to refer to a kingdom in terms of its inhabitants or dominant community (the Mercians, the Hwicce) rather than by its own, separate, name.

Bishops, however, were said to be either of a people or, increasingly in later sources, of a particular see. Therefore, to refer (as modern scholarship does) to 'the bishop of Lindsey' is anomalous when by Lindsey one means the whole area of the kingdom. Bede does not use that title, choosing always to talk of 'the office of bishop of the men of Lindsey'.[47] So when, in marked contrast to his normal practice, Bede speaks simply of Lindsey, he is unlikely to be referring to the kingdom. This he does only twice in his *Historia ecclesiastica*, in describing events of the 670s.[48] After Ecgfrith of Northumbria had defeated Wulfhere of Mercia, Bishop Seaxwulf was driven out of Lindsey (*expulsus de Lindissi*). When a few years later Æthelred re-established Mercian control over the former kingdom, Eadhæd, whom the Northumbrians had put in as bishop in place of Seaxwulf, returned home from Lindsey (*Eadhædum de Lindissi reuersum*) to become bishop of Ripon. In both instances it is clearly the bishop's seat, not the kingdom, which is meant.

The other Anglo-Saxon source which appears to use *Lindissi/Lindesse* as a settlement name is the chronicle of the West Saxon ealdorman Æthelweard, written in the late tenth century.[49] By then it was usual for the former kingdom to be referred to simply as Lindsey.[50] Æthelweard, however, twice speaks of Lindsey as an *urbs* (town) in passages which are basically translations of entries in earlier parts of the *Anglo-Saxon Chronicle*. On the first occasion, in reporting Danish activity in 841 he renders the *Chronicle*'s 'on Lindesse 7 on Eastenglum 7 on Cantwarum' as 'in urbe Lindesse et in Cent prouincia et in Orientalibus Anglis'. Æthelweard could be thought to be using *urbs* loosely here to mean 'region' (the meaning taken by his editor); but that is certainly not his normal practice.[51] In a second instance it seems certain that he is speaking of a town called *Lindesse*. The *Chronicle* records that in 873 the Danish army shifted its base from London to take up winter quarters 'on Lindesse æt Tureces iege', 'in Lindsey at Torksey'.[52] By rendering this as *iuxta Lindissi urbe in Turcesige condicto loco*, 'near the town of *Lindissi* in the place called Torksey', Æthelweard

---

[47] *HE* III.11 and III.27 (pp. 246 and 312); IV.12 (p. 370); and IV.3 (*bis*) and IV.12 (pp. 336, 346 and 370) respectively.   [48] *HE* IV.12 (p. 370).   [49] *Chronicle of Æthelweard*, ed. Campbell.
[50] E.g. *Anglo-Saxon Chronicle* 993 CDE: *Two of the Saxon Chronicles Parallel*, ed. C. Plummer (Oxford, 1892–9) I, 127 (E text) and *ASC* 1013 CDE: *Two Chronicles*, ed. Plummer I, 143 (E).
[51] *ASC* 838 ABC (= 841): *Two Chronicles*, ed. Plummer I, 64 (A); *Chronicle of Æthelweard*, ed. Campbell, p. 31 (he uses *urbs* of London only one sentence later). The D-version of the *Chronicle*, however, has *Lindesige*: see, further, below, p. 32.
[52] *ASC* 873 AB, 874 C: *Two Chronicles*, ed. Plummer I, 72 (A).

seems to be saying something rather different from his source, not simply mistranslating it. Campbell rendered *iuxta Lindissi urbe* as 'the area near Lindsey', i.e. near the region or former kingdom of that name;[53] but that cannot be right, since Torksey certainly lay within Lindsey and Æthelweard can be expected to have known that. Instead it must be the town of *Lindissi*, i.e. Lincoln, less than ten miles away, to which he is referring. Whether it was his deliberate intention to locate Torksey, a little known place, in relation to the nearest major settlement, or whether the phrase was merely an unconscious gloss on the *Chronicle*, it does appear that Æthelweard knew that the name *Lindissi* could be (or at least once had been) used to refer to Lincoln.

It seems, therefore, that there are very good grounds for accepting that *Lindissi/Lindesse* originated as the name of a specific part of Lincoln and of a major settlement which developed there on the 'island' called *Lindesig*. Moreover, the name seems subsequently to have been extended to cover an entire kingdom controlled from there, and to have become conflated with the very similarly sounding *Lindesig* which eventually superseded it. It follows, then, that the see of the bishops of Lindsey would have been at Lincoln too.

LATE ROMAN AND ANGLO-SAXON LINCOLN

Where then was this *ēg*, and why was it so important in the earlier Anglo-Saxon period? To answer these questions it is necessary to look in some detail at Lincoln itself. Roman Lincoln had consisted of two separate walled areas: the *colonia* itself, and the 'lower' or 'new town' to the south.[54] There is adequate evidence of town life at Lincoln continuing to the end of the fourth century; and while little is known of the history of these two areas in the post-Roman period, the general impression is of a continuation of occupation in at least some parts of them, if on a decreasingly urban scale.[55] From the countryside just to the north-east of Lincoln there is, moreover, evidence to suggest considerable agrarian continuity in the town's hinterland throughout the migration period.[56] In view, therefore, of the scarcity of early Anglo-Saxon

---

[53] *Chronicle of Æthelweard*, ed. Campbell, p. 40.

[54] J. Wacher, *The Towns of Roman Britain* (London, 1974), p. 133. Simon Esmonde Cleary points out (pers. comm.) that the archaeological evidence from the lower town suggests that it was seen as part of the *colonia* from the start.

[55] C.M. Colyer and M.J. Jones, ed., 'Excavations at Lincoln. Second Interim Report: Excavations in the Lower Town 1972–8', *AntJ* 59 (1979), 50–91, at 55 and 88–9; M.J. Jones, 'New Streets for Old: the Topography of Roman Lincoln', *Roman Urban Topography in Britain and the Western Empire*, ed. F. Grew and B. Hobley, CBA Research Report 59 (London, 1985), 86–93, at 92.

[56] S. Bassett, 'Beyond the Edge of Excavation: the Topographical Context of Goltho', *Studies in Medieval History Presented to R.H.C. Davis*, ed. H. Mayr-Harting and R.I. Moore (London, 1985), pp. 21–39, at 32–4 and 38.

material in the vicinity of the town, and of the absence of such finds within it, it may well be that Lincoln remained a British centre of some importance in the centuries after 400.[57]

The suggestion is reinforced by the first, apparently pre-Anglo-Saxon, phase of the church of St Paul-in-the-Bail, and its subsequent development focused on a probable high-status burial.[58] There is not the evidence to allow this church, in any of its phases, to be recognized as the one erected in Lincoln by the missionary Paulinus in 625–32 (which could equally have stood here or elsewhere).[59] Its cemetery, however, if not the church itself, may have originated as early as the fifth century,[60] and the site testifies to the continuing (if changing) importance of Lincoln – in all probability one of the four possible metropolitan sees of the fourth century – as a British Christian centre. Paulinus may have visited Lincoln for that reason as well as because of the place's contemporary political status.[61]

Paulinus's first convert in Lindsey was Blæcca, *praefectum . . . Lindocolinae ciuitatis*.[62] He was at least the town's leading official, a man who, from his title and from the importance ascribed to him by Paulinus, can be presumed to have exercised considerable authority in and around Lincoln.[63] Blæcca may even have been a member of the royal family of Lindsey: his name alliterates, for what it is worth, with those of three direct ancestors of Lindsey's only known king, Aldfrith, all three of whom were probably alive in the seventh century.[64] More significantly *praefectus* could indicate a man of royal stock. In 'Eddius' Stephanus's *Vita S. Wilfridi*, for instance, the Northumbrian Berhtfrith whom Bede calls *praefectus* is described as *secundus a rege princeps* ('a prince next in rank to the king'); and in the same source Berhtwald, the nephew of Æthelred, king

---

[57] Eagles, *Anglo-Saxon Settlement of Humberside*, pp. 182–7 and figs. 118–19; and 'Lindsey', *Origins of Anglo-Saxon Kingdoms*, ed. Bassett. Michael Jones informs me that there is still no archaeological evidence of any early Anglo-Saxon occupation of the town.

[58] R.K. Morris, *The Church in British Archaeology*, CBA Research Report 47 (London, 1983), 38–9 and 48; W. Rodwell, 'Churches in the Landscape: Aspects of Topography and Planning', *Studies in Late Anglo-Saxon Settlement*, ed. M.L. Faull (Oxford, 1984), pp. 1–23, at 4 (and refs. cited there); P. Stafford, *The East Midlands in the Early Middle Ages* (Leicester, 1985), pp. 87–8.

[59] *HE* ii.16 (p. 191): *Praedicabat . . . uerbum . . . prouinciae Lindissi*. This church, built in stone and 'of remarkable workmanship', was still standing (though roofless) in Bede's day: *ibid.* (p. 193).   [60] Morris, *Church in British Archaeology*, p. 48.

[61] J.C. Mann, 'The Administration of Roman Britain', *Antiquity* 35 (1961), 316–20, at 318. I have discussed the possible influence of fourth-century diocesan geography on the location of the seventh-century Anglo-Saxon sees in my paper 'Churches in Worcester Before and After the Conversion of the Anglo-Saxons' (forthcoming).   [62] *HE* ii.16 (p. 192).

[63] He is reminiscent of the *praepositus* who showed St Cuthbert around the Roman monuments of Carlisle: see B. Colgrave, *Two 'Lives' of Saint Cuthbert* (Cambridge, 1940), p. 122.

[64] Bubba, Beda and Bisc[e]op/Beoscep: Dumville, 'The Anglian Collection of Royal Genealogies and Regnal Lists', pp. 31, 33 and 37.

of Mercia, is described as *praefectus*.[65] But, royal or not, Blæcca's conversion, like that of kings elsewhere in seventh-century England, is seen by Bede as a major event in the history of the Christian mission, and the prominence he gives to Lincoln in his account of the conversion of the kingdom of Lindsey emphasizes the place's importance within it.

The location of 'Lindesig'

It is not to the Roman walled area but to the part of the town lying south of it that we should look for the '*ēg* of the men of **Lindēs*'. In that area there was a major Roman suburb along Ermine Street, south of the ford by which the road crossed the Witham. From the third century the road's frontages were built up for at least one kilometre from the ford, with several cemeteries nearby.[66]

For the whole of that distance Ermine Street – now High Street – runs along the spine of a narrow finger of land which, projecting northwards into extensive marshland to either side of the Witham, brings the road to its crossing of the river (fig. 1). This small promontory is defined on its western and northern sides by the present course of the Witham (including Brayford Pool), and on the east by what seems to be a former course, now dry. The engineers of Sincil Dyke (date of construction unknown) took advantage of the upper part of this abandoned course when planning the ditch's route from the Witham above Brayford Pool. It is not clear if the promontory was once a true island in a braided river channel, or if much of the present course of the Witham in its vicinity represents a Roman rerouting.[67] In either case, though it may no longer have been surrounded by water in historical times, the feature is entirely appropriate for a place-name in OE *ēg*, which 'most frequently refers to dry ground surrounded by marsh when it occurs in ancient settlements'.[68] No other piece of land in the vicinity of Lincoln has these characteristics. So, although no instance of the name has survived there, it is this low but distinct promontory which must have borne the name *Lindesig* if, as has been proposed here, some part of Lincoln certainly did.

To judge from the relatively few archaeological excavations undertaken there it is clear that the promontory was also important from the Anglo-Danish period onwards, with the banks of Brayford Pool on the Witham being

---

[65] For Berhtfrith, see *HE* v.24 (p. 566), and B. Colgrave, *The Life of Bishop Wilfrid by Eddius Stephanus* (Cambridge, 1927), p. 130. For Berhtwald, see Colgrave, *Life of Bishop Wilfrid*, p. 80; according to William of Malmesbury, Berhtwald was the son of King Wulfhere (*De gestis pontificum*, ed. Hamilton, pp. 351–2).

[66] M. J. Jones, ed., 'Excavations at Lincoln. Third Interim Report: Sites outside the Walled City 1972–1977', *AntJ* 61 (1981), 83–114, at 84; Jones, 'New Streets for Old', fig. 63 on p. 91.

[67] For the latter suggestion, see Hill, *Medieval Lincoln*, p. 6, n. 1.

[68] Gelling, *Place-Names in the Landscape*, p. 34. Dr Gelling lists an impressive number of northern names in which *ēg* seems to be used of a narrow promontory of dry ground (p. 36).

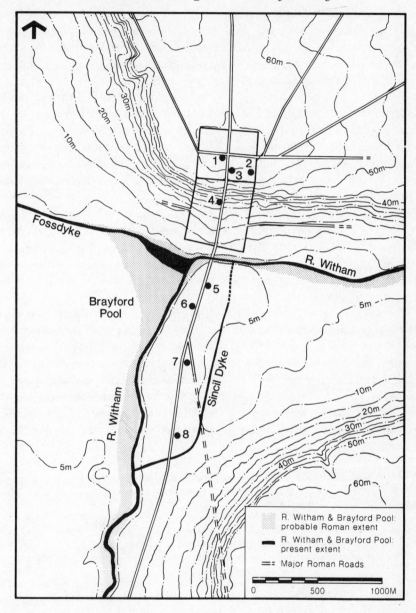

FIG. 1 Lincoln: the natural topography and major early features.
The *ēg* of the *⁸Lindes*, i.e. Lindsey, is outlined by the 5 m contour S. and E. of the Witham. Numbered sites are medieval churches referred to in the text: 1, St Paul-in-the-Bail; 2, Lincoln Cathedral; 3, St Mary Magdalene; 4, St Martin in Dernstall; 5, St Mary-le-Wigford; 6, St Mark's; 7, St Peter-at-Gowts; 8, St Botolph's.

once again developed as a water-front.[69] Sites on and close to Ermine Street seem to have been reoccupied in the late ninth or tenth century. By the middle of the latter century at the latest a cemetery had developed beside the road some 350 m. south of the ford, probably accompanied from the start by a church – the earliest, timber, phase of St Mark's church.[70]

This evidence of considerable Anglo-Danish settlement in the area which became the later medieval suburb of Wigford is conventionally seen as a by-product of the Danish capture of Lincoln in the late ninth century.[71] There is little doubt that Lincoln did make much economic progress from that time; moreover, it is difficult to find any sign in the archaeological record (stray finds apart) of the southern suburb having had much importance beforehand. However, of the seven excavations undertaken there, only four have been in places which would have been dry ground in the early and middle Anglo-Saxon periods, and all but one – an area of some 30 m. by 20 m. in St Mark's church and cemetery – were on a small scale.[72] Large parts of the promontory have had no excavations undertaken in them at all (not least the whole north-eastern area, which had an extensive river frontage below Brayford Pool and the Ermine Street crossing).

There is, moreover, a distinct possibility that little or no pottery was being made in the Lincoln area after (say) the first decade or two of the fifth century until the end of the ninth.[73] This means that early post-Roman (i.e. British) occupation on the promontory, as elsewhere, would be extremely hard to recognize; and early Anglo-Saxon settlers are only likely to be known from the discovery of funerary deposits. It also means that, apart from such relative rarities as glass, distinctive metalwork and imported pottery, there would be no finds by which middle Saxon occupation could be easily recognized. In

---

69 'Excavations at Lincoln. Third Interim Report', ed. Jones, pp. 88–92.

70 B.J.J. Gilmour and D.A. Stocker, *St Mark's Church and Cemetery*, Lincoln Archaeol. Trust [hereafter LAT] Monograph Ser. 13.1 (London, 1986), 3 and 15–17.

71 'Excavations at Lincoln. Third Interim Report', ed. Jones, p. 83.

72 *Ibid.* p. 84 (181–2 High St); J.R. Magilton and D.A. Stocker, 'St Mary's Guildhall', *Archaeology in Lincoln 1981–82*, LAT Annual Report 10 (Lincoln, 1982), 8–16; J.R. Magilton, 'Monson Street', *ibid.* pp. 17–19, at 17; Gilmour and Stocker, *St Mark's Church and Cemetery*, p. 13.

73 To judge by the pottery from excavated sites in Lincoln which has been published so far: G. Coppack, 'The Excavation of a Roman and Medieval Site at Flaxengate, Lincoln', *Lincolnshire Hist. and Arch.* 8 (1973), 87–94; L. Adams, *Medieval Pottery from Broadgate East, Lincoln 1973*, LAT Monograph Ser. 17.1 (London, 1977); Gilmour and Stocker, *St Mark's Church and Cemetery*, pp. 35–40. Findspots of middle Saxon pottery in Lincolnshire (to 1970) are mapped and listed in P.V. Addyman and J.B. Whitwell, 'Some Middle Saxon Pottery Types in Lincolnshire', *AntJ* 50 (1970), 96–100.

other words the absence of archaeological evidence of occupation on the promontory between the end of the Roman period and the late ninth century is not conclusive. There has been too little investigation undertaken there for us to rule out the possibility of its existence.

However, there are other reasons for supposing that such occupation did occur. First, it is inherently likely that the Roman suburb retained a measure of importance well into the post-Roman period, not least because of some continuing role in relation to river transport. There is a little archaeological evidence of major schemes, possibly including the construction of lock gates, in the second and third centuries to control the flow of water in the Witham and its pools to either side of the Ermine Street crossing, and to develop their banks as water-fronts.[74] The Fossdyke was probably dug then to provide a link with the River Trent;[75] and Sincil Dyke may also belong to that period (in whole or in part), since it has the look of a channel designed to by-pass the pools and any system controlling the water levels in them. Therefore, even without skilled maintenance the Witham is likely to have remained navigable as far as Lincoln for boats of shallow draught in the post-Roman period, and the Fossdyke too may have stayed open for a very considerable time.[76]

Secondly, the name Wigford, by which the later medieval suburb on the promontory was known, is further linguistic evidence of there having been early Anglo-Saxon settlement there. Dr Gelling has suggested that Wigford means 'ford by a Romano-British settlement', identifying its first element, OE *wīc*, as a direct loan in this instance from Latin *vicus*.[77] Such a name, therefore, would have been coined early on by Anglo-Saxons who were living, still archaeologically invisible to us,[78] quite close to the ford, and their settlement must have been permanent if we are to account for the name's survival.[79] Presumably it was one which lay on the promontory called Lindsey in or beside the former Roman suburb. Indeed, the suburb itself (rather than the walled area to the north of the river) may have been the *vicus* recognized in the name Wigford, since there is epigraphic evidence to suggest that Roman Lincoln

---

[74] 'Excavations at Lincoln. Third Interim Report', ed. Jones, pp. 88–92; B. Gilmour, 'Brayford Wharf East', *Archaeology in Lincoln 1981–82*, LAT Annual Report 10, 20–4 (where the possibility of Roman lock gates is discussed on p. 22).

[75] Gilmour, 'Brayford Wharf East', p. 20.

[76] Henry I is known to have had the Fossdyke cleaned out; similar work was done on other fenland canals of Roman origin by Cnut: *The Fenland in Roman Times*, ed. C.W. Phillips, Royal Geog. Soc., Research Ser. 5 (London, 1970), 79, n. 35.

[77] Gelling, *Place-Names in the Landscape*, p. 323; M. Gelling, *Signposts to the Past* (London, 1978), pp. 67 and 70.   [78] Eagles, *Anglo-Saxon Settlement of Humberside*, p. 157.

[79] The earliest written record of it is of *c.* 1107: Cameron, *Place-Names of Lincolnshire*, pp. 45–6.

was subdivided into *vici* or wards, one or more of which may have been extramural.[80]

This prompts an awkward question. Why should the name coined for a ford (rather than the name of the promontory itself and of the important early Anglo-Saxon settlement on it) have become that of the prosperous later medieval suburb which developed there? The best answer may be that *wīc*, the first element of Wigford, in time took on a new meaning with the establishment of a market on the promontory, or perhaps that that was as much its original meaning as it was at the handful of major middle Saxon trading centres with names ending in -*wīc*. By the eighth century such markets were appearing at a variety of coastal and similarly accessible riverine sites on the eastern and southern coasts of England, many of them at places where there had been no significant Roman settlement. They included some which were engaged in large-scale international commerce, such as London and York (*Eoforwic*) and, among those on what were effectively new sites, *Hamwic* (Saxon Southampton) and Ipswich.[81] The reference to *Lundenwic*, and to some sort of royal official there called a *wic-gerefa*, in the laws of the Kentish kings Hlothhere and Eadric (673–685?) suggests that *wīc* had already taken on the meaning of market by the later seventh century.[82]

Several of these middle Saxon market centres have now been recognized on riverside sites just outside the walls of former Romano-British towns of the first rank. The first to be tested by excavation is the recently discovered settlement of eighth-century and later date at York, situated along the eastern water-front of the River Foss at its confluence with the Ouse.[83] Settlements of similar function – both perhaps of seventh-century origin – are thought likely to lie in the Aldwych (*Aldewic[h]*) area west of the Roman walls at London,[84] and at Fordwich a short distance down the River Stour from Canterbury.[85]

A trading centre of this sort on the promontory south of Roman Lincoln would have been in a directly analogous location. It would presumably have

---

[80] R.G. Collingwood and R.P. Wright, *The Roman Inscriptions of Britain, 1: Inscriptions on Stone* (Oxford, 1965), nos. 270–1; S. Esmonde Cleary, *Extra-Mural Areas of Romano-British Towns*, BAR Brit. ser. 169 (Oxford, 1987), 113 (where reference is also made to a possible parallel at Trier, where an extramural *vicus* lay at the far end of a river bridge from the *colonia*).

[81] S. Reynolds, *An Introduction to the History of English Medieval Towns* (Oxford, 1977), p. 26; Biddle, 'Towns', pp. 112–20; R. Hodges, *Dark Age Economics* (London, 1982), pp. 66–74.

[82] *The Laws of the Earliest English Kings*, ed. F.L. Attenborough (Cambridge, 1922), p. 22.

[83] R. Kemp, 'Pit your "wics" or how to excavate Anglian York', *Interim* 11.3, York Archaeol. Trust (Autumn 1986), 8–16; 'Redfearns – Where Anglians and Vikings Meet', *ibid.* 11.4 (Winter 1986–7), 12–19.

[84] M. Biddle, 'London on the Strand', *PA* 6.1 (July 1984), 23–7; A. Vince, 'The Aldwych: Mid-Saxon London Discovered?' *CA* 93 (August 1984), 310–12.

[85] T. Tatton-Brown and N. Macpherson-Grant, 'Anglo-Saxon Canterbury: Topography and Pottery', *CA* 98 (Oct. 1985), 89–93, at 90–1.

been accessible both from the sea, *via* the Witham, and from the Humber basin (including York), *via* the Trent and the Fossdyke. Lying at the political and ecclesiastical hub of its kingdom, which later became a major province of landlocked Mercia, it would have been ideally situated for royally controlled international commerce. Its existence would best account for the name of the kingdom's inhabitants, the *Lindesfara* or 'people who resort to a place named *Lindesse/Lindesig*'; and it would put what is otherwise a quite spectacular revival of the former Roman suburb from the later ninth century onwards into a more credible historical context.

A few of the products of such international commerce have already been found at Lincoln, particularly in excavations on Flaxengate in the lower walled area. They include pottery from the Carolingian Rhineland and other western European sources, as well as some from much further afield.[86] However, nowhere near enough imported material of appropriate date has yet been found on sites in and near Lincoln for the existence of a middle Saxon trading centre there to be considered archaeologically proved; the case for one set out here still rests largely on toponymic evidence.

As shown above, the trading centre would have been known as Wigford (whether or not that name had an earlier origin), while the main settlement on the promontory continued to be called *Lindissi* (and/or *Lindesig*). At Saxon Southampton the names *Hamwic* and *Hamtun* represent an analogous situation, the former an important trading centre probably established in the early eighth century on a royal land-unit of the latter name. The two names appear to have been in concurrent use for a long while.[87]

In time *Lindissi* became widely known as the name of a kingdom and see, later on a distinct region under Mercian rule. The former Roman *colonia*, i.e. Lincoln proper, would have begun meanwhile to be re-established as the region's major centre (not least because of its substantially intact walls), taking over the administrative role of the settlement which lay below it on an exposed and indefensible promontory. It is unlikely that a shift of this kind began under the Anglo-Saxon rulers of Lindsey. However, once the Mercians had annexed the kingdom, Lincoln would surely have become one of those fortified centres which they appear to have established throughout the parts of England which

---

[86] D. Perring, *Early Medieval Occupation at Flaxengate, Lincoln*, LAT Monograph Ser. 9.1 (London, 1981), 33. The only comparable imported item (so far published) from excavations on the promontory is a copper alloy ansate brooch, probably a late-seventh- or eighth-century import from mainland western Europe: Gilmour and Stocker, *St Mark's Church and Cemetery*, p. 41.

[87] A.R. Rumble, 'HAMTVN *alias* HAMWIC (Saxon Southampton): the Place-name Traditions and their Significance', *Excavations at Melbourne Street, Southampton, 1971–76*, ed. P. Holdsworth, CBA Research Report 33 (London, 1980), 7, 10 and Table 3.1 on 14.

they dominated in the middle Saxon period.[88] Accordingly, it may well have been Mercians rather than Danes who made the first significant re-use of Lincoln's Roman walls.[89] If so, then the latter would have taken over a refurbished fortification with, one imagines, a defined rural hinterland which already looked to it for protection and by which it was manned and provisioned.

At some time in the earlier tenth century the interior of the whole walled area was substantially replanned and rejuvenated.[90] It is not yet known if this was primarily a Danish or a subsequent English operation. However, its effect is not in doubt, for it must have marked the end of any lingering political importance of the settlement on the Lindsey promontory. Meanwhile its trading centre Wigford continued to thrive, but from then on as a suburb of Lincoln.

THE MAJOR CHURCHES OF ANGLO-SAXON AND NORMAN LINCOLN

The middle Saxon minster

Since the see of Lindsey took its name from this early Anglo-Saxon settlement, one must presume that there was a major minster church on the promontory by the later seventh century. Our present ignorance of it is no doubt largely due to its eventual replacement – whether as a cathedral or simply as the mother church of Lincoln – by a church situated somewhere within the walled area north of the Witham. Thereafter, the former cathedral on the promontory may have disappeared entirely; it is, however, much more likely that it survived to become one of the twelve parish churches of later medieval Wigford,[91] for loss

---

[88] Biddle, 'Towns', pp. 120–2 and refs. cited there; see also J. Haslam, 'Market and Fortress in England in the Reign of Offa', *World Archaeol.* 19.1 (June, 1987), 76–93.

[89] Assuming that they preferred to use them (as Haslam supposes: *ibid.* p. 81 and fig. 2) rather than to fortify the Lindsey promontory. There is no archaeological evidence of early defences on the promontory, but it is nonetheless interesting to note the antiquary Camden's account of Anglo-Saxon activities at Lincoln: 'Old Lincoln of the Britons is supposed to have been on the very peak of a hill, where Nennius . . . records that the warlike Briton Vortimer [son of Vortigern] was buried. But when he had been overthrown, the Saxons at first settled the southern part of the hill, and fortified it from the ruins of its antiquity; they afterwards went down to the river and built in the place called Wigford (*Wickanforde*), which they fenced in with ramparts (*moenibus obsepserunt*) wherever it was not defended by the river' (W. Camden, *Britannia; sive, Florentissimorum regnorum, Angliae, Scotiae, Hiberniae . . . chronographica descripta* (London, 1594), p. 415). Camden's *moenibus* may mean nothing more than Sincil Dyke, but his account has features which tally with the archaeological and place-name evidence for Lincoln's early history and so might just embody a genuine tradition about earthwork defences.

[90] Perring, *Early Medieval Occupation at Flaxengate, Lincoln*, pp. 44 and 46; Jones, 'New Streets for Old', p. 88.

[91] Listed and mapped in Gilmour and Stocker, *St Mark's Church and Cemetery*, fig. 1 on p. 2.

of the see need not have meant an end to the church's existence. As in similar instances elsewhere it could well have retained a parochial function (if only on the promontory itself from then on).

Accordingly, the middle Saxon cathedral may yet be recognized from some slight evidence, so far overlooked, in medieval or later sources showing that it was (or once had been) the senior church in Wigford. None of Wigford's parish churches is recorded until 1107, when seven of them were given by Henry I to the see of Lincoln;[92] while the other five, though undocumented until the later twelfth century, need be of no later origin. For various reasons three of the twelve look likelier than the rest to be early ones – St Mary-le-Wigford, St Peter-at-Gowts, and St Botolph's. They and two other churches, St Benedict's and St Mark's, alone kept their parochial status after the Act of Union of Parishes of 1549, largely because of their greater strength and importance.[93]

The churches of St Mary-le-Wigford and St Peter-at-Gowts have towers which were built in Anglo-Saxon style at some time in the eleventh century, but it is clear in both cases that the tower was added to an existing nave (which at St Peter's was evidently of much earlier date).[94] The medieval fabric of St Botolph's has been demolished, but its dedication to a seventh-century saint could indicate a church of middle Saxon origin. In addition each of the three churches had a parish which included land beyond one or both of the watercourses bounding the promontory. By contrast St Benedict's and St Mark's may not have been so old. At the northern tip of the promontory the tiny parish of St Benedict's church, which also has an eleventh-century tower,[95] looks to have been carved out of the parish of St Mary-le-Wigford; while St Mark's church has now been shown by excavation to be of no earlier than tenth-century origin.[96]

There is at present, therefore, no independent evidence of any church of middle Saxon origin on the promontory (let alone of one which once had the status of a major minster). Three existing parish churches stand out as candidates for identification as the former senior church of Wigford. All, however, are of similar likelihood,[97] so that new evidence would be needed to

---

[92] *Regesta regum Anglo-Normannorum* II, ed. C. Johnson and H.A. Cronne (Oxford, 1956), no. 821 (for the date 1107); *The Registrum Antiquissimum of the Cathedral Church of Lincoln* I, ed. C.W. Foster, Lincoln Record Soc. (Lincoln, 1931), 33 and 262; Hill, *Medieval Lincoln*, p. 144.

[93] Hill, *Medieval Lincoln*, pp. 147–8 and 166.

[94] H.M. Taylor, 'St Mary-le-Wigford, Lincoln', *ArchJ* 131 (1974), 348; H.M. Taylor, 'St Peter-at-Gowts, Lincoln', *ibid.* 348–50.

[95] H.M. and J. Taylor, *Anglo-Saxon Architecture*, 3 vols. (Cambridge, 1965–78) I, 390–1.

[96] Gilmour and Stocker, *St Mark's Church and Cemetery*, pp. 16–17.

[97] See below, pp. 26–7, for further discussion of St Mary-le-Wigford.

discover which (if any) was the correct one among them. That evidence is now likely to come only from archaeological excavation.

The late Saxon minster

The church within the walls which replaced the original head minster on the Lindsey promontory may of course be the Norman cathedral, dedicated to St Mary, which was begun by Bishop Remigius on the transfer of his see from Dorchester to Lincoln in 1072.[98] It has usually been accepted that he used an existing minster church in Lincoln while the new cathedral was under construction.[99] But in a recent paper Dr Dorothy Owen argues that there was no ancient episcopal church in Lincoln at that time, and that later-eleventh-century references to an important church of St Mary can all be explained in terms of Remigius's partly built cathedral.[100] It is true that some of the evidence for an existing minster church adduced by earlier writers is, as she points out, inconclusive, and that one might have expected more and clearer references to it, had it existed. However, it does seem that she has been unduly quick to dismiss the idea, since the evidence of a minster church dedicated to St Mary in Lincoln before 1072 is far stronger than she allows.

In Domesday Book almost all the lands in Lincolnshire of the new see of Lincoln are listed as the bishop's. St Mary of Lincoln is mentioned only rarely: several times incidentally but twice in contexts which suggest that it is not new. The first of the latter entries reports that 'St Mary of Lincoln, in which the bishopric now is, had and has the remaining half carucate of land'.[101] The phrase 'had and has' normally refers in Domesday Book to possession in 1066 and 1086; and one is only forced to give it a different meaning here if 'where the

---

[98] *Regesta regum Anglo-Normannorum* I, ed. H.W.C. Davis (Oxford, 1913), no. 283; *Registrum antiquissimum* I, ed. Foster, 3; *Giraldi Cambrensis opera*, ed. J.S. Brewer, J.F. Dimock and G.F. Warner, RS, 7 vols. (London, 1861–91) VII, 19. Giraldus Cambrensis, too, knew that Lindsey was a place south of the Witham and, it seems, that the Anglo-Saxon cathedral had once been there. In the *Vita S. Remigii*, probably written *c.* 1198 during the three years he spent at Lincoln (*ibid.* p. xi) Giraldus says, 'And so he [Remigius] energetically joined Lindsey, and the whole land between the Witham namely the river of Lincoln and the Humber ('Lindeseiam, terramque totam inter Widhemam scilicet Lincolniae fluvium et Humbriam') to his diocese and the province of Canterbury. And . . . he took care that his cathedral was founded in honour of the blessed virgin on the top of the hill at Lincoln across the Witham ('in summo apud Lincolniam montis vertice trans Widhemam') and was excellently built in a short while' (*ibid.* p. 19).

[99] E.g. Hill, *Medieval Lincoln*, p. 67; D.M. Owen, *Church and Society in Medieval Lincolnshire* (Lincoln, 1981), p. 37.

[100] D. Owen, 'The Norman Cathedral at Lincoln', *Anglo-Norman Studies VI*, ed. R.A. Brown (Woodbridge, 1984), 188–99.

[101] *Lincolnshire Domesday*, ed. Foster and Longley, pp. 4–5.

bishopric now is' is taken to indicate that St Mary of Lincoln is the new cathedral. That church, however, was not ready to be consecrated until 1092,[102] so that the most sensible explanation of the entry is that an existing church, probably of minster status in view of its designation as St Mary of Lincoln, was housing the bishop's seat while his new cathedral was in the course of construction.

The second Domesday entry leaves little doubt that there was an important secular minster church in Lincoln before 1072. It reads: 'Those lands which Alsi and Olgrim had in Lindsey they placed in the church of St Mary of Lincoln, and at the discretion of Bishop Wulfwig; and therefore Bishop Remigius claims them because they [Alsi and Olgrim] had 8 score pounds for these lands T.R.E.'.[103] It is difficult to see how this statement (overlooked by Dr Owen), which proves that the church of St Mary of Lincoln existed before 1066, could be taken to mean other than that it was an episcopal church. Remigius looked on its pre-Conquest possessions as rightly belonging to the see of Lincoln, and there is nothing to show that he was unsuccessful in his claim.

Other evidence also points to the conclusion that St Mary of Lincoln was a minster church, and that it had been the seat of at least the latest of the Anglo-Saxon bishops of Lindsey (the last of whom is not heard of after 1011).[104] A papal bull of 1163, addressed to the dean and canons of Lincoln, included confirmation of their right to what it says is commonly called Marycorn – an annual render of corn from every ploughland which the Lincolnshire parishioners of St Mary's have paid *ab antiquo*.[105] It has been pointed out that this is the only known reference to Marycorn, and that it was said to be levied on all Lincolnshire, not on Lindsey alone – indications perhaps of its novelty.[106] Yet the very absence of other references suggests that by the twelfth century the payment was a firmly and (as the bull states) anciently established one. Its application to the whole of Lincolnshire need not mean that it was of recent origin. Edgar's legislation on the payment of tithes (959–63?)[107] may have provided the mother church of Lincoln with as good an opportunity to raise a levy on the whole shire as it is likely to have had at any later date. Or it could date from as early as the time of the re-establishment (or

---

[102] *Florentii Wigorniensis monachi chronicon ex chronicis*, ed. B Thorpe, 2 vols. (London, 1848–9) II, 30. [103] *Lincolnshire Domesday*, ed. Foster and Longley, pp. 206–7.

[104] *Handbook of British Chronology*, ed. Fryde, *et al.*, p. 219.

[105] *Registrum antiquissimum* I, ed. Foster, 206.

[106] Owen, 'The Norman Cathedral at Lincoln', pp. 194–5.

[107] *English Historical Documents c. 500–1042*, ed. D. Whitelock, 2nd ed. (London, 1979), pp. 431–2.

revitalisation) of the diocese of Lindsey in the middle years of the tenth century, being based on the hinterland of Anglo-Danish Lincoln or on the slightly larger area which became its shire.[108] It could, however, be yet earlier, if the kingdom (therefore the diocese) of Lindsey was not much smaller than the shire established in the tenth century;[109] if so, a liability dating from the pre-Viking period to pay Marycorn could have been easily extended from the one to the other.

Obstacles to accepting St Mary of Lincoln as the head minster of Lindsey

Few obstacles now stand in the way of accepting that the St Mary of Lincoln to which Domesday Book refers had been the episcopal church of at least the tenth- and early-eleventh-century bishops of Lindsey. Only three of them are substantive ones: the alleged unlikelihood of such a church still having its status in the later eleventh century; its apparent lack of endowment then; and finally the vexed question of the St Martin pennies.

It has been suggested that Lincoln would not have retained a head minster with episcopal privileges once the see had been subsumed by Dorchester in the second decade of the eleventh century.[110] But one cannot see why St Mary's should not have kept the status and privileges of a bishop's church, just as former cathedrals which were relegated much later on in that century are known to have done. The see of Lindsey survived at least until 1011; fifty years later the *parochia* of Lindsey was still a reality to which specific reference is made in a bull of Pope Nicholas II in 1061.[111] It is true that the bull does not mention St Mary's itself, but the cumulative effect of the evidence already reviewed here leaves no doubt that it still existed as a major church.

The second obstacle is the almost complete silence of Domesday Book about the pre-Conquest endowments of St Mary's. But this is no different from the treatment which the same source accords to the minster church of St John, Chester, which had a directly analogous status and history to those of St Mary's in the eleventh century. Until 1075 St John's was an important minster church of ancient origin, evidently the principal church of the bishop of Lichfield in Cheshire. Then it became his cathedral until 1102, when the see was transferred to Coventry (at which time a new cathedral church at Chester was in the course of construction but still far from completion). However, Domesday Book mentions St John's only in connection with two parts of a hide in the unidentified rural manor of *Redeclive* and eight houses in the city of Chester. It

---

[108] After the addition of at least the northern part of Stamford's hinterland: Stenton, *Anglo-Saxon England*, p. 338.

[109] See above, pp. 2–3.   [110] Owen, 'The Norman Cathedral at Lincoln', p. 195.

[111] *Registrum antiquissimum* I, ed. Foster, 186.

is probable that all the rest of its possessions were listed with the bishop's own, with which they may have been permanently merged thereafter.[112]

The compilers of Domesday Book may have treated the lands of St Mary of Lincoln in an exactly similar way, which would in itself adequately explain the church's apparent lack of endowments appropriate to its status. It is possible, however, that some of the lands which it had held as the cathedral of the bishops of Lindsey are recorded in Domesday Book as possessions until 1066 of St Mary's, Stow-in-Lindsey, and others as the archbishop of York's.

The minster church of St Mary at Stow was founded by Eadnoth I, bishop of Dorchester from 1006 to 1016.[113] The exact date of foundation is unknown, but it surely cannot have been before the demise of the see of Lindsey (which was still in existence in 1011) and its absorption by Dorchester. Nothing is known of the church which Eadnoth founded,[114] but there can be no doubt that he endowed it with lands of the former see, ones which would have belonged until then to the church of St Mary of Lincoln. Indeed it was probably his intention, in founding a church dedicated to Mary on a site close to Lincoln, that it should act as the caretaker of episcopal lands in Lindsey, or at least of those in the vicinity of Lincoln. It may even have been envisaged as a refoundation of sorts, on a new site, of the former cathedral. If so, it seems not to have been too successful. When Stow church was endowed by Earl Leofric and his wife Godgifu between 1053 and 1055, their charter spoke of it in terms suggestive of its impoverished condition.[115] If much of the land given to it by Eadnoth had been subsequently lost (or never gained in the first place), Leofric may have been doing no more than restoring whatever of Stow's endowment had come into his hands. By 1086 Stow's lands, all lying close to it in an arc around the western and northern sides of Lincoln, were in the hands of Remigius.[116]

Domesday Book shows the archbishop of York with extensive holdings near Lincoln, mainly to the north-east and east of the city.[117] These lands too had presumably belonged until recently to the diocese of Lindsey; and York had already seized the diocese at least once (together, significantly, with Stow

---

112 A.T. Thacker, 'The Church in Cheshire', *A History of the County of Cheshire* i, ed. B.E. Harris, Victoria Hist. of the Counties of England (Oxford, 1987), 268–73; N. Pevsner and E. Hubbard, *The Buildings of England: Cheshire* (Harmondsworth, 1971), p. 149. I am grateful to Dr R.N. Swanson for drawing my attention to St John's, Chester.

113 *Florentii Wigorniensis Monachi chronicon ex chronicis*, ed. Thorpe i, 216; Hill, *Medieval Lincoln*, pp. 74–5.

114 *Ibid.* p. 75. The earliest fabric in the present church is probably of mid-eleventh-century date: E. Fernie, *The Architecture of the Anglo-Saxons* (London, 1983), p. 127.

115 *Anglo-Saxon Charters*, ed. A.J. Robertson (Cambridge, 1939), pp. 213–17.

116 *Lincolnshire Domesday*, ed. Foster and Longley, pp. 47–8.   117 *Ibid.* pp. 25–30.

church) in the course of its lengthy dispute with Dorchester over the control of Lindsey.[118]

It is clear, then, that a considerable amount of the land which the see of Lindsey had held until the early eleventh century had by 1086 passed out of its control, to the obvious detriment of its former cathedral. The foundation of Stow church seems to have eclipsed St Mary of Lincoln – hence perhaps the reference to the one but not the other in Pope Nicholas II's bull of 1061 – and it may only have been the need of Remigius for an appropriate base in Lincoln from 1072 until his new cathedral was up, that brought St Mary's back into temporary prominence.

The third and final obstacle to accepting St Mary's as the cathedral of the late Anglo-Saxon bishops of Lindsey is a small group of Viking coins known as the St Martin pennies, which are taken by some as evidence that there was an episcopal church dedicated to St Martin in Lincoln in the early tenth century. These five silver pennies all have the Lincoln mint signature on them and the legend sci m/arti(*ni*) on the obverse. They are thought to have been struck in the early 920s, and they clearly imitate the type of the second phase of the much better known St Peter coins.[119] The first-phase pennies of the latter series were minted at York probably under the archbishop's authority, bearing the legend s(*an*)c(*t*)i petri mo(*neta*) in commemoration of his cathedral's dedication. Some of the second-phase ones were also struck there; but others (which the St Martin pennies most closely resemble) may not have been, and there is some speculation that they could have been struck at Lincoln.[120]

No bishops of Lindsey are heard of between the later 870s and the middle of the tenth century, so the St Martin pennies are unlikely to have been struck under episcopal authority. That does not mean that the head minster itself on the Lindsey promontory was not still staffed and playing an active role in the Lincoln area if not throughout the diocese.

However, if one were to see these coins as a strict analogue to the St Peter pennies struck at York, not only would they provide further, independent, proof that the see of Lindsey was at Lincoln (as this paper has argued), but they would also show that it was based on a church dedicated to St Martin and that there probably was still (or again) a bishop in office there in the 920s. It would

---

[118] *Registrum antiquissimum* i, ed. Foster, 186; Hill, *Medieval Lincoln*, pp. 65–6.

[119] H.R. Mossop, *The Lincoln Mint c. 890–1279*, ed. V. Smart (Newcastle-upon-Tyne, 1970), pl. i, nos. 7–11; I. Stewart, 'The St Martin Coins of Lincoln', *BNJ* 36 (1967), 46–54, at 46–7 and 54; M. Blackburn, C. Colyer and M. Dolley, *Early Medieval Coins from Lincoln and its Shire c.770–1100*, LAT Monograph Ser. 6.1 (London, 1983), 14.

[120] Stewart, 'The St Martin Coins', pp. 47 and 51; Blackburn, *et al.*, *Early Medieval Coins*, pp. 13–14.

follow from this that the cathedral would have to have been rededicated to Mary at some time during the next century and a half, or else replaced by a different church with that dedication. Neither is out of the question; and if it were to have been the latter, then a case could be made for identifying the superseded church as St Martin in Dernstall. St Martin's appears originally to have had a large parish in the western half of Lincoln's lower walled area, out of which a number of other parishes were formed for later, lesser, churches.[121] If it was indeed the first church in that area, as has been suggested, its dedication to a fourth-century Gaulish bishop may (if an unchanged one) indicate a church which is potentially as early in origin as St Paul-in-the-Bail.

It is, however, most unlikely that St Martin in Dernstall was the cathedral church of the middle Saxon bishops of Lindsey. For reasons already set out here, that must have lain on the promontory to the south of the river since its foundation. A realistic explanation of the St Martin pennies, therefore, is indeed to associate them with the church of St Martin in Dernstall, but to see them as an expression of *esprit de corps* by Lincoln's Danish (or by then Anglo-Danish) community, an aping of its more illustrious neighbour York, rather than as representing any sort of precise ecclesiastical statement.

St Martin in Dernstall was prominently situated at the very centre of the lower walled area, at the junction of Ermine Street and its main east-west Roman street. It is plain that that area was settled and speedily rejuvenated during the Danish occupation of Lincoln,[122] no doubt because its Roman walls afforded much greater security than did the undefended promontory, while allowing unrestricted access to the Witham water-front. If St Martin's was in existence already, it may well have seemed to Danish Christians to be suitably comparable to the minster church of St Peter at York, set at the heart of the legionary fortress. If it was of Danish foundation, its site was well chosen for its purpose. In either case it must have seemed far better situated than the head minster was on the Lindsey promontory below.

Before leaving the subject of coinage it is worth noting an adventurous suggestion made recently about those of the second-phase St Peter pennies which are distinguished by a sword on the obverse (which the St Martin pennies also have) and, on the reverse, by a cross and 'blundered legends that appear meaningless'. It is to the effect that, if these coins were struck not at York but at Lincoln, 'St Peter ... the patron of the Church of York ... may also have been the first dedication of a major church at Lincoln, in which case the SCI M/ARTI(*ni*) legend found on a handful of silver pennies from the early 920s

---

[121] Owen, 'The Norman Cathedral at Lincoln', p. 190, n. 19.   [122] See above, n. 90.

25

could represent an attempt to resolve ambiguities'.[123] However speculative it is, the suggestion acts as a salutary reminder that, as evidence of the dedication and indeed the whereabouts of the cathedral church of Lindsey, the St Martin pennies carry little weight in comparison with other forms of evidence.

The temporary Norman cathedral

It remains to ask where the church was located which Remigius used from 1072 until his new cathedral was completed. It has been usual to assume that St Mary of Lincoln originated *de novo* after the Danish settlement and conversion to Christianity were complete, probably in the tenth century.[124] The extent, however, to which individual churches and the parochial topography in eastern England were destroyed during the ninth century, not merely badly disrupted, can be exaggerated. In areas not directly affected by Viking raids many minster churches of middle Saxon origin were refounded and often rebuilt in the tenth and early eleventh centuries; and in eastern England there was much need of revitalisation for reasons quite apart from Viking depredations.[125] Certainly on occasion entirely new minster churches were founded, but these as often as not supplemented rather than replaced those of much earlier date.[126] There is no need, therefore, to assume that St Mary of Lincoln must have been an entirely new, late Anglo-Saxon, foundation. It is quite likely that it had been the church of the bishops of Lindsey for as long as there had been any. Alternatively, it may well have been the immediate replacement for that church, if it needed effective re-establishment in the tenth century (after quite a lengthy interruption in the succession of bishops of Lindsey) and, in all probability, relocation on a new, more suitable site.

It is not, then, inconceivable that St Mary of Lincoln was situated on the Lindsey promontory throughout the Anglo-Saxon period. If so it can only have become one of the twelve later medieval parish churches of Wigford, since it is most unlikely that a church which had already survived the loss of a see in the early eleventh century and of its last remaining lands by 1086 would not merely have resumed its less elevated role as a parish church in 1092. The only one of the twelve with a dedication to Mary was the church known by the thirteenth century as St Mary in (or of) Wigford, and today as St Mary-le-Wigford; this has already been identified as one of three parish churches likely to be the oldest ones on the promontory.

---

[123] Blackburn, *et al.*, *Early Medieval Coins*, p. 14.   [124] E.g. Hill, *Medieval Lincoln*, pp. 72–3.

[125] *The Anglo-Saxons*, ed. J. Campbell (Oxford, 1982), p. 147. One no longer need believe that 'Not a church was left standing, nor a religious house spared throughout the county': *The Victoria History of the County of Lincoln* II, ed. W. Page (London, 1906), 6.

[126] W. J. Blair, 'Secular Minster Churches in Domesday Book', *Domesday Book. A Reassessment*, ed. P. H. Sawyer (London, 1985), pp. 104–42, at 120–3.

It may be significant, therefore, that St Mary-le-Wigford does not appear to have been one of those many privately owned churches in Lincoln which Bishop Remigius and his first two successors gained through royal patronage. Although it is plainly of pre-Conquest origin (the present structure includes late Anglo-Saxon, probably eleventh-century, fabric), the church does not figure in any of the charters and bulls issued on behalf of the see of Lincoln by the middle of the twelfth century, or in any of the bishops' own charters in the same period.[127] The only comparable later source in which it appears is a confirmation of possessions addressed to the dean and canons of Lincoln by Pope Alexander III in 1163 (the bull which also confirms the see's right to levy Marycorn).[128] This may mean that the church of St Mary-le-Wigford was such a secure possession of the see of Lincoln from 1072 onwards that it did not need to figure in any but the most general confirmation.

It could equally mean, of course, that it was a late acquisition, one of those private churches whose owners could prove their title, and so maintain their ownership, when many similar churches were being given to the bishopric. The notion of its private ownership before the Conquest is prompted by a dedication stone built into the church's late Anglo-Saxon tower (apparently *in situ*) with an inscription that has been translated as 'Eirtig had me built and endowed to the glory of Christ and St Mary'.[129] Though this shows that St Mary-le-Wigford was apparently in private hands for a while in the eleventh century, it need not mean that it could not have passed to the bishopric at some time before 1072. It certainly need not mean that St Mary-le-Wigford originated as a private church: there is nothing in its eleventh-century status to rule out its once having been the cathedral church of the bishops of Lindsey.

On balance, however, St Mary-le-Wigford does seem unlikely to have been the church which Remigius used to house his seat until 1092. That church should, therefore, be sought elsewhere. If it stood within the walls of Lincoln, then it may well have lain close to the site on which the new cathedral had been built by 1092.

The late thirteenth-century chronicler John de Schalby, a canon of Lincoln and bishop's registrar, wrote that the new cathedral was built 'in the place where the church of St Mary Magdalene . . . was situated'.[130] Some scholars have taken Schalby's words to mean that the one replaced the other on the same site, but no pre-Norman fabric has ever been reported found in

---

[127] E.g. *Registrum antiquissimum* I, ed. Foster, nos. 2, 10, 24, 34, 45, 67, 252 and 302.

[128] *Ibid.* p. 205.

[129] Taylor, 'St Mary-le-Wigford, Lincoln', p. 348.

[130] 'In loco autem in quo ecclesia beatae Mariae Magdalenae . . . sita erat': *Giraldi Cambrensis opera*, ed. Brewer, *et al.* VII, 194.

excavations in the cathedral.[131] Moreover, William I's notification of the establishment of the new see stated that he had provided Remigius with 'enough land, free and quit of all customs, for the cathedral and its other buildings'.[132] This implies that they were to be built on a different site from Schalby's church of St Mary Magdalene, one consisting at least in part of land not formerly held by the latter. So if this earlier church was not a figment of Schalby's imagination, it may well have survived for some while, perhaps serving as the cathedral's parish church as other Anglo-Saxon minster churches did elsewhere in not dissimilar circumstances.[133]

It would have been demolished by the later thirteenth century, since Schalby relates that inhabitants of its parish used part of the cathedral nave for their services, and that their children were baptised in its font, until Bishop Oliver Sutton (1280–99) built them a separate church dedicated to St Mary Magdalene in the cemetery.[134] This still stands due west of the cathedral, but is now outside its precinct. It may be on much the same site as its putative Anglo-Saxon predecessor, for one notes that Remigius put his new church hard up against the Roman wall which then bounded the precinct to the east,[135] as if in some way restricted to the west.

St Mary Magdalene's parish at its earliest known extent is considerably larger than those attached to most parish churches of cathedrals. This and the fact that it contained the whole area of Lincoln castle are further indications that it was the anciently established parish of an important church which was already in existence in 1072 when Remigius decided to erect his cathedral there.

It seems, then, that this church could well be the one which housed the bishop's seat until 1092. Only the dedication – to Mary Magdalene not to Mary the Virgin – is wrong. But that information derives from Schalby and need not be correct. The popularity of Mary Magdalene rose sharply in the thirteenth

---

[131] A.W. Clapham, 'Lincoln Cathedral. 1: Explanatory Note', *ArchJ* 103 (1946), 102–3, at 102; J. Bilson, 'The Plan of the First Cathedral Church of Lincoln', *Archaeologia* 62 (1911), 543–64. Two grave slabs of uncertain provenance, now in the cathedral cloister, are thought to be of mid-eleventh-century date: Owen, 'The Norman Cathedral of Lincoln', p. 194.

[132] 'Terram ab omnibus consuetudinibus solutam et quietam sufficienter dedisse ad construendam matrem ecclesiam totius episcopatus et eiusdem officinas': *Registrum antiquissimum* 1, ed. Foster, 3.

[133] As happened, for example, at Winchcombe and Oxford: S.R. Bassett, 'A Probable Mercian Royal Mausoleum at Winchcombe, Gloucestershire', *AntJ* 65 (1985), 82–100, at 88; J. Blair, 'St Frideswide Reconsidered', *Oxoniensia* 52 (1987), 71–127, at 89.

[134] *Giraldi Cambrensis opera*, ed. Brewer, *et al.* VII, 209.

[135] The cathedral was not extended east of the line of the Roman defences until the very end of the twelfth century: D.A. Stocker, 'Excavations to the South of Lincoln Minster 1984 and 1985 – An Interim Report', *Lincolnshire Hist. and Arch.* 20 (1985), 15–19, at 18.

century,[136] so that the dedication to her of a new church at the end of that century need have no direct bearing on the dedication of its late Anglo-Saxon predecessor. (Contrary to some modern historians' claims, Schalby, a contemporary witness, does not say that the altar in the cathedral nave formerly used by its parishioners was dedicated to St Mary Magdalene.) With the cathedral itself (as well as two parish churches in the city) already bearing a dedication to St Mary the Virgin, it would not be surprising if the real possibility of confusion had been avoided by giving a different one to the newly built parish church. What is surprising, however, is that another Mary was chosen rather than any other saint; this may indicate a dim but genuine memory (accurately represented by Schalby) that the original church had also been dedicated to Mary.

The minster church of St Mary of Lincoln is most likely to have been established within the walls as a replacement (immediate or otherwise) for its predecessor on the Lindsey promontory; this probably took place some time in the tenth century, once Lincoln had come back under English control and perhaps in connection with the re-establishment of the see of Lindsey by 953.[137] The dedication to Mary may date from then: only a few middle Saxon churches are reliably known to have borne that dedication, but from the tenth century onwards it rapidly became one of the most popular ones.[138] Meanwhile any superior status which St Martin in Dernstall (in the lower town) may have had during the Danish occupation seems soon to have been lost. It remained one of Lincoln's most important parish churches, but by 1086 was in private ownership.[139]

CONCLUSIONS

There is enough evidence, it seems, to outline a more precise model for the history of Lincoln and the see of Lindsey in the Anglo-Saxon period than has been available before. The *colonia* north of the Witham may have retained something of its former administrative and ecclesiastical role in the first few medieval centuries, but the focus of Lincoln's continuing importance as a regional centre increasingly shifted to the extramural settlement beside its water-fronts. The *Lindenses* (later *Lindēs*), 'the people of *Lindum*', may have been especially associated with that area even before the end of the Roman

[136] F. Arnold-Forster, *Studies in Church Dedications*, 3 vols. (London, 1899) I, 90.

[137] That is, not before late in 918, but perhaps not until the later 920s at the earliest: Stenton, *Anglo-Saxon England*, p. 331; Blackburn, *et al.*, *Early Medieval Coins*, p. 13; *Handbook of British Chronology*, ed. Fryde, *et al.*, p. 219.

[138] W. Levison, *England and the Continent in the Eighth Century* (Oxford, 1946), pp. 263–4; Arnold-Forster, *Studies in Church Dedications* I, 41–2.

[139] *Registrum antiquissimum* I, ed. Foster, 15.

period. They certainly were by the time when the promontory south of the walled town was given its name '*ēg* of the *Lindēs', Lindsey.

There an important settlement developed. By the seventh century its leading family ruled a substantial kingdom which in all probability extended far to the south of Lincoln as well as to the north. The established view has been that its extent was that of the later administrative area called Lindsey. But that is fatally undermined by what has been shown of the early medieval significance of the Lindsey promontory, which lay outside the boundaries traditionally ascribed to the kingdom and diocese. So long as it was thought that Lindsey originated as a district name, the knowledge that later medieval and modern Lindsey was effectively surrounded by water reinforced Stenton's view that the Anglo-Saxon kingdom must have shared the same extent. But once Lindsey is seen to be the name of a specific place, and then the (conflated) name of the settlement there on which the kingdom was centred, it is simple enough to accept that that kingdom could have been a lot larger than the administrative region which eventually inherited its name.

The site of the early Anglo-Saxon settlement on the Lindsey promontory is unknown, but it may have been beyond the former (Roman) suburban sprawl along Ermine Street, in the north-eastern part of the promontory where Lincoln's main commercial activity may always have been concentrated. Its inhabitants were probably of mixed British and Anglo-Saxon stock, even if the leading family, the kingdom's rulers, thought itself Germanic. They may still have been known as *Lindēs, or else they could have had an Old English name *Sȳðe*, 'southern people', appropriate to the location of their settlement across the river from the walled town.

It was adjacent to this settlement that a major market developed in the middle Saxon period, no doubt substantially encouraged by Mercia's extension of overlordship to the kingdom and effective annexation of it. The political and economic significance of the combined royal centre and *wīc* is epitomised in *Lindesfara*, 'people who resort to a place named *Lindesse/ Lindesig*', the name not only of those belonging to the mainland kingdom but also of the inhabitants of an important island off the coast of Bernicia, close to the major Northumbrian royal centre at Bamburgh. But during the Danish occupation of Lincoln in the late ninth century, if not earlier on, this centre's administrative role was transferred to the walled area north of the Witham. Thereafter the Lindsey promontory doubtless quickly reverted to its original status as a suburb of the walled town of Lincoln, becoming increasingly widely known as Wigford.

There, too, stood the church which was the seat of the bishops of Lindsey, probably a minster church of seventh-century foundation typical of most other Anglo-Saxon sees. It is not inconceivable that it remained the head minster of the see (whenever the latter had a separate existence) until the cathedral which Remigius built in the walled town was ready to be consecrated in 1092. It is, however, likelier that the head minster had been moved north of the Witham well before the Conquest – perhaps in the tenth century after Lincoln had been regained from Danish control. If so, the site of the church of St Mary Magdalene, immediately west of the present cathedral, is much the strongest candidate for its location. The site, meanwhile, of the original head minster of the bishops of Lindsey, like that of the settlement it adjoined, still awaits its archaeological rediscovery on the Lindsey promontory.[140]

APPENDIX

THE NAME LINDSEY

MARGARET GELLING

The first element of Lindsey is the British name of Lincoln. This was *Lindon*, 'pool', to which Latin *colonia* was added when the place attained that status in the Roman period. The development of the second part of the name Lindsey has not been satisfactorily explained, however, and this note is a tentative essay which may serve at least as an indication of the shortcomings of previous accounts.

The earliest spellings for Lindsey occur in Bede's *Ecclesiastical History*. Here the name is *(prouincia) Lindissi* and, once, *Lindissae (prouinciae)*. The spelling *Lindissi*, which occurs six times in Bede's text, is a form which presents difficult problems. The -*ss*- and the final -*i* require explanation. The basis of the name Lindsey is generally assumed to be a folk-name derived from the stem of *Lindon* with the addition of the suffix -*enses*. British Latin *Lindenses became *Lindēs, and Jackson says that *Lindēs was taken into Primitive Anglo-Saxon and incorporated in '*Lindesse* etc., Lindsey (Li) and Lindisfarne (Nb)'.[141] The reference to '*Lindesse* etc.' begs the question. A folk-name *Lindenses*, later *Lindēs*, should give a form *Lindis in Bede. Leeds, which is assumed to derive from another folk-name, British *Lātenses, later *Lōdēses, is *Loidis* in the *Ecclesiastical History*.[142]

A form for Lindsey which corresponds to Bede's *Lindissi* appears to have been current until the late ninth century. The *Anglo-Saxon Chronicle's* entry for 873 has *Lindesse*, showing the change of unstressed *i* to *e* which occurred shortly after Bede's time.[143] But there is evidence for another form in the ninth century. Asser calls the province *Lindesig* and *Lindissig*.[144] W.H. Stevenson noted that *Lindesig* was not the

---

140 I am very grateful to the following: Professor N.P. Brooks and Dr Margaret Gelling, for their valuable advice and criticism at all stages in the preparation of this paper; and Dr W.J. Blair, Professor K. Cameron, Professor R.H.C. Davis, Dr A. S. Esmonde Cleary, Mr M.J. Jones and Dr S. Keynes for their many helpful comments and corrections.

141 Jackson, *Language and History in Early Britain*, p. 543.

142 *HE* II.14 and III.24 (pp. 188 and 292); K.H. Jackson, 'On the Name "Leeds"', *Antiquity* 20 (1946), 209–10.　　143 873 AB, 874 C: *Two Chronicles*, ed. Plummer I, 72 (A).

144 *Asser's Life of King Alfred*, ed. Stevenson, p. 34 (in chs. 45 and 46).

same name as Bede's *Lindissi* and the *Lindesse* of the *Chronicle*, and he suggested that it was a later form, 'the name having been wrongly connected with OE *īeg*, *īg*, "island"'.[145] Asser's form can be projected back into the first half of the ninth century. In the annal for 838 the D version of the *Anglo-Saxon Chronicle* has *Lindesige*, where other versions have *Lindesse*.[146] As the D *Chronicle* is believed to have been compiled at York[147] this may reflect local knowledge of an alternative form of the name.

The D *Chronicle's Lindesige* and Asser's *Lindesig* afford a satisfactory basis for the eventual form of the name, and it seems probable that a form with *-īg*, 'island', was current together with *Lindesse*. The majority of Middle English spellings certainly point to derivation from *īg/ēg* (though the exact proportion of eccentric forms and those which are influenced by knowledge of Bede's spelling will not be apparent until the publication of vol. 2 of Professor Kenneth Cameron's *Place-Names of Lincolnshire*).

If Asser's *Lindesig* were due, as Stevenson suggested, to analogical reformation of an earlier name, this would at least be confirmation of the view that the *Lindissi*, *Lindesse* forms have a final element, and are not simple derivatives of a folk-name *Lindēs*. If there had been no final element there would have been nothing for popular etymology to operate on. It seems more likely, however, that *Lindesse* and *Lindesig* were alternative names, formed from *Lindēs* and two alternative final elements, both of which were appropriate to a site near Lincoln, or, more specifically, near the pool of Lincoln.

The final element of Bede's *Lindissi* cannot, unfortunately, be *īg*, *ēg*, 'island'. An archaic nominative of this word was current in Northumbria in Bede's time, and names which contain the element regularly have the spelling *-eu* in the *Ecclesiastical History*. In addition to this objection there is the need to explain the *-ss-*. If we had only the *Anglo-Saxon Chronicle's Lindesse* it would be possible to suggest as final element OE *sǣ*, which meant 'lake' as well as 'sea' and could have been used of the pool at Lincoln. But the *Chronicle* form must be seen as a later development of Bede's *Lindissi*, and *sǣ* does not suit. The final element of Bede's form is unexplained.

The final element of *Lindissi* has been dropped in the compound *Lindisfari*, and in the *Lindesfara* of the 'Tribal Hidage'. But the tribal name only makes sense if it is interpreted as meaning 'people who resort to a place named *Lindesse/Lindesig*'.

---

[145] *Ibid.* p. 242 (n. to ch. 45).
[146] 838 D (= 841): *An Anglo-Saxon Chronicle*, ed. Classen and Harmer, p. 24.
[147] *The Anglo-Saxon Chronicle: A Revised Translation*, ed. D. Whitelock, *et al.* (London, 1961; rev. 1965), p. xiv and ref. cited there.

A new fragment of a ninth-century English bible

MICHELLE P. BROWN

The fragment in question consists of the remains of a bifolium,[1] now a complete single leaf with an irregular stub carrying the ends of three lines of script at its head.[2] The text is Judges v.5–6, vi.6 and x.7 to xi.26. It is undecorated, but written in a highly accomplished Insular cursive minuscule of Phase ii.[3] The fragment, hitherto unpublished, is of importance as the relict of what may have been a bible written in Southumbria during the first half of the ninth century and which on stylistic grounds evidently belongs to the so-called 'Canterbury' or 'Tiberius' group of manuscripts.[4] This group has played a prominent and often controversial role in the evaluation of the ninth century and its contribution to the history of Anglo-Saxon manuscript production.[5]

---

[1] The leaf was offered for sale by Christie, Manson and Woods Ltd on 2 December 1987, as lot 137 of the Estelle Doheny Collection, from the Edward Laurence Doheny Memorial Library St John's Seminary, Camarillo, California. It was bought by Bernard Quaritch Ltd for Prof. T. Takamiya of Keio University, Japan, and is now in the Takamiya Collection, Tokyo. Countess Doheny purchased the leaf from H.P. Kraus. It was previously owned by Dr E.A. Lowe, but does not, however, appear in his masterly survey volumes, *Codices Latini Antiquiores* (11 vols. and supp., Oxford, 1934–71; hereafter *CLA*), perhaps because of the fact of private ownership, but probably also owing to his perception of the chronology of Insular script, which led him, rightly, to omit the 'Book of Cerne' (Cambridge, University Library, Ll. 1. 10) from a survey which was restricted by an artificial upper chronological limit of *c.* 800.

[2] I should like to thank the following for their kind assistance in the preparation of this paper: Professor T. Takamiya, Hans Fellner, Richard Linenthal, Tony Parker, Vanessa Marshall, Marvin Colker, Michael Lapidge, Michael Reeve, Rosamond McKitterick, Mildred Budny, Patrick McGurk and Cecil Brown.

[3] The terminology is that of T.J. Brown; see 'The Irish Element in the Insular System of Scripts', *Die Iren und Europa im früheren Mittelalter*, ed. H. Löwe, 2 vols. (Stuttgart, 1982) I, 101–19, at 113 and 115–16.

[4] For a discussion of the 'Tiberius' group, see K. Sisam, 'Canterbury, Lichfield and the Vespasian Psalter', *RES* n.s. 7 (1956), 1–10, and 8 (1957), 370–4.

[5] For recent discussions which favour a more positive view of the achievements of the ninth century see the following: J. Morrish, 'King Alfred's Letter as a Source on Learning in England', *Studies in Earlier Old English Prose*, ed. P.E. Szarmach (Binghamton, 1986), pp. 87–107, and 'Dated and Datable Manuscripts copied in England during the Ninth Century', *MS* 50 (1988), 512–38; M.P. Brown, 'Paris, Bibliothèque Nationale, lat. 10861 and the Scriptorium of Christ Church, Canterbury', *ASE* 15 (1987), 119–37, and 'Continental

This new evidence sheds further valuable light upon this group of well-known manuscripts, but also raises some interesting new questions. A study of this piece is also of interest as a codicological exercise, which can highlight the ways in which the history of fragments and their varied fortunes may be reconstructed.

PHYSICAL DESCRIPTION

The leaf is housed in a blue morocco-backed buckram case of twentieth-century date, labelled on the spine 'Biblia Latina A–S 1 leaf 1xth cent.', with a Doheny *ex-libris* leather plate on the inside cover.

Measured along the present fore-edge and tail the dimensions are 278 × 200 mm for the full leaf and 278 × 47 mm (maximum) for the stub, which is broadest at its head and which is cut at a gentle curve of seven lines extent, tapering to a thin stub. Heavy trimming has taken place, especially at head and fore-edge, with consequent loss of text. The reconstructed written space would have measured approximately 274 × 209 mm, with two columns of approximately 93 mm width and an intercolumnar space of approximately 23 mm. The present lower margin is approximately 32 mm deep and the gutter margin approximately 9 mm wide. The membrane is prepared in Insular fashion, with little hair/flesh contrast and a slightly suede-like knap.[6] Pricking and ruling are complex, providing double bounding lines for both columns and both margins, at 7 mm spacing. Horizontals are ruled for both head and base lines, with 10 mm spacing between base lines and 4 mm between head and base lines. The latter feature is rare, but may be paralleled in de luxe Insular manuscripts, such as the Lindisfarne Gospels (London, British Library, Cotton Nero D. iv), although these employ a higher grade of bilinear Insular half-uncial script, unlike the quattrolinear cursive minuscule of our fragment. The script is light, with a width:height stroke ratio of 1:4, and with ascenders/ descenders extending to 6 mm and bows to 3 mm width.

At some point in its later history the stub-folding has been reversed; it will therefore be referred to as fol. 1 and the full leaf as fol. 2. It would originally have preceded the full leaf, producing a characteristic Insular quire arrange-

---

Symptoms in Insular Codicology: Historical Perspectives', *Pergament*, ed. P. Ruck (Sigmaringen, forthcoming). See also N. Brooks, *The Early History of the Church of Canterbury* (Leicester, 1984), pp. 111–206; M.O. Budny, 'London, British Library MS Royal 1. E. VI: the Anatomy of an Anglo-Saxon Bible Fragment' (unpubl. Ph.D dissertation, London Univ., 1985), pp. 753–802. For an outline of the case in favour of decline see H. Gneuss, 'King Alfred and the History of Anglo-Saxon Libraries', *Modes of Interpretation in Old English Literature*, ed. P.R. Brown, G.R. Crampton and F.C. Robinson (Toronto, 1986), pp. 29–49.

[6] See T.J. Brown, 'The Distribution and Significance of Membrane prepared in the Insular Manner', *Colloques Internationaux du C.N.R.S.* 547 (Paris, 1972), 127–35. A number of long, straight hairs which remain on the membrane of the fragment suggest that it is not sheepskin.

ment of hair-side facing outwards, with pricking and ruling (in hard point) conducted after folding, on the uppermost hair-side. Horizontal ruling is confined by the columnar bounding lines. Lacunae in the text suggest that three to four lines have been lost from the head, with an original arrangement of two columns of twenty-seven to twenty-eight lines.

A good black ink of carbon and gall was used, with little fading, despite subsequent binding use. The inks used for later additions (see below) either exhibit a greater tendency towards fading and a lower carbon content or are faded brown ferrous inks. Three small copper-stained holes near the centre of the leaf, and at approximately one-third of the height of the present leaf from its head, along with several small and scattered traces, may suggest contact with the pigment verdigris, but are more likely to have been caused by a copper alloy binding mechanism, probably of single strap and pin type.[7] There are a number of worm holes. In the lower right-hand margin of 2r is a faint pencil inscription which appears under ultra-violet light to consist of a rectangular frame containing *Her* (or *n*) *o* (or *g*) *re* (or *m*) *i* (or *d* or *t*)' with the central letters underscored with a wavy line. The first element might be thought to represent a contraction of *Henricus*. Although difficult to date in their present state, the letter forms would suggest a seventeenth- or eighteenth-century date. There is a membrane-strip repair (not recent) to the inner half of the lower margin of 2r. There are also some traces of modern repair tissue. 2v exhibits discoloration and striation caused by paste or glue, but this is absent from 1v (the stub now folded over to partially cover 2v).

The gutter of the fragment supplies useful codicological evidence. The marks found there are of two types: horizontal slits and small round prickings. The slits may be interpreted as the original sewing stations,[8] the head kettle-stitch and the first sewing station having been lost during trimming, the third sewing station slit having been repeated, perhaps due to misplacement or to subsequent re-use, and the final slit relating to the foot kettle-stitch. This would suggest an original sewing on supports, consisting of six single cords, the third and fourth of which were placed closer together than the others, perhaps being thereby intended to reinforce the point of greatest strain.[9] Slits 3, 5 and 6 are each flanked by a pair of prick-marks which may have been added

---

[7] For verdigris, see D.V. Thompson, *The Materials and Techniques of Medieval Painting* (New York, 1956), pp. 163–4 and 167. For single strap and pin, see D. Muzerelle, *Vocabulaire Codicologique* (Paris, 1985), fig. 314.

[8] Slits also appear in this context in the Book of Cerne; see M.P. Brown, 'Cambridge, University Library, MS Ll. 1 10, the Book of Cerne' (unpubl. Ph.D dissertation, London Univ., forthcoming).

[9] It is interesting to note that the Royal Bible (BL, Royal 1. E. VI) was sewn on five cords, although its dimensions were somewhat larger; see Budny, 'Royal 1. E. VI.', pp. 184–98.

as guide-marks for the placing of the sewing stations. Additional holes and the re-use of prickings imply a secondary binding, either when the fragment was part of the original volume or as part of another. The reconstructed dimensions of the leaf would place the copper stains thought to relate to a single strap and pin device almost at a central point and would indicate that this formed part of, or was applied to, the original or secondary binding.[10] Double sets of prickings occur, with one set and a single pricking present at the head and two sets at the foot. These may have been made by a divider and do not relate to the original binding of the volume. They may well relate to the next phase in the fragment's history, when it was reused as a stiffener in a semi-limp binding. They may have acted as guides for the fold-in of a limp cover (traces of the underside of brown leather adhering to 2v may relate to this or to a later binding fold-in), the leaf being trimmed down to the dimensions of this cover with roughly equivalent turn-ins at head and foot. The glue marks indicate, however, that the fragment was not used as a pastedown, since they do not run over the stub which would have acted as a guard or a reinforcement of the hinge. The glue may therefore have been applied to render the fragment a stiffener for a limp cover. A paper pastedown may well have been slid underneath the stub and would account for traces of paper adhering to 2v. The curved head of the stub accommodates a relatively large and almost circular cut near the gutter. The circle is not completed, however, and its centre remains. This cut also pierces fol. 2 and aligns with that of fol. 1 if the stub is reversed to its original position. This hole would have been used to sew the headband onto the limp binding. Finally, the leaf shows signs of later trimming, perhaps associated with a bibliophile 'tidying' of the fragment which would probably also have accounted for the reversal of the stub to bestow a clean and nearly rectilinear appearance when viewed from 2r.

SCRIPT

The script is an elegant and formal version of Insular Phase II cursive minuscule (T.J. Brown's *cursiva media / formata*) of a type written in Southumbria during the first half of the ninth century (see pls. I and II).[11] It exhibits the following noteworthy features:

Aspect and ductus: the aspect is light (1:4) and pointed, an effect which is heightened by the consistent lengthening of ascenders and descenders. Ductus is quite formal for a cursive minuscule script, with few concessions to minimization of strokes through the use of devices such as loops and ligatures.

---

[10] The penetration of the staining would also indicate that at this stage the leaf, still at its original proportions, was near to the binding boards. I am inclined to associate this binding mechanism with the secondary binding, perhaps of thirteenth- to fourteenth-century date.

[11] See above, n. 3.

Reversal of ductus does occur occasionally in **q**, but this feature is employed for calligraphic effect rather than for speed. The impression of formality is increased by the addition of sloping wedges to the heads of ascenders, other than that of round **d**.

Letter-forms: these are of the minuscule range; **a** is pointed and is occasionally left slightly open at its head, representing the most cursive feature of the script; **d** is straight, with a wedge at its head, or round, with an elegantly curved long ascender; **e** has a cross-stroke, as well as an upper bow, which extends to the right, especially at the ends of words. It occasionally enters into ligature with **g** and **i** and assumes a theta shape, as well as entering into the Insular *et* ligature; the cross-stroke of **f** sits low, upon the base-line; **g** has a flat head and an elegant, curved body-stroke which merely hints at a bow and which terminates in a punctus at its foot; **i** is short, except when in ligature with **e**; **l** sits on the base-line; minims of **m** and **n** do not descend below the line to assist legibility, but spacing ensures that the latter is not a problem; the descender of **p** is long, tapering slightly to the left, and its bow remains a little open at its base; **q** generally resembles **p**, with a closed bow, but occasionally exhibits reversed ductus, with its head open and the top-stroke of its bow curving upwards to the left, producing a mild whiplash effect; **r** descends below the line and is of equal length to long **s**, the distinction relying upon the descent of the head-stroke of **r** to the base-line, while that of **s** terminates high; **s** is consistently long and descends below the line; **u** is distinguished from **v**, in numbers, by the manner in which the first stroke of the latter curves outwards to the left; the first leg of **x** descends below the line in the form of a loop.

Litterae notabiliores: these are enlarged, but uncoloured, and assume more elaborate forms: **a** is tall, with a long, curved head-stroke and open upper bow, with the lower bow sometimes left open at its head and hipped on its left-side; **d** is round, but is again hipped; **h** is of minuscule form, but with a high, angular second stroke, which descends below the line; **i** is long and descends; **l** is generously curved and descends; **m** takes a very rounded form; **q** assumes its reversed, whiplash form; **s** is long and descends; **t** has a hipped body-stroke.

Punctuation: original punctuation was by the medial point, except for one case of a triple, triangular group of points, of ultimately Irish inspiration, on 2v to mark a major pause. Patrick McGurk has kindly pointed out that, although the text is well punctuated *per cola et commata*, additional pauses occur, especially following place-names, perhaps indicating another usage. The medial point has generally been converted to a *punctus versus* at a late date and the same hand (probably of the tenth century) adds an occasional *punctus elevatus* and *punctus interrogatus*.

Accents: on monosyllables and occasionally above syllables in words, such as *ípsi* and *oppraessérunt*.

Abbreviations: of restricted use, as one might expect of a formal liturgical manuscript: the Insular *et*-ligature occurs; abbrevation bars denote contraction of *nomina sacra* such as *d(omi)n(u)m* and *d(eu)m n(ost)r(u)m*; p for *p(er)* is the only word or syllable abbreviation symbol, and it is interesting to note that *que*, which was originally written in full, has been consistently altered by erasure subsequently and adapted to one of the most common, and liturgically respectable, *notae communes* of antiquity, q:.[12]

Orthography: there is a common Insular tendency to confuse **s** and **ss**; see also below.

Word division: good, with a sporadic tendency to append monosyllables to following words, a common Insular feature.

Corrections: there have been a number of erasures by scraping, especially in association with *que*, leaving an impression of very generous spacing. Original scribal corrections take the form of interlinear insertions, marked by a point below the line ([*ob*]*tenuit*, 2v, col. 2). The original marginal insertion on 2r is apparently unmarked. A tenth-century hand, using a brown ink, was responsible for alterations to the punctuation and also made certain insertions in an Anglo-Saxon pointed minuscule script which are interlinear and either marked by a medial point (as in *hec*, 2r, col. 1) or unmarked (as in *iept*[*h*]*e*, 2r, col. 2), or by simple addition on the line (as in *cannan*[*ei*], 2r, col. 1). The same hand was also responsible for enclosing parts of words in scratchy boxes (for example, *nos*[*tri*], 2r, col. 2) and the scratchy box and *ic* addition to *scend*[*ic*]*erunt* (2v, col. 1). A hand, perhaps of the late ninth to tenth century, has made two unmarked interlinear insertions, *mis*[*s*]*o* (2r, col. 1) and *ccc* [*os*] *annos* (2v, col. 2), in a black ink. These corrections show that the manuscript was still being studied in England during the first half of the tenth century.

The palaeographical features outlined above serve to place the manuscript within the 'Canterbury' or 'Tiberius' group, of which the closest relatives on grounds of script are BL, Cotton Tiberius c. ii, the Tiberius Bede (*Historia ecclesiastica*) and Cambridge, University Library, Ll. 1. 10, the 'Book of Cerne'

---

[12] I am deeply indebted to Michael Reeve for elucidation on this interesting point and for the following references. He suggests that the erasures have occurred in order to distinguish *que* from *quae* in a period when *ae* was regularly reduced to *e*. The ninth-century scribe of the fragment does not, of course, reduce *ae*, but the later corrector may not have expected all users of the manuscript to be as well aware of the distinction as was the scribe. Professor Reeve has noted a similar feature in two manuscripts of Livy: London, BL, Harley 2493, written in the second half of the twelfth century, and Florence, Biblioteca Medicea, Laur. LXIII.20, of the second half of the ninth century. In these manuscripts corrections have been made at later dates in order to distinguish between *quam*, which, when corrected to abbreviated form, denotes a conjunction, and, when left in full, denotes the feminine accusative of the relative pronoun.

(prayerbook).[13] Of the two it is closer to the latter in its elegant pointed aspect and is generally very close in detail except for several important features. The Book of Cerne exhibits a far greater tendency towards the use of ligatures and frequently employs reversed ductus to link letters and words (on only one occasion in the fragment are two words linked, by the extension of one head of **t** to form that of the next); this discrepancy could of course be explained by the greater formality of the fragment's text. The script of the fragment also lacks certain of Cerne's calligraphic devices, such as the emphasis upon loops and reversed ductus, the tendency to terminate the feet of letters such as **e** and **t** with a point produced by a pen-hold and the frequent graceful descent of **l** below the line. Cerne, in turn, approaches round **d** differently and lacks the elegant long ascender of the fragment, and favours tall **e**. Given the restricted nature of the evidence offered by the fragment it is difficult to be sure that they are not by the same hand, but this seems unlikely, for although Cerne is less formal in certain respects in its approach to script it consistently employs calligraphic features which one might expect to find in the carefully produced formal script of the fragment.

For the closest parallels to the script, one must turn to the evidence of single-sheet charters. In a previous study of an unpublished member of the 'Tiberius' group (Paris, BN lat. 10861, a collection of Latin saints' lives), I suggested that charters provide a useful context for contemporary book-script, and imply a date in the second or third decade of the ninth century for the distinctive and relatively short-lived version of Southumbrian cursive minuscule which I have termed 'mannered minuscule' and which, although frequently associated with documents produced during the episcopacy of Archbishop Wulfred of Canterbury, may well have achieved currency throughout the Mercian *Schriftprovinz*.[14] From the mid-820s the baroque mannerisms of 'mannered minuscule' begin to decline (cf. S 1434 and S 1436).[15] The pointed aspect and relatively formal cursive ductus are retained, resulting in a legible script characterized by its clarity and elegant simplicity, prior to the decline apparent in Christ Church, Canterbury, documents of the mid-ninth century.[16] It is to representatives of this reformed phase of ninth-century documentary cursive script, which is itself very formal in nature, and which occurs in documents of *c.* 825–50, that the script of our fragment finds its closest parallels. The best examples may be seen in BL, Cotton Augustus ii. 94 (S 188; *BM Facs.* ii. 20),

13 See J.J.G. Alexander, *Insular Manuscripts 6th–9th Century* (London, 1978), nos. 33 and 66.
14 See Brown, 'Paris, BN lat. 10861'.
15 Numbers refer to P.H. Sawyer, *Anglo-Saxon Charters: an Annotated List and Bibliography*, R. Hist. Soc. Guides and Handbooks 8 (London, 1968).
16 On this decline see Brooks, *The Early History*, pp. 171–4.

dated 831, and Cotton Augustus ii. 20 (S 1438; *BM Facs.* i. 17), dated 838, with the former forming the closest parallel.[17] These two documents involve both kings of Mercia and archbishops of Canterbury, and, as I have suggested elsewhere, it would be unwise to attempt to restrict these developments to either Canterbury or Mercia, given the complexities of a situation in which the same scribes may well have produced material for both parties, and given the restricted nature of the attestably Mercian material.

The evidence of the script, therefore, implies a date for the fragment of *c.* 825 to 850, on the basis of charter material, and an origin within greater Mercia, which, despite West Saxon intervention, should be taken to include Kent. There is also some evidence to suggest that the closest parallel to the script within a book, the Book of Cerne, may have originated in western Mercia, rather than Kent.

THE BIBLICAL TEXT AND OTHER ANGLO-SAXON BIBLES

The text is from the Vulgate Bible. The stub (1r) carries letters (shown here in italics) from Judges v. 5–6: '| *D(omi)ni et Si*nai a facie Domini Dei Israel. In diebus | *Sam (i)ga*r filii Amath, in diebus Iahel quieverunt | *semi*tae.'. The verso carries letters from Judges VI.6: 'Isra(*h*)*el valde* | in conspectu Madian. Et clamavit ad Dominum *postu* | lans auxilium contra Madianitas qui misit |'. 2r-v has most of Judges x.7–xi.26. There are six standard words to the line and, allowing for variation of between five to eight words in cases where there are abbreviations, it would seem that three to four lines are probably missing from the head of the fragment. This gives an original arrangement of two columns of twenty-seven to twenty-eight lines and a reconstructed written space of approximately 274 × 209 mm. The amount of text which occurs between the beginning of 1r and the end of 2v suggests a length of six folios. This would mean that the fragment either represents the outermost bifolium of a quire of six, or, in accordance with common early Anglo-Saxon usage, the second in a quire of eight.

There are a few minor textual variants from the Vulgate.[18] Apart from variation in the spelling of names (such as *Iordanen* for *Iordanem, ammorrei* for *Ammorrhaei, amalech* for *Amalec, cannan* for *Chanaan, effraim* for *Ephraim*, and so on) and the consistent omission of the final **i** from such words as *Sidonii* or *aegiptii*, the only significant variants are the contemporary marginal addition, by the scribe, of 'usubici|untur | xviii an|nis' beside 'Iordanem' (x.8); the interesting substitution of 'adultera' for 'altera matre' (xi.2); the insertion of 'in' before 'sequebantur' (xi.3); 'nun venimus ad te' for 'nunc ad te venimus'

---

[17] Secondary references are to facsimiles in E.A. Bond, *Facsimiles of Ancient Charters in the British Museum*, 4 vols. (London, 1873–8).

[18] See *Biblia Sacra Vulgatae Sixti V. et Clementis VIII.* (Rome, 1861), vol. VI.

(XI.8); the insertion of 'ut' before 'quod' (XI.10); the omission of 'coram Domino' (XI.11); the substitution of 'ex' for 'de' before 'Aegypto' (XI.16). These are not among the common variations found in early printed editions of the Vulgate.

We may now raise the more interesting question of whether the fragment is the relict of a complete bible. With the exception of those manuscripts known to have been complete bibles (the Codex Amiatinus and other fragments of Ceolfrith's three bible pandects), or reconstructed as bibles (the Royal Bible), there has been little discussion of other Insular manuscripts carrying biblical texts. For purposes of comparison I list, in approximate chronological order, the biblical texts which survive (whole or incomplete) from Anglo-Saxon England, of ninth-century date or earlier:[19] 1. Durham, Cathedral Library, B. IV. 6, fol. 169, a sixth-century uncial fragment of Maccabees (cut to 210 × 125 mm, with a written space width of *c.* 185 mm and two columns of *c.* 30 lines);[20] 2. Florence, Biblioteca Medicea Laurenziana, Amiatino 1, early eighth-century, uncial, complete bible Wearmouth–Jarrow (*c.* 505 × 340 mm, written space 360–75 × 260 mm, two columns of 44–5 lines);[21] 3. London, BL, Add. 37777 and 45025 and Loan ms 81, early eighth-century, uncial, originally complete bible, Wearmouth–Jarrow (*c.* 480 × 335 mm, written space 360 × 255 mm, two columns of 44 lines);[22] 4. Durham, Cathedral Library, C. IV. 7, flyleaves, eighth-century, half uncial, Leviticus, Northumbria (*c.* 260 × 228 mm, written space 240 × 175 mm, two columns of 30 lines);[23] 5. London, BL, Egerton 1046A, eighth-century, cursive minuscule, Proverbs, Ecclesiastes, Song of Songs, Ecclesiasticus, (?) Northumbria (*c.* 310 × 225 mm, written space 260 × 200 mm); 6. London, BL, Egerton 1046B, eighth-century, hybrid minuscule, Wisdom, Ecclesiasticus, (?) Northumbria (*c.* 310 × 225 mm, written space 260 × 200 mm);[24] 7. Cambridge, Gonville and Caius College 820 (h), late eighth-century, cursive minuscule, Minor Prophets (now *c.* 150 × 235 mm, estimated written space 230 × 200 mm, one column of 22–3 lines);[25] 8. Oxford, Bodleian Library, lat. bibl. c. 8 (P) + Salisbury, Cathedral Library, 117 + *olim* Cheltenham, Phillipps Collection 36183 (now Takamiya collection, Tokyo), early ninth-century, cursive minuscule, Numbers and Deuteronomy, Southumbria (*c.* 350 × 260 mm, written space 280 × 190 mm, two columns of 28 lines);[26] 9. Cambridge, Magdalene College, Pepys 2981 (4), ninth-century, minuscule, Daniel (*c.* 315 × 210 mm, 20 lines);[27] 10. London, BL, Royal 1. E. VI, first half of the ninth century, half uncial and hybrid

---

[19] See H. Gneuss, 'Manuscripts Written or Owned in England up to 1100', *ASE* 9 (1981), 1–60.

[20] *CLA* II, no. 153.   [21] *Ibid.* III, no. 299.   [22] *Ibid.* II, no. 177.   [23] *Ibid.* II, no. 154.

[24] *Ibid.* II, no. 194.   [25] *Ibid.* II, no. 129.   [26] *Ibid.* II, no. 259.

[27] M.R. James, *Bibliotheca Pepysiana, III: Medieval Manuscripts* (London, 1923), p. 117.

minuscule, New Testament, Southumbria (Canterbury) (*c.* 470 × 345 mm, written space 345 × 265 mm, two columns of 42 lines).[28]

The dimensions are of great importance in establishing relationships within this group. BL, Royal 1. E. VI (the Royal Bible), as a key member of the 'Tiberius' group, is an obvious candidate for comparison with the fragment. The dimensions of the former are certainly larger, but some allowance should be made for the script, which is larger and of a more formal nature than the cursive minuscule of the fragment. Dr Budny has pointed out that the use of minuscule script in Carolingian bibles of the ninth century entailed a difference in proportions and enabled far greater economy of space.[29] The number of volumes into which a complete bible might be divided would also affect the proportions. Nonetheless, it must be said that the discrepancy in dimensions between those manuscripts known or thought to have been complete bibles and other members of the group, including our fragment, is still considerable. The written spaces of the complete bibles measure around 360 × 260 mm, whilst our present fragment, Egerton 1046, Pepys 2981 (4), Gonville and Caius 820 (h) and Bodleian lat. bibl. c. 8 (P) all measure approximately 230–80 × 200 mm and are wholly or partly in minuscule script.[30] Carolingian bibles are also generally larger than the latter group, with London, BL, Add. 10546 (the Moutier-Grandval Bible) measuring *c.* 510 × 375 mm overall, Paris, BN, lat. 1 (the Vivian Bible, or First Bible of Charles the Bald) measuring approximately 495 × 345 mm, BN lat. 2 (the Second Bible of Charles the Bald) measuring approximately 430 × 335 mm, with two columns of 52 lines, and BN lat. 3 (the Bible of Rorigon) measuring approximately 500 × 372 mm with two columns of 51–2 lines. These dimensions are closer to those of the Royal Bible than to those of our fragment and its group.

This raises several interesting questions concerning the nature of Insular biblical volumes. Given the comparatively large number of complete or fragmentary English gospel books which survive from before *c.* 900, it is not unlikely that the other books of the bible may have circulated separately or been grouped into volumes, such as complete Old Testament volumes, which might have warranted a slightly smaller format and less formal script than that applied to complete large format bibles, or even to gospel books. Alternatively, the biblical items which employ the smaller format and minuscule scripts all date to around or after *c.* 800 and, regardless of whether they formed part of complete or partial bibles, may bear an interesting relationship to the

---

[28] *CLA* II, no. 214.   [29] See Budny, 'Royal 1. E. VI', p. 751.

[30] It is worthy of note that the dimensions of the latter (*CLA* II, no. 259) are extremely close to those of the reconstructed fragment and that its script has been compared to that of Oxford, Bodleian Library, Hatton 93, which I suggest was probably from the same scriptorium as the Book of Cerne; see M.P. Brown, 'Book of Cerne', and *CLA* II, no. 241.

upgrading of minuscule scripts for general and high-grade use in Britain and on the Continent. British experiments in the use of minuscule scripts for important liturgical manuscripts as well as for private devotional and library books would certainly appear to be contemporaneous with, or perhaps even anterior to, similar developments in Caroline minuscule for use in projects such as the Tours bibles. This could reflect an early manifestation of Carolingian influence, which is also apparent in certain examples of pre-Alfredian art (such as the Royal Bible and the Book of Cerne), and in texts such as the 'Primum in Ordine' mass-text of Oxford, Bodleian Library, Hatton 93.[31] Similarly, there may have been a more specific Insular contribution to the formulation of Carolingian reforms of script than the general artistic debt and half-uncial influence which is already acknowledged.[32]

CONCLUSIONS

Our present fragment is an important addition to the 'Tiberius' group of manuscripts. Although it has no decoration of the calligraphic beast variety associated with the group, its elegant script and the formality of its layout serve to indicate that it formed part of an important biblical volume, perhaps even part of a complete (if not a single-volume) bible. Its script raises a number of interesting questions concerning the development of minuscule script in Britain. Its association with certain Southumbrian documents and with the Book of Cerne indicate a Mercian or Kentish origin (as part of a Mercian *Schriftprovinz*) between *c.* 825 and 850. As such it must be taken into account in any discussion of manuscript production during the ninth century, an era for which every piece of evidence counts. A new find (or the re-interpretation of a better known piece) may thus offer a definite contribution to our understanding of this difficult and controversial period.

---

[31] *CLA* ii, no. 241.

[32] Further work on the nature of transmission of biblical texts in Anglo-Saxon England would be of use. A fruitful approach could be an initial study of references in medieval library catalogues.

An eleventh-century English missal fragment in the British Library

K.D. HARTZELL

Derek Howard Turner in memoriam

In the introduction to his edition of the New Minster Missal (Le Havre, Bibliothèque municipale, 330), Derek Turner tells us that the manuscript he is editing 'is one of the five fairly complete mass-books of probable English provenance remaining from before 1100, and the oldest true missal'.[1] By 'missal' he means, of course, that Le Havre 330 is a mass book of the sort which usually contains a suitably integrated ordering of texts and chants of the sacramentary, the lectionary and the gradual according to the various traditional propers and ordinaries of the temporal and sanctoral arranged to accompany the church year; normally there are also some votive masses after the main corpus of the book.

The statement that Le Havre 330 (s. xi²) is the 'oldest' surviving English missal will strike many as nothing unusual. Being a compendium of the type I have just outlined, the missal is frequently considered a late phenomenon, one incapable of telling us very much about the evolution of early medieval liturgy. Since liturgical history in England prior to 900 depending on a study of contemporary service books is almost entirely bound up with whatever manuscripts may be said to have found their way to Germany and still survive there or in Paris – except for a striking group of Insular gospel books produced and still found in the British Isles – some would also say that manuscripts as late as the eleventh century[2] do not count toward the elucidation of this difficult field.

---

[1] *The Missal of the New Minster, Winchester*, ed. D.H. Turner, HBS 93 (London, 1962), vi; see also H. Gneuss, 'A Preliminary List of Manuscripts Written or Owned in England up to 1100', *ASE* 9 (1981), 1–60 (no. 837), and 'Liturgical Books in Anglo-Saxon England and their Old English Terminology', *Learning and Literature in Anglo-Saxon England*, ed. M. Lapidge and H. Gneuss (Cambridge, 1985), pp. 91–141 (no. A.1).

[2] The oldest book representing what we call a missal is the fragment, Monte Cassino, Archivio della Badia, 271 (s. viii); see A. Wilmart, 'Un missel grégorien ancien', *RB* 26 (1909), 281–300; the text is printed in A. Dold, *Vom Sakramentar, Comes und Capitulare zum Missale*, Texte und Arbeiten 34 (Beuron, 1943). It is z6 in *SG* (see below, n. 9), and item 701 in K. Gamber, *Codices*

This point is all very well but it is very false, as is the notion that the missal is a late book, and as a late book was not copied in substantial numbers before the high middle ages of the thirteenth century and beyond. That few missals survive must not convince us they were not written. The missal is, par excellence, the missile of the expanding church, the missionary church, the crusading church, the church in motion. The early missal in the homogenized form is not the book reflecting directly the buzzing hives of ecclesiastical hierarchy at Reims, Tours or Mainz, but rather the Schwarzwald and the Fens, and more precisely, the ecclesiastics who brought organized worship to the backward parts of a sprawling medieval diocese, to the people.

Why then is Le Havre 330 the oldest English missal we have if missals were so common? There is no simple answer to that. Being more utilitarian than other, more magnificent books, they had no beautiful decoration to save them for later collectors. Since they were conceivably the amalgamation of at least three different books, whenever there were changes in those parts, for whatever reason, marginal annotation and entries *in rasura* may have made them scruffy and unsightly. If the institutions using them eventually inclined to elaborate ceremonial, they could have passed them on to others less developed, *ad infinitum*. Finally, since the work was often entrusted to less competent scribes, errors and major corruptions could have crept in and made them the burden of later generations.

The oldest English missal fragment of the post-900 period of which we have any scholarly account is the fragment published in full almost twenty-five years ago by Lilli Gjerløw.[3] Two others were published earlier, one by Frederick Warren and Léopold Delisle almost simultaneously, the other by

---

Liturgici Latini Antiquiores, 2nd ed., 2 vols. (Freiburg, 1968) (henceforth *CLLA*). See also A. Chavasse, 'Les fragments palimpsests du Casinensis 271 (Sigle z6). A coté de l'Hadrianum et du Paduense, un collatéral, autrement remanié', *Archiv für Liturgiewissenschaft* 25 (1983), 9–33. Another early book, the earliest witness to a homogenized text, has been published by K. Gamber, 'Fragment eines mittelitalienischen Plenarmissale aus dem 8. Jahrhundert', *Ephemerides liturgicae* 76 (1962), ʾ35–41, and his discovery has been discussed by S. J.P. van Dijk, 'Gregory the Great, Founder of the Urban *Schola Cantorum*', *Ephemerides liturgicae* 77 (1963), 335–66, at 355–6, and 'Recent Developments in the Study of the Old-Roman Rite', *Studia Patristica* 8 (Berlin, 1966) II, 299–319, at 309–10. It is *CLLA*, no. 1401. For these books and others consult O. Nussbaum, *Kloster, Priestermönch, und Privatmesse: ihr Verhältnis im Westen von der Anfängen bis zum hohen Mittelalter* (Bonn, 1961), pp. 178–85; M. Huglo, in *The New Grove Dictionary of Music and Musicians*, ed. S. Sadie, 20 vols. (London, 1980) XII, 365–7 (s.v. 'Missal'), and P. Jeffery, 'The Oldest Sources of the Graduale: a Preliminary Checklist of MSS copied before about 900 AD', *Jnl of Musicology* 2 (1983), 316–21. For the missal 'phenomenon', see J.A. Jungmann, *Missarum Sollemnia*, 2nd ed., 2 vols. (Vienna, 1949) I, 269–94, and S. J. van Dijk, *The Origins of the Modern Roman Liturgy* (London, 1960), pp. 45–66.

[3] L. Gjerløw, *Adoratio Crucis, the Regularis Concordia and the Decreta Lanfranci. Manuscript Studies in the Early Medieval Church of Norway* (Oslo, 1961), pp. 29–67; Gneuss, 'A Preliminary List', no. 872.

Toni Schmid, but neither of these books has had its complete text published.[4] Recently a number of important Anglo-Saxon missal fragments which found their way to Norway in the early period have been published by Mrs Gjerløw in their entirety.[5] Others remain unpublished.[6] Aside from its value as the earliest tenth-century missal fragment which we have, Oslo Mi1 is unique in that it is the only manuscript to contain the three prayers of the 'Adoratio crucis' prescribed by the *Regularis concordia* as well as the seven penitential psalms of the Good Friday service. Further, Mrs Gjerløw's conclusion regarding the text of the whole fragment is just as significant: 'it is quite possible that the sacramentary underlying Mi 1 represents the sacramentary in use at Old Minster in St. Aethelwold's Winchester, and also before him'.[7] Missals were written and they can tell us things about the tenth century and earlier that other books have yet to do. We now turn to the subject of this paper, a fragmentary missal in the Royal collection in the British Library.

DESCRIPTION OF THE ROYAL MISSAL FRAGMENT

At the beginning of London, British Library, Royal 5. A. XII, there are four leaves of a noted *missale plenum* (henceforth Roy). It is clear at a glance that they are not related to the rest of the book.[8] The basic manuscript belonged to

---

[4] For the first, now Worcester, Cathedral Library, F. 173, see F.E. Warren, 'An Anglo-Saxon Missal at Worcester', *The Academy* 28 (July–December 1885), 394–5; L. Delisle, 'Mémoire sur d'anciens sacramentaires', *Mémoires de l'Académie des inscriptions et belles-lettres* 32 (1886), 57–423, at 272; C.H. Turner, 'The Churches at Winchester in the Early Eleventh Century', *JTS* 17 (1916), 65–8; C.E. Hohler, 'Some Service Books of the Later Saxon Church', *Tenth-Century Studies*, ed. D. Parsons (London and Chichester, 1975), pp. 60–83 and 217–27, at 224, n. 55; and Gneuss, 'A Preliminary List', no. 764 (not a sacramentary). For the other, now preserved as fragments, see T. Schmid, 'Smärre Liturgiska Bidrag, viii', *Nordisk Tidskrift för Bok- och Biblioteksväsen* 31 (1944), 25–34; Gneuss, 'A Preliminary List', no. 936.

[5] One fragment is ed. L. Gjerløw, 'Missaler brukt i Bjørgvin bispedømme fra misjonstiden til Nidarosordinariet', *Bjørgvin bispestol*, ed. P. Juvkam (Oslo, 1970), pp. 73–128; Gneuss, 'A Preliminary List', no. 789. For others, see her 'Missaler brukt i Oslo bispedømme fra misjonstiden til Nidarosordinariet', *Oslo bispedømme 900 ar. Historiker studier*, ed. F. Birkeli, A.O. Johansen and E. Molland (Oslo, 1975), pp. 73–142; Gneuss, 'A Preliminary List', nos. 871 and 875.

[6] Gneuss, 'A Preliminary List', nos. 143, 212 (not a sacramentary), 255 (almost unreadable, perhaps a missal; see N.R. Ker, 'A Palimpsest in the National Library of Scotland: Early Fragments of Augustine "De Trinitate", the "Passio S. Laurentii" and other Texts', *Trans. of the Edinburgh Bibliographical Soc.* 3 (1948–55), 169–78), 454, 524, 572 and 649.

[7] Gjerløw, *Adoratio Crucis*, p. 50. A section of Gamber, *CLLA*, is devoted to a list of *missalia plenaria*. As the list makes clear, Italy is the true home of the full missal, but this is precisely what we should expect of the centre of Western Christendom: the creation of a book designed to be used by individual clergy intent on fulfilling their pastoral duties in the field. In laying out his material, however, Gamber has neglected to cite any English or Scandinavian fragments, making the picture he paints of the diffusion of this important liturgical book very distorted. Furthermore, it is unreasonable to postulate on negative evidence that the Franks did not use the *missale plenum* soon after it was available to them.

[8] The basic book, s. xv on vellum, contains primarily sermons of St John Chrysostom.

William Neel, vicar of Blockley, appointed by the bishop of Worcester, at the end of the fifteenth century (d. 1510). In 1533 it was presented to the nearby monastery of Hayles by Neel's executor. In the seventeenth century it was owned by John Theyer, who owned many manuscripts from that part of the country, and it came to the Royal Library with others of his manuscripts.

The four leaves are bifolia numbered iii–vi. Their proper order is iv, iii, vi, v, and when rearranged – taking into account lacunae in the texts – they constitute leaves 2, 3, 6 and 7 of a regular quire of eight. They measure 243 × 172 mm but they have been cut down in the outer margins. The original measurements may have been 270 × 220 mm. The writing space is 223 × 139 mm within double bounding lines. Line spacing is approximately 7–8 mm. There are 30 long lines per page but trimming has left only 28 or 29 lines on certain pages. Ruling is by dry point on the flesh side. Punctuation is by medial point, semi-colon and inverted semi-colon (*punctus elevatus*), the medial point being altered to one of the other forms on occasion.

The script is the round Anglo-Caroline minuscule (Bishop Style I) practised in the tenth and eleventh centuries at monasteries established or re-established by St Æthelwold (see pl. III). The hand of the main scribe slants slightly to the right. Descenders of **p** and **q** sometimes draw to the right and in conjunction with adjacent ascenders (as in *plorans* and *adimpleretur*) give the script a mild yawing aspect. In **a**, the main stroke, frequently very high, arched, and ungainly in initial positions – less so in medial and final positions – stays slightly left of the vertical. The bowl usually extends only halfway up the ascender. The ligatures **ct**, **st**, **rr**, **ra** and **rra** occur; **nt** ligatures are used at the ends of lines. A following **r** is a double **c** or horned form. Ampersands are used medially and finally. Ascenders are clubbed; most of the time they are vertical. **F** and long **s** lean to the right. The tail of **g** begins in the centre of the round bowl, draws slightly to the left, then comes around in a generous sweep, the final part running parallel to the writing line; it terminates with a short ascending nick which draws to the right. Letters following **e** are very closely written. **Y** has a dot. Tailed **e** is sporadically used, mostly to signify the genitive feminine case ending. Round **r** with a tail and stroke through it is found only after **o** and only to signify the genitive plural. Aside from common marks of suspension and abbreviation, ÷ for *est* comes only at the ends of lines. Specialized marks of abbreviation and suspension at line endings reveal an experienced scribe anxious to maintain a regular right-hand margin.

Besides the hand of the main scribe, whose performance we may date to the eleventh century without modification, there are hands of two scribes of the next generation and of one or more scribes who corrected the book in the late twelfth or early thirteenth century. The first slightly later scribe, Hand B, wrote fol. iv recto, lines 1–5, in an upright, firm, well-placed script. The final descenders of **m** and **n** resemble the exaggerated horseshoe-like arm written by scribes active in the early eleventh century. The parchment of these five lines is darker than the rest of the page. Punctuation is by low point (slightly above the line). **Y** is distinctive. The other scribe, Hand C, wrote fol. v recto, lines 9–18 (along with parts of 8 and 19), and fol. v verso, lines 24–6. His work is not so regular. It does not begin well – minims are uneven lengths and the spacing is imprecise; **a** has many forms – but it improves by the last few lines on v recto. The script slants slightly to the right. This scribe entered new marginal initials and rubrics.

The layout of the book reflects an intelligently planned and executed exemplar. The original rubrics are written in uncials in a faded and deteriorated metallic red. In some places the script has not faded, due perhaps to different ink, to different preparation of the parchment at that place on the page (vi recto), or to an entirely new scribe. Rustic capital has been used in two places. Before original rubric *Lectio ad Hebreos* for the epistle for the third mass of Christmas, a scribe has entered *Lectio Epistole (Beati) Pauli Apostoli* in that script. The ink is vegetable red. The second instance of rustic capital (by Hand C) is far more important and we shall dwell on that later. Capitals in red, green, and blue in the left margin are two, three, four, or five lines high depending on whether they preface a prayer or an epistle or gospel lection. Lines of text may be indented after a marginal capital. New texts begin at the left-hand margin except for the supplementary prayers included after the main listing for the third mass of Christmas where they follow one another, line by line. Hardly any lines are left uncompleted. Pages appear neat without being overly crowded. The only major blank space will be discussed later.

We may now consider the liturgical contents of Roy. I shall discuss in turn the elements constituting the sacramentary, lectionary and gradual, and then offer some observations on Roy's musical notation.

THE LITURGICAL CONTENTS OF THE ROYAL FRAGMENT
The sacramentary

The text of the sacramentary portion of our manuscript is, with a few notable exceptions, fundamentally the text of a Gregorian Sacramentary. There appears to be no reason to prefer any version of that text other than the one represented by the so-called Hadrianum. Modifications to the Gregorian Sacramentary introduced over the course of the ninth century are present as they are in many so-called 'mixed' sacramentaries of the tenth century and later. Besides the evidence of the basic text there is some additional evidence that the scribe of Roy's exemplar may have consulted the *Hucusque*-Supplement, attributed in recent years to Benedict of Aniane. One would not suspect that a fragment of four leaves could provide us with enough material to make a study of the prayers anything more than a mild exercise in textual analysis, but that suspicion is unjustified, as we shall see.

In addition to comparing the texts to those in Jean Deshusses's admirable edition of the Gregorian Sacramentary and in other printed editions,[9] I have used three English manuscripts dating from the tenth and eleventh centuries, of which two have been published. The earliest of the published books is the 'Leofric Missal', an early tenth-century sacramentary to which a number of other sections were added over the span of a century and a half.[10] It is called by the name of Leofric because it is one of the books given to his cathedral by Leofric, bishop of Exeter, in the mid-eleventh century. The second manuscript is the 'Missal of Robert of Jumièges', an early eleventh-century sacramentary presented to Jumièges by a Robert who has often been identified with a Norman of that name who became bishop of London in 1040 and ultimately, although briefly, archbishop of Canterbury.[11] The third manuscript is Orléans, Bibl. mun., 127 (105), a late tenth-century sacramentary of Winchcombe Abbey taken to Saint-Benoît-sur-Loire soon after it was written.[12] There are two additional books to which we could turn. The first is the 'Missal of the New Minster' but this has a lacuna at the point where our texts would have

---

[9] The editions are:

Ge = Sacramentary of Gellone (Paris, Bibliothèque Nationale, lat. 12048), ed. A. Dumas, *Liber Sacramentorum Gellonensis*, 2 vols., CCSL 159 and 159A (Turnhout, 1981).

Go = Missale Gothicum (Vatican City, Biblioteca Apostolica Vaticana, Reg. lat. 317), ed. L.C. Mohlberg, *Missale Gothicum* (Rome, 1961).

Ha = Hadrianum (*SG1*, 83–348).

SG1 = *Le Sacramentaire Grégorien: ses principales formes d'après les plus anciens manuscrits*, ed. J. Deshusses. 1: *le Sacramentaire, le Supplément d'Aniane* (Fribourg, 1971).

Sg = Sacramentary of St Gall (St Gallen, Stiftsbibliothek, 348), ed. L.C. Mohlberg, *Das frankische Sacramentarium Gelasianum in alamannischer Überlieferung* (Münster, 1918).

Sp = The Supplement to the Hadrianum (*SG1*, 349–605).

Tc = *Textes complémentaires pour la messe* [*SG11*] (Fribourg, 1979).

Va = The Vatican manuscript of the Gelasian Sacramentary (Vatican City, Bibl. Apost. Vat., Reg. lat. 316), ed. L.C. Mohlberg, L. Eisenhöfer and P. Siffrin, *Liber Sacramentorum Romanae Aeclesiae ordinis anni circuli* (Rome, 1960).

[10] Oxford, Bodleian Library, Bodley 579 (s. x–xi); *The Leofric Missal as used in the Cathedral of Exeter*, ed. F.E. Warren (Oxford, 1883). The main part of this book (c. 900) will be cited as LeofA.

[11] Rouen, Bibl. mun., Y.6 (274) (s. xi^in); *The Missal of Robert of Jumièges*, ed. H.A. Wilson, HBS 11 (London, 1896) (cited below as Jum).

[12] This manuscript (cited as O) and the sacramentary of Giso of Wells are cited as Whc. and Vit. in *Missale ad usum ecclesie Westmonasteriensis*, ed. J.W. Legg, 3 vols., HBS 1, 5 and 12 (London, 1891–7) III; D. Grémont and L. Donnat, 'Fleury, le Mont Saint-Michel et l'Angleterre à la fin du Xe et au début du XIe siècle à propos du manuscrit d'Orléans No. 127 (105)', *Millénaire monastique du Mont Saint-Michel*, 4 vols. (1966–71) I, 751–93. The fundamental study of these books and the period is Hohler, 'Some Service Books'.

corresponded.[13] The second is the sacramentary of Giso of Wells, now London, BL, Cotton Vitellius A. xviii, of the mid-eleventh century.[14] This book has been utilized only in the discussion of the mass for St Mary.

The third mass of Christmas

Our fragment opens imperfectly in this mass. No collect has survived. The secret and the post communion follow the Hadrianum as do the preface and the *communicantes*. Here as elsewhere the text has been corrected. Sometimes the correction is contemporary, sometimes it is twelfth-century or perhaps later; in the edition (ptd in the Appendix, below, pp. 91–7) I distinguish the age of the hands. In the secret, because of the amount of room taken up by the later script, the original reading may have been *tui nativitate sanctifica nosque per haec* as in LeofA and Jum. These books read together against the sources used by Deshusses in *SG*. The preface in Jum is *Cuius divinae nativitatis*, found in the Supplement for the vigil. In our preface, the standard one for Gregorians, the rewritten part stems from the omission in many early books of the *in* before *invisibilium*. The reading *celebrantes qua* of the *communicantes* was originally *celebrantes in quo*. A later scribe expunged the 'in' and turned the 'o' of *quo* into an 'a' by adding a single stroke. The original reading, found in Va and Ge, is not part of the Gregorian tradition which has *quo*.

After the post communion we find a group of six optional prayers. The first of these is the normal collect in standard Gregorians based on the Hadrianum. Since the collect to our mass is missing, it is tempting to speculate on what prayer might have served in that spot. In the Frankish Gelasianum represented by Sg, the first of two collects is *Omnipotens sempiterne deus qui hunc diem* (Sg 24). This prayer is one of the optional collects in the Hadrianum (Ha 58); it is missing in our manuscript. The second of the two collects in Sg (25) is the standard Gregorian collect which in our manuscript is optional. Thus Sg 24 (Ha 58) may have been the collect for this mass in our manuscript. Some reinforcement is given by the Winchcombe Sacramentary which follows Sg exactly in this regard.

The second prayer is not found in the Hadrianum represented by manuscript A, although it occurs in some other ninth-century witnesses. It is also not in any of the English books we have been using, nor is it in Sg or Va. The fourth prayer is again not in any of the English books, and, surprisingly, it is not in any of the witnesses to the Gregorian Sacramentary used by Deshusses. It must have come from the Gelasian tradition. The fifth prayer originally read *famulis tuis fidei et securitatis* in common with the Winchcombe Sacramentary alone of the English books. The use of this phrase distinguishes

---

Gregorians before modification by the Supplement and a few of the important Gelasian manuscripts. Three blank lines follow the sixth prayer.

Holy Innocents

The secret for this mass has a portion rewritten. In common with LeofA, Jum and O, our manuscript must have read *et munera nostra conciliet* with most of the other Gregorians.

Turning to the preface, we discover that all of the beginning has been rewritten. Only near the end does the corrector become satisfied with the original reading. The notes in *SG* reveal the reason. In the Hadrianum there was no proper preface for Holy Innocents. The redactor of the Supplement borrowed the preface for this feast from the Frankish Gelasians and emended it. The text in Roy as corrected is little different from that in the Supplement. In other words, what was originally written must have been quite different and probably resembled the Gelasian text. In view of the heritage of our manuscript, it conceivably may have been closest to that in the Leonianum. But this solution is not complete. The uncorrected end of the preface in Roy is that of the text of the Supplement. The scribe must have begun the old preface and when he got to the words *pro suo nomine* was told to follow the Supplement; which he did. He then returned to the bulk of the text and corrected it by erasure and addition, much as the corrector of Sg did with the complete text of the old preface. In the twelfth century this mess was eradicated and written over. Oddly the later scribe retained the reading *magis sola* (which must have been before him) instead of the more modern *sola magis*.[15]

Commemoratio de Sancta Maria in Nativitate

We come next to a mass under the rubric *Commemoratio de Sancta Maria in Nativitate*. The rubric (in rustic capitals) is not original, and the three prayers under it have been entered by the scribe which I have called Hand C and whose work is found elsewhere.

COMMEMORATIO DE	Deus qui salutis eterne beate maria
SANCTA MARIA IN	Suscipe sacrificium domine
NATIVITATE	Libera nos ab omni malo

---

[15] Work on this text was greatly facilitated by the comprehensive edition of the Roman prefaces by E. Moeller, *Corpus Praefationum*, 5 vols., CCSL 161, 161A–D (Turnhout, 1980). That it took so long to unravel was due to the fact that the editor prints (as no. 739) the version of this preface from the Leonianum (L), but neither the eighth-century text based on it nor the ninth-century revision. As a consequence, one must reconstruct those texts from the notes provided for no. 739. The editor also cites the version of this preface from Vat. lat. 3325 (ed. H.M. Bannister, 'Liturgical Fragments', *JTS* 9 (1908), 398–421, at 414–15) under both nos. 291 and 739. Despite this, the text is no. 739 alone. Bannister states that 'on the whole the fragment agrees mostly with L' (p. 415); but in light of Moeller's work it can be linked to the received text of most of the Frankish Gelasians.

What mass is this? In the Hadrianum the sequence of masses after Holy Innocents and continuing to Epiphany is:

13 Silvester
14 Octave of Christmas
15 Oratio in alia dominica
16 Item alia in dominica
17 Epiphany

There is no mention of a mass in honour of Mary.

Before we attempt to determine why this mass has been entered here, we should list the feasts in the remainder of this fragment, the formulae of which will assist us in our task. The succeeding masses are:

IN OCTAVAS DOMINI   Deus qui nobis nati salvatoris
                             Presta quaesumus domine ut per haec munera
                             Presta quaesumus domine ut quod salvatoris

DOMINICA PRIMA IN   Omnipotens sempiterne deus dirige (all present)
NATALE DOMINI

It is important to realize that our mass occurs directly before that of the octave of the Lord's Nativity (Christmas).

Among the English sacramentaries and missals roughly contemporary with or later than Roy, some also contain a mass for Mary in this season. The sacramentary of Giso of Wells reads: *In Commemoratione S. Marie, In Octavas Domini, Dominica I post Natale Domini.* The late eleventh-century missal of St Augustine's, Canterbury, has: *In die Circumcisionis, De sancta Maria, Dmc I post ND*, and the slightly later missal from Bury St Edmunds reads similarly: *In octabas natale domini, Missa de sancta Maria, Dmc I post ND*.[16] Books from the English secular tradition of Sarum Use prescribe masses in honour of Mary at different seasons of the year but do not indicate on what days they are to be said.[17] None of these liturgical philosophies are reflected in LeofA, Jum, or O.

In addition to the English witnesses there are continental books reflecting an interest in Mary at the Christmas season. The eleventh-century sacramentary in the Rossi collection at the Vatican has two masses on the octave of which one is a Marian mass: *In Octabas Domini de sancta Maria, Alia missa in OD.* It is the first manuscript I have so far encountered which stipulates

---

[16] Cambridge, Corpus Christi College 270: *The Missal of St Augustine's, Canterbury*, ed. M. Rule (Cambridge, 1896); Laon, Bibliothèque municipale, 238 (s. xii¹).

[17] J.W. Legg, *The Sarum Missal* (Oxford, 1916), pp. 387–91. Mrs Gjerløw has published a fragment of a twelfth-century English noted missal from the diocese of Bergen which has [*Sexta die post Natali Domini*], *Missa de Sancta Maria per Nativitatem Domini, In Circumcisione Domini*: 'Missaler brukt i Bjørgvin', pp. 93–7.

a mass for Mary on 1 January.[18] Others are as vague in their assignations as the English books. An eleventh-century missal from Saint-Martin at Tours has *Missa de sancta Maria, In Octabas Natale Domini*.[19] The oldest missal of Bayeux has *In Octavas Domini, De sancta Maria*.[20]

We are thus able to say that in a few places in England and on the continent a mass for Mary was observed during Christmastide. The appearance of a mass in Roy for a similar purpose should cause no alarm. One continental book even goes so far as to tell us that the mass for Mary would have been celebrated on the octave, one of two for that day.

The mass *Commemoratio de Sancta Maria in Nativitate* is not in the first hand and we must determine what was originally entered in its place. In the list previously given of masses in the Hadrianum the only mass between Holy Innocents and the octave of Christmas is Silvester (31 December). Since this is the proper place for it, it is compelling to surmise that our mass has been written over one for that saint. If there is another possibility, it must be one permitting Silvester to appear elsewhere. In England there was a tradition extending back to the end of the ninth century (but probably observed earlier) of having a separate sanctoral in the manner of the Vatican Gelasian.[21] This usage was observed on the continent in the same century. All three English mass books we have been using have separate sanctorales extended idiosyncratically to include all the saints' days in Christmas week. The English graduals of this period (and well after it) also have separate sanctorales. In the twelfth-century missal of Rennes, Silvester's feast comes after four Sundays of Epiphany.[22] This admittedly odd arrangement is very old. It is found in the fragment of a ninth-century gradual from Fulda.[23]

If Silvester's was not the mass expunged and written over, what mass could it have been? The logic by which we removed Silvester would also remove feasts of other saints. The only mass of the temporal I have discovered in Christmas week is one entitled *Sexta die* in some books,[24] *Dominica infra Octavas Domini* in others,[25] or *Dominica prima post Natale Domini*. But we already have a

---

[18] Vatican City, Bibl. Apost. Vat., Ross. lat. 204 (s. xi); ptd *Sacramentarium Rossianum*, ed. J. Brinktrine, *Römische Quartalschrift*, Supplement-Heft 25 (Freiburg im Breisgau, 1930).

[19] Tours, Bibliothèque du Petit Séminaire, without signature. The Petit Séminaire in Tours has been closed for some years, but this precious book and others formerly in its collection are now safely at the Bibliothèque municipale.

[20] Paris, Bibliothèque Mazarine, 404 (s. xii).

[21] Hohler, 'Some Service Books', pp. 61–2.   [22] Paris, BN, lat. 9439.

[23] B. Opfermann, 'Un frammento liturgico di Fulda del IX secolo', *Ephemerides liturgicae* 50 (1936), 207–23.

[24] *Sexta die* is the rubric in the Sarum Missal and in the Sarum Gradual, *Graduale Sarisburiense*, ed. W.H. Frere (London, 1894), pl. 18.

[25] The twelfth-century gradual of Rouen (Paris, BN, lat. 904) calls this Sunday *Dominica infra*; facsimile in *Le Graduel de l'église cathédrale de Rouen au XIIIe siècle*, ed. H. Loriquet *et al.*, 2 vols. (Rouen, 1907).

in manus philistin & filiorum ammon ad
plicatiq; sunt & uehementer opprimerentur per
annos x & un. Omnes qui habitabant trans
Iordanen interra ammorrei: quae est in
Galaad intantum ut filii ammon iordane
trans misso uastarent iudam & beniamin
& effraim. Adflictusq; est israhel nimis.
Et clamantes ad dnm dixerunt: peccauimus
tibi quia dereliquimus dnm nrm & seruiuim;
baalim. cuibus locutus est dns: Numquid non
aegyptii & ammorrei filii quoq; ammon & phi
listin: Sidonii quoq & amalech & cannan
oppresserunt uos & clamastis ad me & erui
uos demanu eorum. Et tamen reliquistis me
& coluistis deos alienos. Idcirco non addam
ut ultra uos liberem: Ite & inuocate deos
quos elegistis ipsi uos liberent intempore
angustiae. Dixeruntq; filii israhel ad dnm.
peccauimus: redde tu nobis quicquid placet
tibi tantum nunc libera nos: quae dicentes
omnia de finibus suis alienorum deorum
idola proiecerunt & seruierunt do. quidoluit
super miseriis eorum. Itaque filii ammon con
clamantes in galaad fixere tentoria.

erat dux populi galaad. Fuit illo
tempore galaaditis unus repperimus.
filius meretricis mulieris quem
habuit autem galaad & uxorem
speciem filiorum. qui post quam creui
tempore dicentes. Neque indomo p...
non poteris: quia de adultera n...
natus es: quos ille fugiens atq; d...
uit interra tob. Congregatiq; s...
uiri inopes & latrocinantes & q...
sequebantur. In illis diebus p...
ammon contra israhel: & cuibus
instantibus perrexerunt maiores...
ut tollerent in auxilium suum iep...
tob. dixeruntq; que ad eum ueni &...
noster & pugna contra filios am...
ille respondit: Nonne uos estis...
& secistis de domo patris mei. Et
tis ad me necessitate compuls...
que principes galaad adie...
causam nunc uenimus ad te ut p...
nobiscum & pugnes contra filios...
siqui dux omnium qui habitant...
tempore quoque dixit eis: Si uere ue...

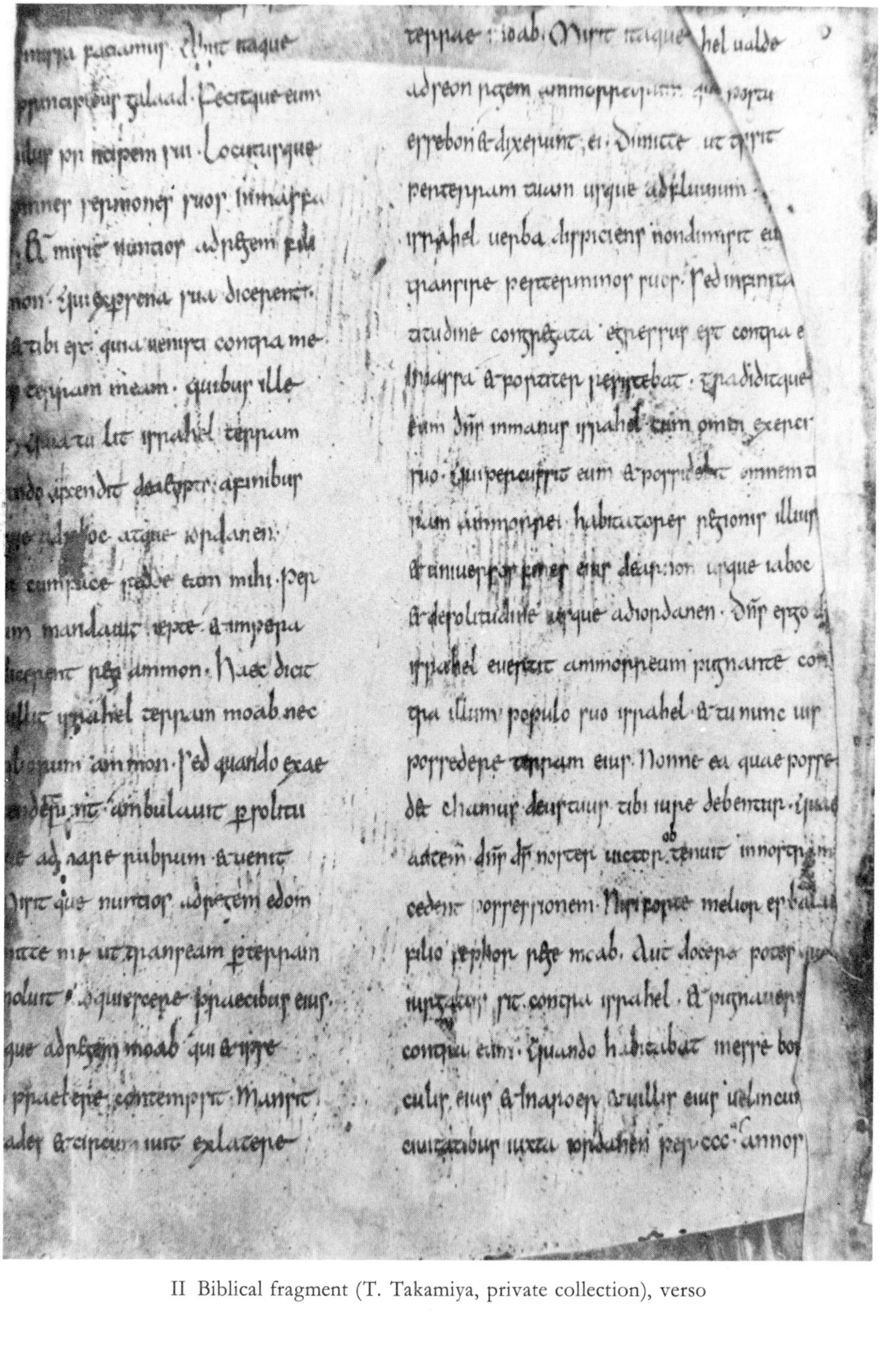

II Biblical fragment (T. Takamiya, private collection), verso

u Inhumiliasti sicut uulneratum superbum · & in uirtute brachii tui dispersisti inimicos

tuos · firmetur manus tua & exaltetur dex

Oblata dne munera noua unigeniti tui natuitate sanctifica ;

nosq; a peccatorum nostrorum maculis emunda · p eund ·

Aeterne ds · Quia p incarnati uerbi mysterium noua

mentis nostre oculis lux tue claritatis infulsit · ut dum

uisibiliter dm cognoscim? p hunc in inuisibilium amore ra

piamur · Et ideo cum angelis & archangelis · cum thro

& dominationibus · Cumque omni militia celestis exer

citus hymnum glorie tue canimus sine fine dicentes ;

Communicantes & diem sacratissimum celebrantes

qua beate marie intemerata uirginitas huic mundo

edidit saluatorem · Sed & memoriam uenerantes inp

mis eiusdem glose semp uirginis marie genitricis d · & ·

dni nri ihu xpi · Sed & beatorum apostolorum ac martyrum

tuorum · &c · Uiderunt omnes fines terre saluatare

Presta quesumus omps ds · ut natus hodie saluator mundi

sicut diuine nobis generationis est auctor · ita & immortalita

tis sit ipse largitor · qui tecum · ORAT

oncede qs omps ds · unosunigeniti tui noua p carnem nati

uitas liberet · quos sub peccati iugo uetusta seruitus tenet · q

Concede qs omps ds · ut quos sub peccati iugo uetusta ser

uitus tenet · eos unigeniti tui noua p carne natiuitas li

beret · p eundem · Respice nos misericors ds · & men

tibus · clemenc humanis nascente xpo sui me ueritatis

lumen ostende · p eund · Largire qs frequentamus

saluacionis humane primordia quia eius celebritates beate

comparate mysteriis uirginitatis p dnm

largire qs dne familis tuis fidospei & caritatis augmentum

III London, British Library, Royal 5. A. XII, iii r

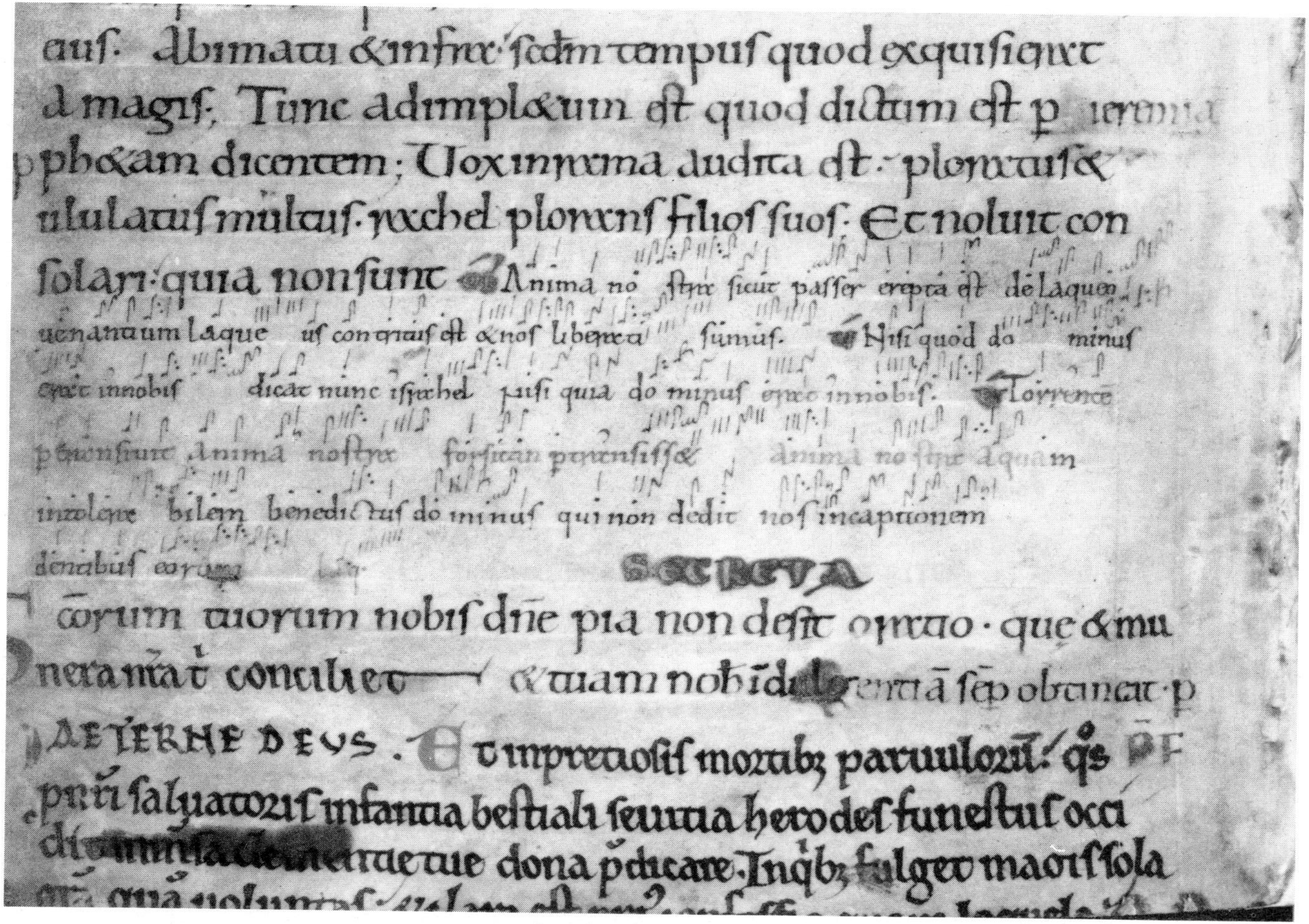

IV London, British Library, Royal 5. A. XII, vi v

Sunday after Christmas in Roy, a mass placed in this case after the octave, and thus this possibility is ruled out.[26]

Having determined that Silvester's mass lies under the mass we are discussing, we need to make a crucial observation before proceeding to the prayers themselves. The first prayer for *Dmc I post N.D.*, the only surviving prayer for that feast in Roy, is also the work of Hand C. Should we consider the mass for Mary and the rewriting of the collect for the Sunday after Christmas in the same breath? Is the latter dependent on the former?

There are two traditions of mass formulas for the Sunday after Christmas. In one, represented by Ge, Sg and the Supplement to the Hadrianum (Sp), the prayers are:

> Deus qui salutis aeternae;
> Muneribus nostris quaesumus domine precibusque;
> Da nobis quaesumus domine deus noster, ut qui.[27]

In the other, represented by a number of different books, the prayers begin with *Omnipotens sempiterne deus, dirige*, and follow with differing prayers depending on their tradition.[28] Since *O.s.d. dirige* is on an erasure, the prayer under it must have been *Deus qui salutis*.

The reason for expunging *Deus qui salutis* is not entirely clear. One possibility is that the scribe wanted to bring the mass into conformity with other books. Another, equally strong in my opinion, was that he did not wish to have two mass formulas liturgically close to each other beginning with the same prayer, something which had happened for centuries in the Roman church, as we shall see. After we attempt to assess our fragment *in toto*, it may be possible to choose between these two hypotheses.

The mass in the sacramentary of Giso of Wells is prayer for prayer the mass for the octave in the alternate form of the Gregorian Sacramentary contained in Paduense.[29] The mass in Roy is not. The first prayer, *Deus qui salutis*, is the same; the others are different. To what should we attribute this?

---

[26] This usage, the common appellation for this Sunday and a standard position for it, is that of the Gregorian Sacramentary modified by the Supplement.

[27] Ge 10, Sg 10 and Sp v.

[28] Tours, Bibliothèque Municipale, 184, a ninth-century sacramentary of Tours, has *O.s.d. dirige, Muneribus, Da nobis*. The books of Sarum use have *O.s.d. dirige, Accepta domine quaesumus sacrificium, Sumpto sacrificio domine*. In the books cited in the previous note, a mass *O.s.d. dirige, Concede quaesumus domine ut oculis, Per huius domine operationem mysterii*, is employed for the second Sunday after Christmas.

[29] The formulae are *Deus qui salutis, Muneribus, Da nobis*, the very prayers used in the Eighth-century Gelasians for the Sunday after Christmas; see above, n. 27. The masses in the two English books cited earlier (n. 16), are the prayers in the Hadrianum. For Paduense (Pa), see *SG1*, 50–60 and 607–84. It needs to be pointed out that Dom Deshusses has printed Pa as a table of incipits and has supplied variant readings in the notes to Ha; he has not reedited the manuscript.

The earliest mass I have discovered having the three prayers in Roy in the same order and in similar form is a votive *Missa in Honore Sanctae Mariae* in Paris, BN, lat. 2290 (s. ix), a sacramentary of Saint-Denis (*SG*: R; formulae Tc 1853–5). It is the only one of the seventeen principal manuscripts used by Deshusses to contain this mass as part of the main corpus. I have also found it in the following sources earlier than or contemporary with Roy: sacramentary of Fulda (s. x), ed. Richter and Schönfelder, no. 318 (votive);[30] Paris, BN, lat. 9434 (s. xi), a missal from Tours, 273v (votive); and Tours, Petit Séminaire, without signature (s. xi), a missal from Tours, fol. 38 (liturgical).

Since we have met the first prayer before, we will not discuss it and instead will concentrate on the others. The second prayer is very old. It is found in the Leonine Sacramentary, in the Gelasianum for Cecilia, in the sacramentary of Angoulême for Cyriacus, and in other early books. The direct ancestor of the prayer in R, however, would appear to be Sg 1090, the super oblata for the vigil of the Assumption.

Sg 1090	R (Tc 1854)
Suscipe domine sacrificium	Suscipe domine sacrificium
placationis et laudis	placationis et laudis
quod nos interveniente	quod nos interveniente
sancta tua semperque	beata dei genetrice maria,
virgine Maria, cuius	
festivitatem prevenimus	
et perducat ad veniam	et perducat ad veniam
et in perpetua gratiarum	et in perpetuam gratiarum
constituat actione. Per.	constituat actionem. Per.

The versions in the sources from Tours follow R with minor variants.[31] That in Roy is a reworking of the text of R and Fulda.

The last prayer has an even more restricted orbit. The only precursor to the version in R is in the Missale Gothicum.

Go 540	R (Tc 1855)
Libera nos a malo	Libera nos ab omni malo
domine christe iesu	domine iesu christe
corpus tuum	qui corpus tuum sanctum
pro nobis crucifixum aedimus	pro nobis crucifixum edimus
et sanguinem sanctum tuum	et sanguinem tuum

---

[30] *Sacramentarium Fuldense*, ed. G. Richter and A. Schönfelder (Fulda, 1912); rptd as HBS 101 (London, 1980) with a new introduction by D.H. Tripp.

[31] 4 beata dei] beatae BN lat. 9434 | maria] *add.* offerimus *Petit sem.*

pro nobis effusum bibimus.	pro nobis effusum bibimus,
	oremus benignissime domine
	ut per merita et intercessionem
	gloriosissimae mariae virginis,
fiat nobis corpus sanctum tuum	fiat nobis corpus tuum ad salutem
in salute et sanguis sanctus tuos	et sanguis tuus ad remissionem
in remissione peccatorum, hic et	peccatorum. Qui cum patre.
in aeterna saecula saeculorum.	

The sources from Fulda and Tours are close to this version.[32] That in Roy is quite different.

There is a reasonable explanation for these differences in Roy. The scribe of the mass, Hand C, knew that he wanted a mass in honour of Mary at this particular place. The only way to fit it in was to excise the mass for Silvester, and because of that, the space available for entering the replacement mass was limited. He could not use the mass commonly chosen for this celebration, the formulae of which are identical to the mass for the octave in the Hadrianum, because the prayers were too long to fit into the space he had available. They could not be altered because of their familiarity and authority. He discovered a votive mass for Mary beginning with the same prayer as that traditionally used for the octave, and sensing that no one would be the wiser, since the other prayers were totally obscure, he pruned and recast the secret and the post communion to fit his space. If this explanation is correct, it follows that our scribe, if he was the redactor, was also a priest and that he had enough command of Latin to carry out his task. There could not have been many like him. If we can locate the place where this manuscript was used, it might be possible with a little work to identify him.

In Octavas Domini

The mass for this feast is that of the Eighth-century Gelasian Sacramentary, which in turn obtained it from Va. It was adopted by many mixed

[32] 8 ut] *om.* BN 9434 *Petit sem.* | et] *om.* BN lat. 9434 | 9 mariae virginis] virginis mariae *Petit sem.* | 11 tuus] tuis *Fulda* | 12 Qui] qui te BN lat. 9434, qui vivis et regnas cum deo *Petit sem.*

If we care to consider Saint-Denis as the place where the prototype of our mass was compiled, then Fulda and Tours are obvious places where it could have gone. The celebrated sacramentary of Fulda has been determined to belong to a family of sacramentaries called provisionally the family of Saint-Amand. 'The St. Amand type of sacramentary is frequently, and in particular at Fulda, found associated with a set of masses for non-Roman saints which must have been compiled at or with some reference to the monastery of St Denis near Paris' (C. Hohler, 'The Type of Sacramentary used by St. Boniface', *Sankt Bonifatius* (Fulda, 1954), pp. 89–93, at 92). Our early source for this mass from Saint-Denis is a sacramentary written for it at Saint-Amand (R), a book sharing numerous singular variants in the text of the Supplement with books of Tours.

sacramentaries of the tenth century and later in order to avoid juxtaposing two masses with the same collect for *In Octavas Domini* and *Dmc I post N.D.*, a usage promoted by the Supplement to the Hadrianum. It gradually became the usual mass for this feast all over Europe. The steps by which it became the norm have not been elucidated. The impetus to use the Gelasian mass in the Gregorian tradition is first observed in the ninth-century sacramentary of Saint-Vaast, Cambrai, Bibliothèque municipale, 162–3 (s. ix²; *SG*: S). This is the only manuscript of those used by Deshusses for his edition to choose this mass.

The preface has one unusual reading: *virgo et mater* for the normal *mater et virgo*. I find this only in Paris, BN, lat. 9436 (s. xi), a sacramentary and gradual intermixed of Saint-Denis.

The lectionary

In considering the lectionary in Roy I have compared the choices of lessons for these masses to those cited in a number of manuscripts of the seventh and eight centuries. For the epistles I have used the Würzburg codex,[33] Alcuin's *Comes*,[34] and the epistolary of Corbie in Leningrad.[35] For the gospels the Würzburg Evangeliary has been used,[36] and for both epistles and gospels the *Comes* of Murbach, a Gallican list and the ancestor of the modern Roman lectionary.[37]

This comparison, admittedly of marginal value in the context of the other discussions, reveals the Murbach list as the basic model for our fragment. It has the octave of Christmas; the Würzburg epistle-list and Alcuin do not. The lesson here for *Dmc I post N.D.* is given for *Dmc II* by Alcuin. For the octave Roy has an alternate epistle from Philippians: *Fratres; Nos enim sumus circumcisio* (III. 3–8), a lesson I have not located in other books.

The gradual

The texts of this portion of Roy follow the order of the oldest graduals published by Dom Hesbert with one exception. Chants are preserved for the third mass of Christmas (*AMS* 11), Stephen (*AMS* 12), Holy Innocents (*AMS*

---

33 G. Morin, 'Le plus ancien Comes ou lectionnaire de l'église romaine', *RB* 27 (1910), 41–71; A. Chavasse, 'Les plus anciens types du lectionnaire et de l'antiphonaire romains de la messe', *RB* 62 (1952), 3–94, at 65–72 and 84–5; and 'L' épistolier romain du codex du Wurtzbourg. Son organisation', *RB* 91 (1981), 280–331.

34 A. Wilmart, 'Le lectionnaire d'Alcuin', *Ephemerides liturgicae* 51 (1937), 136–97, and Chavasse, 'Les plus anciens types', pp. 49–58.

35 W.H. Frere, *The Roman Epistle Lectionary*, Studies in Early Roman Liturgy 3 (Oxford, 1935), 1–24.

36 G. Morin, 'Liturgie et basiliques de Rome au milieu du VIIe s. d'après les listes d'évangiles de Wurzbourg', *RB* 28 (1911), 296–330; Chavasse, 'Les plus anciens types', pp. 28–49, and 'L'evangéliaire romain de 645: un receuil', *RB* 92 (1982), 33–75.

37 A. Wilmart, 'Le Comes de Murbach', *RB* 30 (1913), 25–69.

15), the octave of Christmas (*AMS* 17bis; only M, S and R) and the first Sunday after Christmas (*AMS* 17). Of the masses that are normally part of this season we are missing the two for John the Evangelist (*AMS* 13, 14) and that for Silvester (*AMS* 16).[38]

The chants have been selectively compared to those in a number of manuscripts from England and Northern France for texts and music. Two of these are available in facsimile: the manuscript of Mont-Renaud (s. x), a gradual and antiphoner written perhaps at Saint-Denis (Eli), and Paris, Bibliothèque Mazarine, 384 (s. xi), a gradual from Saint-Denis (Den1).[39] The other sources are:[40]

CC	Cambridge, Corpus Christi College, 473 (*c.* 1000), a troper from the Old Minster, Winchester
Bo	Oxford, Bodleian Library, Bodley 775 (s. xi^{med}), a troper from the Old Minster, Winchester
Cor	Paris, BN, lat. 18010 (s. xi^2), a gradual from Corbie
Den4	Paris, BN, lat. 9436 (s. xi), an integrated sacramentary-gradual of Saint-Denis, written and notated at Saint-Vaast
Dur	Durham, University Library, Cosin v.v.6 (s. xi^{ex}), a gradual of Durham cathedral priory, written at Christ Church, Canterbury
Iri	Oxford, Bodleian, Rawlinson c. 892 (s. xii^{med}), a gradual from Downpatrick, Ireland
Vor1	Worcester, Cathedral Library, F. 160 (s. xiii^1), a gradual of the cathedral priory

Other manuscripts have been used where we have thought it necessary to include them.

---

[38] R.-J. Hesbert, *Antiphonale missarum Sextuplex* (Brussels, 1935) (henceforth *AMS*). Both masses for John were undoubtedly included. The mass for Silvester may have consisted only of cues. In setting out the texts of some of the chants, the scribe uses a point at certain places to separate one word from another or, more commonly, the first syllable of a word from the other syllables. He may do this in the middle of a text or at the very end. The precise meaning of this usage is obscure. The chants in which it occurs (for which see the edition in the Appendix, below) are:

1. CO. *Viderunt omnes* for Christmas (III)
2. part of a *versus ante officium* for Stephen beginning with *Alleluia Nunc levite*
3. GR. *Anima nostra* for Holy Innocents
4. Alleluia *Te martyrum* for Holy Innocents.

[39] *Le Manuscrit du Mont-Renaud*, Paléographie musicale 16 (Solesmes, 1955), and G.M. Beyssac 'Le Graduel-Antiphonaire de Mont-Renaud', *Revue de musicologie* 40 (1957), 131–50. R.-J. Hesbert, *Le Graduel de Saint-Denis. Manuscrit 384 de la Bibliothèque Mazarine de Paris*, Monumenta musicae sacrae 5 (Paris, 1981).

[40] The sigla Cor, Den1, Den4, Eli, Iri and Vor1 are those of the Abbaye de Saint-Pierre at Solesmes, *Le Graduel romain* 11: *Les Sources* (Solesmes, 1957).

Some explanation must be given for choosing these particular manuscripts to compare with Roy. With respect to the mass, for which we are solely concerned, great strides in understanding the unfolding of regional musical differences were made with the publication in 1960 of a major study of manuscripts by the Benedictines of Solesmes, France, the congregation responsible for the modern restoration of the chant; and other scholars have used these results for their own purposes.[41] It is possible to choose those sources most likely to be comparable to Roy based on that work. However, since Roy is a fragment, there is no way of determining exactly which sources are close to it under the methods of determining affinity. There is also no reason why other types of comparisons should be neglected.[42]

Some of these manuscripts lack some of the chants in Roy so that a full comparison of textual, musical and notational variants is not possible. This is especially true of CC and Bo, which are different from the other books in intent and format. As in the case of the sacramentary, we shall not discuss every situation but only those which are distinctive.

The third mass of Christmas

The introit to this mass is missing. The other chants are very standard, but there is one exception and it is a noteworthy one. The Alleluia is the celebrated bi-lingual *Ymera agiasmeni–Dies sanctificatus*, a famous text found in other English sources. It has been studied in detail by Dom Louis Brou and Egon Wellesz.[43]

The text is laid out in particularly striking manner. The top of the page is divided into two colums of uneven width. On the left side the Greek text is written phrase by phrase, one phrase per line; on the right the Latin equivalent is set out in the same fashion, the last part of the third phrase being written underneath the Greek in order to make way for the rubric of the gospel. The use of capitals for the Greek and minuscules for the Latin is especially striking.

---

[41] *Le Graduel romain, édition critique par les moines de Solesmes*, IV, *Le Texte neumatique*, 1: *Le Groupement des manuscrits* (Solesmes, 1960). An earlier volume listed all the sources, even those not used in the study, and assigned sigla to them. See above, n. 40, as well as K.D. Hartzell, 'An Unknown English Benedictine Gradual of the Eleventh Century', *ASE* 4 (1975), 131–44; D. Hiley, 'The Norman Chant Traditions – Normandy, Britain, Sicily', *Proc. of the R. Musical Assoc.* 107 (1980–1), 1–33. See also below, n. 119.

[42] D.H. Turner compared the post-Pentecost Alleluia list in Le Havre 330 with those in manuscripts from England and northern France: see *New Minster Missal*, ed. Turner, pp. xx–xxiv.

[43] L. Brou, 'L'Alléluia gréco-latin *Dies sanctificatus* de la messe du Jour de Noël', *Revue Grégorienne* 23 (1938), 170–5; 24 (1939), 1–8, 81–9 and 202–13; E. Wellesz, 'Eastern Elements in English Ecclesiastical Music', *Jnl of the Warburg and Courtauld Inst.* 5 (1942), 44–55; and *Eastern Elements in Western Chant* (Boston, 1947), pp. 36–44.

Along the left column at the margin, the first letters of the second and third lines have been omitted, yet the text of each of the three phrases are in line, one with another. From this we may conclude that our scribe was copying his source exactly since the larger, perhaps slightly ornamented letters beginning the second and third lines in his exemplar may never have been filled in. The same situation holds for the first initials of each of the Latin phrases.

There are two ways of interpreting this layout. From the point of view of the letter forms we might conclude that the Greek text would be sung completely through first and the Latin would follow. Dom Brou knew of ten manuscripts preserving the Greek text.[44] Another, from Nevers, was noted by Peter Wagner who published the Greek text in 1901.[45] There is a second manuscript from Nevers which also has the Greek text.[46] Of these twelve manuscripts only two have Greek and Latin sung integrally one after the other, and of these, only one has the Greek first. Neither of these sources is English and in neither case is the Alleluia part of the main manuscript.[47]

Another manner of performance, a phrase of Greek followed by a phrase of its Latin equivalent, is equally possible, and, on the basis of evidence from other manuscripts, more likely. Of the sources remaining from the above list, seven have this type of alteration.[48] They are (in chronological order):

CC, 2v (the first of two; the second is the usual chant)
CCᵒ, fol. 163 (a polyphonic voice for an organum)
Cambrai, Bibl. mun., 75 (s. xi²/⁴), a gradual from Saint-Vaast (Vaa1), 34v
Bo, 76v (as in CC)[49]
Iri, 9v (the second of three; the first is the usual chant, the third is *Multiphariae*)

---

44 Brou, 'L'Alléluia', p. 2.

45 P. Wagner, *Ursprung und Entwicklung der liturgischen Gesangsformen*, 2nd ed. (Leipzig, 1901), and consequently in the English translation of that volume, *Origin and Development of the Forms of the Liturgical Chant* (London, 1907), p. 47. The manuscript is Paris, BN, nouv. acq. lat. 1235 (s. xiiⁱⁿ), 123r.

46 This manuscript was also known to Wagner but evidently he missed this text in it. See N. van Deusen, *Music at Nevers Cathedral*, 2 vols., Musicological Stud. 30 (Henryville, Pa., 1980). The manuscript is Paris, BN, lat. 9449 (s. xiᵐᵉᵈ), 17r.

47 See H.M. Bannister, *Monumenti Vaticani di Paleografia Musicale Latina*, 2 vols. (Leipzig, 1913) II, pl. 63b. The other manuscript is Erlangen, Universitätsbibliothek, 10.ii, 39v.

48 The two manuscripts from Nevers have the Greek text on its own; the other has the Latin first and then the Greek. For the third manuscript (from Beauvais): London, BL, Egerton 2615, 47r, see Brou, 'L'Alléluia, p. 8. The chant from this manuscript is also given in Wellesz, *Eastern Elements in Western Chant*, pp. 41–2. In Wellesz, 'Eastern Elements in English Ecclesiastical Music', p. 46, the author says 'there are MSS. giving the melody with the Greek text without a break, e.g. Codex Cambrai 61, f. 21v', and then he cites Brou, 'L'Alléluia', p. 4, where the Greek tune with Latin text (as in the manuscript) is transcribed. The source of the Greek tune with Greek text transcribed by Wellesz into eighth notes and printed by him (p. 46) is unknown to me.

49 Facsimile in Wellesz, 'Eastern Elements', pl. 17.

Arras, Bibl. mun., 444 (s. xiii), a missal from Saint-Vaast (Vaa3), fol. 60
Vor1, 299v (for the octave)

In view of the evidence of the English witnesses, it is reasonable to include Roy
in this list. It will be noticed that England and Saint-Vaast, the ancient Flemish
monastery at Arras, are the only places to have preserved this particular form.

I have written out the texts and melodies of these sources and have
compared them. We shall preface our discussion by considering the
(hypothetical) text of the Greek.

> Hēmera hēgiasmenē epiphanē hēmin
> Deute ta ethnē kai proskyneite ton Kyrion,
> Hoti sēmeron katebē phōs mega epi tēn gēn.

The Greek is transliterated here from the reconstruction provided by Dom
Ugo Gaisser and reproduced by Henri Villetard and Wellesz.[50]
There are several things wrong with beginning our study with this text.
Dom Gaisser reconstructed his ideal version from the text of the Erlangen
manuscript in comparison with that in Bo and in the twelfth-century source
from Nevers. His reconstruction correctly maintains the accusative, *epi tēn gēn*,
where the ninth-century (or earlier) prototype of the text in the manuscript has
the genitive, *epi tis gis*. Aside from orthography and deterioration due to
elision, the text in the manuscript is thus not classical Greek but Greek on the
way to modern Greek. It is significant that in none of the papers discussing this
text is the argument based on the transliteration I have given above. None of
the manuscripts have anything like it.

Consequently we should choose a version from the manuscripts and use it as
a basis for comparison. Wellesz printed the text from Bo in 1942, but in 1947 he
selected that from CC and I give that here.[51]

> Ymera agias me ni epifanimon
> Teutheta ethni keprosceni teton kirrion.
> Otis imeron katabifos mega epitis gis.

Although Wellesz's text is orthographically correct, with one important
exception, he has not observed the syllabification as carefully as we need to and
so I give his transcription in an emended form as well as the texts in the other
manuscripts.[52]

---

[50] U. Gaisser, 'Brani greci nella liturgia latina', *Rassegna Gregoriana* 1 (1902), 109–12 and 126–31, at 111. H. Villetard, 'L'"Alleluia: Dies sanctificatus" en grec et en latin', *Rassegna Gregoriana* 5 (1906), 5–12, at 8; Wellesz, 'Eastern Elements', p. 46.

[51] Wellesz, *Eastern Elements*, p. 41, n. 1.

[52] There are no hyphens in the manuscripts. I have added them where I have felt the notation clearly indicates that the syllables are supposed to be considered part of the same word. This

CC   Ymera agias me-ni epifanimon
CC⁰ Ymera agias me-ni epifan i mon
Bo   Ymera agias me-ni epiphanimon.
Vaaı Ymera agiasme-ni epiphani mon.
Iri   Ymera agios me .ni epiphani immon.
Vaaʒ Imera agyasme-ni. epyphan y mon.[53]
Vorı Ymera agyos me-ni epiphani mon.

CC   Teutheta &hni keprosceni teton kirrion.
CC⁰ Deutheta &hni keprosceni teton kirrion.
Bo   Teutheta &hni. kepros keni teton kyrrion.[54]
Vaaı euteta &hni keproscheni teton kirrion.
Iri   Theutheta ethni keproskeni teton kirrion
Vaaʒ Deute ca ethni keproskeni-te. ton kyrrion.
Vorı Teutheta et ni kepros chenite ton. kyrrion.

CC   Otis imeron katabifos mega epitis gis
CC⁰ Otis imeron katabi fos mega epitis gis
Bo   Otissimeron katabi fos mega epitis gis.[55]
Vaaı tissimeron catabifos mega epitisgis.
Iri   Otissimeron kata biphos mega epitisgis.
Vaaʒ Otysimeron katabi fos mega epy ti gis.
Vorı Otissimeron kata bifos mega epitis gis.

Of the seven texts, that in Vaaʒ is closest to a hypothetical prototoype. It maintains a proper word separation in most cases. At the end of the first phrase, if the 'i' of *imon* was in the original spelling, it is one of two manuscripts to resist elision. At the beginning of the third phrase it elides the first two words but in a way – with only one 's' – which is believable. Clearly it has evolved along different lines from Vaaı. Of all the sources it is the only missal.

Vaaı is close to the English books but has a few idiosyncrasies not shared by the early English sources. In common with them it uses the ligature 'et' and treats *teton* as one word, but it spells *epi tis gis* as one word.

Bo and CC are close and we would expect that, even though Bo originally read *catabi* in the third phrase. It does, however, have some other

is moderately easy to sense in manuscripts having neumes *in campo aperto* because the music scribe will frequently write them along an imaginary ascending line so as to leave room for the notation appropriate to the next syllable, in case the number of notes for the preceding syllable exceeds the space left for them by the text scribe.

[53] There is an erasure immediately before *mon*. The 'i' may have been erased.
[54] The scribe may have separated *keproskeni* to give room for writing the 'k' of *keni*; the original spelling was *kyrion* (possibly corrected by the main scribe).
[55] The original spelling was *catabi*.

orthographical variants as against CC and CC⁰ which are even more similar. CC and CC⁰ have *epifanimon, keprosceni* (but see Vaa1 and Vor1) and *Otis imeron* and these are not shared by other books.

Iri and Vor1 are idiosyncratic. The former reads *immon, theutheta,* and *biphos,* while the latter has *agyos* and *chenite.* They share the breaking up of *kata* and *bifos* (*biphos*). But there is one unsuspected relationship here, that of Vaa3 and Vor1. Despite the strange syllabification of Vor1 in phrase two, it separates *chenite* and *ton* and has a mark of punctuation after that word, although it is clearly most similar to the early English manuscripts, CC, CC⁰ and Bo.

Let us now return to Roy, which has the following text:

> YMERA. AGIAS. MENI. EPIPHANI. MON.
>
> EUTE. TA ETH NI. KEPROSKENITE. TON KYRION.
>
> TI. SIMERON. KATAVIFOS. MEGA. EPITIS GIS.

Regarding syllabification we find the following parallels:

agias meni	CC, CC⁰, Bo, Vor1
epiphani mon	Vaa1, Iri, Vor1
eute ta	Vaa3
eth ni	Vor1
keproskenite	Vaa3
ton kyrion	Vaa3, Vor1
katavifos	CC, Vaa1
epitis gis	CC, CC⁰, Bo, Vor1

The text is more similar to Vor1 (5 ×), CC (3 ×), and Vaa3 (3 ×) than to the others. More interesting than this is the number of variants it has with only one manuscript or at most two, and these are usually either the Worcester Gradual or the missal from Saint-Vaast or both. We have already noticed that Vaa3 and Vor1 separate *chenite* and *ton,* and they utilize points of demarcation (punctuation) to assure some sort of syllabification.

Thus Iri cannot be linked convincingly to any of the other sources. CC and CC⁰ represent one source, and while this is similar to Bo, Bo is not its model. They represent two branches of the same tree. Vor1 is related to those branches but distinct from them. They perhaps have a common ancestor. Vaa1 is a friendly relative. Vaa3 is not related to the Winchester books but it is to the Worcester Gradual, and Roy is most clearly linked to these two books.

On the basis of these observations, we may draw the following tentative conclusions. The versions of *Ymera agiasmeni* in Roy and Vaa3 are more archaic than the others and for that reason are undoubtedly closer to the original. When this text entered England is not known. If the model were similar in layout to that in Roy, it was rewritten at Winchester to conform to ideals in which musical considerations superseded textual ones. In the second phrase *teton* is a typical Winchester syllabification and has an exact parallel elsewhere in CC and Bo when prepositions in a modifying phrase are elided to the beginning of the succeeding word. But this usage is not unique to Winchester and can be found on the continent. It is certainly conceivable that the models for CC and Bo came already modified in the manner I have described.[56]

It will be of interest to discover whether the textual groupings we have established will be borne out by the melodic traditions of the seven sources. Although I reserve discussion of the notational peculiarities of Roy for the moment (see below, pp. 71–5), it is useful here to group the sources according to their notational status, and with that in mind, they are grouped as follows:

> Anglo-Saxon neums: CC, Bo and Roy
> Saint-Vaast neums: Vaa1
> notation on lines: Iri, Vor1 and Vaa3

The three Anglo-Saxon manuscripts have a few melodic differences. In phrases one and two on *me*ni (sancti*fica*tus) Roy has aEF where Bo and CC have aFF.[57] At the words me*ga* and mag*na* in phrases five and six, Roy ends the melisma on D, FGED'D, whereas Bo and CC end it on C, GFED'DC (or as in CC, EFED'DC). This version of CC is not an error in the manuscript. The notation must be interpreted to give these pitches, and the scribe must have used them since the melodic shape EFED is common in other parts of the chant. CC also has EFED in the jubilus where every other source has GFED.

The melody in Vor1 and in the other sources is close to this. In line one at *mon* (no*bis*) it reads uniquely F'FED.[58] *Teutheta* is three syllables in Vor1 and four in the others. Here, as in all the late sources, the quilismas have been dropped. It follows Roy on me*ga* and mag*na* alone of the other manuscripts.[59]

Vaa1 exhibits subtle differences at the beginnings of lines. It does not have the pitch preparatory to the quilismata in lines three and four, and it uses liquescents where none of the other sources have them.

Vaa3 (like Vaa1) follows Roy on *me*ni and sancti*fica*tus. In phrases five and

---

[56] On the other hand, England and Saint-Vaast being the only places to preserve the form Greek, Latin, Greek (and so forth), it is also conceivable that this form was invented in England.

[57] The notational scheme for representing pitches is that adopted in *Monumenta Monodica Medii Aevi* (Kassel, 1956–). It is based on the anonymous *Dialogus de musica* (*c.* 1000), for which see the convenient article by R.L. Crocker, 'Alphabet Notations for Early Medieval Music', *Saints, Scholars and Heroes: Studies in Medieval Culture in honour of Charles W. Jones*, ed. M.H. King and W.M. Stevens, 2 vols. (Collegeville, Minn., 1979) II, 79–104, at 99.

[58] See also cheni*te* (adora*te*), lines 3 and 4, where the motive is the same.

[59] There is an extra note preceding the climacus on sancti*fica*tus (line 2) which must be an error. It is not at the identical place on line 1. Another error, this time in the text, occurs in line 4 where the syllable *te* of *adorate* is written four pitches too soon.

six (like Vaa1) it follows Bo on me*ga* and mag*na*. It has no liquescents in the last phrase where the other manuscripts do.

Iri has an oddly notated jubilus which is missing notes. On me*ga* it follows the sources which end on C.[60]

Roy, therefore, while similar to Bo and CC, goes its own way, one paralleled in one case by Vor1, but this book also goes its own way in one distinctive case. Vaa1 has a related but distinct profile, whereas Vaa3 seems close to Roy. We shall discuss notational variants in this chant later on.

St Stephen

Before the nearly total capitulation to square notation in the thirteenth century, notational and musical practices were quite distinctive, and we are given the opportunity to examine another piece making that point even more obvious.

What we broadly call tropes came in various sizes and configurations, as we are realizing more and more. Such disparity of form and usage is difficult to classify. For instance, in the case of the piece we shall now examine, rather than trope pure and simple, it has been called *versus ante officium* by the scribes of two of the manuscripts in which it is given.[61] The title is liturgical and just; the piece leads directly to the first introit trope rather than to the introit itself as in the case of most of the proper tropes to that chant. Alejandro Planchart has pointed out that these pieces, preceding as they do the entire service, take on a function similar to processional antiphons preceding mass.[62]

The *versus ante officium* in our manuscript, *Cui adstat candida contio*, has been noticed in only eleven sources: three English, seven French and one Italian. On the basis of readings, there are three groups.

Group A: CC, Bo, Vaa1, Roy and a manuscript we have not considered heretofore: Paris, BN, lat. 13252 (s. xi), a troper from Saint-Magloire, Paris;

Group B: the two manuscripts from Nevers;

Group C: four manuscripts from Aquitania and Italy: Paris, BN, lat. 887, 909, 1084, and Ivrea, Biblioteca Capitolare, 60.

Alejandro Planchart, to whom we owe this grouping, has postulated that the tradition of development proceeds from area A to B to C.[63] In fact the text from

---

[60] There is a severe textual muddle in line 3 where, as on line 4 in Vor1, *te* of *keproschenite* is brought in four notes too soon. The following *ton* is also brought in four notes too soon.

[61] CC and Bo.

[62] A.E. Planchart, *The Repertory of Tropes at Winchester*, 2 vols. (Princeton, 1977) I, 235.

[63] *Ibid.* II, 31; *Tropes du propre de la messe, I: Cycle de Noël*, ed. R. Jonsson, Corpus Troporum I (Stockholm, 1975), 70.

Saint-Magloire is undoubtedly closest to the textual idea. The one significant variant in CC, Bo and Roy (*paraphonistae dicite* for *paraphonista dic domne*) was undoubtedly chosen so the text could reflect the elaborate directions for performance in CC and Bo, that is, rubrics specifying antiphonal performance rather than responsorial. Interestingly, the final *e* in Roy has been erased.[64]

With respect to the music, the five closely related sources from Group A give the same melody, but the English books do have some departures from the other two (which are similar in some ways), and it is difficult to believe that the two groups could be directly related.[65]

Holy Innocents

In the Carolingian period there was no Alleluia for this feast. The rubric in the Senlis manuscript (S) reads IN NATALE INNOCENTIUM GLORIA IN EXCELSIS DEO NON CANITUR NEC ALLELUIA SED QUASI PRO TRISTITIA DEDUCITUR DIES ILLA (*AMS* 15). Even as late as the twelfth century some churches did not sing an Alleluia. In the tenth century, or possibly in the ninth, when an Alleluia made its way into this mass, *Te martyrum candidatus* was usually chosen by churches in the northwestern part of France. *Te martyrum* belongs to the oldest layer of the Alleluia repertory, although it occurs in only two of the six graduals in *AMS*, once for Felix and Adauctus (K) and once as part of a list of Alleluias *per circulo anni* (C), where it was clearly part of the group intended to be used for the common of saints.[66] Later, but no later than the eleventh century, some churches had composed their own Alleluia. A number of these chants have a very restricted usage. To give only two examples, *Hodie sancti innocentes*, the first of two Alleluias in Dur, is not listed by Karl-Heinz Schlager in his comprehensive catalogue of Alleluias written before 1100, although it is found later in books from Abingdon, Sherborne and Whitby.[67] The only chant for this feast in the Saint-Magloire troper, *Herodes iratus*, is found in the Paris Missal and in books of the Dominican order. *Te martyrum* is found in Roy, CC, Bo, Iri and Den4; Vor1 has the same Alleluia as Dur; Cor has *Iudicabitur sancti*; Den1 and Eli have no chant. In the context of our discussion, then, *Te*

---

[64] In *Tropes*, ed. Jonsson, the editor prefers *paraphonista dic domne*. I read *obtamus* and *paraphonista* in Vaa1.

[65] The melody for this trope from Paris, BN, lat. 887 (s. xi¹), a Troper from Saint-Géraud at Aurillac, is found in G. Weiss, *Introitus-Tropen I: Das Repertoire der südfranzösischen Tropare des 10. und 11. Jahrhunderts*, Monumenta Monodica Medii Aevi 3 (Kassel, 1970), no. 21. The version in this manuscript omits the last stanza of Planchart's Group A. The attribution to Aurillac is given in *Tropes*, ed. Jonsson, p. 47. In the latest volume of *Corpus Troporum* (1982) this attribution is queried.

[66] For a list of Roman Alleluia verses in the oldest repertory, see K.-H. Schlager, in *The New Grove Dictionary*, ed. Sadie, 1, 269–76 (s.v. 'Alleluia').

[67] K.-H. Schlager, *Thematischer Katalog der ältesten Alleluia-Melodien* (Munich, 1965).

martyrum is not an unusual choice. What follows it in Roy, on the contrary, is quite extraordinary.

Following the text of *Te martyrum* the scribe has written the word TRACTUS and after it a piece known previously only from an organal voice in CC.[68] A tract for Holy Innocents, while perhaps being more appropriate for this feast than an Alleluia, is uncommon. I have found only three instances:

Angers, Bibl. mun., 91 (83) (s. x), a gradual inserted in a sacramentary possibly from Saint-Pierre d'Angers, 44v: *Posuerunt* (not part of the earliest repertory of texts)[69]

Angers, Bibl. mun., 96 (88) (s. xii[in]), a gradual from Saint-Aubin d'Angers, fol. 4: *Laus tibi christe* (also not early)

Paris, BN, lat. 9449 (of Nevers and cited earlier), fol. 15: *Qui seminant* (usually for Virgins)

The text of this tract, while given in full in the edition (below, p.94), must be given here as well.

Vidi supra montem sion agnum stantem et cum eo centum quadraginta quattuor milia. VERSUS. Habentes nomen eius et nomen patris eius scriptum in frontibus suis. VERSUS. Et cantabant canticum novum ante sedem dei et resonabat terra in voces illorum.

Those familiar with the liturgy will recognize this as part of the epistle for the day, taken from ch. XIV of Revelation. The decision to set it as a tract must be one of the more remarkable in the history of medieval chant, and it is not at all surprising that it has such a limited distribution. We would be safe in concluding that it is an English piece were it not for the fact that it is found in Den4, the integrated sacramentary-gradual from Saint-Denis cited earlier in connection with textual variants in the prayers. The ramifications of this discovery will be discussed below (pp. 76–7).

The octave of Christmas

With the exception of the gradual from Rheinau, this feast is not found in the oldest graduals. Yet as we have seen there is a mass in the Hadrianum *In Octavas Domini* reflecting its adoption by the papal liturgy in the seventh century. The

---

[68] A. Holschneider, *Die Organa von Winchester* (Hildesheim, 1968), p. 44.

[69] Theodore Karp kindly informs me that the tract presently assigned to Holy Innocents (*Effuderunt*), although it has multiple assignments in the medieval period, is ascribed to that feast in the following manuscripts: Paris, BN, lat. 903; Rome, Bibl. Angelica, 123; Vatican City, Bibl. Apost. Vat., Ross. lat. 231; Milan, Bibl. Ambrosiana, s. 74 sup.; and Benevento, Bibl. Capitolare, VI.34. For a list of the earliest tracts, see H. Hucke, in *The New Grove Dictionary*, ed. Sadie, XIX, 108–10 (s.v. 'Tract').

reason for its omission in the early graduals could be that, unlike the papal sacramentaries, they used the mass of the day for the octave without change, and this decision has held good for all of the chants in this mass from an early date except the Alleluia.

As we know, the Alleluia for Christmas (III) is *Dies sanctificatus*. It is assigned to that mass in all six of the graduals in *AMS*. The Gregorian melody for this piece is one of the most widely used in the entire repertory, serving for nine other texts in the oldest layer alone. Initially it may have been used for the octave, although curiously, the Rheinau manuscript has *Dominus regnavit decorem*, the Alleluia for Christmas (II) and for the Sunday after Christmas. When we examine one of the oldest lists of Alleluias once more, that in manuscript C (Compiègne), we find the following order approximately half way through:

ALL. Dies sanctificatus
ALL. Video celos
ALL. Hic est discipulus
ALL. Vidimus stellam

These chants are for Christmas (III), Stephen, John the Evangelist, and Epiphany, respectively. The same order is found in the list of Alleluias in Bo (76r–87v) and, except for *Te martyrum*, in CC (2v–8v).

At some point an undoubtedly prestigious church in the West decided that instead of the normal Alleluia *Dies sanctificatus* for Christmas (III), they would sing an Eastern melody with a Greek text. Perhaps the Latin equivalent would then have been sung, in the manner of the bilingual singing mentioned in the early *ordines Romani* which describe a papal mass. We could view this method of performance as a substitute for the earlier practice of just singing the Gregorian tune and text on its own. But this logic may be backward. It is easier, and according to these same *ordines Romani* more historically accurate, to place the alternation of texts as the earlier practice and the reduction to a single Latin text and tune as the simplification of this elaborate procedure.[70] We should ask, therefore, whether any of the chants for the proper were ever sung in Greek, and why a Greek Alleluia was introduced in the first place, but these questions are more appropriate to an extended study of this important chant on its own.

At some point Greek and Latin became artificially integrated to the point where we have the form preserved anachronistically in Roy and the other seven sources. Where this Alleluia held sway, the natural tendency was to take

---

[70] Wellesz, *Eastern Elements*, esp. 11–18, 36–44 and 50–67.

the Gregorian tune and its purely Latin text and use it for the octave. It is this situation which is reflected in our manuscript.

To return to the point that the Alleluia for the octave has not remained stable we may turn to the Cosin Gradual (Dur) which has Alleluia *Multifariam*. In the ninth century when the repertory of Alleluias began to expand, a number of them became associated with a single feast. In the eleventh and twelfth centuries we have an abundance of chants, almost too many to use. Alleluia *Multifariam* became the Alleluia for the octave for those churches not using the Greco-Latin *Dies sanctificatus* for the day. Of course it would have been possible to scrap the Gregorian *Dies sanctificatus* altogether but I am not aware of a situation where that happened. Some churches which did not use the Greco-Latin chant never expanded their repertory of Alleluias to include *Multifariam*. We would expect their repertory of Alleluias to have remained very limited.[71]

It has been stated often enough to become 'law' that where we find two Alleluias with different texts for a single feast, the second is the older: if not the older in the repertory, the older in the usage of the particular manuscript containing the pieces, and by extension, in the usage of the institution for which the manuscript was copied.[72] Although this is undoubtedly true in some cases, where a church observed a feast with an octave it is almost certainly wrong, especially if no mass for the octave is given in its proper place. One unusual example will reinforce this. In Vatican City, Biblioteca Apostolica Vaticana, lat. 4770 (s. x–xi), an Italian noted missal perhaps from Subiaco (Sub), there are two Alleluias for Christmas (iii), *Dies sanctificatus* and *Multifariam* (*Multifariae*; the tradition is variable). After this mass, the scribe has written the mass for the octave where we would normally expect to proceed to that for Stephen, but even more unusually, he has given the chants of the *Vultum tuum* mass (*AMS* 16bis), accorded the rubric *Natale Sanctae Mariae* in *AMS*. The traditional Alleluia for this mass is *Specie tue* and it is found here. This being accomplished we pass to Stephen and so on. Clearly this scribe was following what was now considered a standard procedure – writing two Alleluias for Christmas, the second intended to be sung on the octave – but wanting to make certain that a Marian mass was also observed on 1 January, he included the whole mass for that day immediately after the main mass: an extraordinary procedure to reinforce an unusual liturgical situation. Normally, of course, by this time the octave would have been relabelled the feast of

---

[71] There are some exceptions to this theory provided by four of the manuscripts cited in Brou, 'L'Alléluia', pp. 3–4, as sources for the Greek tune: 11, 13, 14 and 21. Iri also has *Multiphariam* but the usage of this manuscript is confusing.

[72] I am freely interpreting here the 'loi des doublets' identified by A. Baumstark, G. Beyssac, and A. Chavasse, and articulated by M. Huglo, *Les Tonaires* (Paris, 1971), p. 296.

the Circumcision, although this practice was not uniformly observed until later.

The notation and the other chants

So far we have considered a number of musico-liturgical anomalies in the gradual and have said nothing about the melodic versions of the more standard chants. We turn to that subject now. Before we do, something must be said about the notation and the notational idiosyncrasies this fragment possesses.

The neumatic notation in Roy belongs to a family broadly called French and more specifically Northern French. It seems to have been written across the northern part of Francia from the ninth century onwards, with the exception of those places using a more primitive system recently called palaeo-Frankish or an almost contemporary elaboration of palaeo-Frankish which we now call Breton. Although the most systematic study of French notation has not yet been published, a map showing the results is available in Solange Corbin's 1977 handbook, *Die Neumen*.[73] The notation used in Lotharingia inevitably found its way into this region. In one celebrated Parisian house a recognizable mélange of French and Lotharingian neumes was common.[74]

Northern French neumes and other musical notations found their way to England, which by the beginning of the tenth century had not developed its own. These neumes were written at Winchester and other places and were adopted by most institutions having a musical tradition relating to the standard Gregorian repertory. For this reason scholars have called them 'Anglo-Saxon'. The term is useful although there has never been a study sufficiently detailed to determine whether England augmented or revised the Northern French system in any way. One reason for that might be that we have more and better examples of Anglo-Saxon neumes than we do of Northern French neumes which can be compared directly to them.[75]

---

[73] S. Corbin, *Die Neumen*, Palaeographie der Musik 1.3 (Cologne, 1977). There are earlier maps: G.M. Suñol, *Introduction à la Paléographie musicale Grégorienne* (Paris, 1935), pl. B; *Les Sources* (see n. 35), map 2 (reproduced in *Die Neumen*). Corbin's study is derived from her doctoral dissertation submitted to the Sorbonne in 1957, 'La notation musicale neumatique. Les quatres provinces lyonnaises: Lyon, Rouen, Tours, et Sens.' This work has been cited by E. Jammers in *Tafeln zur Neumenschrift* (Tutzing, 1965), in *Die Neumen*, and by Corbin and her fellow editors in her series *Répertoire de manuscrits médiévaux contenant des notations musicales*, but since it has never been available to the public, these citations are meaningless.

[74] Saint-Maur-des-Fossés, represented by Paris, BN, lat. 12584; a folio is reproduced in colour in B. Stäblein, *Schriftbild der einstimmigen Musik* (Leipzig, 1977), p. 113; see also Corbin, *Die Neumen*, p. 123. For Lotharingian neumes generally, consult J. Hourlier, 'Le Domaine de la notation Messine', *Revue Grégorienne* 30 (1951), 96–113 and 150–8.

[75] On Anglo-Saxon neumes see the works of Planchart and Holschneider (above, nn. 62 and 68), and my 'A St. Albans Miscellany in New York', *Mittellateinisches Jahrbuch* 10 (1975), 20–

The notation in Roy is an excellent example of Anglo-Saxon neumatic notation (see pl. IV). The axis is upright with a slight tilt to the right. The virga is mostly straight and pointed at both ends like a quill; there is some tendency for the stem to curve slightly at the tip. For the podatus, the foot is appended to the stem; it is not consistently placed. The foot is also found frequently curved and without a toe: scarcely wedge-shaped. The join to the stem is not smoothly executed, and the angle of the join varies. The punctum-virga form of the neume is also found. The stem of the clivis is straight, the head rounded on top; the descender runs parallel to the stem and then occasionally draws left. Only once or twice is there a tendency to buttonhook. The puncta inclinata of the climacus run at about a forty-five degree angle to the stem, which terminates in a short turn to the right. The torculus is straightforward, as is the porrectus, which mostly is just three straight lines, the middle one of which is very short. The oriscus is the familiar 'lazy' s. It is used in a pressus, a salicus, and the virga strata. In the pressus the scribe begins it sometimes even with but usually lower than the top of the virga, while with a clivis it begins opposite the end of the loop. Distropha and tristropha are always represented as bivirga and trivirga. The quilisma is written in one stroke, the curls being depressed slightly from the line of text. Sometimes they run parallel to it.

So far these forms are standard though individual. There are others, however, which are refinements or modifications of these: (a) scandicus of punctum and pes (regular or liquescent); (b) pes stratus; (c) porrectus flexus (a clivis with an additional loop to the right of the first) either on its own or praebipunctis; (d) climacus with loops; (e) clivis of regular shape or as a slightly tilted circumflex, above a bivirga. The circumflex shape also occurs above a pes and a scandicus; (f) the trigon, either the standard three dots or four; (g) torculus resupinus with a large loop; (h) bivirga with praepunctum, with two puncta (a sort of scandicus), or with three puncta; (i) torculus subpunctis with a resupinus virga capped to the left; (j) torculus subpunctis resupinus in the cursive form; (k) ancus; (l) an oriscus in pressus configuration with two subpunctis or three; (m) climacus-clivis in cursive form; (n) virga strata. Many of these are found in the two manuscripts of the Winchester Troper.

In compiling this list I have been guided by the following factors. There are eighteen chants on the eight pages of Roy. Three of these are cited by incipit.

61; see also S. Corbin, 'Paléographie musicale', *Ecole pratique des hautes études. Annuaire 1967–68* (Paris, 1969), pp. 329–41; *Die Neumen*, pp. 131–40; and *The New Grove Dictionary*, ed. Sadie, XIII, 128–44, at 143 (s.v. 'Neumatic Notation, I–IV'). Mlle Corbin prefers the title 'English neumes', quoting P. Wagner approvingly in 'Neumatic Notation' to the effect that they are 'not old enough to be described as Anglo-Saxon'. See also Suñol, *Introduction*, pp. 283–91, and the comprehensive descriptions of two Anglo-Saxon neume styles in Bannister, *Monumenti Vaticani* I, nos. 226 and 227.

One is incomplete and in damaged condition. Three more are special chants with limited distribution which we have already discussed. One is a duplicate. Eliminating these, we are left with ten chants where comparisons of usage and melody are possible. Going beyond the observance of usage in Roy by itself, two of the ten chants are found in all three English books: Roy, CC and Bo. Not surprisingly they are both Alleluias. All six neumed manuscripts – Roy, CC, Bo, Cor, Den 1 and Eli – have one of these: *Dies sanctificatus* for the octave. The other, *Te martyrum*, is not in Cor and Den 1. But there are eight other chants – three introits, one gradual, two offertories and two communions – where Roy and the three continental books can be compared. We may now proceed to analyse the results of the comparison of these four books.

Den 1 (s. xi) is an immaculately produced book. The neumatic style is French but meticulously refined. As Dom Hesbert observed in the facsimile edition, the scribe – undoubtedly a professional – does not differentiate between scandicus and salicus, between punctum and strophicus. The trigon is absent, the quilisma has a restricted usage, the sign for the last (prolonged) pitch of a climacus is a virga with a flag at the top descending to the left (see especially the gradual *Anima nostra*), and there are various other sorts of prolongations of final notes of simple neumes. At *de* in the Offertory *Anima nostra* the scribe has written a rare neume before the beginning of the quilisma which is probably meant to signify the preceding pes.[76] The scribe uses a pes of virga and foot. If the style of neumes in this book represents the old Saint-Denis style, then the type of neums in Roy, Cor and Eli never resembled it, but there is no reason to believe that it does. It probably was adopted in the eleventh century, possibly after 1008, when there is Cluniac influence at the abbey.[77]

Cor, also an eleventh-century book, is not so well written. The virga has a typical eleventh century cap or flag to the left. The neumes are very close together. This book is frequently cited as the model for the style of neumes adopted in England.[78] There are many similarities. The axis is almost vertical. There are many cursive forms, such as the climacus and its various compound elaborations. But for all the similarity in style, the usage is not Roy's. Cor does not use the trigon, nor does it usually differentiate salicus and scandicus – sometimes it writes them as pes-virga – and it frequently omits quilismata or uses them where the other manuscripts do not. One of its idiosyncrasies is the nearly suprascript clivis in the circumflex form.

---

[76] Hesbert, *Le Graduel de Saint-Denis*, pl. 13, line 16. Compare BN, lat. 12584, in Stäblein, *Schriftbild*.

[77] The style of the Cluniac Gradual (Paris, BN, lat. 1087 (s. xi)) is recognizable in the neumes of Den 1; see Corbin, *Die Neumen*, pls. 40 and 41.

[78] Corbin, 'Neumatic Notation', p. 143.

Eli is the oldest of the three continental manuscripts we have been comparing with Roy. The basic book is of tenth-century date, but the notation seems to have been added sometime later, although still in that century. Of the three manuscripts, both its style and its usage are closest to Roy. It differentiates scandicus and salicus, uses the trigon, prefers roughly the same mixture of cursive climacus (with elaborations) and virga and puncta inclinata as does Roy, uses the punctum-virga form of the pes predominantly as does Roy, follows Roy in the use of the quilisma and prefers to avoid a pressus of oriscus-punctum. But although it is close to it, Roy is not a carbon copy of Eli. It does not stress the final punctum in a climacus where other sources call for it; it uses the circumflex clivis where Eli will write the small regular clivis to the right of the second of the bivirgae; it has the pes stratus; and there are small differentiations in usage which distinguish the two books. Despite this they are clearly representatives of the same basic notational heritage.

One idiosyncrasy reinforces this, one does not. In the first case, in *Etenim sederunt* for Stephen, the penultimate neume at the final cadence, a porrectus in the *Graduale Romanum*, is written in all four neumatic sources as a pressus followed by a virga. In Eli the scribe has written the oriscus, punctum and virga in such a way that they form a scandicus; this has been followed by Roy. The exact same cadence occurs on a different pitch in *Dum medium silentium* (silen*ti*um), and it is handled in a similar way. In the second case, in the communion *Viderunt* for Christmas (III), Eli uses what is essentially a square-notation virga as a clivis. The same usage is found in two chants shared by all six sources but not yet discussed, the two Alleluias: *Te martyrum* (end of Jubilus) and *Dies sanctificatus* (three places in the verse). Roy has nothing like this.

In addition there is an error in Roy which must be interpreted as a misunderstanding of the Eli tradition. In the communion *Vox in Rama*, on *no*luit, Eli has virga-oriscus-virga with the second virga in suprascript position. The *Graduale Romanum* reads b bc, and this is what is intended in Eli but the grouping is bb′c. In Roy this place is unreadable, but on the first syllable of the next word, *con*solari, we have a similar situation. This time in Eli we have virga-oriscus-liquescent virga with the elements in the same position as before. Roy has interpreted this as a scandicus. The pitches are cc′ca. Cor and Den1 have nothing similar. Interestingly, Roy does use a scandicus in other places for b′bc or for other pitches in a similar configuration (e.g., offertory *Tui sunt caeli*, iustiti*a*).

It is time to introduce the two Alleluias into the discussion. *Te martyrum* is missing in Cor and Den1. Bo and Roy are usually closer than Bo and CC, and they are closer to Eli with the exception of the peculiar use of the clivis noted earlier. In *Dies sanctificatus*, the allegiances are changed around. Bo and CC are closer to each other than either is to Roy; Eli seems to be closest to Bo except again, where it has the strange clivis. *Dies sanctificatus* is in both Cor and Den 1 but the traditions of those books are of lesser importance here.

Notational differences apart, the melodic shapes of the sources are very similar. There are a few eccentricities. Cor has distinct readings in the introit *Etenim sederunt*. In the gradual *Anima nostra* the scribe of Den 1 has written the cadence formula for the second *est* over the first *est*, and the scribe of Cor has done just the opposite. The end of the verse in Cor has the notes arranged in strange ways. Eli is missing the last four notes of the jubilus of the Alleluia *Te martyrum* and, by extension, the last four notes of the verse. In the communion *Vox in Rama* Cor and Den 1 have single notes on u*lula*tus, and all four sources show variation on *noluit consolari*. In the Alleluia *Dies sanctificatus*, Cor, alone of all six sources, has a clivis on sancti*fi*catus.

Summary of the liturgical contents

On the basis of the preceding discussion, we may draw some definite conclusions about the eleventh-century English *missale plenum* that Roy once was. Behind the sacramentary portion lies the Gregorian Sacramentary, but the compiler retained usage from an earlier period and introduced novelties of the ninth century, one of which became standard practice for all service books of this type. In the original book there was no Prophecy for the third mass of Christmas, there was a mass for St Silvester, and the collect for Christmas (III) was probably that associated with the Eighth-century Gelasians. The large blank space after this mass was left so that local practice could be catered for and the priest whose book it was could enter some of his favourite prayers, perhaps some of his own authorship. The format of the group of six supplementary prayers – run-on, not marginal beginnings – encourages this view. The lectionary is a standard series of lessons despite the alternate epistle for the octave. The gradual generally follows the convention, too, although it should be observed that there was far less flexibility in the gradual than in the sacramentary during the early Middle Ages.

Soon after it was written, the standard Prophecy for Christmas, Is. LII. 6–10, was written over something (and I am unsure what it may have been), the mass for Silvester was erased, and a new mass in honour of Mary was entered. Some textual emendation was done but the basic text was retained into the following century, when someone rewrote the beginning of the preface for Holy Innocents and made substantial alterations in the texts of many of the prayers. Two of these come in the group of supplementary prayers for Christmas (III). The lectionary did not escape emendation at the same time. In the introit for

Holy Innocents, the reading *latentium* may have been chosen in the earlier period. Thus all substantial changes in wording were done at the same time, and few may be attributed to the period immediately after the Conquest.

It is possible to estimate the original readings underlying some of the changes. The most striking of these are in the preface for Holy Innocents where, on the basis of scribal practice, we may postulate a text dating from the eighth century or earlier retained anachronistically until the eleventh. In some of the prayers there are readings implying similarity to readings in the Leofric Missal and the missal of Robert of Jumièges, as well as to an eleventh-century sacramentary–gradual from Saint-Denis. Significantly, the three books rarely share such readings. In the fifth of the optional prayers at Christmas the main scribe has changed his wording from one shared by the Winchcombe Sacramentary alone of the English books.

Despite what has been said about the text of Roy, there are some intriguing idiosyncrasies. The original preface for Holy Innocents has already been mentioned. Some of the supplemental prayers for Christmas are extremely rare. The second is not from the tradition of the Eighth-century Gelasian. It is not in any of the English books. In Dom Deshusses's edition of the Hadrianum, his note indicates that it occurs in ten of the ninth-century witnesses to that text. Six of these are Belgian-German-Swiss, one is Italian (Verona) and three are French (Paris, from the Court of Charles the Bald, which ended up at Nonantola, Senlis and Tours). Among the German books is the sacramentary of Trent. Clearly, this implies at least an early ninth-century distribution. The fourth prayer also takes us back to the eighth century. Remarkably it is not in any of the ninth-century witnesses to the Gregorian Sacramentary used by Deshusses.

Readings in the Christmas prayers take us further toward their possible sources. In the third supplemental prayer, *nostris* is read in only four of the books used by Deshusses: two from Verona, a fragment from Benedictbeuern, and the Senlis book, of which Deshusses remarks 'ce sacramentaire mérite à peine le nom de grégorien'.[79]

Aside from these readings and the usage in the group of supplemental Christmas prayers, the greatest idiosyncrasies come in the gradual. For the third mass of Christmas the compiler has chosen a rare but splendid bilingual Alleluia. He has also displayed it in the manuscript in a remarkable way. Before the mass for St Stephen he has included the full text of a *versus ante officium* which has an equally restricted usage. But the most remarkable of the musical choices is a tract for Holy Innocents which I have located in only one other

---

[79] *SG*I, 41.

regular service book, Den4, although an organal voice for this chant is found in the Cambridge manuscript of the Winchester Troper (CC).

THE ORIGINS OF THE ROYAL MISSAL FRAGMENT

Having described the basic text and presented some of the most important alterations and idiosyncrasies, it is time to discuss the origin of Roy: its script and notation, its format and sources, why we have the text we do, and its importance.

After comparing eleventh-century manuscripts from centres for which we have securely attributable sources, the greatest affinity to the main hand of Roy is shown by London, BL, Cotton Nero E. i (pts 1 and 2), a two-volume passional written and used at the cathedral priory of Worcester in the mid-eleventh century. The script of the missal is more accomplished. The main strokes of **r**, **s**, and **f** are unterminated where in the passional they usually have serifs. The scribe was perhaps less overwhelmed with the task of writing the missal. The missal probably antedates the passional, although, if this is correct, the relationship is close enough to posit a dating of the mid-eleventh century for it also. The script of other liturgical manuscripts attributed to Worcester in this period has a decidedly different cast.

As with book-hand under the control of a conscientious and gifted scribe, it is possible to identify music scribes who exhibit regularity in their work. The music scribe of Roy is one such. His notation is that of pp. 315–620 and selected chants thereafter in the well-known Portiforium of St Wulstan (Cambridge, Corpus Christi College, 391 (s. xi^med)), a manuscript known to have been written and used at Worcester cathedral priory, and which has been dated more precisely by some scholars to 1065–6 on account of markings in the calendar.[80]

---

[80] *The Portiforium of St Wulstan*, ed. A. Hughes, 2 vols., HBS 89–90 (London, 1958–60). A fair amount of this manuscript was earlier published in *The Leofric Collectar II*, ed. E.S. Dewick and W.H. Frere, HBS 56 (London, 1918). The calender is in *English Kalendars before A.D. 1100*, ed. F. Wormald, HBS 72 (London, 1934), no. 17. A facsimile of p. 643 is seen in W.H. Frere, *Bibliotheca Musico-Liturgica* 1 (London, 1901), pl. 15.

In a brief paper, 'The Provenance of the Oldest Manuscript of the Rule of St Benedict', *Bodleian Library Record* 2 (1941–9), 28–9, repr. *Books, Collectors and Libraries: Studies in the Medieval Heritage* [by] N.R. Ker, ed. A.G. Watson (London and Ronceverte, 1985), pp. 131–3, the late Neil Ker gave a small list of mid-eleventh-century books containing writing in a 'round, upright English hand' which he assigned to Worcester. After describing the characteristics of the script, and being careful not to imply that parts of these books where this script is found were all written by the same scribe, he proposed the hand of London, BL, Add. ch. 19801 (dated A.D. 1058) as the basic script. Initially the scribe of Roy did not observe its canons, but he came to observe some of them by the time he wrote the Cotton passional. We may compare CCCC 391, p. 591/1–20, the hand of a scribe whose work is similar to that

An attribution to Worcester, already secure, is reinforced by recalling that Royal 5. A. XII was once the property of a clergyman directly appointed by the bishop of Worcester, that his executor presented it to a nearby monastery, and that it eventually came directly to John Theyer, whose connection with manuscripts from the west midlands is well known. In addition, many manuscripts at Worcester in the twelfth century were books of an older period whose usefulness was prolonged through textual emendation.[81]

The sources from which the original scribes of Roy were working (and potentially the text and music scribes may be the same person) need careful examination. Perhaps it would be best to begin by discussing the reason why we have the book in its present format. From the point of view of usage the most singular anomaly is that in a missal we have a *versus ante officium* for St Stephen. To my knowledge this is the only occurrence anywhere of this combination. Moreover, the number of missals having the text of a 'proper' trope included in the very chant to which it belongs must be extremely small. Outside of Roy and a thirteenth-century missal of Saint-Denis, there do not appear to be any other than those of Italian origin.[82] *Cui adstat candida contio* must be here because the man using the book needed it here. There was room left for it so that more prayers could be added to the mass for Christmas (III), and when the volume became this man's book, it seemed natural to enter the trope since he was expected to perform and teach it. In other words, he must have been the precentor at Worcester. By the same token, *Hodie inclitus martyr* was not written out in Roy; it was in his troper. Aside from the inclusion of this chant, the format of the book poses no problems.

For the source or sources of the sacramentary we need to posit the availability of a book or books with specific characteristics. Its basis was a Gregorian Sacramentary with the mass of the octave of Christmas taken from the Eighth-century Gelasians. Furthermore it had the Gelasian collect for Christmas,[83] a text of the *communicantes* for that feast with some unusual wording, and a version of the preface for Holy Innocents earlier than that in the Supplement. Then we have the six supplemental prayers for Christmas.

---

of the charter, with p. 591/21–30, probably the scribe of Roy. Similarly, cf. CCCC 146, the 'Pontifical of Bishop Sampson' (Old Minster, Winchester, s. xi[in] and xi/xii; provenance Worcester), p. 57/10–24 (= Roy's scribe) with p. 57/25–30, a more characteristic Worcester hand. This suggests that in this group of manuscripts the passional represents later work and that material added to CCCC 146 at Worcester was begun not late in the eleventh century but in the middle, as Ker suggested in 1941.

[81] N.R. Ker, *English Manuscripts in the Century after the Norman Conquest* (Oxford, 1960), pp. 52–3.

[82] I owe this information to Mr Planchart; see now his 'Italian Tropes', *Mosaic* 18 (1985), 11–31. The Saint-Denis missal is Paris, BN, lat. 1107 (s. xiii²).

[83] None of the manuscripts collated by Deshusses has it.

	Ha	Pa	Sg	Va
(a) Concede q.o.d. ut nos unigeniti	49	17	25	6
(b) Concede q.o.d. ut quos sub peccati	53b	—	—	—
(c) Respice nos misericors deus	54	20	9	11
(d) Leti domine frequentamus	—	—	29	9
(e) Largire q.d. famulis tuis fidei	55	21	32	25
(f) Deus qui de beate marie virginis	56	22	37	10

The first prayer is the standard collect in Gregorians. In the Eighth-century Gelasians it is an *alia*. In a book where only one prayer is given for each function, it is not surprising to find it heading our list. Prayers (b), (c), (e) and (f) have the same order in a number of the ninth-century Gregorians, and except for (b), the same order as they do in Paduense (Pa). If prayer (b) was an addition in an early source serving as an eventual model for Roy, it is surprising that it should have been entered in exactly the same place as in the ninth-century Gregorians which have it. We can eliminate the sacramentaries of Nonantola and Trent from the list given earlier since they have textual omissions not shared with Roy. Given the distribution it is tempting to associate its particular form – it is based on eighth-century prayers – with Alcuin, and the distribution from Tours to Belgium, Germany, and Switzerland, even perhaps Austria. Prayer (d) was probably added in the lower margin of a folio in some manuscript serving as an ancestor of Roy. Our scribe is unlikely to have entered it since he would logically have placed it after prayer (f). The format I have hypothesized could be that of his exemplar, therefore.

A crucial textual variant in prayer (c) was mentioned earlier, and all of the significant variants in these prayers must now be discussed.[84]

(a) per eundem . . .] qui X
(b) qui tecum] per eundem X V
(c) mentibus] *add.* nostris B Z1 X
(e) et securitatis B N X ZL Ω *et cet.*
(f) venientis B X Ω *et cet.* | per Y Ge Sg

Three of the six variants are choices of the concluding formula. For the standard Gregorian collect (a), the Senlis book (X) is the only one to indicate the shortened form of the standard 'classical' formula for conclusion. By itself this would not mean too much, but when we look over the list we see that this manuscript is more conspicuous than any of the others. B signifies two related

[84] The sigla are: B = Verona, Biblioteca Capitolare, 91 (B1) and 86 (B2); N = Paris, BN, lat. 2292; V = Cologne, Bibliothek des Metropolitankapitels, 88 (V1) and 137 (V2); X = Paris, Bibliothèque Sainte-Geneviève, 111; Y = Florence, Biblioteca Medicea Laurenziana, Edili 121; Z1 = Munich, Bayerische Staatsbibliothek, Clm. 6333; Ω = Trento, Castel del Buon Consiglio, without signature.

manuscripts from Verona, the best representatives of the 'corrected' Hadrianum. Z1 is a fragment at Munich related to the text of the uncorrected Hadrianum. X is also the only one of the manuscripts containing the Supplement to have *nostris*. Deshusses links it to sources from Cologne but also to books from Saint-Denis and Paris.[85] In view of this it is interesting to discover that it also contains an antiphoner of the mass, or gradual, which was almost certainly written at Saint-Denis.[86]

The *communicantes* for Christmas (III), to which we now turn, has a number of singular readings. *Celebrantes in quo* is the reading of Sg for the vigil, and it must have been retained from an Eighth-century Gelasian, but the specific text of the *communicantes* in Sg bears little relationship to that in Ha or this one.

The compiler of the *Missa in Commemoratio de Sancta Maria in Nativitate* could not have produced his mass without the model provided by Tc 1853–5, and specifically the versions associated with R (Paris, BN, lat. 2290, from Saint-Denis). It is reasonable to suspect they were available to him in Roy.

When we bring these points together it seems clear that a manuscript related in some way to the liturgical books of Saint-Denis lies somewhere behind the text of Roy. It is unlikely to have been a book similar to X, for that manuscript (and N alone of all the ninth-century witnesses) calls the Hadrianum mass for the octave, *Dominica Prima post Natale Domini*, and has no mass for the octave. It is unlikely to have been a manuscript like R, for R lacks two of the supplementary prayers for Christmas (III), namely nos. 2 and 4. More strikingly it is unlikely to have been a book directly modelled on S, the sacramentary of Saint-Vaast, for S lacks all of the supplementary prayers. Of course, if it were based on an idiosyncratic book similar to X, it would have been possible at some stage to insert the Gelasian mass for the octave for which S is the only Gregorian witness surveyed by Deshusses.

The relationship between the sacramentary portion of Roy and the English books is most strikingly reflected in a number of places where it and O (Orléans 127: the sacramentary of Winchcombe) have common usage.[87] O has the Gelasian collect for Christmas (III) and Roy almost certainly shared that usage. The original reading in supplementary prayer (e) is found also in O. In comparison, there are few distinctive readings shared by the other two English books and Roy, and places where they agree against Roy. They also do not have supplementary prayers (b) and (d), although neither does O, and O has an unusual reading in the preface for Christmas (III) not found in any of them.

---

[85] *SG1*, 74.   [86] *AMS*, pp. xxiii–xxiv; in Hesbert's edition it is S.

[87] Hohler has hypothesized that O (= Orléans 127: see above, n.12) may be a Saint-Denis sacramentary rewritten for use in England: 'Some Service Books', pp. 65–6.

Roy, therefore, seems to represent a separate strain in England, one not represented by the well-known books.

Turning to the sources of the gradual we encounter a whole new set of difficulties. Roy is related to Eli among the continental books, in terms both of the style of its neumes and of their specific usage. But Roy is not closely similar to Eli. They reflect a similar approach to the notation of a gradual and they may share a common geographical heritage. In the facsimile edition of 1955 (above, n. 39), Eli was assigned to Noyon and, so far as I am aware, this assignation has never been challenged. The place of origin was more difficult to determine, but Corbie was suggested on the basis of neumatic variants and neume styles. Shortly thereafter, Dom Gabriel Beyssac argued comprehensively for Saint-Denis, and although some of his arguments are weak, the Saint-Denis origin has been generally accepted.[88] It was reinforced in pt IV of *Le Graduel romain* in 1960, and adopted by Michel Huglo in a number of articles.[89] Despite these endorsements, Corbie cannot yet be dismissed. Robert Bautier, for example, feels that an attribution to that monastery on palaeographical grounds is very possible.[90] The neume styles are compelling evidence as well. What makes all arguments based on neumes and melodic variants doubtful is that good examples of Saint-Denis neumes before Den1 have not been published,[91] and that Eli was a 'manuscrit rattaché', that is, it was one of the manuscripts omitted from the main sorting due to lacunae. The fact that it and Den1 were chosen side by side for the second sorting and that they are very close to each other in that sorting does not necessarily imply they are both associated with the same foundation. It is certainly possible that Eli was written for a particular place; but it might not have been. If it were, it may have been written where it was intended to be used; but it might not have been. More work needs to be done.

In *Le Groupement des manuscrits*, Vor1 and Iri are linked most closely with the Saint-Denis – Corbie sphere.[92] In fact those two books are closer to Den1 than other manuscripts from Saint-Denis. As we know, Vor1 is the thirteenth-century gradual of Worcester. Roy was written at Worcester and was used there. It is tempting to conclude that Roy was in the lineage which produced

---

[88] See above, n. 39.

[89] *Le Groupement des manuscrits*, pp. 214 and 245. They revised their estimate of the date of the notation from s. x^ex to s. xi^in in light of Beyssac's arguments (p. 290). See also M. Huglo, *The New Grove Dictionary*, ed. Sadie, 1, 484 (s.v. 'Antiphoner'), and 'Les Chants de la Missa Greca de Saint Denis', *Essays Presented to Egon Wellesz*, ed. J. Westrup (Oxford, 1960), pp. 74–83.

[90] In Huglo, *Les Tonaires*, p. 91, n. 2.

[91] I do not consider seriously the neumes identified as possibly from Saint-Denis published by Bannister, *Monumenti Vaticani*, pl. 46a. They are not in the least calligraphic.

[92] *Le Groupement des manuscrits*, chart opposite 213, and 245.

Vor1 and thus must preserve, in the repertory of chants used for comparisons, variants in common with it.

If Roy did not have three distinctive chants, we would need to stop here, but we can pursue the gradual a bit further by looking at these chants as a group. Alleluia *Ymera agiasmeni–Dies sanctificatus* is found in this form only in manuscripts from England and Saint-Vaast at Arras. The text in Roy is closest to that in Vor1 and Vaa3, a thirteenth-century missal of Saint-Vaast. The melody in Roy, while being similar to that in Bo and CC, is nevertheless distinctive. The melody in Vor1 has one unique reading, but we can allow that. Let us tentatively hypothesize that the textual version of this chant in Roy might have come from a missal, and that the tune was meant to work with the textual model of a missal and not a gradual. Thus the missal tradition of Roy and Vaa3 could go back to a common textual ancestor, and this could be a book related to books of Saint-Denis.

The version of the *Cui adstat candida contio* in Roy is common to CC, Bo, Vaa1 and an eleventh-century troper from Saint-Magloire in Paris. Textual variants make it identical to CC and Bo and distinct from the other two sources of which Vaa1 is corrupt in one place. All of these books have the same melody. The three English books are close in usage but Bo and Roy are closer than either is to CC although they are not exact replicas one of the other. In three cases Roy has readings different from the one they share. I have pointed out above that the occurrence of such a chant in a missal is unique, and it therefore must have come from a gradual or a troper. Worcester had its own troper; the rubric in Roy tells us that. From where did they get it? Since the textual version is identical to that in the Winchester books, I suspect that they obtained it from there. When they obtained it cannot be determined without considering the context of all the arguments.

The last musical idiosyncrasy is also the rarest. The tract *Vidi supra montem* has a concordance only in CC of the English books, meaning that it was available to be set polyphonically as an organum *c.* 1000. It is not in Bo, which probably means it was not in Bo[a].[93] From where did Roy obtain it? Winchester is the logical conclusion. The only other source for the chant is Den4. The melodies are related but not similar. From where did Den4 obtain it? It may have been available in the model sent to Saint-Vaast from Saint-Denis but we do not know that for certain. It could have been available at Saint-Vaast to be entered in Den4 at the personal whim of the scribe.[94]

The urge to have a striking tract for Holy Innocents is uncommon. This particular one is based on the epistle for the feast, a lesson going back at least to

---

[93] Bo[a] is the siglum used by Professor Planchart to designate the prototype of Bo: see *The Repertory* I, 40–3. [94] For this manuscript, see Corbin, *Die Neumen*, p. 123.

the late sixth century.[95] In the *Comes* now at Leningrad, printed by Frere at the beginning of his study of the Roman epistle list, there is musical notation over the beginning of this epistle.[96] The manuscript is from Corbie and was written *c.* 780 during the abbacy of Maurdramnus.[97] The neumes are good examples of Corbie notation, and for the tenth century, which is when I would date them, they appear to be without rival.[98] The impetus to generate this tract, therefore, could have come from Corbie. Perhaps it was an attempt to elevate the liturgical variety and importance of the liturgy of Holy Innocents to that of John and Stephen. In the Corbie *Comes* there are neumes over the epistles for these saints as well, and these three are the only ones in the book to have neumes. In the case of John, who has two epistles because his day has two masses, only the first epistle has neumes. If we take this phenomenon and pair it with the citations for Stephen and Holy Innocents, there is a perfect parallel to these observances in the organa of CC. Organa nos. 57–9 are settings of the Alleluias for Stephen, the first mass for John, and Holy Innocents. It is thus possible for *Vidi supra montem* to have been a legacy of Corbie brought to England. This could have occurred in the 950s, when monks from Corbie came to Abingdon to teach psalmody. But we are not yet ready to leave this intriguing chant.

It has been suggested to me by Theodore Karp that *Vidi supra montem* dates to the tenth century. It is part of a layer of second-mode tracts which he labels the fourth stratum. His detailed observations about the differences in structure between the versions in Roy and in Den4 are exceedingly important. Given the paucity of sources, it may be that the piece was carried to England in some singer's head during the tenth century. Since it is based on a well-known model, this hypothesis is certainly plausible. It was written down at

---

[95] It is in the Würzburg *Comes*; see Morin, 'Le plus ancien Comes'.

[96] See above, n. 34. There are facsimiles of 15v in *Paléographie musicale* 13, 78 and of 15v and 16v in A. Staerk, *Les Manuscrits Latine du Ve au XIIe siècle conservés à la Bibliothèque Impériale de Saint-Petersburg*, 2 vols. (St Petersburg, 1910), pls. LX and XXI.

[97] *CLLA*, no. 1005. The date must be emphasized. Corbin would have it eleventh century (*Die Neumen*, p. 130), and Frere and the *Paléographie musicale* would have it tenth.

[98] D. Escudier has examined ninety manuscripts of Corbie in the Bibliothèque Nationale in Paris dating from the eighth to the beginning of the twelfth century. He found notation in thirty-nine. Of these, five are liturgical books. In addition to lat. 11522, 12052, and 18010 (listed in Corbin, *Die Neumen*), he includes 11589 and 12051. The last is the 'Missale S. Eligii', the manuscript chosen by Ménard as the basis for his edition of the Gregorian Sacramentary. It is a Corbie book of s. ix² which has tenth-century neumes over the same text as that in the sacramentary of Ratoldus (BN, lat. 12052, 45r; reproduced in *Paléographie musicale* 13, 76). Escudier's study is reported in 'Des Notations musicales dans les manuscrits non liturgiques antérieurs au XIIe siècle', *Bibliothèque de l'Ecole des Chartes* 129 (1971), 27–48, and two plates. I should like to thank M. Escudier for sending me photocopies of prints from BN, lat. 12052.

Winchester, used in CC, and ended up in Roy. The point made earlier about Corbie would certainly fit this scheme.

It will be seen that any conclusion regarding the origin of Roy involves the evidence of books from many institutions including Corbie, Saint-Denis, Saint-Vaast, Senlis and Winchester. Is there one hypothesis which will bring these institutions and their legacies together and help us to arrive at a conclusion which is plausible and realistic? There may be one, but before we advance it, we need to consider Roy in the liturgical context of Worcester and discuss the singular fact of its being a Worcester fragment.

The following is a list of liturgical manuscripts for the mass and the office associated with Worcester during the earlier Middle Ages. In rough order they are:

1. London, BL, Cotton Claudius A. iii, fols. 31–86 and 106–50 (s. x, 4th quarter, according to Turner): the so-called Claudius Pontifical I, written in an unknown English centre and at one time in the keeping of Wulfstan, bishop of Worcester (1003–16) and archbishop of York (1003–23).[99]

2. Cambridge, CCC 146 (s. xi^{in} and xi/xii), a pontifical written at the Old Minster, Winchester, and used at Worcester after the middle of the eleventh century; also called the 'Pontifical of Bishop Sampson'.[100]

3. Oxford, Bodleian Library, Hatton 93, fol. 42 (s xi^{med}), the only surviving leaf of a sacramentary written and used at Worcester. Two other leaves were formerly used as pastedowns in Hatton 30, but are now missing.

4. Worcester, Cathedral Library, F. 173 (s. xi^{med}), a fragment of a noted *missale plenum*, written at the Old Minster, Winchester. The first leaf is from a Gallican psalter written in Square minuscule, the text of which has been provided with a commentary in Latin and a number of Latin glosses.[101]

5. Cambridge, CCC 391 (s. xi^{med}), the 'Portiforium of St Wulstan', written and used at Worcester and based on a Winchester exemplar.[102]

6. Cambridge, CCC 9 + London, BL, Cotton Nero E. i, pts 1 and 2 (s. xi^{med}), a two-volume passional now bound in three volumes, written and used at Worcester. There is a kalendar prefixed to the Cambridge volume.[103] The second volume of the Cotton manuscript contains a noted office for St Nicholas followed by his mass (153v–155v).

7. London, BL, Cotton Claudius A. iii, fols. 9–18 and 87–105 (s. xi²) part of an English pontifical, written either at Christ Church, Canterbury, and brought

[99] *The Claudius Pontificals*, ed. D.H. Turner, HBS 97 (London, 1971).
[100] For the estimate of the date of its arrival at Worcester, see above, n. 80.
[101] See above, n. 4, and Gneuss, 'A Preliminary List', no. 764.   [102] See above, n. 80
[103] Printed in Wormald, *English Kalendars*, no. 18.

to Worcester, or (less securely) at Worcester and based on a Christ Church, Canterbury, exemplar: Claudius Pontifical II.[104]

8. Oxford, Bodleian Library, Hatton 113, ii^v–xi^r, a kalendar dating perhaps to 1070 prefixed to the first of a two-volume collection of homilies in Old English written at Worcester. The second volume has the shelfmark 114.[105]

9. Cambridge, CCC 198, 377v (s. xi^{ex}), part of a noted office for St Guthlac written at the end of a collection of homilies in Old English from Worcester (s. xi^{in}).

There are also various homilies and collections of homilies (and other materials) of various dates with a Worcester connection: CCCC 178; London, BL, Cotton Otho B. x, fols. 29–30; Oxford, Bodleian Library, Barlow 4 and Hatton 115; Worcester, Cathedral Library, F. 91 and Q. 21.[106]

In addition there are books and fragments either of foreign origin or whose connection with liturgical usage is questionable. These are:

1. Worcester, Cathedral Library, Q. 78b (s. x^{in}), a leaf of a lectionary, written in Northern France. The date, with which Francis Wormald concurred, was advanced by Bertram Schofield in a letter on deposit in the Cathedral Library.

2. London, BL, Royal 4. A. XIV, fols. 3–106, (s. x^{med}), a commentary on Psalms 109–49 written in Square minuscule. At Worcester at least by s. xii.[107]

3. London, BL, Royal 4. A. XIV, fols. 1* and 2* (s. x^{in}), two leaves of a missal in long lines and continental script containing portions of Passiontide: part of *feria v, feria vi, sabbato* ('vacat quando elemosina datur'). The first recto and the last verso are very rubbed. The dating given in the catalogue of Royal manuscripts is too late.

---

[104] See above, n. 99.   [105] The calendar is in Wormald, *English Kalendars*, no. 16.

[106] Peter Clemoes had kindly provided the following notes: CCCC 198 has textual connections originally with the southeast, but seems to have been in the west of the country by the time certain additions were made in the second half of the eleventh century; it was certainly at Worcester by the thirteenth century when it was annotated by the 'tremulous' Worcester hand. CCCC 178 was written s. xi^1 in an unknown place, probably in the Worcester area, and was at Worcester by the third quarter of the eleventh century. Cotton Otho B. x, fols. 29–30, were written at an unknown place, s. xi^{med}, and were at Worcester by the thirteenth century when they were annotated by the 'tremulous' Worcester hand. Hatton 115 was similarly written at an unknown place (s. xi^2), but was annotated in the thirteenth century by the 'tremulous' Worcester hand.

[107] N.R. Ker, *Catalogue of Manuscripts containing Anglo-Saxon* (Oxford, 1957), no. 250. It may have been there late in the eleventh century when an unknown scribe copied a list of books at the end of Oxford, Bodleian Library, Tanner 3. We do not know where this list was written but there is a distinct possibility it was at Worcester. Item 46, an 'expositio psalterii', fits Royal 4. A. XIV perfectly: see M. Lapidge, 'Surviving Booklists from Anglo-Saxon England', *Learning and Literature*, ed. Lapidge and Gneuss, pp. 33–89, at 69.

This is a substantial collection. It is particularly strong in vernacular homilies and in pontificalia, but by way of comparison we note and must remember how many surviving Latin liturgical manuscripts are Winchester books or are derived from Winchester books.

The leaves at the beginning of Royal 4. A. xiv, which were listed above, are the oldest witnesses in England to a *missale plenum*.[108] In view of the provenance of the manuscript in which they are presently bound, they have a bearing on the present argument. The main manuscript, also referred to above, was written by the scribe of Royal 2. B. v, a Psalter in the Roman version commonly called the Regius Psalter and the source of an influential gloss in Old English discussed in detail by Celia and Kenneth Sisam and by other scholars.[109] This book was not listed since its possible connection with Worcester has never been established. It contains 'seven preliminary leaves written in the first half of the eleventh century. Their contents, especially f. 7, indicate that they were added to the Psalter in early times, and that they were written at Winchester, probably at Nunnaminster.'[110] At the end (as well as at the beginning) there is material in Old English of a later date connected with Christ Church, Canterbury.

Since the Sisams came to no firm conclusion as to the original home of these manuscripts, it would be impertinent of me to reassess the evidence presented by them. If we wish to go further we must introduce other arguments. Did any surviving books known to have been written at Worcester in the Old English period end up at Winchester? To judge from the list published by Helmut Gneuss, the answer must be no. Did books from Worcester end up at other places? Royal 13. C. v (Bede, s. xi²) went probably to Gloucester, and Oxford, Corpus Christi College 197 (*Regula S. Benedicti*; s. x² and not located, but Worcester is a very strong possibility), went to Bury. Despite significant activity in its scriptorium, Worcester was hardly an exporter of books.[111] By

---

108 Gneuss, 'A Preliminary List', no. 454. The only other sources with which they might be compared are: (1) Exeter, Cathedral Library, 3548A, fragments of a *missale plenum* in two columns in a continental hand, for which see N.R. Ker, *Medieval Manuscripts in British Libraries* II (Oxford, 1977), pp. 839–40 (not a sacramentary); and (2) Cambridge, University Library, Gg.3.32, the last leaf, pasted down, another fragment of a missal in two columns written in a continental hand. Regarding this last leaf, I do not know when the parent manuscript may have come to England and include it here only for completeness. The format is close to the Exeter fragments.

109 Ker, *Catalogue*, no. 249. *The Salisbury Psalter*, ed. C. and K. Sisam, EETS os 242 (London, 1959), *passim* but esp. 52–6.   110 *The Salisbury Psalter*, p. 53.

111 For the scriptorium at Worcester in the tenth century, see T.A.M. Bishop, 'The Copenhagen Gospel Book', *Nordisk Tidskrift för Bok- och Biblioteksväsen* 54 (1967), 33–41, at 38, and *English Caroline Minuscule* (Oxford, 1971), p. xxii and nos. 18, 19, 20 (and p. xxv), 21 and 22. We should not neglect three books cited by Gneuss, 'A Preliminary List', nos. 341, 383 and 412, which may have been produced either at Worcester or York, but they hardly alter the picture.

comparison, we have at least eleven books from Winchester which went to Tavistock(?), Worcester (2), Christ Church, Canterbury (3), Sherborne, Durham, St Augustine's, Canterbury, Ramsey (?), and Thorney. Besides books from Winchester, Worcester obtained Hatton 30 from Glastonbury and Cathedral Library, Q. 5 from Christ Church, Canterbury. These observations are probably not a just estimate of the traffic in books involving Worcester and Winchester in the tenth and eleventh centuries, but they do allow us to infer with due caution that Winchester is far more likely than Worcester to have produced both Royal 2. B. V and Royal 4. A. XIV. This conclusion is consistent with Ker's feeling that 2. B. V is perhaps a Winchester manuscript.[112]

Were the leaves at the beginning of Royal 4. A. XIV part of a Winchester book brought to Worcester at the time the other liturgical books were brought, or might they have been taken from a discarded Worcester book and used as binding leaves after the manuscript went to Worcester? The leaves at the rear of the volume may be of some help. Fols. 107–8 are from a copy of Felix's *Vita S. Guthlaci* (s. viii/ix). On one of them is an Old English gloss which Ker says is 'in a pointed hand contemporary with the text'. He adds that the leaves are probably from Worcester.[113] Linking what we have observed, we can say that the leaves at the beginning of Royal 4. A. XIV, a manuscript probably written at Winchester and available at Worcester in the twelfth century if not before, were available at Worcester when the manuscript was rebound in the Middle Ages. As part of the whole manuscript they may have been at Worcester since the early tenth century. In fact, the manuscript could have been Roy's exemplar.

But if Roy is witness to a tradition of mass books stretching back to the early tenth century, where does Worcester Cathedral F. 173 fit in? Why is its presence at Worcester in the mid-eleventh century, soon after it was written, of such importance for this study?

No one leafing through Cuthbert Turner's loving study of early Worcester manuscripts can fail to be struck with the wealth of early manuscripts and fragments still to be found in the cathedral library.[114] Nor can they fail to notice that these manuscripts and fragments were at Worcester early on and some

---

112 Gneuss has noticed some 'striking correspondences' between the Old English interlinear gloss in Royal 2. B. V and the vocabulary of the Old English Benedictine Rule, known to have been the work of Æthelwold: 'The Origin of Standard Old English and Æthelwold's School at Winchester', *ASE* 1 (1972), 63–83. The earliest copy of the OE Rule is contained in Oxford, Corpus Christi College 197 (siglum x), a book possibly written at Worcester as I have said above, and for which consult M. Gretsch, 'Æthelwold's translation of the *Regula Sancti Benedicti* and its Latin Exemplar', *ASE* 3 (1974), 125–51. x belongs to a group including w (Cambridge, CCC 178, pp. 287–457; s. xi¹, from Worcester) and j (London, BL, Cotton Titus A. iv, fols. 2–107; s. xi^med, possibly from Winchester).

113 Ker, *Catalogue*, no. 251. 114 C.H. Turner, *Early Worcester Manuscripts* (Oxford, 1916).

perhaps were written there. Worcester, clearly, was an institution to reckon with as early as the seventh century, and it retained its prestige in learning at least to the age of Alfred at the end of the ninth. After that time we encounter a gap such as exists in the history of other institutions in the tenth century. And then we come to the age of Roy and the two-volume passional, of the Portiforium of Wulstan and eventually the Worcester Antiphoner. Is it possible from these materials to reconstruct a notion of pre-Conquest liturgical observance at Worcester?

The simplest response is to cite those parts of Byrhtferth's *Vita S. Oswaldi* which refer to the liturgy. There are many of these. They have been known for some time, although a recent paper by Susan Millinger is the first to comment on them in many years.[115] Then there is the scattered evidence of the medieval library assembled by Neil Ker and of books possibly written there recently identified by Alan Bishop. This evidence is more obscure, especially in light of the *Vita S. Oswaldi*. Hatton 48, the oldest copy of the *Regula S. Benedicti*, was possibly written at Worcester in the eighth century.[116] The earliest copy of Æthelwold's Old English translation of the Rule (s. x²), however, is more probably Worcester work. Together with bringing Germanus from Fleury to instruct in the Rule, it may represent Oswald's attempt to encourage the community to embrace a strict monastic ideal. Nevertheless, aside from Claudius Pontifical I (a bishop's book, not a chapter book) and collections of homilies, we have no newly written liturgical books attributed to Worcester in the period of the reform and after it until we reach the mid-eleventh-century collection set out above. One needed a substantial number of books to celebrate the Office fully, as it was celebrated at Fleury, and Oswald may have decided not to press for complete compliance at Worcester. The case set out by Armitage Robinson in 1919 and upheld by Peter Sawyer in 1970 emphasizes the geniality of Oswald's reform there.[117] He may simply have retained those liturgical books he found, deciding to devote more energy to the founding of

---

[115] S.P. Millinger, 'Liturgical Devotion in the *Vita Oswaldi*', *Saints, Scholars and Heroes*, ed. M.H. King and W.M. Stevens, II, 239–64. The attribution to Byrhtferth of the *Vita S. Oswaldi* has been accepted by M. Lapidge, 'The Hermeneutic Style in Tenth-century Anglo-Latin Literature', *ASE* 4 (1975), 67–111, at 90–3.

[116] For the provenance, see the paper cited in n. 80. Ker did not go so far as to claim an origin at Worcester for Hatton 48, but a good case can be made for believing it was written there: P. Sims-Williams, 'Cuthswith, seventh-century abbess of Inkberrow, near Worcester, and the Würzburg manuscript of Jerome on Ecclesiastes', *ASE* 5 (1976), 1–21, at 4–5.

[117] J.A. Robinson, *St. Oswald and the Church of Worcester*, British Academy Suppl. Papers 5 (London, 1919), and P.H. Sawyer, 'Charters of the Reform Movement: the Worcester Archive', *Tenth Century Studies*, ed. Parsons, pp. 84–93 and 228, supporting Robinson against Eric John. See also N. Brooks, 'Anglo-Saxon Charters: the Work of the Last Twenty Years', *ASE* 3 (1974), 211–34, at 228–9.

Ramsey, the restoration of Winchcombe, and to the archdiocese of York, his most challenging pastoral care. This does not mean, of course, that the level of Worcester's liturgical observance was narrow, merely that it is likely to have been more traditionally English, filled more with the strengths and weaknesses of the Anglo-Saxon past, than was consciously perpetuated at other English houses attempting to adopt the standards of Fleury, Ghent and Brogne.

In this light the presence of Worcester F. 173 and the other Winchester and Winchester-based books at Worcester at mid-century makes perfect sense. Bishop Wulstan (1062–95) wanted to bring Worcester into the present.[118] He could do it most effectively by introducing books lent or given by the most liturgically advanced diocese in England. There is every reason to believe he was more or less successful. The possible importance of F. 173 in this period of intellectual ferment awaits further study.

To return at last to a hypothesis. Roy's exemplar was a missal and a well-planned one. It was written in England, probably at Worcester, in the tenth century, a period during which the concept of the *missale plenum* imported from the Continent came of age. Adhering to standard methods of organizing the feasts of Christmastide, it may have followed the format of its model exactly. It had the sacramentary portion of Roy and its lectionary was the same as Roy's. Its gradual had all of Roy's chants except *Cui adstat candida contio* and *Vidi supra montem*. In the course of being written it was notated in Northern French neumes which we now call Anglo-Saxon when applied to manuscripts notated in England. These neumes were related to those in Eli and slightly distinct from those in Bo[a]. Based on the comparative studies of notation, I would judge them to be earlier than those in Bo[a]. They preserved the musical dialect associated with Vor1.

Eventually this exemplar was copied by our scribe, Hand A. It was undoubtedly on the initiative of the precentor of Worcester that the *versus ante officium* for the feast of Stephen, *Cui adstat candida contio*, was entered along with the incipit of the following trope before the mass for that feast. He must have obtained it from one of the manuscripts containing tropes written at Winchester, one which undoubtedly found its way to Worcester in the same period as the models for some of the books listed previously. That troper was evidently noted, or else he would not have had the music we see in this fragment. The stimulus provided by the newly received books to recopy and

---

[118] A. Gransden, 'Cultural Transition at Worcester in the Anglo-Norman Period', *Medieval Art and Architecture at Worcester Cathedral*, Brit. Archaeol. Assoc. Conference Trans. 1 (1978 for 1975), 1–14. I support Miss Gransden except where her characterization of Worcester during the bishopric of Oswald (p. 2) runs counter to the views of Robinson and Sawyer cited in the previous note.

emend Roy's exemplar extended to *Vidi supra montem* which was undoubtedly available in one of them. This rare tract was ultimately made available for Den4 in the same manner as it originally was in England, something which would account for the disparity in the versions in Roy and that manuscript.

From where did the musical text come, the gradual, the ultimate source of the chant in Roy? If Roy is in the lineage of Vor1, then it must have come from Saint-Denis or an institution whose chant was very similar to that of Saint-Denis in the early part of the tenth century.

In the hierarchy of liturgical books, missals have been passed by more often than not. They are not spectacular in the manner of Æthelwold's Benedictional, nor are they likely to be of the same painstakingly beautiful stock as a gospel book. They do have a tale to tell, in this case a short, intricate one, and we must listen closely to catch the details. Not all of the fascinating tale Roy can tell 'of the makers of our race and country' has been told here, but at least we have gathered its gist.[119]

---

[119] I should like to thank friends and scholars who gave me information, suggestions and encouragement over many years, and who may have read this paper in whole or in part at various stages of its preparation: P. Clemoes, T. Karp, R.W. Pfaff, A.E. Planchart, H. Pohlsander, A.G. Watson and especially C. Hohler.

Between the completion of this paper (June 1986) and its publication, a substantial contribution by D. Hiley has appeared: 'Thurstan of Caen and Plainchant at Glastonbury: Musicological Reflections on the Norman Conquest', *PBA* 72 (1986), 57–90. His estimate of the possible influence of William of Dijon at Glastonbury at the time of the Conquest is well argued and convincing. In preparing the background to the infamous massacre at Glastonbury in 1081, he discusses many of the manuscripts I have been using. A few observations on that discussion are in order.

(1) [pp. 61–2] Monks from Corbie did not '[come] in the tenth century to help improve the performance of the liturgy in England', they came specifically to Abingdon to instruct the monks there in psalmody and the 'proper' manner of reciting lessons. (2) [p. 65] The 'Corbie musical family' is a misleading collective obscuring the precision intricate arguments require. (3) [p. 65, n. 5] The manuscript used to represent Corbie is, surprisingly, not Paris, BN, lat. 18010, as we would expect, but the manuscript of Mont-Renaud. No evidence is presented substantiating this choice. (4) [p. 67, n. 1] The collation of Amiens, Bibliothèque municipale, 115 (Paléographie musicale 12, 105, n. 2) was completed and the results reported in a note to p. 110 printed in that volume on p. [181]. (5) [p. 81 and the accompanying explanatory note] It is only here, when we see Corbie paraded next to Dijon, Bec, and Cluny, *and* read the note, that we realize that Saint-Denis has been dropped from the argument because, although it 'had an almost identical practice, [it] is not known to have had strong English links'.

APPENDIX

THE TEXT OF THE ROYAL MISSAL FRAGMENT

The text is printed from the manuscript with as little correction as possible. As it stands it is a twelfth-century text. Passages in italic not dated in the notes should be inferred to date from that approximate period. The readings of the original manuscript, where they are able to be determined, must be sought in the notes.

I have identified the hands of two correctors. B is a slightly later scribe and C wrote more or less in the same period.

The numbering of the masses is editorial. The texts of the prayers have been compared to those in the printed edition of Jum and the manuscripts of LeofA and O, the texts of the chants to the nine music manuscripts cited by sigla. Of these, only Bo, Den1, Den4, Dur and Eli have offertory verses. Alleluia *Ymera agiasmeni–Dies sanctificatus* and tract *Vidi supra montem* are special cases. The layout of the bilingual Alleluia for the main mass of Christmas and of the *versus ad officium* and the following cue for the trope before the introit for the feast of St Stephen follow the layout in the manuscript.

The following signs are conventional:

< >	enclose words and letters which have been supplied in the transcription where the manuscript is deficient through damage.
( )	enclose words and letters which have been supplied where the scribe has omitted them by mistake.
[ ]	for my own additions
ˋ ˊ	for added words or letters
⊢ ⊣	for deleted words or letters

Medial points and low points are reproduced as periods, the punctus elevatus as a semicolon. Since in editions of missals complete texts of the lessons are rarely printed, I have indicated editorial omissions with ellipsis periods.

Note finally that footnote numbers and apparatus are keyed to individual prayers, not to individual lemmata; thus all the variant readings in any one prayer are grouped together under the one number.

I

<IN NATALI DOMINI>

<IN DIE AD MISSAM.

Puer natus. . . .

ORATIO. .

PROPHETIA DOMINI NOSTRI IESU CHRISTI. Hec dicit dominus. Propter
iv^{r} hoc sciet . . . Quam pulchri . . . predicantis> | *salutem dicentis*; *Syon. regnabit deus tuus. Vox speculatorum tuorum. Levaverunt vocem*; *simul laudabunt. . . . Et videbunt omnes fines terre*; *salutare dei nostri.*[1]

[1] *text by Hand B; see above, pp. 48–9*

LECTIO EPISTOLE. PAULI. APOSTOLI. LECTIO AD HEBREOS. [1.1–12]
Fratres; Multifari*am* multisque modis olim deus loquens patribus in prophetis;
. . . Thronus tuus deus in seculum seculi; virg*a equitatis* virga . . . ole*o exultationis*
pre particibus tuis . . . Tu autem idem ipse es. et anni tui non deficient.[2]

GR. Viderunt omnes fines terre salutare dei nostri iubilate deo omnis terre. /

iv^v < V. Notum fecit dominus salutare suum ante conspectum gentium revelavit
iustitiam suam.

ALLELUIA. >

YMERA. AGIAS. MENI. EPIPHANI.   (D)ies sanctificatus illuxit nobis.
MON.

(D)EUTE. TA ETH NI. KEPROSKENITE.   (V)enite gentes et adorate dominum
TON KYRION.

(O)TI. SIMERON. KATAVIFOS. MEGA.   (Q)uia hodie descendit lux.
EPITIS GIS.   magna super terram.[3]

SEQUENTIA SANCTI EVANGELII SECUNDUM IOHANNEM. [1.1–14] < I > n principio
erat verbum; Et verbum erat apud deum; et deus erat verbum; Hoc erat in
principio;. . . Plenum gratie; et veritatis.

OF. Tui sunt celi et tua est terra orbem terrarum et plenitudinem eius tu fundasti
iustitia et iudicium preparatio sedis tue. V. Magnus et metuendus super omnes
qui in circuitu eius sunt. tu dominaris potestatis maris motum autem
fluc < tuum > eius tu mitigas. V. Misericordia et veritas preibunt ante

iii^r < fa > ciem tuam et in beneplacito tuo exaltabitur cornu nostrum. / V. Tu
humiliasti sicut vulneratum superbum et in v⊦ i ⊦rtute brachi tui dispersisti
inimicos tuos firmetur manus tua et exaltetur dextera tua. iustiti < am >.[4]

S < ECRETA. > Oblata domine munera nova unigeniti *tui nativitate sanctifica*;
nosque a peccatorum nostrorum maculis emunda. per eundem.[5]

< PREFATIO. > VD Aeterne deus; Quia per incarnati verbi mysterium nova
mentis nostrae oculis lux tue claritatis infulsit; Ut dum visibiliter deum
cognoscim*us*. *per hunc in in*visibilium amore rapiamur; Et ideo cum angelis et
archangelis cum thro(nis) et dominationibus; Cumque omni militia celestis
exercitus hymnum glorie tue canimus sine fine dicentes;[6]

< INFRA ACTIONEM. > Communicantes et diem sacratissimum celebrantes.
⊦ in ⊦ qu*a* beate marie intemerata virginitas huic mundo edidit salvatorem. Sed
et memoriam venerantes. In primis eiusdem gloriose semper virginis marie
genitricis dei et domini nostri iesu christi. Sed et beatorum apostolorum ac
martyrum tuorum.[7]

---

[2] Multifariam] *orig.* Multifarie
[3] KATAVIFOS] *orig.* KATAVIEOS *corr. by main scribe*
[4] maris] naris Den4 | nostrum] *add.* iustitia Bo Eli (iustitiam) | brachi] brachii Bo Den1 Den4
Dur Eli | exaltetur dextera] *add.* dei cum patre sempiterna sine tempore. terris hac die apparens
ex semper virgine semper sanctae hanc serva plebem. benedicens sancta dextera Bo |
iustiti < am >] iustitia Bo | iustiti < am > (*final time*)] dom < inaris > *is written above and to the*
right ⁓   [5] nosque] *add.* per haec Jum LeofA
[6] infulsit] effulsit O | hunc in] *omit* in Jum (*first Mass*) LeofA O SG (*many wit.*)
[7] qua] *orig.* in quo Va Ge | quo SG, qua Den4 (*first Mass*) Jum LeofA | In primis] *omit* Jum
LeofA O SG, In primis gloriose Den4 | genitricis eiusdem dei Den4

co. Viderunt omnes fines terrae salutare dei nostri.[8]

POST COMMUNIO. Presta quesumus omnipotens deus. ut natus hodie salvator mundi. sicut divine nobis generationis est auctor. ita et inmortalitatis sit ipse largitor. qui tecum.

ORATIO. Concede quesumus omnipotens deus. u't' nos unigeniti tui nova per carnem nativitas liberet. quos sub peccati iugo vetusta servitus tenet qui.

< ALIA. > Concede quesumus omnipotens deus ut quos sub peccati iugo vetusta servitus tenet eos unigeniti tui. nova per carnem nativitas liberet per eundem.[9]

ALIA. Respice nos misericors deus. et mentibus ⊦ nostris ⊣ clementer humanis nascente christo summe veritatis lumen ostende. per eundem.[10]

ITEM. Leti domine frequentamus salutis humane principia quia trina celebratio beate competit mysteri < um > trinitatis per dominum.[11]

ITEM ALIA. Largire quesumus domine famulis tuis fidei. *spei et caritatis* augmentum < ut qui nativitate > filii tui domini nostri gloriantur et adversa mund < i > / te gubernante non sentiant. et que temporaliter celebrare desiderant sine fine percipiant. *per eundem.*[12]

iiiᵛ

ITEM ALIA. < Deus > *qui de* beate marie virginis partum sine humana concupiscentia procreatum in filii tui membra venientes paternis fecisti preiudiciis non teneri. presta quesumus ut huius creature novitate suscepta vetustatis antique contagiis exuamur. per.[13]

2

(.III. KAL. IAN. NATALE SANCTI STEPHANI MARTYRIS)

< C > UI ADSTAT CANDIDA CONTIO OMNISQUE EXPECTAT CATERVA DARE VOCES IN EXCELSO.

< O > ptamus regi regum dicere odas qui sic in suo milite truimphat hodie.

< L > audabile est christo psallere nunc iubilando paraphonist*a* dicite

< A > lleluia Nunc levite exultantes iubilemus stephano quem elegit summus apex in septeno numero eia dicite. TROPUS. Hodie inclitus martyr. require ut non plenum scriptum.

[A.] Etenim sederunt principes et adversum me loquebantur et iniqui persecuti sunt me adiuva me domine deus meus quia servus tuus exercebatur in tuis iustificationibus. P[s]. Beati inma[culati.][14]

ORATIO. < D > a nobis quesumus domine imitari quod colimus. ut discamus et

---

8 dei nostri] dei. nostri (sic) 9 *not in A (of* SG); *also lacking in* Jum LeofA O
10 nostris] *omit* Jum LeofA O
11 Sg 29 Va 9; *not in* Jum LeofA O | mysterium] *this completion is justified by the space left for the two letters*
12 spei et caritatis] *orig.* et securitatis (*corr. due to main scribe* (?)) | et securitatis O
13 qui de] qui per LeofA | de] *omit* Jum O | concupiscentia] *a first attempt at this word has been partially erased* | venientes] *orig.* venientis | *three lines have been left blank after this prayer*
14 paraphonista] *orig.* paraphonistae (?) | apex] a. pex (sic) | plenum] *I cannot decipher what the manuscript reads; it is possibly* plentem

inimicos diligere. quia eius natalicia celebramus. qui novit etiam pro
persecutoribus exorare. (per) dominum nostrum iesum christum.[15]
LECTIO ACTUUM APOSTOLORUM. [VI.8–10; VII.54-] In diebus illis; Stephanus
plenus gratia et fortitudine; faciebat prodigia et signa . . . Exclamantes autem
voce magna; con/

3

<.VI. KAL. IAN. NATALE SANCTI IOHANNIS EVANGELISTE>

vi[r] < ORATIONES. Deus qui per os beati apostoli tui iohannis verbi tui > / nobis
archana reserasti. presta quesumus. ut quod ille nostris auribus excellenter
infudit. *intelligentie* competentis eruditione ca*piamus. per eundem.*[16]
ITEM ALIA. Beati iohannis evangeliste quesumus domine supplicatione placatus.
et veniam nobis tribue. et remedia sempiterna concede. per dominum.[17]

4

.V. KL. IAN. SANCTORUM INNOCENTUM

[A.] Ex ore infantium deus et latentium perfecisti laudem propter inimicos tuos.
P[S]. Domine dominus noster.[18]
ORATIO. Deus cuius hodierna die preconium innocentes martyres non loquendo
sed moriendo confessi sunt. omnia in nobis vitiorum mala mortifica. ut fidem
tuam quam lingua nostra loquitur. etiam moribus vita fateatur. per dominum.
LECTIO LIBRI APOCALIPSIS IOHANNIS APOSTOLI. [XIV.1–5] In diebus illis.
Vidi supra montem sion agnum stantem. et cum eo centum quadraginta
quattuor milia. habentes nomen eius et nomen patris eius scriptum in frontibus
suis; . . . Sine macula sunt; ante thronum d*ei*.[19]
GR. Anima nostra sicut passer erepta est de laqueo venantium. V. Laqueos
contritus est et nos liberati sumus adiutorium nostrum in nomine domini qui
fecit celum et terram.[20]
ALLELUIA. Te martyrum candidatus laudat exercitus domine.[21]
vi[v] TR. < Vidi supra montem sion agnum stantem > et cum eo centum
quadra < gin > /ta quattuor milia. V. Habentes nomen eius et nomen patris eius
scriptum in frontibus suis. V. Et cantabant canticum novum ante sedem dei et
resonabat terra in voces illorum.
SECUNDUM MATHEUM. [II.13–18] In illo tempore; *A*ngelus domini apparuit in
sompnis ioseph; dicens; Surge . . . Ut adimpleretur quod dic*tum est. a domino*; *per*

---

[15] *the first phrase of this prayer is in capitals* | quesumus domine] domine quesumus LeofA |
celebramus] caelebramus O   [16] eruditione] eruditionem Jum   [17] *not in* Jum
[18] latentium] *orig.* lactentium (?), lactantium Cor Den1 Eli Iri, lactentium Den4 Dur Vor1
[19] dei] *orig.* dn (sic)
[20] erepta] erecta Cor | laqueos] laqueus *all other sources* | sumus] su. mus (sic)
[21] domine] do. mine (sic) | *Opposite* Alleluia *in the far right margin a later hand has added* Mirabilis (*no notation*)

ieremiam prophetam dicentem. . . . Tunc adimpletum est quod dictum est per *ieremiam pro*phetam dicentem; Vox . . . quia non sunt.[22]

OF. Anima nostra sicut passer erepta est de laqueo venantium laqueus contritus est et nos liberati sumus. V. Nisi quod dominus erat in nobis dicat nunc israhel nisi quia dominus erat in nobis. V. Torrentem pertransivit anima nostra forsitan pertransisset anima nostra aquam intolerabilem benedictus dominus qui non dedit nos in captionem dentibus eorum. Laqueus.[23]

SECRETA. Sanctorum tuorum nobis domine pia non desit oratio. que *et munera nostra tibi conciliet* et tuam nobis *indulgentiam semper obtineat. per.*[24]

PREFATIO. VD *Aeterne deus. Et in pretiosis mortibus parvulorum; quos pro(pter) nostri salvatoris infantia(m) bestiali sevitia herodes funestus occidit inmensa clementie tue dona predicare. In quibus fulget magis sola gratia quam voluntas; et clara est prius confessio quam*

v[r] *loquela < Ante passio quam membra idonea passioni. Existunt testes / christi qui eius nondum fuerant agnitores. O infinita benignitas. > o ineffabilis misericordia; que pro suo nomine trucidatis meritum glorie p < er > ire* non patitur. sed proprio cruore perfusis. et salus regenerationis adhibetur. et imputatur corona martyrii. Et ideo cum.[25]

CO. Vox in rama audita est ploratus et ululatus. rachel plorans filios suos noluit consolari quia non sunt.

POST COMMUNIO. Votiva domine dona percepimus. que sanctorum nobis precibus et presentis *quaesumus vite* pariter et aeterne tribue conferre subsidium. per.[26]

5

COMME < MORATIO > DE SANCTA MARIA IN NATI < VITATE >

< ORATIO. > Deus qui salutis eterne beate marie virginitate fecunda humano generi premia prestitisti. tribue quesumus. ut ipsam pro nobis intercedere sentiamus. per quam meruimus auctorem vite suscipere. dominum nostrum.[27]

SECRETA. *Suscipe sacrificium domine quod nos interveniente beata dei ge < ne > trice maria. et perducat ad veniam. et in perpetuam gratiarum consti < tuat > actionem. per.*[28]

POST COMMUNIO. *Libera nos ab omni malo domine iesu christe per merita et intercessionem gloriose virginis marie de qua veram carn < em > assumere dignatus es. ut fiat nobis corpus tuum ad salutem. et sanguis tuus ad remissionem omnium peccatorum. qui vivis.*[29]

---

[22] Angelus] *orig.* Ecce angelus | est per ieremiam pro] *orig.* per prophetam *Correction due to main scribe* (?)   [23] erepta] erecta Cor | intolerabilem] intollerabilem Bo

[24] tibi] *omit* Jum LeofA O Den4 | indulgentiam . . . per] *rewritten by original scribe* (?)

[25] in pretiosis] impreciosus LeofA | magis] maois Roy | magis sola] sola magis Jum LeofA O Den4 | prius] passio O | ineffabilis] *corr. from* inestabilis | que pro] qui pro Jum

[26] quaesumus vite] vitae quesumus LeofA

[27] *the texts and rubrics to this mass are by Hand C; see above p. 57* | Tc 1853 (MS. R): Missa in honore sanctae Mariae | Deus qui salutis *for* DMC I post N.D. Jum LeofA O | prestitisti] praetulisti Jum | per quam] ex quam LeofA

[28] Tc 1854; *not in* Jum LeofA O   [29] Tc 1855; *not in* Jum LeofA O

6

IN OCTAVAS DOMINI

[A.] *Puer natus.*

ORATIO. Deus qui nobis nati salvatoris diem celebrare concedis octavum. fac quesumus nos eius perpetua divinitate muniri. cuius sumus carnali commercio reparati. *qui tecum vi*[*vit*].[30]

EPISTOLA. [ad Titum II.II] Karissimi. Apparuit gratia dei.

ALIA EPISTOLA AD PHILIPENSE < S. > [III.3–8] Fratres; Nos enim sumus circumcisio qui spiritu de*o* servimus et gloriamur in christo iesu. et non in carne fiduciam habentes; quamquam ego < habeam confidentiam et in carne. > Si quis alius videtur confidere . . . que in lege est conver/ < satus sine querella . . . > omnia detrimentum esse; . . . scientiam. iesu christi domini mei;[31]

GR. Viderunt omnes. V. Notum fecit dominus.

ALLELUIA. Dies sanctificatus illuxit nobis venite gentes et adorate dominum quia hodie descendit lux magna super terram.

SEQUENTIA SECUNDUM LUCAM. [II.21] In illo tempore; Postquam consummati sunt dies octo . . . priusquam in utero conciperetur.

OF. Tui sunt cel*i*.

SECRETA. *Presta omnipotens deus. u*t per hec munera que domini nostri iesu christi archane nativitatis mysterio gerimus. purificate menti*s* intelligentiam consequamur. *per eundem.*[32]

PREFATIO. VD Aeterne deus per christum dominum nostrum; Cuius hodie circumcisionis diem et nativitatis octavum celebrantes. tua domine mirabilia veneramur; Quia que peperit et virgo et mater est. qui natus est et infans et deus est; Merito celi locuti sunt. angeli gratulati. pastores letati. magi mutati. reges turbati. parvuli gloriosa passione coronati. Et ideo cum angelis.[33]

< CO. > Viderunt omnes fines terrae salutare dei nostri.

POST COMMUNIO. *Presta quesumus omnipotens deus*; ut quod salvatoris nostri iterata sollempnitate percepimus. perpetue nobis redemptionis conferat medicinam. per *eundem.*[34]

7

DOMINICA PRIMA POST NATALE DOMINI

[A.] Dum medium silentium tenerent omnia et nox in suo cursu medium iter haberet omnipotens sermo tuus domine de celis a regalibus sedibus venit. P[S]. Dominus regnavit decore.[35]

---

[30] IN OCTAVAS DOMINI. Puer natus. Oratio.] *Hand C* | celebrare] caelebrare Jum | quesumus nos] nos quaesumus Jum LeofA | qui tecum vi] *another contemporary hand or perhaps the main scribe* · [31] deo] *orig.* dei | habeam . . . carne] *erased and written over in scrawl*

[32] Presta omnipotens deus] Praesta quaesumus domine Jum LeofA O Den4 | mentis] *orig.* mentibus | intelligentiam] intelligentia Jum

[33] virgo et mater] Den4 *there are construing marks in Roy, so it would appear, indicating the words should have their order reversed*, mater et virgo Jum LeofA O

[34] Presta quesumus omnipotens deus] Praesta quaesumus domine Jum LeofA O Den4

[35] nox] nos Den4 | haberet] haberent Den4 Iri

ORATIO. *Omnipotens sempiterne deus. dirige actus nostros in beneplacito tuo ut in nomine dilecti filii tui mereamur bonis operibus habundare. per eundem dominum nostrum iesum christum.*[36]

LECTIO EPISTOLE BEATI PAULI APOSTOLI AD GALATHAS. [IV.1–] Fratres; Quanto tempore heres parvulus est; nihil differt a servo cum sit dominus omnium. Sed sub tutoribus et actoribus /

---

[36] *the text of this prayer is by Hand C* | Per . . . christum] *the work of the later corrector*

The unknowable audience of the Blickling Homilies

MILTON McC. GATCH

Manige men beoð þe beforan oþrum mannum hwæthugu god begangaþ 7 raþe hie hit anforlataþ, forþan þe Crist sylfa cwæþ þæt he nelle gehyran þæs gimleasan 7 þæs forgytenan mannes gebedrædene. Ne þæt to nahte nyt ne bið þæt man godne mete ete oþþe þæt betste win on gebeorscipe drince gif þæt gelimpeþ þæt he hit eft spiwende anforlæteþ, þæt he ær to blisse nam 7 to lichoman nyttnesse. Swa we þonne þa gastlican lare unwærlice ne sceolan anforlætan, þe ure saul big leofaþ 7 feded bið. Swa se lichoma buton mete 7 drence leofian ne mæg, swa þonne seo saul gif heo ne bið mid godes worde feded gastlice hungre 7 þurste heo bið cwelmed. Forþon myccle swiþor we sceolan þencan be þæm gastlicum þingum þonne be þæm lichomlicum.[1]

This passage from the fifth sermon in the Blickling collection invites reflection on the audience to whom the Old English sermon was addressed. It seems to imply that its hearers would know something about feasts at which over-indulgence in meat and drink was commonplace – feasts, we instinctively infer, like those attended by Beowulf and Cædmon. By their apparent topicality, passages like this have inclined commentators to assume that they refer to

---

[1] Blickling homily v (Dominica V in Quadragesima), MS (see below) 33r4–v3 (Morris 57/1–14; see below). ('There are many who, in the presence of others, do some good and promptly abandon it. For that reason, Christ himself said that he would not hear the prayers of any negligent or forgetful man. Nor is it of any use if one eat good meat or drink the best wine at a feast, if it comes to pass that he later, vomiting, loses what he took for merriment and for the body's use. Just so, then, we should not carelessly lose the spiritual teaching that our soul lives and is fed by. Just as the body cannot live without meat and drink, so the soul, if it is not fed with the word of God, is killed by spiritual hunger and thirst. We must, therefore, meditate much more on spiritual than on bodily things.')

For texts of Blickling sermons in this article, I follow the typescript edition of the late R.L. Collins, citing parenthetically as 'Morris', by page and line, the edition of R. Morris, *The Blickling Homilies*, EETS os 58, 63 and 73 (1874–80). Abbreviations are silently expanded, and punctuation and capitalization are modernized. Translations are mine, although I have kept an eye on Morris's published translation. For description of the manuscript, now Princeton, New Jersey, Scheide Library, 71 (s. x/xi), see N.R. Ker, *Catalogue of Manuscripts Containing Anglo-Saxon* (Oxford, 1957), no. 336, and 'A Supplement to *Catalogue of Manuscripts Containing Anglo-Saxon*', *ASE* 5 (1976), 121–32, at 125; *The Blickling Homilies, the John H. Scheide Library, Titusville, Pennsylvania*, ed. R. Willard, EEMF 10 (Copenhagen, 1960), 13–41; and R.L. Collins, *Anglo-Saxon Vernacular Manuscripts in America* (New York, 1976), pp. 52–7.

everyday life and to specific abuses the preacher wanted to reform. This passage and others like it seem to invite us to consider what the Blickling Homilies may have to say about everyday life in Anglo-Saxon England or (more specifically) about the audience for whom this complex and often mystifying collection was made.[2]

I attempted to address one aspect of the subject of the audience of the sermons in Old English in my *Preaching and Theology in Anglo-Saxon England: Ælfric and Wulfstan.*[3] The issues raised in that book were primarily liturgical: what, if any, was the liturgical setting in which the sermons were intended to be read? Is there evidence for regular preaching at Mass in the early Middle Ages? In view of their monastically based sources, can the sermons have been intended for the edification of the laity? The evidence drawn upon was based primarily in manuscripts and liturgical practice. The nature and construction of the books were studied in an effort to learn what Old English and contemporary Latin texts may teach us about the practice of preaching and the use of homiliaries.[4]

In this article, I propose to look in a cursory way at the contents of four of the sermons in the Blickling Book in an effort to determine what they may indicate about the audience which the preachers, adapters or anthologizers of these sermons from the Latin had in mind.[5] This exercise is a necessary prolegomenon to a new edition of the Old English collection. The late Professor Rowland L. Collins was for many years at work on a new edition, which (in fulfilment of his request) I plan to complete. Collins's idea was to present the text of the Blickling manuscript, transcribed correctly but only lightly edited, and to give the modern reader a sense of the book as it was intended to be used by preachers addressing Christian congregations in the tenth century. It thus needed, Collins thought, comparatively little *apparatus criticus* and references to parallel texts in Old English only as they were needed

[2] On the history of the compilation of the Blickling Book and its relation to other manuscripts and to the homiletic corpus as a whole, see D.G. Scragg, 'The Homilies of the Blickling Manuscript', *Learning and Literature in Anglo-Saxon England*, ed. M. Lapidge and H. Gneuss (Cambridge, 1985), pp. 299–316, and 'The Corpus of Vernacular Homilies and Prose Saints' Lives before Ælfric', *ASE* 8 (1979), 223–77, esp. 233–5.

[3] Toronto, 1977; see esp. pp. 24–59.

[4] The discussion of the designations for liturgical manuscripts has been carried further, with some useful corrections and distinctions, by H. Gneuss, 'Liturgical Books in Anglo-Saxon England and their Old English Terminology', *Learning and Literature*, ed. Lapidge and Gneuss, pp. 91–141.

[5] This paper originated as 'post-prandial divagations' delivered at the conference dinner of the International Society of Anglo-Saxonists, Toronto, 22 April 1987. I am grateful to Professor Roberta Frank for the commission to prepare it and to her and Dr Ann Hutchison for gracious care during the conference. I am also grateful to Professor Jane Rosenthal for an invitation to read another version of this paper to the Medieval Seminar of Columbia University in 1987–8.

to supply gaps in the Blickling manuscript. On the basis of my reflections in *Preaching and Theology in Anglo-Saxon England*, I disagreed with this approach and with the assumption that the Blickling anthology had as its clearly intended audience a congregation or congregations of lay folk of all sorts and conditions. Collins and I had, indeed, many a lively conversation on the subject. And it has now, alas, been left to me to resolve the question without the benefit of his great erudition and lively curiosity. If I am correct in my inclinations about the matter, the editorial task will be much more difficult than Collins had thought, for to attempt a full understanding of the book it will be necessary to learn as much as possible about the history of the texts – their ultimate Latin sources, their textual and palaeographical histories – before we can venture hypotheses concerning the intended uses of the book and the precise nature of its contents.

To approach the issue of internal evidence for the condition and needs of the audience of the sermons of the Blickling collection, as has already been noted, four sermons have been selected for attention. Although one of the four, no. XI, explicates scripture (at the outset, at least), they are mainly not exegetical but catechetical sermons.[6] This is to say that they are not efforts to expound the readings from the gospel for a Sunday or a feast and not adaptations of the *acta* of saints for reading on their feast days. Rather, these sermons were intended as basic instruction on fundamentals of the faith for Christian people. Not necessarily the only items in the collection that might be designated as catechetical, nos. IV, V and X were probably assigned to Lent and Rogationtide, seasons in which general instruction is most often to be found. No. XI, on the other hand, contains the famous dating passage which raises our hopes for other and more specific contemporary and topical allusions. Were the writers or translators of the sermons anthologized in the Blickling Book attempting to speak to contemporary conditions, these materials and times of the year would, thus, be the most likely to invite reflection on the specific needs of the audience or congregation and, indirectly, upon its character and compositon.

Blickling homily IV: the sermon for III Lent

This sermon also occurs in Oxford, Bodleian Library, Junius 85 + 86 (s. xi^med), 40v–61v.[7] It is assigned to the third Sunday in Lent in the Blickling Book only, but it was probably also known to the Junius compiler in a Lenten

---

6 On catechesis and catechetical writing, see my 'Basic Christian Education from the Decline of Catechesis to the Rise of the Catechisms', *A Faithful Church; Issues in the History of Catechesis*, ed. J.H. Westerhoff III and O.C. Edwards, Jr (Wilton, Connecticut, 1981), pp. 79–108, and V. Day, 'The Influence of the Catechetical *Narratio* on Old English and some other Medieval Literature', *ASE* 3 (1974), 51–61.

7 Ker, *Catalogue*, no. 336, art. 7; see also R. Willard, 'The Blickling–Junius Tithing Homily and its Sources', *Philologica: the Malone Anniversary Studies*, ed. T.A. Kirby and H.B. Woolf

context. The Blickling and Junius copies of the sermon were both clearly taken from earlier exemplars. Thus, in attempting to learn something about the audience for which the Blickling Book was intended, we must not only look for ways in which the Latin texts that were adapted to English as sermons were changed to meet the needs of an Anglo-Saxon audience but also remember that there might be some distance in time and place between the originally intended Anglo-Saxon audience and the audience in mind for the Blickling Book when it was prepared in the later years of the tenth century. By the time Junius 85 + 86 was written in the middle decades of the eleventh century there had been further distancing between the original Anglo-Saxon audience and the audience for whose edification and use that particular copy was prepared.[8]

The sermon, at the beginning and end, adapts a sermon on tithing by Caesarius of Arles.[9] Caesarius's sermon was originally assigned to the feast of the Birth of St John the Baptist (24 June); later it seems to have been attached to a nearby Sunday. Its subject, tithing or the devotion of a portion of the produce of agriculture to ecclesiastical and charitable use, was suitable to the harvests which were just beginning at that time of the year in the south of France. The Old English sermon begins with a sentence introducing the sermon as derived from 'the worthy teacher' ('se æþela lareow')[10] and treating tithes, 'manna teoþungceape': 'He cwæþ, Nu nealæceþ þæt we sceolan ure æhta 7 ure wæstmas gesamnian. Don we þonne geornlice drihtne þancas þe us þa wæstmas sealde, 7 syn we gemyndige þæs þe us Crist sylfa bebead on þyssum godspelle. He cwæþ þæt we symle emb twelf monaþ ageafon þone teoþan dæl þæs þe we on ceape habban.'[11] The first clause is a fairly straightforward translation of the Latin source, Caesarius's 'De reddendis decimis', but it obscures the reference to the harvest season in the original. The anachronistic reference to the time of harvest becomes in the Lenten setting of the Anglo-Saxon translation a figure for offering. The sermon of Caesarius, in other

(Baltimore, 1949), pp. 65–78. Morris's homily XVI is a misbound singlet that has now been properly inserted as fol. 30 in no. IV at Morris 53/2; see *The Blickling Homilies*, ed. Willard, p. 22.

[8] The dating for Junius is Ker's. For Blickling, Ker allows for activity into the eleventh century; but Collins prefers a tenth-century terminus despite some correctors' entries of later date, and Scragg implicitly agrees.

[9] No. XXXIII in the edition by G. Morin, CCSL 103, 143–7.

[10] Junius reads 'se godes lareow' (Willard, 'Tithing Homily', p. 72). The use of 'æþela lareow' in Blickling needs to be studied closely. (See also below, n. 14.) Here it clearly means not the apostle Paul (as is assumed at Morris 38/1) but the major authority on whom the sermon relies; see Willard, 'Tithing Homily', p. 66.

[11] 22r1–10 (Morris 39/1–7). ('He said, Now the time approaches when we ought to gather our possessions and fruits [of the field]. Then let us eagerly give thanks to the Lord who gave us those fruits, and let us be mindful of what Christ commanded in this gospel. He said that we always once a year give back a tenth of what we possess.')

words, was originally addressed to a subject appropriate to the occupation and life-setting of its audience at the season intended for its delivery; but the assignment of an adaptation of it to general, catechetical use as a Lenten sermon in tenth-century England did away with the original setting and relationship to the lives of the intended congregation. In this passage, at least, little was done by the redactor preparer of the Old English version to adapt the content of the sermon to the lives of its new audience.[12]

The opening of the sermon in Old English contains a reference to 'þyssum godspelle'; but the sermon is not, in fact, an exegetical one, and the words about tithing that follow the reference to the gospel are not quoted from any of the gospels but are adapted from a phrase in Caesarius: 'de offerendis, immo de reddendis decimis cogitemus'.[13] The use of *godspel* in this context is mystifying. If it is intended to refer to a canonical gospel, it is erroneous. The sermon is not a commentary on a liturgical reading from the gospels, a pericope; but perhaps the adapter thinks of 'a gospel' in the sense of a text that is being adapted for delivery to a congregation in their vernacular language. If so, Caesarius is referred to as *godspel* here. Indeed, the sermon translates Caesarius with amplification and explanation as though it were an explication of 'De reddendis decimis'. This kind of false, or (more exactly) confused, citation is a characteristic of this sermon that has not been adequately attended to by critics.[14]

When one examines the structure and content of this Blickling sermon, however, it becomes clear that it is not simply an expanded version of Caesarius's 'De reddendis decimis'. After the sermon has followed Caesarius for little more than three manuscripts pages, its 'theme suddenly changes to pastoral care', as Rudolph Willard observed.[15] After a sentence about the eternal benefits of almsgiving, there occurs the first of at least two passages

---

[12] Willard ('Tithing Homily', p. 78, n.) suggests it may have been assigned to Lent because plough-alms were due in England a fortnight after Easter. This suggestion seems to me strained. In any case, the harvest references are out of place.

[13] CCSL 103, 143, lines 3–4.

[14] To take examples only from the opening section of Blickling IV, cf. 22v15–16 (Morris 41/4–5), 'sægþ on þissum bocum þæt dryhten sylf cwæde', introducing a paraphrase of Exodus XXII.29; 23r1–2 (Morris 41/8), 'cwæþ se æþela lareow', introducing a quotation of Proverbs III.9–10; and 23v1–2 (Morris 41/23), 'on þyssum godspelle sægþ', introducing a passage based on Caesarius. Note that where Blickling refers to 'se æþela lareow', Junius (Willard, 'Tithing Homily', pp. 72–3) reads 'on ðissum bocuum' or 'on bocum'. The term also occurs in the section of this Blickling sermon that is based on the *Visio Pauli*: 23r1–2 (Morris 43/5); 24r5–6 (Morris 43/32); 25v3 (Morris 45/12–13), with *goda* for *æþela*; 25v19 (Morris 45/24); 26v10 (Morris 47/10), *halga*; and 27v13 (Morris 49/9). It seems throughout (although the sources are not always known) to be a tag to indicate quotation from a main source.

[15] 'Tithing Homily', p. 65.

based upon the apocryphal *Visio Pauli*.[16] The clergy, both bishops and priests, are exhorted to perform their offices well. Christians – lay and clerical – who do not give alms and do not fast will perish, and (citing the *Visio*) those who forsake the church will not be cared for by the church. The clergy must be diligent in teaching penitential discipline and giving other instruction, showing no special favour to the rich. Posthumous punishments of negligent clergy are recited from the *Visio Pauli*, and admonitions to careful fulfilment of priestly and pastoral offices are given. Piety is to be encouraged by the clergy. For example, people are to be taught to sign themselves with the cross seven times daily. In language that sounds as though it were derived from synodal councils, the bishops are urged to enjoin priests to teach the people faithfully.[17] Layfolk and clergy who fail to heed these admonitions are to be disciplined. A passage preparing for a return to adaptation of Caesarius's tithing homily admonishes the audience to give alms and stresses the rewards, or other consequences, of response to the requirement of almsgiving.[18]

Thus at the centre of the Blicking adaptation of the Caesarius sermon on tithing the address shifts from a presumably general congregation gathered in Lent to receive catechetical instruction on an aspect of the Christian life to an audience of clergy, who are admonished to perform the pastoral office well and faithfully. Almsgiving or tithing is simply one aspect of the teaching which the clergy are expected to give to the people. The writer of the Old English sermon clearly had sources for his precepts here. They may in part have been canonical or synodal; the passage is in some ways reminiscent of the pastoral or canonical writing associated with Wulfstan and Ælfric some years later. Perhaps, as Willard suggested,[19] the sermon was prepared in connection with a movement to impose tithes as a legal obligation, a tax. If so, the compiler of Blickling IV must have been assembling materials for the use or instruction of the clergy – a preacher's handbook such as Ælfric had in mind in the second series of the *Sermones catholicae*, for example.[20]

It is not necessary to comment extensively here on the last third of the sermon, which returns to adaptation of Caesarius on tithing. Whereas the first portion had expanded its sources, this final section is more selective, becoming in effect a condensation of the source, with one added passage that may have

16 A. diPaolo Healey, *The Old English Vision of St Paul*, Speculum Anniversary Monographs 2 (Cambridge, Mass., 1978), 51–2. Note, however, that at 27v30 (Morris 49/14) St Paul is named as the source of material derived from Matthew XVI.19 and XVIII.18.

17 27r7–13 (Morris 47/24–8).   18 28r3–8 (Morris 49/18–22).

19 'Tithing Homily', pp. 70–2.

20 M.R. Godden, 'The Development of Ælfric's Second Series of *Catholic Homilies*', ES 54 (1973), 209–16.

been drawn, once again, from the *Visio Pauli*.[21] It concludes with an apparently independent paragraph on the values of almsgiving.[22] Wealth rightly acquired is allowed because it gives the opportunity for expressions of generosity, which please God.

The sermon as it has come to us in the Blickling and Junius manuscripts must be regarded as containing only confused, and therefore confusing, evidence concerning its audience. It mixes apparent address to laity with address to the clergy. It cites sources in difficult and misleading ways. Its use of *godspel* for a source that is not a pericope from the canonical gospels is especially worrisome. It is true, as Marcia A. Dalbey argued cogently some years ago, that Blickling IV (like x, which also has a source by Caesarius) moderates the harshness of the moral exhortation in its original.[23] Yet, however winsome the Blickling sermon may be (comparatively) as an example of moral suasion, examined closely it seems very deeply flawed and confused both conceptually and rhetorically. It has found a new and less appropriate liturgical occasion for its teaching and has not been completely or coherently adapted to the new season. It has mixed address to laity and to clergy so that one suspects the clerical audience has become central: the clergy, it seems, were expected to make use of the text in their instruction of the layfolk. Finally, it is misleading and wrong in its citation of authority, even by the standards of the age.

What *is* clear is that the function of this sermon in a preaching book is ambiguous. Coming to some clarity about the purpose of the piece and its relation to the rest of the volume will be a difficult matter that requires nothing less than careful and complete presentation of the sources and of the text in Junius alongside the one in Blickling.

Blickling homily v: the sermon for V Lent

This second sermon for examination is one that does not occur elsewhere in the manuscripts containing Old English sermons and whose sources are basically unknown.[24] At its beginning and again near its middle the authority for its

---

[21] 30v5–21 (Morris 195/17–26). I had drafted this sentence before becoming aware that Paul Acker had argued the same point in 'The Going-Out of the Soul in Blickling Homily IV', *ELN* 23.4 (1986), 1–3.   [22] 31v3–21 (Morris 53/19–33).

[23] M.A. Dalbey, 'Hortatory Tone in the Blickling Homilies: Two Adaptations of Caesarius', *NM* 70 (1969), 641–58. For a summary of what is known of uses of Caesarius by writers of Old English, see J.B. Trahern, Jr, 'Caesarius of Arles and Old English Literature', *ASE* 5 (1976), 105–19, at 114–19.

[24] 'A Probable Source for the *ubi sunt* Passage in Blickling Homily v (Morris 59/15–21)' was identified by L. McCord, *NM* 82 (1981), 360–1. (The passage is at 35r7–17.) The source is pseudo-Basil, *Admonitio ad filium spiritualem*, VIII (PL 103, col. 690). I am grateful to Professor

teaching is referred to as 'se æþela lareow'.[25] Because of its similarity in this regard to Blickling IV, it was once tempting to posit that Blickling IV and V had the same source and probably derived from the same homiliary or the same author.[26] But D.G. Scragg, by means of an examination of the physical evidence of the manuscript, has recently shown that, although both Blickling IV and Blickling V were copied by the same scribe, nos. V and VI were copied at the same time and before IV. III was copied after IV. Thus the compiler seems to have worked backward from Easter, no. VIII, to complete a series of sermons for the Lenten season.[27] The Easter sermon, to complicate matters even further, was prepared before nos. V and VI, for the fifth Sunday of Lent and Palm Sunday, respectively, which were prepared as a unit. Thus it can no longer be easily assumed that 'se æþela lareow' in nos. IV and V refers to the same author or source document. Even though we know very little about the sources of V, an examination of the text shows that this sermon has interesting implications for the question of audience. Even without knowing its Latin sources in detail, one must conclude that it is so conventional in content that it was probably little adapted to the special conditions and spiritual needs of an Anglo-Saxon congregation of the tenth century.

The sermon announces itself at the outset as addressed to the necessity of not only hearing the word but also 'æfter þon ful medomme wæstm agifan 7 agildan'[28] – a sentence evocative of scripture (e.g. James 1.22 and Matthew XIII.8) but not directly quoting it. These ideas are repeated with variation, and ps. XV.3–4 is quoted, epitomizing the faithful person who knows the word of God and performs it, not deceiving neighbours or friends. Deceit of neighbour is defined as being often a tendency to say what the neighbour wants to hear, not the truth that should be heard. God's word is useless for the unbelieving and those who do not pay attention to what they hear. In this context the passage quoted at the beginning of this article is introduced: if one hears but does not heed the word of God, one is like a person who eats fine victuals and drinks good wine at a feast but retches it afterwards. Sustenance has served no purpose for such a person, and, whether physical or spiritual, sustenance is needed for life. This observation introduces a passage on the superiority of the spiritual to the physical life.

J.E. Cross for confirming my recollection on this matter in a personal letter, 2 March 1987. Cross, of course, published the basic study of '"Ubi sunt" Passages in Old English – Sources and Relationships' *Vetenskaps-societeten i Lund, Årsbok* (1956), 25–44, esp. 40.

[25] 32r1 and 36r17 (Morris 55/1 and 61/19).

[26] M. McC. Gatch, 'Eschatology in the Anonymous Old English Homilies', *Traditio* 21 (1965), 117–65, at 120.

[27] 'The Homilies of the Blickling Manuscript', pp. 300–1 and 304.

[28] 32r5–6 (Morris 55/3–4, 'afterwards to give back and offer up worthy fruit').

Everything to this point seems quite conventional, drawn from common-place Christian moral teaching. The word *gebeorscipe* in the colourful passage about feasting might be thought local colouring, a beer-word in a wine-setting; but a glance through the Old English concordance[29] shows that the expression is really quite common in Ælfric and other ecclesiastical writers for banquets and other social meals and (occasionally) for spiritual fellowship. So there is no sign thus far of an Anglo-Saxon audience whose special conditions and needs are addressed in the English sermon. Even if the piece to this point were free composition, which one may doubt, it is thoroughly conventional and without detectable local colouring.

As has already been stated, the sermon shifts at this point to a discussion of the superiority of the spiritual to the physical. The passage is suffused with reflections of themes popular in Anglo-Saxon homiletic writings.[30] The body will be severed from the things of this world, but the soul will live spiritually and be reunited with the body at Doomsday, when both will atone for their physical or worldly deeds. Many hear the word of God but fail to live by it. So one must contemplate the fate of the body when it is separated from the soul and from the beauty of things in the world. Paraphrasing the Epistle of James 1.11,[31] the author declares that flowers and plants wither and disappear and their fragrance is dissipated in the heat of summer – a Mediterranean, not an English observation. In youth, in the bloom of *geogoðlustas*,[32] one should be mindful of age and death, of the decay of the body, which begins in life. There follows the one passage whose source we know, in a general way, and should guess if we did not know. It is an *ubi sunt* passage: 'Hwær bið la þonne se idla lust 7 seo swetnes þæs hæmedþinges þe he ær hatheortlice lufode?'[33] The closest source that has been found is a monastic text, the *Admonitio ad filium spiritualem* of pseudo-Basil,[34] which was known in England somewhat later, at least, and adapted by Ælfric.[35] The monastic origins of this source may give one pause about the audience intended for Blickling v.

The universal hardships and sorrows of human life are recounted from

---

29 *A Microfiche Concordance to Old English*, ed. A. diPaolo Healey and R.L. Venezky (Newark, Delaware, 1980).

30 See Gatch, 'Eschatology', and 'Two Uses of Apocrypha in Old English Homilies', *Church History* 33 (1964), 379–91, for discussion of eschatological motifs in the preaching traditions. As Scragg observes ('Corpus of Vernacular Homilies', pp. 266–7), 'the tradition was an extraordinarily narrow one'.

31 This scriptural passage – like others – is attributed in Blickling v to 'Crist sylfa', 34v1–2 (Morris 59/1). The passage also recalls Isaiah XL.6–9.   32 34v16–17 (Morris 59/9).

33 35r8–10 (Morris 59/15–17). ('Where then will be the frivolous desires and the sweetness of sex that he loved so hotly before?')

34 See above, n. 24. The pseudo-Basil text is ptd in PL 103, col. 690.

35 *The Anglo-Saxon Version of the Hexameron of St Basil . . . and the Saxon Remains of St Basil's Admonitio ad Filium Spiritualem*, ed H.W. Norman (London, 1848), pp. 31–55.

generation and birth through the labours of a lifetime. The same devils that tempt us to sin in our lifetime will torment us hereafter unless we repent. The exhortation to repentance is extended by means of lists of those who will be found in hell. The lists are conventional, but the stress on judges, *gerefan*,[36] is interesting, for they seem to be singled out for special attention. This passage is conventional in content but not in emphasis. Perhaps an audience of rulers was in the mind of the author of the source or the English adapter. Harsh though the judgement of false judges may be, the sermon takes care to point out that not all judges are evil and that some, in fact, attempt to encourage the doing of God's word. Without knowledge of the source or sources of this passage, one cannot know whether the sermon was intended to be delivered to secular judges or rulers, or simply repeats a Latin source's injunctions to rulers. The audience does sound secular, but need not absolutely have been so. Words with local and legal evocations, such as *gerefa*, are used; but so is *dema*, which (according to the new dictionary) is usually ecclesiastical in its connections.[37] The digression on judges and their judgement leads to a conclusion envisaging the last judgement and using the language of Matthew xxv. 21 and 23. We shall have to account for our sins, both great and venial. After reflections on variations of murder, which observes *inter alia* that vices are equivalent to murder, the sermon concludes with evocations of the blessings of the coming, eternal realm.

There is much that we need to learn about the sources of this sermon, much that would help us to know whether any attempt was made to adapt it to interests and concerns peculiar to an Anglo-Saxon setting and audience. Yet on the basis of what we presently know, fairly clear conclusions are to be drawn. The sermon's contents are thoroughly conventional and – beyond coincidence of vocabulary – contain no discernible, peculiarly Anglo-Saxon details or cultural characteristics. Its one known source is monastic in origin and had originally a monastic audience. If in its concerns for judges and rulers it seems to presume a secular audience, then at some stage elements of monastic piety may have been adapted to instruction of the laity. Although we can document conventions and hypothesize about sources for this sermon, we shall be able to speak definitively about its audience only when we can compare actual sources with the Old English text.

Blickling homily x: a probable Rogation sermon

This sermon is part of what D.G. Scragg calls 'block **b**' of nos. VIII–XV, which begins after Easter and continues to Pentecost and into the *sanctorale*, or items for saints' days.[38] No. x is the third in this run; and although it does not have a

---

[36] 37r9 (Morris 61/26).
[37] 38v8 (Morris 63/20). *Dictionary of Old English*, fascicle D, ed. A. Cameron *et al.* (Toronto, 1986), *s.v. dema.*   [38] 'The Homilies of the Blickling Manuscript', p. 303.

rubric, it falls just before a sermon for Ascension Thursday, and therefore, almost certainly, was intended for one of the three Rogation Days that precede the Feast of the Ascension. The Rogation Days, called *in letania maiore* in the Anglo-Saxon liturgical and homiletic manuscripts, are three days before the Ascension and are marked by recitation of the litany in procession (in later English usage, with agricultural associations).[39] Hence the days were known in English as *gangdagas*, days for going on processions to say litanies. Among the preachers, Rogationtide became an occasion for treating general subjects, indeed matters usually associated with catechetical instruction, such as the creed, the *Pater noster* and basic moral concepts, which are more normally associated with Lent; and an extraordinary number of Old English sermons – at least twenty-four – is assigned *in letania maiore*.[40] It is not known why this should be so unless somehow the catechizing of those to be baptized at Pentecost, the second Sunday after the Ascension, had come to be associated with these days, on which the liturgy had a penitential tone and character comparable with those of Lent. Whatever the case, Blickling x immediately precedes a sermon designated for the Ascension and is most likely to have been meant for the third Rogation Day (Wednesday), which is also the eve of the Ascension.

Its subject is the imminence of Doomsday. Indeed, its earliest editor, Richard Morris, gave it a title taken from early in the sermon's text: 'Þisses middangeardes ende neah is'.[41] One would normally assume that a sermon warning of the impending end of the world, of the advent of Doomsday, would speak of the conditions that lead the preacher to this prophecy. One would expect to be told rather specifically and graphically about the condition of the world in which the preacher's audience lives; no. x invites examination for traces of information about the situation of the late-tenth-century audience being addressed by the preacher.

The opening address of the sermon garners for itself a wide audience of all sorts and conditions; 'ge weras ge wif, ge geonge ge ealde, ge snotre ge unwise, ge þa welegan ge þa þearfan'.[42] Mercy will be shown to those who recognize their sinfulness and repent. Thus it is important for all to know that

þisses middangeardes ende swiþe neah is 7 manige frecnessa æteowde 7 manna wohdæda 7 wonessa swiþe gemonigfealdode. 7 we fram dæge to oþrum geaxiað

---

[39] For some discussion of Rogationtide among the Anglo-Saxons and of preaching texts for the season, see the introduction to *Eleven Old English Rogationtide Homilies*, ed. J. Bazire and J.E. Cross (Toronto, 1982), pp. xiv–xxv. The list of items for the occasion is based on Ker, *Catalogue*, p. 529. To this list, Willard (*The Blickling Homilies*, pp. 39–40) added Blickling ix–x, which lack rubrics. The comment of Bazire and Cross that Willard's conclusion is speculative (*Eleven Homilies*, p. xvii) seems over-cautious.

[40] *Ibid.* pp. xxiv–xxv, and Gatch, 'Basic Christian Education', pp. 93–9.

[41] Morris, p. 107.

[42] 65r5–7 (Morris 107/7–8; *Bright's* 2–3, see below; 'male or female, young or old, wise or

ungecyndelico witu 7 ungecynlice deaþas geond þeodland to mannum cumene, 7 we oft ongytaþ þæt arisep þeod wiþ peode 7 ungelimplico gefeoht on wolicum dædum. 7 we gehyraþ oft secgan gelome worldricra manna deaþ þe heora lif mannum leof wære 7 þuhte fæger 7 wlitig heora lif 7 wynsumlic. Swa we eac geaxiað mislice adla on manegum stowum middangeardes 7 hungres wexende; 7 manig yfel we geaxiaþ her on life gelomlican 7 wæstmian, 7 nænig god awunigende 7 ealle worldlicu þing swipe synlicu; 7 colaþ to swiþe seo lufu þe we to urum hælende habban sceoldan 7 þa godan weorc we anforlætaþ þe we for ure saule hæle began sceoldan. Þas tacno þyslico syndon þe ic nu hwile big sægde be þisse worlde earfoþnessum 7 fræcnessum, swa Crist sylfa his geongrum sægde: þæt þas þing ealle geworpan sceoldan ær þisse world ende.[43]

The preacher continues with an exhortation to amended life, not with the purpose of averting the coming Doom but to assure oneself a place among those found acceptable at the Judgement. Thus liberality and charity, peacefulness, right rearing of children, humility and similar virtues are enjoined.

Passages like this are intended to be applicable to all people at all times, and they are effective according to the rhetorical urgency the writer or speaker conveys. The passage is carefully constructed for rhetorical effect. But, however one might want to rank this passage for the success of its rhetorical strategies, it must be recognized that, despite the dated qualities of its assumptions concerning social structures and relationships, its descriptions are absolutely general and quite as applicable to our own age as to the tenth century in Europe. Rooted in the language of apocalyptic passages of the synoptic gospels, this warning of the end of the world says nothing specific about the reasons why the end is 'swyþe neah' on the basis of the writer's observation of current events. Yet it evokes cogently the universal sense that humankind is sinful and the times are perilous.

---

unwise, rich or needy'). For this homily I also supply references (as *Bright's* by line) to text no. 9 in *Bright's Old English Grammar and Reader*, ed. F.G. Cassidy and R.N. Ringler, 3rd, corrected, ed. (New York, 1971), at pp. 196–203, which has some variant readings from Cambridge, Corpus Christi College 198, 314r–316r (s. xi¹ and xi²).

[43] 65v2–66r5 (Morris 107/21–109/8, *Bright's* 12–25). ('The end of this world is very near, and many calamities have appeared and men's crimes and woes greatly multiplied. And from one day to the next we hear of monstrous plagues and deaths occuring throughout the country, and we often see that nation rises against nation and unfortunate fighting gives rise to iniquitous deeds. And we hear very frequently of the death of men of substance, whose life was dear to men, and whose life seemed fair and beautiful and pleasant. We are also informed of various diseases in many places in the world and of increasing famines; and many evils, we learn, are becoming general and flourishing in this life, and no good abides here, and all worldly things are very sinful; and the love that we ought to have for our Lord cools greatly, and we abandon the good works that we should observe for our soul's health. Such are the signs which I mentioned earlier concerning this world's tribulations and calamities, as Christ said to his disciples that all these things should come to pass before this world's end.')

The preacher next observes that amendment must take place during one's earthly lifetime:

Ne þearf þæs nan man wenan þæt his lichama mote oþþe mæge þa synbyrþenna on eorþscrafe gebetan, ah he þær on moldan gemolsnaþ 7 þær wyrde bideþ hwonne se ælmihtiga god wille þisse worlde ende gewyricean; 7 þonne he his byrnsweord getyhþ 7 þas world ealle þurhslyhþ 7 þa lichoman þurhsceoteð 7 þysne middangeard tocleofeð 7 þa deadan up astandaþ, biþ þonne se flæschoma ascyred swa glæs, ne mæg ðæs unrihtes beon awiht bedigled.[44]

Right faith is important, and faith makes possible works that may lead to redemption. Thus one must remember that the world and its wealth are transitory. The soul is parted from the body at death, leaving the physical body nothing but 'wyrma mete'.[45] An *ubi sunt* passage laments the wealth and vanities of worldly life.

There follows an exemplum of a rich and successful man who died. One of the rich man's kinfolk went into exile because of his grief for the departed man and continued to grieve for a long time. He determined at length to return to this homeland to view the tomb and remains of his friend, but the bones of the dead man admonish him to be mindful of the transitoriness of life and wealth. Enlightened by this *dustsceawunga*, the mourner is converted and, by his preaching and teaching, earns not only grace for himself but also the deliverance of his friend's soul. Thus, the preacher concludes, we ought to take to heart this example and know that 'þeos world is eall gewiten'.[46]

A final paragraph contrasts the beauty and joy of the world before the fall with the grief of the transitory, fleeting world of historical time. For this, the composer of the English version apparently drew on a passage of a sermon of Gregory the Great for the feast of two martyrs, SS. Nereus and Achilleus.[47] Gregory had contrasted the age in which those martyrs lived with the misery of

---

[44] 66v17–67r7 (Morris 109/30–111/1; Bright's 43–8). ('Nor should anyone think that his body can or will change the burdens for sin in the grave, but there he shall moulder in the earth and await the great event, when the almighty God shall bring this world to an end. And when he will draw his burning sword and smite right through this world and shoot through the bodies and cleave this world and the dead rise up, then flesh will be as clear as glass [and] no trace of unrighteousness can be hidden.')

[45] 86r10 (Morris 111/33; Bright's 76; 'food for worms').

[46] The exemplum is 68r20–69v9 (Morris 113/4–115/4; Bright's 83–111). (69r7, *dustsceawunga*, 'vision of dust'; 69v6–8, 'þeos . . . gewiten' ('this world is altogether transitory').) The source for this passage, Caesarius's 'De elemosinis' (CCSL 103, 135) or a version of the same circulating in pseudo-Augustine, *Ad fratres in eremo* (PL 40, cols. 1352–3), is discussed by J.E. Cross, 'The Dry Bones Speak – a Theme in some Old English Homilies', *JEGP* 56 (1957), 434–9, at 438–9.

[47] J.E. Cross, 'Gregory, Blickling Homily X and Ælfric's *Passio S. Mauricii* on the World's Youth and Age', *NM* 66 (1965), 327–30, at 328–9. The passage of Gregory is *Homilia in evangelia* XXVIII (PL 76, cols. 1212–13).

his own time, but the Blickling adapter made the contrast one between the pre-lapsarian time and the present, last, days without adequately editing the text. A later transcriber of this portion of the Blickling text had to cut and reshape it quite radically to make sense of it.[48] In other words, not only did the Old English adapter fail to render his text appropriate to the lives of his immediate audience, but he failed even to edit his sources adequately to make them comprehensible in their new context.

Once again in Blickling x, then, all is general and commonplace. Sources are known for only a few passages, but the traditions of the address of the body to the soul, of the *ubi sunt*, of the transitoriness of wealth, are as common as those of the signs of the impending Doom. They tell us that the author expected the audience to respond to his tried and true rhetorical commonplace in the appropriate way, but they reveal no specific facts about the lives and conditions of the persons for whom the sermon was written. Of them, little more can be said than that the writer thought his sermon suitable for their admonition and edification during the Rogation season.

Blickling homily XI: for the Ascension

Finally, it is in order to look briefly at the Ascension sermon, which, in the manuscript, follows immediately on the sermon that has just been discussed. It will not be necessary to treat this in great detail; but it is the locus of the famous dating passage of the Blickling manuscript, and so it seems important at least to ask whether there is some information to be gleaned from it about the conditions of life in the year 971.

The Ascension sermon begins with an exposition of the account of the event commemorated on the feast, Acts I.I–II. Professor J.E. Cross has argued that the sermon is 'freely-written'. The opening exposition of the epistle for the Ascension is enriched by clear recollections of Gregory the Great's homily on the gospel of the day and by echoes of Bede's *Expositio super Actuum Apostolorum*, both of which were anthologized in homiliaries.[49] This leads to reflection on the expectation of the second coming of Christ and the last judgement. All of the signs of the apocalypse have come to pass except the coming of Antichrist; and thus the sixth, present age of history must be approaching its end.[50] Most of the last age has passed: 'efne nigon hund wintra 7 lxxi in þys geare'.[51]

---

[48] On the adaptation of CCCC 198, see the apparatus at *Bright's*, pp. 201–2.

[49] 'On the Blickling Homily for Ascension Day (No. XI)', *NM* 70 (1969), 228–40. Bede on Acts is now available in CCSL 121, 3–91.

[50] Cross ('On . . . Ascension', p. 233) corrects Morris's and my earlier reading of 71v17–72r15 (Morris 117/29–119/4).

[51] 72r10–11 (Morris 119/2, 'even nine hundred and seventy-one years in the present year').

Dating by *annus domini* is not common in the era of the Blickling manuscript, although its use here may derive from the practice of the *Anglo-Saxon Chronicle*, within the century preceding the writing of the sermon book.[52] Here there is no sense of a millenarian literalism. The writer says that the ages of history were of uneven length: some three thousand winters, some less and others more. Further, it is not known what God now intends, 'hwæþer þis þusend sceole beon scyrtre ofer þæt þe lengre'.[53] When the Lord told the faithful that it was not for them to know when the end would be, he also promised them the gift of the Holy Spirit, which came to them at Pentecost, ten days (as it is observed liturgically) after the Ascension. Thus the people were given the strength to endure the sufferings and uncertainties of the world. The exposition of Acts I ends with observations about the cloud in which Jesus ascended and which presages his return on the last day in a cloud as well, and of his reception by angels. The conclusion of the passage has exhortations to right living in the light of the work of Christ and of the expectation of Doomsday.

As far as this conclusion, the sermon is mainly expository. This section up to this point is, indeed, one of the most strictly exegetical passages in the whole collection, paraphrasing and explaining the passage that describes the event being commemorated liturgically. The reference to the present as being 971st year of the Christian era is quite simply part of the exposition of the passage in Acts, in which Jesus tells his followers that they are not to know when the Parousia, or Second Coming, is to occur. If it tells us anything about the conditions of the tenth-century English church, it is that there was not evidently a millenarian expectation focused on the approaching *annus domini* 1000; and that is, if fact, precious and important information concerning the tenth-century audience, although it is not rich in detail.

The sermon finishes with an account of the site of the Ascension, based ultimately on the recollections of a pilgrim bishop, Arculf, as recorded in Adamnan's *De locis sanctis* I.xxiii.[54] This passage is detailed, and it accurately

---

52 The *Chronicle* derived this scheme of dating from its sources, annals kept in Easter tables; see F.M. Stenton, *Anglo-Saxon England*, 3rd ed. (Oxford, 1971), pp. 15–16. Bede, also influenced by Easter tables, was the first significant user of the *annus domini*; see P.H. Blair, *The World of Bede* (London, 1970), pp. 268–70.

53 72r18–19 (Morris 119/5–6, 'whether this thousand is to be shorter or longer than that'). Cross ('On . . . Ascension', p. 234) thinks 'þreo þusend' must be scribal error.

54 On the source of this section, see Cross, *ibid* pp. 235–40, which advances the identification first made by R. MacG. Dawson, 'Two New Sources for Blickling Homilies', *N&Q* ns 14 (1967), 130–1. The best text of Adamnan is the ed. by D. Meehan, Scriptores Latini Hiberniae 3 (Dublin, 1958); see also J. Wilkinson, *Jerusalem Pilgrims before the Crusades* (Warminster, 1977), pp. 166–7 and 193–4 and pl. 2, and translation at pp. 100–1; both reproduce the manuscript schema for the church at the site of the ascension of Jesus, which greatly helps in visualizing the description in the sermon.

reflects descriptions of the church on the Mount of Olives with its open roof and the footprints of Jesus, from which he ascended. There is a clear expectation that the audience will be interested in details about the holy place – as Christians commonly were in the early Middle Ages, shaping their liturgical observances in many ways in imitation of what was done in Jerusalem at the sites of the original events:

Ond nu men þa leofestan þeah þe we nu þær andweardene syn æt þære halgan stowe þe ic nu sægde, þehhweþre we magon on þyssum stowum þe we nu on syndon gode [7] medeme weorþan for urum drihtne gif we nu soþ 7 riht on urum life don willaþ. Forþon æghwylc man sy þær eorðan þær he sy þurh gode dæda Gode lician sceal, 7 ælc man sceal his godan dæda ahebban gif he sceal god 7 medeme weorþan.[55]

The pilgrimage motif is carried further in the conclusion, for the writer urges the audience 'beon ælmesgeorne 7 ærdæde wiþ earme man, 7 eaþmode us betweonan',[56] so that one may be better than one now is when the season of the Ascension returns a year hence, as though in the annual liturgical cycle one were living the cycle of pilgrimage of the Jerusalem church at the holy places.

Perhaps one can learn something about the author's interests from the passage on the site of the Ascension at the Mount of Olives and the church that has stood there. Perhaps, too, this antiquarian knowledge would have appealed to the interest of the audience for Blickling xi. But the dating passage tells us only when the sermon – or, more likely, the Blickling manuscript – was written and gives no further information about the audience, its conditions, its spiritual needs and its interests.

CONCLUSION

It is an attractive assumption that books can tell us something about the people for whom they were written. But it is not necessarily the case that authors will tailor their materials to the special needs and conditions of those who will read their writings or hear them read. The nature and purpose of the Anglo-Saxon sermon books are very difficult and complex matters. The fact that the books were written in English is perhaps the most useful datum we have concerning the audience and its culture. Those who provided sermon texts for the church in England clearly felt a greater need to communicate in the vernacular – or, at

---

[55] 80r4–14 (Morris 129/29–35). ('And now, beloved, although we are not now present at the place of which I just spoke, nevertheless in these places where we are gathered we can become good [and] worthy before our Lord if we will do what is true and right in our life. Therefore every person, wherever he may be on earth, must please God through good deeds, and each must lift up his good works if he will become good and worthy.')

[56] 80r17–19 (Morris 131/1–2, 'to be charitable and merciful to the poor and humble amongst ourselves').

least, to record materials in written form in the vernacular language – than did their counterparts elsewhere in Europe.[57] But it does not follow that, because one writes for an audience in the native tongue of its members, one has also carefully fitted the fabric of the discourse to the audience. This examination of four sermons from the Blickling manuscript suggests that little sense of a specific congregation or reading audience prevails in this collection of ancient and commonplace materials for the instruction of Christian folk. It also suggests that the questions of the nature and purpose of the Blickling and other collections are so difficult that their texts cannot be edited or considered in isolation from variant texts and collections or from their sources in the Latin literature of the Christian church. We need to know as much as can be learned about how Latin, ecclesiastical – often, indeed, monastic – conventional materials were prepared and transmitted to serve the needs of Anglo-Saxon Christians. In the present state of knowledge, we have to accept that the audience for the Blickling sermons is 'unknowable', as in my title.

---

[57] See Gatch, 'The Achievement of Ælfric and his Colleagues in European Perspective', *The Old English Homily and its Background*, ed. P.E. Szarmach and B.F. Huppé (Albany, 1978), pp. 43–73.

Holofernes's head: *tacen* and teaching in the Old English *Judith*

ANN W. ASTELL

Ælfric's *On the Old and New Testament* includes a brief synopsis of the story of Judith, the Hebrew widow who decapitated the Assyrian general, Holofernes. In it, Ælfric refers his friend Sigeweard to an English version of the *Liber Judith* which has been written 'eow mannum to bysne, þæt ge eowerne eard mid wæmnum bewerian wið onwinnendne here'.[1] Ælfric thus defines the tropology or moral lesson of the Judith story as a timely call to men such as Sigeweard to resist the invading army of Danes. Most scholars agree that Ælfric is alluding to his own homily about Judith ('on ure wisan gesett'), not the Old English poem celebrating the same heroine.[2] Nevertheless many have held that Anglo-Saxon auditors of the poem derived the militaristic moral from it that Ælfric draws from the poem's biblical source.[3]

Judith, extant in a fragment of 349 lines, follows *Beowulf* in London, British Library, Cotton Vitellius A.xv. Its recent editors, Elliott Van Kirk Dobbie and B. J. Timmer, both assign a late, tenth-century, date to the poem on linguistic and metrical grounds.[4] As Ian Pringle observes: 'The homily, the Letter to Sigeweard, and the poem must all have been written within at most a century of one another, and the likelihood is that they were rather closer than that.'[5] The historical climate in which the poem was written and read, then, carefully encouraged others besides Ælfric to perceive a parallel between their situation

---

[1] Ælfric, 'Letter to Sigeweard', *The Old English Version of the Heptateuch*, ed. S.J. Crawford, EETS os 160 (1922), 48.

[2] See B. Assmann, 'Abt Ælfric's angelsächsische Homilie über das Buch Judith', *Anglia* 10 (1888), 76–104, and I. Pringle, '*Judith*: the Homily and the Poem', *Traditio* 31 (1975), 83–97.

[3] See C.L. Wrenn, *A Study of Old English Literature* (London, 1967), p. 181; T.G. Foster, *Judith: Studies in Meter, Language and Style*, Quellen und Forschungen 71 (Strassburg, 1892), 90–103; and E.E. Wardale, *Chapters on Old English Literature* (New York, 1965), esp. pp. 215–17. They suggest that the poem was written in honour of Æthelflæd, the widow of Æthelred of Mercia, who successfully led the Mercian troops against the Danes between 915 and 918. For a more cautious view, see K. Sisam, *Studies in the History of Old English Literature* (Oxford, 1953), p. 67.

[4] See *Beowulf and Judith*, ed. E.V.K. Dobbie, ASPR 4 (New York, 1953), lxii–lxiv, and *Judith*, ed. B.J. Timmer, rev. 2nd ed. (Exeter, 1978), pp. 6–11. See now also F. Wenisch, '*Judith* – eine westsächsische Dichtung?' *Anglia* 100 (1982), 273–300.

[5] Pringle, 'Homily and Poem', p. 92.

and Judith's, to be encouraged by her example and to undertake action 'mid wæpnum' analogous to hers.

The question remains: does the poem itself – apart from the general historical context and the coincidence of the Letter to Sigeweard – employ rhetorical strategies appropriate to a militaristic tropology? If heroic action is being urged, how does the poem move its auditors to that end? Does internal evidence, in short, support the supposition that the poem was written 'to exhort man and woman to the utmost resistance' against the Danes?[6]

How one answers that question essentially depends on one's reading of the poem's embedded allegory. The poet explicitly associates Judith with Christ, Holofernes with Satan. Some critics, on the basis of that identification, have treated the poem as a religious allegory – that is, a composition which says one thing (military conflict) and means another (spiritual conflict). They insist that the poem's moral message is an exhortation to virtuous (in particular, chaste) living.[7] Other critics, eager to see *Judith* as a patriotic poem with literal reference to the contemporary situation, have de-emphasized the allegorical component altogether.[8] They treat the poem, along with *The Battle of Maldon*, as a heroic secular work – in contrast to the first group of scholars, who typically classify *Judith* as a saint's life, comparable to *Juliana* and *Elene*.[9] Scholars, in short, have generally found the Christological allegory of the poem incompatible with a militaristic tropology.[10] A better understanding of religious allegory in relation to *historia*, however, will help us to reconcile the two, to reconstruct the sacred basis for Ælfric's secular moral and to review the *Judith* poet's own historical/rhetorical uses of allegory.

The allegory embedded in the literal text of *Judith* supports, rather than nullifies, the literal meaning of military conflict and presents it as a holy

---

6 Cf. *Judith*, ed. Timmer, p. 8.

7 See R. Woolf, 'The Lost Opening to the *Judith*', *MLR* 50 (1955), 168–72; G.K. Anderson, *The Literature of the Anglo-Saxons*, 2nd ed. (New York, 1966), p. 134; J.J. Campbell, 'Schematic Technique in *Judith*', *ELH* 38 (1971), 155–72; J. Doubleday, 'The Principle of Contrast in *Judith*', *NM* 72 (1971), 436–41; and B.F. Huppé, *The Web of Words* (Albany, NY, 1970), pp. 157 and 173 and *passim*.

8 See D. Chamberlain, '*Judith*: a Fragmentary and Political Poem', *Anglo-Saxon Poetry*: *Essays in Appreciation for John C. McGalliard*, ed. L.E. Nicholson and D.W. Frese (Notre Dame, IN, 1975), pp. 135–59, at 156.

9 Cf. *Judith*, ed. Timmer, p. 8, and C.R. Sleeth, *Studies in 'Christ and Satan'*, McMaster OE Stud. and Texts 3 (Toronto, 1982), p. 72.

10 Pringle is, I believe, the only critic who has attempted to harmonize the allegory of the Judith story with the poem's patriotic motive. He does so artificially, however, by dividing *Judith* into two poems, appealing to *oratores* and *bellatores* respectively. According to Pringle, the initial treatment of Judith 'as an example of the triumph of chastity' (p. 97) underscores the need for monastic reform as a precondition for Anglo-Saxon victory over the Danes, as it is represented in the heroic Israelite/Assyrian combat of the second half.

warfare against an enemy that is at once historical and eternal, political and religious, Danish and demonic. The poet, who Christianizes Judith through the allegorical subtext, establishes a series of parallels between the heroine and his Anglo-Saxon audience which promotes not only sympathy for her, but also a share in her way of thinking, her submission to God's headship and her confident militancy. As Judith leaves her fear behind and radically opposes in attitude and action the frame of mind found in Holofernes, the audience in turn is moved to follow her example and confront, with comparable courage, the invading Danes.

The kind of historical thinking which understands the temporal conflicts of nations and individuals to be a participation in the eternal warfare waged between God and Satan finds its theoretical rationale classically expressed in the seven rules of Tyconius, which were preserved for the Middle Ages in summary form in St Augustine's influential *De doctrina Christiana*. The first rule, 'Of the Lord and his Body', has its counterpart in the seventh and last rule, 'Of the Devil and his Body'. According to this Tyconian guide of interpretation, historical figures must be seen not only in their abstract sign value as emblems of good and evil, but also as the timely exponents of the divine or demonic head to whom they have allied themselves. As St Augustine puts it, Satan 'is the head of the impious, who are in a way his body, and who will go with him to the tortures of eternal fire, in the same way that Christ is the head of the church, which is his body and will be with him in his kingdom and everlasting glory'.[11] Both Christ and Satan have their earthly bodies, their incarnations in others, and as a result historical human conflict is inherently apocalyptic as the expression and means of cosmic oppositions.

According to Gerald Bonner, Tyconius's method of interpretation 'dominated all commentary on the Book of Revelation' for eight hundred years and directly influenced Bede, who quotes Tyconius's rules and relies upon his exegesis as a major source.[12] Because 'Tyconius understands the Book of Revelation not so much as prophecy of the end of the world than as an image of the church in the world', his vision of history tends to see behind all temporal events 'the struggle of the true church, the city of God, against the church of the devil, whose members include both open enemies of the church and false

---

[11] St Augustine, *On Christian Doctrine* III.37, trans D.W. Robertson, Jr (Indianapolis, IN, 1958 and 1983), pp. 116–17. St Augustine's own view of history, as articulated in *The City of God* was, to be sure, much more complex than that of Eusebius, who envisioned a virtual identification of church and state, of divine and human powers, in the person of the Christian king (*Christus et Caesar*). Nevertheless, the notion of two supra-temporal principles at play, co-determining the events of earthly history behind the scenes, is thoroughly Augustinian and inclusive of the demand for human cooperation.

[12] G. Bonner, *Saint Bede in the Tradition of Western Apocalyptic Commentary*, Jarrow Lecture, 1966 (Jarrow upon Tyne), pp. 5 and 13.

friends within'.[13] While Tyconius (unlike his fellow Donatists) upholds the orthodox position that the church-in-time is a mixed reality, composed of saints and sinners who will be separated into two camps and thus visibly distinguished only on the Day of Judgement, his method nevertheless leaves 'intact the sense of an immediate expectation of the end of the world'.[14]

During the tenth century in England, the onslaught of the Danish forces and the political/social upheaval which it precipitated awakened in many a fear of the final days. They saw in contemporary events the awesome *foretacen* of the Apocalypse. Under that stress, the Tyconian interpretation of history, with its behind-the-scenes *telos* toward two opposing divine and diabolic bodies, modulated quickly into an incarnational/compositional allegory of the present. That is to say, the temporal forces of good and evil were no longer seen as mixed realities, requiring allegoresis with reference to the absolute; they appeared in stark separation from each other, already bearing the mark of judgement. One did not have to interpret them; one had only to decide for or against them and act accordingly. To submit to the Danes was to join oneself to the body of the Antichrist.

Scholars such as Pringle have noted the increasing general tendency in England 'to regard the Vikings as embodiments or manifestations of diabolical forces', citing as examples the letter of Abbot Lupus to Æthelwulf, king of Wessex (852), Asser's accounts of the Danish wars, the translation of Orosius's *Historia adversus paganos*, Ælfric's Life of St Edmund, Wulfstan's sermons and *The Battle of Maldon*.[15] The implications of that identification for Anglo-Saxon poetry have not been sufficiently recognized, however. We may chart a general pattern of development, moving from instructive works oriented toward allegoresis (that is, the abstract interpretation of events within a dogmatic frame) to compositional allegories oriented toward the application of dogma. The former emphasize the appeal of *logos*, moving from the letter to its gloss, while the latter evoke the pathetic by personifying truths and clothing them in moving images.[16] In Cynewulf's *Juliana*, for instance, the devil himself appears alongside the saint's human persecutors and teaches us to perceive an instrumental dependence between their misguided actions (in the foreground) and his malice (in the background). Characterization is bare, action ritualistic, to make the text as a whole diaphanous to the structure of hidden meaning: the cosmic struggle between Christ and Satan.[17] In *Judith*, on the other hand, Holofernes becomes the devil incarnate – not a transparent

---

[13] *Ibid.* p.5.   [14] *Ibid.*   [15] Cf. Pringle, 'Homily and Poem', pp. 87–8.

[16] J. Whitman makes a useful distinction between allegoresis and compositional allegory as two inverse literary kinds within the allegorical tradition in *Allegory: the Dynamics of an Ancient and Medieval Technique* (Oxford, 1987), at pp. 1–5.

[17] See D.G. Calder, 'The Art of Cynewulf's *Juliana*', *MLQ* 34 (1973), 355–71.

type of Satan, pointing beyond himself and inviting allegoresis, but a Satanic embodiment requiring tropological resistance.

The *Judith* poet systematically allegorizes the tale as he tells it *literaliter* – a procedure which displaces allegory as the story's spiritual (hidden or unstated) meaning and leads the reader directly into its tropological dimension. The poet aims at his audience's application, not discovery, of truth. When, for instance, the poet tells us outright that Holofernes is 'Nergende lað'[18] and 'se deofulcunda' (61b), he obviates the need to discover the demonic, allegorical significance of the character, while using allegory in a direct way to heighten the emotional response of his audience. In its tropological dimension, then, the poem exerts upon its audience in an immediate way both the logical and ethical appeal included in the allegory (which assimilates Judith to God, Holofernes to the devil) and the pathetic appeal found in the *prima facie* meaning, the sound and sequence of the heroic tale – rhetorical appeals fused by the poet in the body of the text and directed toward a single final cause: the arousal of resistance in his auditors against a real and pressing foe.

Even as the poet minimizes the distinction between the tale and its interpretation by re-literalizing the allegory, embedding it in the very letter of his text, homilists such as Wulfstan exhort their auditors to see the devil taking flesh around them in an incarnational descent: 'He byð sylf deofol 7 ðeah mennisc man geboren. Crist is soð God 7 soð mann, 7 Antecrist bið soðlice deofol 7 mann. Ðurh Crist com eallum middanearde help 7 frofer, 7 ðurh Antecrist cymð se mæsta gryre 7 seo mæste earfoðnes þe æfre ær on worulde geworden wearð.'[19] Wulfstan takes care to teach his auditors to see the Antichrist ('Godes wiðersaca', 'contrarius Christo') not merely as a single legendary person, but as each and every one who abandons the true faith ('Godes lage 7 lare forlæt') gives himself over to a life of sin and tempts others to evil-doing. While few perhaps will encounter Antichrist himself face to face, God's faithful ones ('Godes þeowas'), suffering in the midst of heathens ('on hæðenum þeodum'), can readily see and recognize the limbs of Satan's body on earth: 'And ðeah þæt sy þæt fela manna Antecrist sylfne næfre his eagum ne geseo, to fela is þeah his lima þe man wide nu geseon 7 ðurh heora yfel gecnawan mæg, ealswa hit on þam godspelle geræd is: *Surgent enim pseudocristi.*'[20]

Given this view of the Danish invasion as a Satanic entering into time and space through a body of unbelievers, it is not surprising that the poet has seized upon the central icon of the Judith story, the severed head of Holofernes, and converted it into a *tacen* for teaching and moving his audience. Through a kind

---

[18] *Judith*, ed. Timmer, 45b. This edition is cited throughout.
[19] *The Homilies of Wulfstan*, ed. D. Bethurum (Oxford, 1957), p. 128.
[20] *Ibid.* pp. 116–17.

of thematic punning on the notion of headship, the poet retells the biblical story as the corporate conflict between two heads and their members. He sets God's authority against Satan's tyranny; Judith's sapience in opposition to Holofernes's wicked intent, befuddled thinking and lack of insight; Judith's inspired leadership within the Israelite community in contrast to Holofernes's headship within the *comitatus*; the attitude of the victorious Jews against that of the defeated Assyrians. His rhetorical strategy aims at incorporating his audience anew into the body of believers. The marked emphasis on mental and emotional state, which distinguishes the poem from its biblical source, helps to promote within his readers an attitude of courageous followership that is ready to enter into battle believing in victory. Even as the allegorical associations connected with the cross support the militaristic vision 'In hoc signo', the allegory of the *heafod* supports a triumphant tropology of Christian resistance to heathen invaders.

This pattern of assimilation becomes evident when we examine four major scenes in which the poet departs from his biblical source in order to establish Holofernes's head and headship as a moving sign of contradiction: (1) the feast, (2) the beheading, (3) the display of the head and (4) the battle.

The feast

The *descriptio* of the feast, one of the most memorable in Old English poetry, differs considerably from the Vulgate account. In the biblical version Judith is present at the banquet, coolly playing the coquette and accepting Holofernes's offer to drink: 'Bibam, domine, quoniam magnificata est anima mea hodie.'[21] The Vulgate briefly notes that Holofernes, lusting after her, drinks more than he has ever drunk before: 'Et iucundus factus est Holofernis ad illam, bibitque vinum nimis multum, quantum numquam biberat in vita sua.' In the poem Judith is absent, and the drunken revelry of the men in the hall is described at great length.

The change reflects a selective assimilation of the exegetical writings in support of the poet's overall rhetorical aim. St Ambrose's commentaries, in particular, place a primary importance on Judith's sobriety and complete abstinence from drink. In his *De viduis* he uses Judith as an example, urging widows to practice temperance as a safeguard for their chastity: 'casta primo a vino, ut possis casta esse ab adulterio'.[22] In *De Elia et ieiunio liber unus*, St Ambrose draws a contrast between Holofernes's men, whose drinking symbolizes their moral capitulation to his leadership, and Judith, whose sober clear-headedness enables her to resist him successfully: 'Denique bibebant

---

[21] Passages from the Vulgate *Liber Judith* are quoted from *Biblia sacra iuxta vulgatam versionem* VIII (Rome, 1950), 210–80.   [22] PL 16, cols. 246–7.

vinum in ebrietate potentes, qui Holopherni principi militiae regis Assyriorum se tradere gestiebant; sed non bibebat femina Judith.'[23] While Fulgentius, like St Jerome and Prudentius, places great emphasis on Judith's chastity, he also contrasts Holofernes's drunkenness with her sobriety: 'Ille pugnabat armis, ista ieiuniis; ille ebrietate, ista oratione.'[24] Hrabanus Maurus, whose *Expositio in librum Judith* is the only full-length commentary on the biblical text, twice quotes the passage from I Peter 5 which urges sober vigilance in the face of the enemy: 'Sobrii estote et vigilate, quia adversarius vester diabolus tanquam leo rugiens circuit quaerens quem devoret, cui resistite fortes in fide' – and he does so to explicate the tropological significance of Judith's display of Holofernes's severed head.[25]

Thus, while the commentaries do present Judith as a 'castitatis exemplar' (to use Hrabanus's phrase), they also emphasize her sober counsel, temperance and prudence. As St Ambrose puts it: 'Sobrii vigore consilii abstulit Holophernis caput, servavit pudicitiam, victoriam reportavit.'[26] The poet of the Old English *Judith* has clearly seized upon the latter element in the exegetical writings and altered the original plot accordingly, stressing Judith's sobriety and Assyrian drunkenness. David Chamberlain is right in observing that chastity *per se* is de-emphasized by the poet.[27] As Jane Mushabac has shown, the epithets for Judith characteristically focus attention not on her purity but on her ability to think clearly.[28] She is 'seo snotere mægð' (125a), the 'gleawhydig wif' (148a), the 'searoðoncol mægð' (145a), the 'snoteran idese' (55a), 'seo gleawe' (171a), 'ferhðgleawe' (41a) and 'gleaw on geðonce' (13b). This kind of on-going narratorial commentary on Judith encourages the audience to approve her way of thinking and to assume her fundamental attitude in the face of similar danger presented by the Danes (who were, by the way, notorious for their excessive drinking).

Whereas Judith abstains completely from drink, Holofernes and his men drink themselves into a stupor. The Vulgate merely states that the Assyrians were drowsy from wine ('omnes fatigati a vino'). The poet, however, expands upon the Ambrosian notion that their drunken sleep not only foreshadows their impending death but also symbolizes their spiritual destruction. The 'bealde byrnwiggende' (17a) are Holofernes's companions in misery (*weagesiðas*); the 'rofe rondwiggende' (20a) are doomed (*fæge*). While Ambrose uses the Vergilian language of death ('somno sepultis', 'vino sepultus') to describe the Assyrian stupor, the poet makes the comparison

---

[23] PL 14, col. 707.   [24] *Epistola II ad Gallam viduam*, PL 65, cols. 319–20.
[25] PL 109, cols. 573 and 575.   [26] *De Elia*, PL 14, col. 707.
[27] 'A Fragmentary and Political Poem', p. 156.
[28] '*Judith* and the Theme of *Sapientia et Fortitudo*', *Massachusetts Stud. in Eng.* 4 (1973), 3–12.

explicit, stating that Holofernes 'oferdrencte his duguðe ealle, swylce hie wæron deaðe geslegene, / agotene goda gehwylces' (31–2a).

Holofernes, their head, is described as the source of evil polluting the *comitatus* which exists as a corporate entity joined to him. We are told that Holofernes frequently exhorted his men ('manode geneahhe / bencsittende') to merry-making, that he drenched and drowned his retainers with wine ('dryhtguman sine drencte mid wine, . . . / oferdrencte his duguðe ealle') and that he commanded his attendants to serve drink to his troop ('het . . . / fylgan fletsittendum'). The boisterous behaviour of the thegns, who answer Holofernes's invitation to the feast and follow his lead in drinking, must be inferred from Holofernes's own conduct. It is he who laughs, clamours, roars, rages, yells and makes a general din: 'hloh 7 hlydde, hlynede 7 dynede, / . . . / . . . styrmde 7 gylede' (23–5b). The poet stresses Holofernes's headship over his *comitatus* and their moral identification with him. When he summons them, they come; what he commands, they perform:

> Hie ðæt ofstum miclum
> ræfndon rondwiggende, comon to ðam rican þeodne
> feran, folces ræswan (10b–12a);

> Hie hraðe fremedon
> anbyhtscealcas, swa him heora ealdor bebead,
> byrnwigena brego (37b–9a).

Like Satan in the Blickling homily *Dominica prima in quadragesima*, Holofernes as *heafod* of the Assyrians is the source of unrighteous deeds, and his thegns, in a grim parody of the *corpus Christi mysticum*, are his extended self, his members, his limbs: 'se awyrda gast is heafod ealra unrihtwisra dæda, swylce unrihtwise syndon deofles leomo.'[29]

The poet's language again and again stresses Holofernes's leadership, calling him 'se gumena baldor' (9b), 'folces ræswan' (12a), 'se rica' (20b), 'egesful eorla dryhten' (21a), 'goldwine gumena' (22a) and 'se gumena ealdor' (32b). At the same time the poet emphasizes Holofernes's lack of insight and inability to think clearly. He and his men are doomed 'þeah ðæs se rica ne wende' (20b). He is mead-foolish (*medugal*), insolent (*swiðmod*), perverse (*inwidda*) and confused with wickedness ('niða geblonden'). The darkness of night and the dizziness of drink surround him as an outward sign of his spiritual condition.

When Holofernes's men bring Judith at his bidding to the pavilion ('to træfe þam hean'), the poet digresses to describe at length the golden fly-net ('eallgylden fleohnet') which hangs about Holofernes's bed. The *Liber Judith* makes mention of a canopy (*conopeum*), hanging from the bedposts, which

---

[29] *The Blickling Homilies of the Tenth Century*, ed. R. Morris, EETS os 58, 63 and 73 (1874–80), 33.

Judith takes down and uses to wrap Holofernes's severed head. In the biblical account she displays the *conopeum* as well as the *caput*, using it as an emblem of Holofernes's *luxuria*: 'Ecce conopeum illius, in quo recumbebat in ebrietate sua.'

The poet's reworking of the source material converts the *conopeum* into a strange and wonderful *fleohnet* which, as an emblematic representation of Holofernes's inner state,[30] reflects not so much his *luxuria* as his self-delusion. Baleful (*bealofulla*) and renowned for evil ('niðe rofra'), Holofernes has provided a false security for himself in the form of the 'fleohnet fæger' (47a) which enables him to see anyone who approaches his bed while keeping him from being seen. The fly-net as a two-way mirror thus takes on the significance it has in Hrabanus Maurus's *Expositio*: 'Et conopeum, hoc est, rete muscarum, insidias significat dolosae cogitationis.'[31] Holofernes is destroyed by the treachery of his own deceitful thoughts which betray him into a false carefreeness. Hrabanus Maurus describes him lying on a couch of impious security ('in lecto nefandae securitatis'), trusting that he can sin with impunity ('se impune peccare posse') and heading blindly toward eternal perdition: 'ad perditionem perpetuam improvidus'.[32] The poet, incorporating Hrabanus's interpretation into the actual plot, literalizes the allegory in the form of the fly-net, fusing the *sententia* with the letter in a single, rhetorically potent image.

The Vulgate account has nothing to say about Holofernes's inner reaction to the news of Judith's enclosure in his chamber. It merely states that he fell down, unconscious, on the bed. The poet, on the other hand, specifies his attitude and wicked intent:

> þa wearð se brema on mode
> bliðe, burga ealdor, þohte ða beorhtan idese
> mid widle 7 mid womme besmitan (57b–9a),

and links his sinfulness to his approaching death at Judith's hand:

> Gewat ða se deofulcunda,
> galferhð gumena ðreate,
> bealofull his beddes neosan, þær he sceolde his blæd forleosan
> ædre binnan anre nihte. Hæfde ða his ende gebidenne
> on eorðan unswæslicne, swylcne he ær æfter worhte,
> þearlmod ðeoden gumena, þenden he on ðysse worulde
> wunode under wolcna hrofe (61–7a).

The poet thus links Holofernes's mortal sins to his cruel end (*swylcne*) and contrasts his intention to seduce Judith with the actual outcome, his own

---

[30] See C.T. Berkhout and J.F. Doubleday, 'The Net in *Judith* 46b–54a', *NM* 74 (1973), 630–4.
[31] PL 109, col. 573. [32] *Ibid.* col. 572.

destruction. In so doing, the poet again demonstrates a selective use of the biblical commentaries. St Augustine, for instance, notes that Holofernes, captivated by Judith's beautiful face ('mulieris vultu captivus') and out of his senses with lust for her ('solutus est sensibus'), was destined to lose his soul along with his head: 'animam cum capite perditurus'.[33] Similarly, Hrabanus Maurus, commenting on the fact that Judith pulls Holofernes by his hair and kills him with his own sword, stresses the self-destructiveness of Holofernes's attitude: 'Gladius, qui in ea ligatus pendebat, malitia est iniquae intentionis. Coma capitis est elatio superbae mentis.'[34]

The beheading

Unlike Holofernes, who is so drunk ('wine swa druncen') that he can no longer think or maintain consciousness ('he nyste ræda nanne / on gewitlocan'), Judith is exceedingly mindful ('þearle gemyndig') of her plight and seeking a way to overcome her enemy. In her distress she prays. Once again the poet's version differs considerably from the Vulgate. While the biblical Judith invokes the Lord God of Israel ('Domine Deus Israhel'), the Old English heroine addresses the Blessed Trinity ('frymða God 7 frofre Gæst, / Bearn Alwaldan'). The change demonstrates the poet's literalization of the allegory associated with the story. Hrabanus Maurus, like the other exegetes, treats Judith as a type of the church. Ælfric's brief *moralité*, appended to his homily on Judith, affirms the analogy: 'þæt is Cristes cyrce.'[35] The poet's christianized Judith speaks as *ecclesia*, professing 'soðne geleafan' (89a) even as she asks for the gift of faith. Her prayer, moreover, uses language which links the beheading of Holofernes to the salvation event foretold in Genesis: 'Ipsa conteret caput eius' – a text cited by Hrabanus and others in their writings on the *Liber Judith*.[36] The poet calls Judith the Saviour's handmaid ('Nergendes / þeowen þrymful'); he describes her calling upon the Saviour of all ('Nergend ealra / woruldbuendra'); and he places upon her lips a petition for salvation: 'Geunne me minra gesynta' (90b).

The same pattern of allegorical assimilation controls the characterization of Holofernes, who is likened more and more to Satan and the serpent. Hrabanus, St Jerome and Ælfric all draw a parallel between Judith's decapitation of Holofernes and the church's triumph over the devil: 'in typo Ecclesiae diabolum capite truncavit'.[37] The *Judith* poet incorporates the traditional interpretation into his rendition of the story, calling Holofernes 'Nergende lað' (45b), 'deofulcunda' (61b), 'unsyfra' (76b) and the giver of deadly crime ('morðres brytta'). In the *Liber Judith* Holofernes is a proud, licentious man; in

---

[33] *Sermo de Judith*, PL 39, col. 1839. [34] *Expositio*, PL 109, col. 573.
[35] Assmann, 'Ælfric's Buch Judith', p. 103. [36] Cf. *Expositio*, PL 109, col. 575.
[37] St Jerome, *Epistola LXXIX ad Salvinam*, PL 22, col. 732.

Judith he is rhetorically reduced to bestiality. The epithets for Holofernes become increasingly negative. When Judith finally kills him she kills a monster ('þone atolan'), a heathen hound ('þone hæðenan hund'), a malignant-minded and hostile enemy ('þone feondsceaðan', 'heteþoncolne').

Besides the invocation to the Trinity ('þrynesse þrym') and allegorical colouring, three other features distinguish the *Judith* prayer from its biblical source. First of all, the Vulgate mentions that Judith wept as she prayed ('orans cum lacrymis') without making any further comment on her state of mind. Indeed, her recorded prayer is simply a petition for strength ('confirma me') to carry out her preconceived plan: 'et hoc, quod credens per te posse fieri, cogitavi, perficiam'. The poet, on the other hand, considerably expands Judith's prayer and alters its tone. Unlike Cynewulf's Juliana, the heroine of *Judith* opens her heart to God and to the poem's auditors, revealing emotions of fear, sorrow and distress:

> þearle ys me nu ða
> heorte onhæted   7 hige geomor,
> swyðe mid sorgum gedrefed   (866–8a).[38]

She is 'torn on mode,/hate on hreðre' (936–4a). The insight the poet gives his audience into Judith's troubled mental state not only registers a pathetic appeal and awakens sympathy for her; it provides a basis for identification with her. After all, his Anglo-Saxon listeners, like Judith, are frightened and at the mercy of pagan invaders.

At the close of Judith's oral prayer, the poet interrupts the narrative to moralize its action:

> Hi ða se hehsta Dema
> ædre mid elne onbryrde,   swa He deð anra gehwylcne
> herbuendra,   þe Hyne him to helpe secað,
> mid ræde 7 mid rihte geleafan   (94b–7a).

Here we find a clear, universally applicable statement of the poem's ethical teaching. The poet affirms that God will inspire with courage anyone who believingly seeks his help. Judith's experience offers a convincing proof of God's power to work a miracle of inner transformation. She, who had been sad and frightened, suddenly becomes 'rume on mode, / haligre hyht geniwod' (97b–8a). The change effected in Judith's attitude anticipates the transformation the poet hopes to bring about in his auditors through the *tæcing* of the

---

[38] Calder notes that Cynewulf's Juliana, unlike the suffering and emotionally expressive saint in the *Acta*, 'is only described by the poet as full of unflinching steadfastness'; see 'The Art', p. 365.

poem as a whole and provides a pointed indication of his aim. Neither the miracle nor the associated *moralité* appears in the Vulgate text, and its addition strongly enforces the rhetorical emphasis on faith as a basis for courageous action.

Unlike Holofernes's thegns who submit to his headship and thereby lose right reason, Judith becomes 'rume on mode' (97b) in her humble submission to God's authority. In the Vulgate account the Israelites act under Ozias's leadership; in *Judith* they have no *dryhten* but the Lord. The titles given him by the poet emphasize his leadership over all creatures and invite a comparison with Holofernes's tyrannical leadership. God is 'mihtig Dryhten' (92b), the 'torhtmod tires Brytta' (93a), 'se hehsta Dema' (94b), the 'dugeða Waldend' (61a), the 'cyninga Wuldor' (155a), the 'swegles Ealdor' (124a) and the 'þearlmod Þeoden gumena' (91a). Holofernes plans to defile Judith but, the narrator interjects, 'Ne wolde þæt wuldres Dema / geðafian, þrymmes Hyrde, ac he him þæs ðinges gestyrde' (59b–60). God himself opposes Holofernes, but he does so through Judith whom he inspires with valour.

Judith's instrumental relationship to God stands in contrast to the blind discipleship exercised by Holofernes's thegns. The poet calls her the 'scyppendes mægð' (78a) and the Saviour's *þeowen* (74a), even as the exegetes treat her as a type of the church whose head is Christ: 'Christus Ecclesiae sponsus'.[39] The poet stresses the coordination between Judith and her divine *Dryhten* in the next two narrative units which recount Judith's actual beheading of Holofernes (98–111a) and the subsequent torments of his soul in hell (111b–21). The former considerably expands and rhetorically heightens the matter-of-fact Vulgate account: 'Et percussit bis in cervicem eius, et abscidit caput eius', stressing the link between 'þæt heafod' (110b) which rolls upon the floor and Holofernes's hateful, hostile frame of mind (*heteþoncolne*). The graphic description of Holofernes in hell ('wyrum bewunden, witum gebunden') is the poet's own addition. Judith's violent physical action against Holofernes anticipates his eternal torment in hell and thus becomes an *imitatio Dei*, an act of holy devotion. In opposing her enemy Judith fights against God's foe, and she does so in his power. In a summary statement at the end of these two passages the narrator explicitly unites divine action with human cooperation, noting that 'Iudith æt guðe' attained outstanding success 'swa hyre God uðe' (123b).

---

[39] The phrase is from Hugh of St Victor's *Allegoriae in Vetus Testamentum* XI, PL 175, col. 747. The idea is much older. St Jerome, for instance, likens Judith to Mary in her virginal espousal to Christ (PL 22, col. 408). Ælfric calls Judith, as a type of the church, Christ's 'an clæne bryd' ('Ælfric's Buch Judith', ed. Assman, p. 103). St Paul, of course, describes the bridal relationship between the church and Christ in a classical way in Ephesians v.21–33.

The display of the head

The literalization of allegory in the first part of *Judith*, together with a calculated pathetic appeal which encourages the audience's identification with Judith, prepares the way for tropological assimilation in the middle and concluding sections of the poem. Judith's maidservant places 'þæs herewæðan heafod swa blodig' (126) in a pouch, and the two walk quietly homeward through the enemy lines. The poet describes their inner elation (*collenferhðe*) and, in a moving addition to the Vulgate account, tells how the women behold the walls of Bethulia shining in the distance:

> hie sweotollice geseon mihten
> þære wlitegan byrig weallas blican (136–7).

The image provides a striking contrast to Holofernes's newfound *ham* (121a) in hell and recalls Hrabanus Maurus's allegorical treatment of Bethulia as a type of heaven and the church. 'Hic pervenit ad portam civitatis, quia ille pertingit ad introitum regni coelestis.'[40] Here within the walls of Bethulia, Judith will reveal Holofernes's head, teach the people and inspire them with courage, incorporating them into the miracle of her own inner transformation.

In the *Liber Judith* the heroine reaches the city gate, asks to be admitted ('Aperite portas') and then proceeds to display Holofernes's head and canopy to the assembled people. The poet expands the account by describing the emotional reaction of the sentries ('weras wæccende') whose exceeding joy at Judith's safe return matches their previous sorrow (*geomormodum*) at her departure. Judith is well loved, 'leof to leodum' (147a), and the guards welcome her warmly, even as Beowulf's thegns throng around him when he returns victorious from the mere. Thus the warriors model the favourable response to Judith that the poet desires from the audience.

The poet then adds a speech (152b–8), not found in the Vulgate, which Judith addresses to the guards as a preface to her later speech to the whole populace. Again, the emphasis is on a change of emotional state: 'ge ne þyrfen leng / murnan on mode' (153b–4a). Judith proclaims God's favour to her people and predicts that soon the whole world will know how the Measurer has given them *wuldorblæd* (156b) in exchange for injuries (*læðða*) long endured. The reference to the universal audience ('þæt gecyðed wearð / geond woruld wide') assimilates the poem's audience into the text and disposes them to hear Judith's address along with the Israelites. The poet then expands upon the Vulgate account of the general assembly (159–70), stressing the emotional

---

[40] *Expositio*, PL 109, col. 573.

responses of the people, young and old alike, who gather around Judith. They are 'on lustum' (161b), *bliðe* (159a) and 'mod areted' (167b). The poet's auditors, imaginatively experiencing the same event, are invited to respond similarly.

A dramatic pause, during which the crowd makes way for Judith, increases the solemnity of the moment when Judith's handmaid unwraps the bloody *heafod* to display (*ætywan*) it as a sign ('to behðe'). Unlike the biblical Judith, who displays the head herself and then praises the Lord for preserving her chastity and enabling her to kill the Assyrian general, the poet's Judith emphasizes Holofernes's past crimes against the nation and his intent to inflict more injuries:

> Holofernus   unlyfigendes
> þe us monna mæst   morðra gefremede,
> sarra sorga   7 þæt swyðor gyt
> ycan wolde;   ac him ne uðe God
> lengran lifes,   þæt he mid læððum us
> eglan moste   (180–5a).

In treating the beheading as a defensive action undertaken by the Lord on behalf of his afflicted and threatened people, Judith identifies herself completely with her nation as its exponent. She then urges the Israelites to arm themselves, go out from Bethulia at dawn and attack the Assyrians, assuring them that they will obtain victory even as she has:

>   ge dom agon,
> tir æt tohtan,   swa eow getacnod hafað
> mihtig Dryhten   þurh mine hand   (196b–8).

Unlike the *caput* in the *Liber Judith* which offers proof of a victory already accomplished, the *heafod* in *Judith* is a sign inspiring belief in a victory still to be won. The Israelites can share in Judith's conquest of Holofernes, but only if they join her actively seeking God's help 'mid ræde 7 mid rihte geleafan' (97a). Victory over their enemies depends, in the first place, on their vanquishing their own fear and unbelief, on their becoming 'rume on mode' (97b). This is the very attitude the poet hopes to inspire in his auditors, and the response of the Israelites to Judith's speech and proffered *tacen* provides a model for audience response.

The literalization of allegory in the first part of the poem prepares the reader to associate Holofernes's *heafod* with the cross as a symbol of Christian victory over the forces of darkness. Judith prophesies that the Israelites will triumph over their enemies 'swa eow getacnod hafað / mihtig Dryhten þurh mine hand' (197b–8); similarly, the angel in Cynewulf's *Elene* points to the cross that appears in the sky, calling it a 'sigores tacen' and assuring Constantine: 'Mid þys beacne ðu / on þam frecnan fære feond oferswiðesð.'[41] The battle-cry 'In hoc signo' sounds in both poems and reflects a historical tendency to literalize the allegory of the cross, converting a supra-temporal spiritual victory over Satan, sin and death into a temporal triumph over pagan foes. Ælfric, for instance, records that St Oswald erected a cross before entering into battle and urged his thegns to join him in praying for military victory: 'Uton feallan to ðære rode and þone Ælmihtigan biddan þæt he us ahredde wið þone modigan feond.'[42]

Furthermore, as we have seen, the allegorical colouring of the Judith story as the poet tells it *literaliter* involves the use of loaded language that encourages in the audience unqualified support for Judith and opposition to Holofernes as agents of God and Satan. Having aroused a strong emotional response within an ethically unambiguous context, the poet then directs that energy on to the battlefield through the enacted tropology of the Israelite advance against the Assyrians.

The battle

The battle that follows Judith's speech has no parallel in the *Liber Judith*. In the biblical account the Israelites follow Judith's advice and wait until the Assyrians, horrified at the discovery of Holofernes's decapitated body, take flight. They then pursue the fleeing soldiers, cutting them down from behind. In *Judith*, on the other hand, the Israelites, trusting in God's assistance, go out

---

41 *Cynewulf's 'Elene'*, ed. P.O.E. Gradon, rev. 2nd ed. (Exeter, 1977), lines 85a and 92b–3. There is, by the way, a traditional allegorical association between *heafod* and *rod* that supports the poet's attempt to make Holofernes's head, like the cross of Constantine's vision, a rousing sign of victory for his Anglo-Saxon audience. The Genesis prophecy, 'Ipsa conteret caput eius', after all, finds its fulfilment on Calvary when Mary's son vanquishes Satan. Bede presents David decapitating Goliath as a type of Christ separating souls from Satan, the head of sinners and the source of unrighteousness in his members. See *In I Samuhelem, Opera exegetica* II.2, CCSL 119 (Turnhout, 1962), 159. The Blickling homily *Dominica tertia in quadragesima* urges the faithful to bless themselves 'mid Cristes rode tacne' and thus exorcise the devil who dreads the cross more than an executioner 'mid sweorde wiþ þæs heafdes' (*The Blickling Homilies*, ed. Morris, p. 47).

42 Ælfric, *Lives of Three English Saints*, ed. G.I. Needham, rev. 2nd ed. (Exeter, 1976), p. 28. Bede tells the story of Oswald's erection of the cross at Heavenfield in *Historia ecclesiastica* III.2. In Bede's account, miracles of physical healing and miracles of military victory over barbarians are both associated with the cross, which stands as a sign of the king's faith in God's assistance. Similarly, in *Historia ecclesiastica* I.20, the army of the Britons, still wet with baptismal water and full of faith in the Easter triumph, advances under the leadership of Bishop Germanus against the vastly superior forces of the invading Picts and Saxons – and miraculously overcomes them. Clearly the English at the time of Bede and Ælfric had little difficulty in connecting the allegory of salvation, so often described as a battle against the foe, with actual defensive warfare against pagan invaders – a connection explored in the incarnational art of *Judith*.

boldly against the Assyrian army. As the narrator observes, they who formerly endured the abuse of aliens ('elþeodigra edwit'), the blasphemy of pagans ('hæðenra hosp'), now advance to the front to repay the Assyrians. Once the Israelites were afraid; now they are *styrnmode* (227a) and *stercedferhðe* (227b). Once they suffered defeat at the hands of the Assyrians; now they obtain victory. The poet's language, which establishes a conflict between native inhabitants (*landbuende*) and invaders (*elþeod*), Christians and heathens, sober warriors (*styrnmode*) and drunken thegns (*medowerige*), facilitates the assimilation of the audience into the poem at the tropological level, inviting them to fight as courageously against the Danes as the Israelites do against the Assyrians.

The Assyrians, startled at the hard and unexpected attack, send word back to the camp, asking for help. Holofernes's retainers, roused from their drunken slumber (*medowerige* and *werigferhðe*), crowd around his pavilion, seeking to warn him. In a masterful integration of his material, the poet uses pictorial panels, shifting from the warriors at Holofernes's tent back to the battlefield where the Israelites with sharp swords ('heardum heoruwæpnum') are paying back the Assyrians for old grudges, and then back to the waiting, anxious retainers.[43] With bitter dramatic irony the poet thus links the *heafodweardas* (239b) at the battlefront with the thegns guarding their headless head. The gloom which weighs upon Holofernes's men (*sweorcendferhðe*) due to the Hebrew attack foreshadows their reaction to his murder and inseparably unites the victories of Judith and the Israelites.

Even as Holofernes's head stands as a token of victory for the Israelites, his headless body becomes a sign of destruction for the Assyrians. The unnamed thegn who dares to enter the bedchamber and discovers the corpse announces:

> Her ys geswutelod   ure sylfra forwyrd,
> toweard getacnod,   þæt þære tide ys
> mid niðum neah geðrungen,   þe we sculon nu losian,
> somod æt sæcce forweorðan.   Her lið sweorde geheawen,
> beheafdod healdend ure   (285–9a).

His speech, like Judith's *tæcing* in Bethulia, links the outcome of the battle to the *tacen* of Holofernes's head. Lacking their leader, the Assyrians are affected in mind and spirit, becoming *hreowigmode* (289b) and *werigferhðe* (290b). They throw down their weapons and flee before the Israelites who continue to experience God's assistance: 'Him feng Dryhten God / fægre on fultum, Frea ælmihtig' (299b–300). With a final, irresistible pun, the narrator reports that the 'head-count' (*heafodgerimes*) of fallen Assyrians was great (cf. 308b).

---

[43] A. Renoir ('*Judith* and the Limits of Poetry', *ES* 43 (1962), 145–55) compares the poet's typological panelling to the split-screen technique used in modern cinema.

Unlike the *Liber Judith* which concludes with Joachim's speech in Judith's honour and her own extended canticle in God's praise, the poem places its emphasis on the national victory won 'þurh Iudithe gleawe lare' (333) and faith in God. While the sapience of the biblical Judith manifests itself in calculating cleverness, the wisdom of the poem's heroine shows itself in blind trust and the courage to confront one's enemies, relying on the aid of the Almighty. This is the lesson the Israelites learn through her instruction and the *tacen* of Holofernes's head and, by way of *assimilatio*, the lesson the poet's audience also learns.

CONCLUSION

Headship in *Judith*, as we have seen, includes an intersecting range of vertical/ horizontal meanings. On the vertical axis, defined by the higher or deeper *sensus* (depending on the metaphor one prefers), headship recalls the head/ member relationship between Christ and the church, Satan and the church's persecutors. On the horizontal axis defined by the *sensus literalis*, headship denotes God's fatherly authority over Israel, Holofernes's tyrannical hold over his thegns. The poem generates its power from the constant intersection of these two axes, the fusion of the allegorical and narrative lines. Holofernes's threat reifies Satan's, even as God's protection of Judith communicates the help and comfort of Christ to the poem's beleaguered audience. The literalized allegory provides the basis, the necessary *scientia* (as Hugh of St Victor later calls it) for personal application. The *pathos* of the literal tale encourages the reader's identification with Judith, even as the embedded allegory ('þæt is Cristes cyrce') defines that placement objectively. Thus the poet unites the story's allegorical meaning closely with its psychological valence. Ultimately, however, the tropological meaning of headship belongs outside the text in the *historia* of one's own experience. Whether one becomes 'rume on mode' through a Judith-like trust in God, or fearfully submissive to God's Danish/ demonic adversary, depends on one's response to the poem's *tacen*.

Rutland and the Scandinavian settlements: the place-name evidence

BARRIE COX

A cursory glance at a map of Rutland shows a surprising lack of place-names containing Scandinavian themes. When Rutland's place-names are studied in historical detail, this dearth becomes truly startling, especially when we consider the geographical position of the county, lying as it does between the Danish boroughs of Leicester, Lincoln, Nottingham and Stamford and surrounded by heavy Norse settlement in Leicestershire and Lincolnshire and a not inconsiderable spread in Northamptonshire to its south.

Today, the boundaries of Rutland enclose a compact land unit which has every indication of being very ancient indeed. Stamford's town lands lying north of River Welland and west of River Gwash were clearly once part of this territory, for these rivers constitute its natural limits at this point (fig. 2). By Domesday, Rutland's modern extent was divided into three wapentakes, the north-westerly two of Alstoe and Martinsley (comprising the Domesday Book *Roteland*) being carucated and regarded as part of Nottinghamshire for tax purposes. The third, the south-easterly Witchley, was hidated and then an integral part of Northamptonshire. Domesday *Roteland* was also connected closely with Lincolnshire. Stamford had seventy residences which lay in *Roteland* and itself contained outlying dependencies of Hambleton in Martinsley wapentake. In addition, we may note that eight of the twelve lands in Alstoe wapentake are duplicated in the Lincolnshire folios.[1]

But such divisions appear to be a late reorganization of the region we know as Rutland. For example, Phythian-Adams has argued convincingly that the district which was to comprise the Forest of Rutland in the later Middle Ages and contain much of the land of both Martinsley and Witchley wapentakes was once the dower land of the Anglo-Saxon queens.[2] The place-name Edith Weston which contains the personal name of Edward the Confessor's wife is a memory of this royal demesne which ignored the later boundary between Martinsley and Witchley.

---

[1] *Domesday Book: Rutland*, ed. F. Thorn (Chichester, 1980).
[2] C. Phythian-Adams, 'Rutland Reconsidered', *Mercian Studies*, ed.
  A. Dornier (Leicester, 1977), pp. 63–84, esp. 67–73.

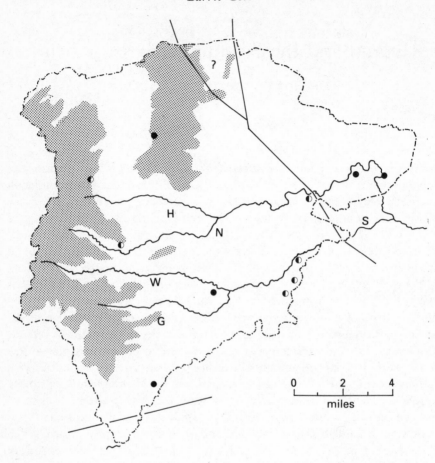

FIG. 2 Rutland

H = Hambleton, N = Normanton, G = Glaston, W = Wing, S = Stamford; ? = possible name in *-bý*,
● = *þorp* names recorded in Domesday Book or earlier, ◑ = *þorp* names recorded only post
Domesday Book. Roman roads are indicated. Land over 400ft is stippled.

At the time of the Scandinavian incursions, Rutland was part of the
kingdom of Mercia. However, at a much earlier period, it may well have
comprised the territory of a small kingdom of the Middle Angles, perhaps that
of the eponymous *Rōta*. Place-names along its western boundary such as
Wardley on its hill-top (OE *weard* 'watch, protection'), Belton (OE *bēl* possibly
'a beacon'), Flitteris (OE *(ge) flit* 'strife, dispute', hence 'brushwood region of
disputed ownership') and Twitch Hill in Ridlington (OE *tōt-hyll* 'a look-out
hill') suggest an ancient frontier region demarcating its territory from that of
unfriendly neighbours in what was to become Leicestershire. Above and along
River Welland, the hill-top barrows of Barrowden, Seaton and Thorpe by

Water signalled a south-easterly demarcation of the kingdom in much the same way as those of Sutton Hoo and Snape marked the boundaries of the Wuffingas in East Anglia.

Central to the territory of Rutland is the major site of Hambleton (OE *hamel-dūn* 'the flat-topped hill') which bears one of the very early Old English place-name types in *-dūn*.[3] As late as Domesday, the manor of Hambleton was the most important and valuable in *Roteland* and Phythian-Adams observes that by 1086 Oakham as a royal vill would have been quite a recent development.[4] Hambleton on its splendid hill-top site may well have been the ancient royal stronghold and *caput* of Rutland. Indeed, to its immediate north is Burley, OE *burh-lēah* 'woodland belonging to or near to a stronghold', surely not a reference to low-lying Oakham in the Vale of Catmose, but rather to a fortified Hambleton. If, as Phythian-Adams suggests, the boundaries of Rutland could have their origins in the Iron Age,[5] it may be worthwhile exploring the possibility of the presence of an oppidum of the Coritani on the hill of Hambleton. But more relevant to our present focus is perhaps the siting of Normanton (OE *Norðmanna-tūn* 'the tūn of the Norwegians') so close to this dominating and important centre (fig. 2).

Having established some sort of identity for early Anglo-Saxon Rutland, let us turn to such Scandinavian place-names as survive within its territory for any light that they may throw on what happened within its frontiers during the period of the Viking incursions and settlements.

It is probable that the earliest Scandinavian settlements in the Danelaw are represented by the so-called Grimston-hybrids, place-names compounded of (usually) a Danish personal name and OE *tūn*.[6] In Rutland, there is only one place-name which appears at first sight to be of this type; that is Glaston, 'the tūn of Glaðr'. But significantly, the personal name Glaðr is Norwegian and occurs otherwise only in Norwegian place-names.[7] There is no evidence for its early use by Danes. Glaston shares its northern boundary with Wing, which is Scandinavian *vengi*, a derivative of *vangr*, 'a field', used in this case, I believe, of one of the great fields of an estate or village. It is reasonable to suppose that Glaston with Wing and perhaps Bisbrooke once formed a large Anglo-Saxon land unit. The western boundary of Wing appears to continue that of

[3] B. Cox, 'The Place-Names of the Earliest English Records', *Jnl of the Eng. Place-Name Soc.* 8 (1975–6), 12–66.

[4] Phythian-Adams, 'Rutland Reconsidered', pp. 75–6.   [5] *Ibid.* p. 78.

[6] K. Cameron, 'Scandinavian Settlement in the Territory of the Five Boroughs: the Place-Name Evidence. Part III, the Grimston-Hybrids', *England before the Conquest: Studies in Primary Sources Presented to Dorothy Whitelock*, ed. P. Clemoes and K. Hughes (Cambridge, 1971), pp. 147–63. Reprinted in *Place-Name Evidence for the Anglo-Saxon Invasion and Scandinavian Settlements: Eight Studies*, ed. K. Cameron (Nottingham, 1975), pp. 157–71.

[7] E.H. Lind, *Norsk-Isländska Personbinamn från Medeltiden* (Uppsala, 1920–1), pp. 110–11.

Bisbrooke whose eastern boundary with Glaston indicates a later tit-for-tat adjustment. That the Glaston settlement is more ancient than Glaðr's village or estate is shown by the pagan Anglo-Saxon inhumation cemetery west of the village.[8] Glaston is only one among a striking group of place-names in *-tūn* concentrated in the south-western quarter of the county.[9] Such a concentration suggests both a break-up of early large estates and later assarting in heavily wooded land in this area.

The early Anglo-Saxon name for the larger land unit was most probably Thornham (OE *þorn-hām*, 'the hām or estate where hawthorns grow'). The name survives in *Thornhám bróc* in the Old English bounds of a charter for neighbouring Ayston, dated 1046.[10] This brook I take to be the nameless stream which separates Wing from Glaston and which flows into River Chater just north of South Luffenham.[11]

The earliest reference to Wing occurs in the bounds of the same charter where we find a ford on this stream called *wengeford*, that is, 'the ford to the field'. As its name implies, Wing did not originate as a habitation site. It could not have been a primary Scandinavian settlement. I take the Glaston territory to have originated in the late division of an earlier Anglo-Saxon estate and that, as with Wing, it probably does not represent initial Scandinavian expropriation of land. Indeed, by the date of Thornham's division, Glaðr need not have been of Norwegian stock, but it is worthwhile noting his possible connection with Normanton some four miles away. Normanton, 'the tūn of the Norwegians', is the only other possible early Scandinavian settlement site in the county. Normanton is, of course, a place-name created by English speakers

---

8 T.Mck. Clough, A. Dornier and R.A. Rutland, *A Guide to the Anglo-Saxon and Viking Antiquities of Leicestershire including Rutland* (Leicester Museum, 1975), p. 80.

9 B. Cox, 'The Major Place-Names of Rutland: to Domesday and Beyond', *Rutland Record* 7 (1987), 227–30, fig. 2.

10 P. Sawyer, *Anglo-Saxon Charters: an Annotated List and Bibliography* (London, 1968), no. 1014 (J.M. Kemble, *Codex Diplomaticus Aevi Saxonici*, 6 vols. (London, 1839–48), no. 784).

11 I agree with Phythian-Adams, 'Rutland Reconsidered', p. 81, that Finberg's interpretation of the Ayston bounds (in C.R. Hart, *The Early Charters of Eastern England* (Leicester, 1966), pp. 108–9) is incorrect. However, Phythian-Adams's alternative solution perhaps needs slight amendment. The *ræd weg* (bound 6), which is OE *ræde-weg* or *rād-weg* 'road suitable for riding on' (and not 'Red Way' as per Finberg and Phythian-Adams), I take to be the major route through Uppingham and Preston which appears in Scandinavianized form, with ON *gata* for OE *weg*, as *le Redegate* in Uppingham in 1290 and 1376 (forms collected by J.E.B. Gover from unpublished Forest Proceedings in the Public Record Office). I believe that the boundary followed Phythian-Adams' identified line of *holebroc* 'stream in a hollow' (bound 4) to its confluence with the northern stream at Ayston Spinney at 852016, the site of *brocholes* 'the badger setts' or 'the burrows at the brook' (bound 5), thence along this stream to the *ræde-weg* at 867014; *(into) wenge forde* (bound 7) is at 884015 and *þornham broc* (bound 1) is the stream separating Wing from Glaston but forking at 888014. Clearly, the present parish bounds of Ayston are not those of the charter.

and signified specifically non-Danish settlers. But we do not know precisely enough what sort of date to give names in Normanton.[12] There is no firm evidence to place them among the initial Scandinavian settlements. However, it may be significant that this solitary example in Rutland is situated beside Hambleton which seems to have been the early Anglo-Saxon *caput* of the territory. By Domesday, Normanton was a berewick of Hambleton. We shall return to it later.

If we move next to what some scholars consider to be a colonization phase of Scandinavian settlement, Cameron's period of secondary migration, characterized by place-names in -*bý*,[13] we find that there are *no* villages in Rutland with names of this type. The only real possibility of an early site of such a kind is that of Hooby Lodge in Stretton parish, one mile from the Roman Ermine Street and one mile from the northern county boundary with Lincolnshire. Its earliest appearance is in a terrier of field names for neighbouring Thistleton of 1633.[14] If Hooby is not a family name[15] or a transferred name from the Leicestershire Hoby (pronounced Hooby), it is a hybrid place-name compounded of OE *hōh* and Scandinavian *bý*, hence 'the *bý* at the headland'. There is indeed a low spur of land to the east of Hooby Lodge and the shape of the parish boundaries of Stretton suggests that Hooby's territory which is to the west of the Roman road may have been absorbed into it at some late date. But even if Hooby is an early place-name, its hybrid character and position on the northern periphery of Rutland's territory do not proclaim Scandinavian presence of any significance.

Apart from Normanton, it is only with some of its names in *þorp* that we get any real sense of Scandinavians in Rutland. Such names, of course, belong to a later stratum of name-giving than those in -*bý*, and are of a period of greater integration between the native English and Scandinavian settlers.[16]

There are five Rutland place-names in *þorp* that appear in Domesday Book: *Alsthorpe* (in Burley), Belmesthorpe (in Ryhall), Sculthorpe (in North Luffenham), Tolethorpe (in Little Casterton) and Thorpe by Water. Their

---

[12] G. Fellows-Jensen, *Scandinavian Settlement Names in Yorkshire* (Copenhagen, 1972), pp. 189–94, discusses the Norwegian presence in the settlements.

[13] K. Cameron, *Scandinavian Settlement in the Territory of the Five Boroughs: the Place-Name Evidence*, Inaugural Lecture (Univ. of Nottingham, 1965). Reprinted in *Place-Name Evidence for the Anglo-Saxon Invasion and Scandinavian Settlements*, pp. 115–38.

[14] Northampton, Northants. Record Office, Brudenell ASR 562.

[15] Sir Thomas Hoby's famous Renaissance translation of Castiglione's *Il Cortigiano* was published in 1561. To what extent his name would have been widely known some seventy years later is open to question.

[16] K. Cameron, 'Scandinavian Settlement in the Territory of the Five Boroughs: the Place-Name Evidence. Part II, Place-Names in Thorp', *MScand* 3 (1970), 35–49. Reprinted in *Place-Name Evidence for the Anglo-Saxon Invasion and Scandinavian Settlements*, pp. 139–56.

compounded personal names are respectively OE (E)alhstān and Beornhelm and Scandinavian Skúli and Tóli, while Thorpe by Water was always simplex: thus they provide an equal ratio of English to Scandinavian personal names in their composition. Only Thorpe by Water became a modern parish. *Alsthorpe* is lost, Sculthorpe survives as the name of a small spinney, Tolethorpe as the name of a country house.

Eight place-names in *þorp* are recorded initially later than 1086: they are Barleythorpe, the lost *Fregsthorpe* (in Ketton), Gunthorpe, Ingthorpe (in Tinwell), Kilthorpe (in Ketton), the lost *Manthorpe* (in Ketton), Martinsthorpe, and Westhorpe (in Wing). Barleythorpe, Gunthorpe and Martinsthorpe are modern parishes, although Martinsthorpe is now deserted. Barleythorpe originally was a simplex place-name in *þorp* later prefixed by OE *bærlic*, 'barley'. Gunthorpe is 'Gunni's outlying farmstead', a completely Scandinavian place-name. Martinsthorpe is recorded only from 1205, but the forms *Martinestoch* 1176 and *Martinstok* 1286[17] suggest that what was once an Old English place-name ('the outlying farmstead of Martin') had its final theme *stoc* replaced by its Scandinavian equivalent *þorp* in the course of the thirteenth century. Martin may have been an important Anglo-Saxon landowner of the Christian period. Martinsthorpe/-*stoc* lies in Martinsley wapentake, while a *Martines hó*, 'Martin's headland', is present in the bounds of the 1046 Ayston charter. (Ayston, of course, also lies in Martinsley wapentake.) Phythian-Adams points out, however, that both Martinsthorpe and Lyndon churches in the wapentake were dedicated to Saint Martin.[18] At least it seems reasonable that we should place Martinsthorpe's initial settlement firmly in the pre-Viking period.

While Martinsthorpe appears to be an original Anglo-Saxon foundation, Westhorpe seems very late. It is not recorded until 1296.[19] 'The west farmstead', it lies at the western edge of the village of Wing whose name, as we have seen, denoted a field of one of the neighbouring settlements.

Our final four names in *þorp* are all sited in the vicinity of the Danish borough of Stamford. Personal names of Norse origin are to be expected and we probably get them. The lost *Fregsthorpe* and Kilthorpe, both in Ketton parish, are compounded with the Scandinavian personal names Friðgestr (but also found as Friðegist in late Old English sources) and Ketill respectively. Ingthorpe in Tinwell probably contains Scandinavian Ingi (but could perhaps

---

[17] *Pipe Rolls* (Pipe Roll Soc.) in progress and *Placita de quo warranto*, Publ. of the Record Commission (London, 1818).   [18] Phythian-Adams, 'Rutland Reconsidered', p. 76.
[19] London, Public Record Office, Subsidy Rolls for Rutland (from a collection of J.E.B. Gover).

have OE Ingeld as its prototheme).[20] So even here we have to reckon with possible English personal names. Also in Ketton is the lost *Manthorpe*. It appears to be comparable with the two nearby surviving Lincolnshire examples of Manthorpe, with either the Scandinavian personal name Manni as its first element or alternatively the Old English or Scandinavian genitive plural *manna*, 'of the men'.[21]

The distribution of Rutland names in *þorp* is significant (fig. 2). Discounting Martinsthorpe which is most likely a modified Old English name in -*stoc* and Westthorpe which I take to be a late example, sited as it is on the western edge of Wing village, we find seven of the remaining eleven *þorp* settlements just inside the south-eastern boundary of the county, with six of these in an arc around Stamford, whose town land to the north and north-west was doubtlessly carved out of Rutland's territory at some early date, presumably prior to the establishment of the *þorp* sites. In the west, Barleythorpe is just a little over a mile from the county boundary. Only Gunthorpe on its tiny patch of Northampton Sands but with its fields on clay, *Alsthorpe* on the Boulder Clay north of Burley and Sculthorpe also on clay between North Luffenham and South Luffenham are situated in the interior of the county. Even the distribution of the place-names in *þorp*, then, suggests a region already heavily exploited by men of English stock.

Two other names on our map of Rutland have a hint of the Scandinavian about them: Osbonall Wood in Clipsham parish on the north-eastern boundary of the county and Turtle Bridge which crosses its south-eastern boundary, River Welland, between Barrowden and Northamptonshire's Harringworth. Speed's county map of 1611 is the earliest recording of Osbonall Wood (*Osburneall Wood*). Possibly we have here the Scandinavian personal name Ásbjǫrn with an anglicized first theme Ōs-, but its later medieval reflex Osbern is just as likely. Turtle Bridge is *Thurkelbregge* in 1298, *Turtles Bridge* in 1762.[22] Ralph *Turcle* is mentioned in connection with Harringworth in 1274[23] and the name of the bridge is surely to be associated with his family. The surname, of course, is a reduced form of the Scandinavian personal name Þorketill (giving Þorkell).

Scandinavian field names in Rutland reflect the poverty of major

[20] The earliest form *Ingelthorp* of 1189, in a copy of 1332 (*Calendar of Charter Rolls*) is unique and may be erratic. The usual forms from 1203 onwards are *Inget(h)orp(e)*. Late forms in *Inglethorp(e)*, 1547 and 1553 (*Calendar of Patent Rolls*) do, however, occur.

[21] G. Fellows-Jensen, *Scandinavian Settlement Names in the East Midlands* (Copenhagen, 1978), pp. 114 and 129 where Manthorpe's grid reference should read SK 9238.

[22] Lincoln, Lincs. Archives Office, Ancaster 5 Anc 1/6/61/24.

[23] London, PRO, Assize Rolls for Rutland (from a collection of J.E.B. Gover).

Scandinavian place-names in the county. Unfortunately, few terriers survive from before 1400. By chance, six of the eight discovered to date belong to parishes close to the county boundaries where perhaps Norse influence from outside the territory would be most strongly felt. These are for Barrowden, Bisbrooke, Caldecott, Little Casterton, Lyddington and Market Overton.[24] All show with monotonous regularity a minimum of the common Norse or Scandinavianized themes to be expected in the East Midland dialect of Middle English: *dík* 'a ditch', *gata* 'a road', *holmr* 'a water meadow', *sík* 'a ditch', *vangr* 'an in-field' – but little else of note.

Again by chance, the two remaining early terriers are for Glaston and Tolethorpe.[25] That for Glaston is of the fourteenth century. Of the twenty-eight items contained, ten have Norse or Scandinavianized themes, but again the dearth of earlier Norse speakers seems evident: we find *gata* (x 5), *holmr* (x 2), *sík* (x 3). There is nothing to distinguish Glaston's terrier from the pattern of the previous six. Only that for Tolethorpe is a little more encouraging, suggesting perhaps a former settlement of Norse speakers. It is of very early fourteenth or late thirteenth century date. Of its twenty-four names, eleven contain Norse or Scandinavianized themes: *gata*, *holmr*, *sík*, *storð*, *topt*, *vangr* (x 5), *vrá*. This is the same kind of package as before, though with the addition of three more specific items: *storð* 'a young wood', *topt* 'the site of a building' and *vrá* 'a corner of land'. But we must not forget that Tolethorpe is only two miles from Stamford from which we would expect a strong Scandinavian linguistic influence.

The weight of the place-name evidence concerning Scandinavians in Rutland suggests that the territory was largely unaffected by them in a region of heavy Danish settlement. We have so few historical facts for Rutland in the period of the Viking incursions that we can only speculate as to why the county seems to have remained inviolate. The following scenario is only one possibility.

We learn from the Anglo-Saxon Chronicle how, in 877, a Viking host first apportioned the kingdom of Mercia: '*þa on herfeste gefor se here on Myrcena land and hit gedældon sum and sum Ceolwulfe sealdon*'.[26] Ceolwulf II, '*anum unwisum cynges*

---

[24] For Barrowden: Belvoir Castle, Duke of Rutland's archives, Add. 98 and Add. 105; Bisbrooke: Rutland 2715, 2732, 5263 and 5385; Caldecott: Oxford, Queen's College 366; Little Casterton: London, PRO, Exch. Augm. Office AD B.B. 16; Lyddington: Queen's 366; Market Overton: PRO, Ministers' Accounts for Rutland (ex-Gover).

[25] For Glaston: Northampton, Northants. Record Office, Brudenell E xxi 56; Tolethorpe: T. Blore, *History and Antiquities of the County of Rutland* (Stamford, 1811), p. 214.

[26] *Anglo-Saxon Chronicle* 877: *Two of the Saxon Chronicles Parallel*, ed. C. Plummer, 2 vols. (Oxford, 1892–9) I, 74; 'then in the harvest season the army went away into Mercia and shared out some of it and gave some to Ceolwulf' (*The Anglo-Saxon Chronicle: A Revised Translation*, ed. D. Whitelock *et al.* (London, 1961; rev. 1965), p. 48).

þegne'[27] as he is described in the annal for 874, had received temporary rule of Mercia in that year from the Viking host so that '*hit him gearo wære swa hwilce dæge swa hi hit habban woldon*'.[28] It may have been that he was not so *unwis* as to realize that Rutland was a prime portion of real estate and that from the 877 bargaining and division of the kingdom he retained the territory intact as a jewel in his crown. We do not know, of course, whether prior to the Viking incursions, Rutland was the dower land of the queens of *Mercia* and whether its later becoming that of the queens of England merely perpetuated its reginal demesne status.

By 894, Rutland appears either to have passed into or be about to pass into the control of the Vikings of York rather than of the Five Boroughs. In Æthelweard's Chronicle we find that in that year, Ealdorman Æthelnoth

adit in hostes Euoraca urbe, qui non parua territoria pandunt in Myrciorum regno loci in parte occidentali Stanforda. Hoc est inter fluenta amnis Vueolod et condenso syluæ quæ uulgo Ceostefne nuncupatur.[29]

The *territoria* so described must have constituted Rutland, the streams of River Welland being the Eye Brook which forms the south-western boundary of the

---

[27] *ASC* 874 (= 873): *Two Chronicles*, ed. Plummer I, 73; 'a foolish king's thane' (*Anglo-Saxon Chronicle*, ed. Whitelock *et al.*, p. 48). Ceolwulf had been a thegn of Burgred, king of Mercia. As Dr Simon Keynes has pointed out to me in correspondence, one should bear in mind that *unwis* is likely to represent a West Saxon attitude current *c.* 890 as opposed to an attitude current in the mid-870s. Ceolwulf seems to have been taken quite seriously during his reign and was clearly more than a puppet king. He issued charters in his own name and had a sound coinage, sharing moneyers and coin types with Alfred of Wessex. The precise denotation of *unwis* as here used by the chronicler is unclear. Professor Christine Fell suggests that perhaps 'impulsive' rather than 'foolish' would be nearer the mark.

[28] *ASC* 874 (= 873): *Two Chronicles*, ed. Plummer I, 73; 'that it should be ready for them on whatever day they wished to have it' (*Anglo-Saxon Chronicle*, ed. Whitelock *et al.*, p. 48).

[29] *The Chronicle of Æthelweard*, ed. A. Campbell (London, 1962), p. 51. Campbell translates: 'In the city of York, he contacted the enemy who possessed (*pandunt*) large territories in the kingdom of the Mercians, on the western side of the place called Stamford. This is to say, between the streams of the river Welland and the thickets of the wood called Kesteven by the common people.' Campbell's rendering of *pandunt* is questioned in S. Keynes and M. Lapidge, *Alfred the Great: Asser's 'Life of King Alfred' and other Contemporary Sources* (Harmondsworth, 1983). They offer as an alternative translation of this passage, 'At the city of York he comes upon the enemy who are plundering no small territories in the kingdom of the Mercians to the west of Stamford; that is, between the waters of the river *Weolod* (Welland) and the thickets of the wood which is commonly called Kesteven' (p. 190). They note: 'The transmitted *pandunt* is nonsense, and Campbell's translation of it ("possessed", literally "opened out") is impossible: *pando* is intransitive and cannot govern the accusative *territoria*. We suggest emending to *praedantur*, "they plunder"' (p. 337). However, Æthelweard most frequently uses the verb *vastare* when he refers to plundering and the verb *pandere* is indeed commonly transitive. Although we may ponder Æthelweard's precise

county and the rivers Chater and Gwash which flow eastwardly through it. All three streams are tributaries of River Welland. Is this the date at which *Norwegian* Vikings from York established a unique settlement of Scandinavians at Normanton beside the ancient *caput* of the territory? Was it by chance that it was so sited and that no *Danish* occupation is apparent in the county? Certainly the York-Dublin Norse axis was developing by 892 when Sihtric, son of Ivar the Boneless, invaded England. Perhaps the fact that Glaston, the only hybrid *tūn* in Rutland, had as its owner a man with a Norwegian personal name indicates that it was only Norwegian Vikings who settled early in Rutland and that it was Norwegian York which continued to hold sway over an English Rutland until the reconquest of the territory by Edward the Elder in 918.[30]

Our Rutland *þorp* sites, nudging warily over the county boundaries in the south-east and north-west are to be ascribed to the period when Anglo-Saxons and Scandinavians were living more harmoniously in a kingdom of England. But by this date there seems to have been little worthwhile undeveloped land in the territory for the taking.

It is possible to argue that place-name creation depended on the *proportion* of English to Scandinavian speakers in Rutland during the period of the settlement. Large numbers of Scandinavians settling in an already highly populated area could possibly have been swamped linguistically. But by 1086, at least in the Martinsley and Witchley wapentakes, the density of population in Rutland was similar to that of much of the more southerly

---

meaning, his verb *pandere* is correctly inflected in its context and consistent with his style. There the problem of *pandunt* must rest.

Whether the York Vikings already held sway over Rutland at this date or whether they were overrunning it prior to taking it into their possession, the territory appears to be regarded by Æthelweard as English and still part of the kingdom of Mercia. Certainly it does not seem to be a province occupied by Danes. It is most unlikely that York Vikings would be plundering the possessions and settlements of their fellow Scandinavians living in the East Midlands. Hugh Pagan has suggested that after the 877 division of Mercia, Ceolwulf still controlled Lincoln (see *Anglo-Saxon Monetary History*, ed. M.A.S. Blackburn (Leicester, 1986), p. 63 and n. 33). This is difficult to accept. Even so, the conventional historical wisdom that when Mercia was divided in 877, Ceolwulf retained only the western part of the kingdom and the Danes took the entire East Midlands (as well as land further south and south-east, i.e. dependent land around Northampton, Bedford and London) must at present be held in serious question. At just what date Stamford, whose town lands were once so obviously part of the ancient territory of Rutland, became a Danish borough also remains a problem.

30   We may also note the lost *Normandale* in Tixover parish on River Welland, six miles south-west of Stamford. Although first recorded as late as 1770 (Lincoln, Lincs. Archives Office, Aswarby D/13/4), this is most probably OE *Norðmanna-dæl* 'the valley of the Norwegians'.

Northamptonshire[31] where we find a fair spread of early major Scandinavian place-names. It is difficult, therefore, to accept that Scandinavians were linguistically absorbed in Rutland but not in neighbouring Northamptonshire unless the Anglo-Saxon population of pre-Viking Northamptonshire was for some reason exceptionally sparse and that for Rutland exceptionally dense. It is instructive also to note the difference in kind of the Scandinavian place-names of Northamptonshire in contrast to those of Rutland. Discounting its thirty-three later place-names in *þorp*, Northamptonshire boasts six (possibly seven) Grimston-hybrids as well as three Carlton-hybrids and sixteen place-names in -*bý*.[32] This indicates early Scandinavian expropriation of land on a significant scale in the county as well as some considerable settlement.

Overall, the thrust of the evidence suggests that Rutland retained its English integrity throughout the period of the Scandinavian invasions and settlements and that what was once the territory of Rōta continued, apparently without hindrance, to be extensively exploited by Anglo-Saxon husbandmen.

APPENDIX

A GAZETTEER OF SCANDINAVIAN PLACE-NAMES IN RUTLAND

Abbreviations

Abbreviations in italics denote manuscript sources.

Ass	Assize Rolls for Rutland in the Public Record Office, London. (Place-name forms collected by J.E.B. Gover.)
Ass	Assize Rolls in various publications
BCS	W. de G. Birch, *Cartularium Saxonicum*, 3 vols. (London, 1885–93)
Blore	T. Blore, *History and Antiquities of the County of Rutland* (Stamford, 1811)
Bru	Brudenell Manuscripts in Northamptonshire Record Office, Northampton
Ch	*Calendar of Charter Rolls* (PRO), (London, 1903–27)
Ct	Court Rolls for Rutland in PRO, (ex-Gover)
Cur	Curia Regis Rolls (PRO), in progress.
Dane	F.M. Stenton, *Documents Illustrative of the Social and Economic History of the Danelaw* (London, 1920)
DB	*Domesday Book: Rutland*, ed. F. Thorn (Chichester, 1980)
DC	Dean and Chapter of Lincoln Cathedral Muniments in Lincolnshire Archives Office, Lincoln
Dugd	W. Dugdale, *Monasticon Anglicanum*, 6 vols. (London, 1817–30)

---

[31] *The Domesday Geography of Midland England*, ed. H.C. Darby and I.B. Terrett (Cambridge, 1954), p. 378.
[32] Fellows-Jensen, *Scandinavian Settlement Names in the East Midlands*, pp. 244–57.

el.	Place-name element
FF	Feet of Fines for Rutland in PRO, (ex-Gover)
For	*Select Pleas of the Forest*, Publ. of the Selden Soc. 13 (1901)
Ipm	*Calendar of Inquisitions post mortem* (PRO), in progress
IpmR	*Inquisitiones post mortem*, Publ. of the Record Commission (London, 1808–28)
KCD	J.M. Kemble, *Codex Diplomaticus Aevi Saxonici*, 6 vols. (London, 1839–48)
Lei	Miscellaneous deeds in Leicestershire Record Office, Leicester
Misc	*Calendar of Miscellaneous Inquisitions* (PRO), in progress
OIcel	Old Icelandic
P	*Pipe Rolls* (Pipe Roll Soc.), in progress
(p)	Place-name used as a personal name (e.g. Willelmus de Westhorp')
Pat	*Calendar of Patent Rolls* (PRO), in progress
pers.n.	Personal name
Pleas	*Select Civil Pleas A.D. 1200–3*, Publ. of the Selden Soc. 3 (1890)
PRO	(Publ. of) the Public Record Office
QW	*Placita de quo warranto*, Publ. of the Record Commission (London, 1818)
Reg	*Regesta regum Anglo-Normannorum* (Oxford, 1913, 1956).
RHug	*Rotuli Hugonis de Welles Episcopi Lincolniensis*, Publ. of the Lincoln Record Soc. 3 and 6 (1912 and 1913)
S	P.H. Sawyer, *Anglo-Saxon Charters: an Annotated List and Bibliography* (London, 1968)
Sale	Sale particulars for Ketton, Leics. Record Office, DE 1797/4/124.
Scand	Scandinavian
Speed	J. Speed, *The Theatre of the Empire of Great Britain* (London, 1611–12)
SR	Subsidy Rolls for Rutland in PRO, (ex-Gover)
Surv	A survey of Greetham, Leics. Record Office, DE 7/1/71
Terrier	A terrier for Ketton, Lincs. Archives Office, Ter 20/13
Val	*The Valuation of Norwich*, ed. W.E. Lunt (Oxford, 1926)
WDB	'Westminster Domesday Book', London, Westminster Abbey, W.A. Muniment Book 11
Wyg	Wyggeston Hospital Records, Leics. Record Office

Major names

ALSTHORPE (lost – Burley)	Alestanestorp 1086 DB, Alestanthorp 1282 IpmR, Alestorp 1232 RHug. The first el. is the OE pers.n. *(E)alhstān*.
BARLEYTHORPE	Thorp iuxta Ocham *c.*1200 *WDB*, Bolaresthorp 1203 *FF*, Barlithorp 1286 *Ass*. Originally the simplex Scand *þorp*, 'outlying farmstead', but also known by the family name of John *le Bolour* who is mentioned in connection with Oakham *c.*1200 *WDB*. Later, the alternative OE prefix *bærlic* 'barley' was added.
BELMESTHORPE (Ryhall)	Beolmesðorp 1042–55 (12) KCD 927, S 1481, Belmestorp(e) 1086 DB, 1230 Blore.

The first el. is the OE pers.n. *Beornhelm*.

FREGSTHORPE
(lost – Ketton)

Fregisthorp(e) 1322 *Wyg*, 1550 Pat, Fregthorp 1611 Speed, Fregsthorpe 1638 *DC*.

The first el. is a Scand pers.n. *Friðgestr* which appears in late Old English sources as *Friðegist*, *Freðegyst*. According to Domesday Book, one Fredgis held land in Empingham (which is in the same wapentake) in the reign of Edward the Confessor.

GLASTON

Gladeston 1086 DB, Glathestun *c*.1100 Dugd, Glaðestunne mid-12 BCS 22, S 68, Gladston 1203 *FF*.

The first el. is the Scand pers.n. *Glaðr*, found only in Norwegian place-names.

GUNTHORPE

Gunetorp' 1200 Pleas, Gunnetorp 1269 Pat.

The first el. is the Scand pers.n. *Gunni*.

INGTHORPE
(Tinwell)

Ingelthorp 1189 (1332) Ch, Ingetorp 1203 Ass, Ingethorpe 1227 Ch.

The first el. is probably the Scand pers.n. *Ingi*. But if the 1189 form is significant, the first el. could be the OE pers.n. *Ingeld* or Scand *Ingjaldr*.

KILTHORPE
(Ketton)

Ketelistorp *c*.1250 *Ct*, Ketelesthorp 1296 *SR*, Ketillisthorp 1296 *SR* (p).

The first el. is the Scand pers.n. *Ketill*, an original by-name; cf. OIcel *ketill* 'cauldron, cauldron-shaped helmet'.

MANTHORPE
(lost – Ketton)

Manthorpe Bridge 1677 *Terrier*, Manthorpe Hill 1919 *Sale*.

The first el. is either the Scand pers.n. *Manni* or the Scand or OE gen. pl. *manna* 'of the men'.

MARTINSTHORPE

Martinestorp' 1206 Cur (p), 1218 For, Martinstorp' 1254 Val, (Martinestoch 1176 P (p), Martinstok 1286 *Ass*, 1286 QW).

The first el. is the medieval Latin pers.n. *Martin* which was borrowed into Old English. An earlier place-name in OE *stoc* 'a dairy farm' seems to have been Scandinavianized to a name in *þorp* 'an outlying farmstead'.

NORMANTON

Normenton 1180 P (p), Nort(h)manton 1295 Ipm, 1327 *SR*, Normanneton 1375 Misc.

An Old English place-name whose first el. is *Norðman*, -*manna* (gen. pl.) 'a Norwegian, of the Norwegians'.

SCULTHORPE
(N. Luffenham)

Sculetorp 1086 DB, Scultorp' *c*.1160 Dane.

The first el. is the Scand pers.n. *Skúli*.

THORPE BY WATER

Torp 1086 DB, Thorp 1297 Ass, -by the Watre 1428 *FF*.

A simplex Scand *þorp* 'outlying farmstead'; later distinguished by its proximity to the waters of River Welland.

TOLETHORPE
(Little Casterton)

Toltorp 1086 DB, Toletorp 1202 Ass.

The first el. is the Scand pers.n. *Tóli*, a short form of names such as Þorlakr, Þorleikr, Þorlaugr.

WESTHORPE
(Wing)

Westhorp' 1296 *SR* (p).

'The western outlying farmstead'.

WING

Weng(e) 1136–9 Reg, 1202 Ass, (cf. into wengeforde 1046 (12) KCD 784, S 1014).

This name is the Scand appellative *vengi* a derivative of *vangr* 'a field', probably used here of one of the large fields of a village.

Minor names

HOOBY LODGE
(Stretton)

Hooby(e), Hoobie 1633 *Bru*, the Hubyes 1646 *Lei*, Hoobye Hedge furlong 1652 *Surv*.

Perhaps a compound of OE *hōh* 'a spur of land, a headland' with Scand *bý* 'a farmstead'. Otherwise a family or transferred name.

OSBONALL WOOD
(Clipsham)

Osburneall Wood 1611 Speed.

The first el. is possibly the Scand pers.n. *Ásbjǫrn* with anglicization by substitution of the cognate OE *Ōs-* for Scand *Ás-*. But equally we may have here its later medieval reflex *Osbern*. This was also common in Normandy and brought to England by the Normans after the Conquest.

TURTLE BRIDGE
(Barrowden)

Thurkelbregge 1298 Ipm, Turtles Bridge 1762 *Anc*.

The first el. is a reduced form of the Scand pers.n. *Þorketill* (giving *Þorkell*) used as a family name. Ralph *Turcle* is mentioned in connection with the neighbouring Northamptonshire parish of Harringworth in 1247 *Ass*.

The Five Boroughs of the Danelaw: a review of present knowledge

R.A. HALL

The increase in urban archaeological work during the last twenty years has both illuminated many facets of pre-Norman life and demonstrated the development of individual sites to an extent hardly conceivable before.[1] Nevertheless, the only well-defined group of sites to have received concentrated attention has been the *burhs* of Wessex. Prompted by Biddle's work at Winchester and Hill's elucidation of the *Burghal Hidage*, the establishment of a network of fortified centres and its development into an urban hierarchy in which the component sites variously played commercial, industrial, administrative and ecclesiastical roles has been charted in some detail.[2] Beyond the frontiers of Wessex, Atkin has drawn together the available data from East Anglia.[3] Rahtz has briefly presented the excavated evidence from the towns of the West Midlands, 'English Mercia';[4] within the area of Mercia that was to become the south-eastern Danelaw (Bedfordshire, Cambridgeshire, Huntingdonshire and Northamptonshire), Williams has surveyed the new evidence for the urban development of Northampton, the best understood centre in the region,[5] while Haslam has suggested that Bedford and Cambridge are examples of a group of sites, numbering a dozen or more and spread across pre-Viking Mercia, where urban origins can be traced back to deliberate

---

[1] Compare *The Erosion of History*, ed. C.M. Heighway (London, 1972); *Recent Archaeological Research in English Towns* ed. J. Schofield and D. Palliser, CBA Research Report (London, 1981); and *Urban Archaeology in Britain*, ed. J. Schofield and R. Leech, CBA Research Report 61 (London, 1987), for an index of the scale of recent work.

[2] See, e.g., M. Biddle and D. Hill, 'Late Saxon Planned Towns', *AntJ* 51 (1971), 70–85; F. Barlow, *et al.*, *Winchester in the Early Middle Ages*, Winchester Stud. 1, ed. M. Biddle (Oxford, 1976); and D. Hill, 'Trends in the Development of Towns During the Reign of Ethelred II' *Ethelred the Unready* ed. D. Hill, BAR Brit. ser. 59 (Oxford, 1978), 213–26.

[3] M. Atkin, 'The Anglo-Saxon Urban Landscape in East Anglia', *Landscape Hist.* 7 (1985), 27–40.

[4] P. Rahtz, 'The Archaeological of West Mercian towns', *Mercian Studies*, ed. A. Dornier (Leicester, 1977), pp. 107–30.

[5] J.H. Williams, 'From "Palace" to "Town": Northampton and Urban Origins', *ASE* 13 (1984), 113–36; see also his 'A Review of Some Aspects of Late Saxon Urban Origins and Development', *Studies in Late Anglo-Saxon Settlement*, ed. M.L. Faull (Oxford, 1984), pp. 25–34.

foundation by Offa.[6] North of the Humber, York has a singular position; it is the only important Northumbrian urban centre mentioned in late Anglo-Saxon historical sources, and seems to have achieved a sustained regional pre-eminence greater even than that of Winchester in Wessex. It has recently been reviewed;[7] there is also a recent study of London.[8]

Within the East Midlands, 'the essential Danelaw',[9] there is contemporary historical evidence for the existence of a well-defined group of *burhs* (see fig. 3). This is the Five Boroughs, the modern towns of Derby, Leicester, Lincoln, Nottingham and Stamford, which all lie within the area settled by part of the Viking *micel here* in 877, and which were regained for the English by Æthelflæd's campaigns of 917 and 918.[10] Historical sources do not shed light on the status of any of the Five Boroughs in the Viking period of their existence, and following their recapture there is a further silence until they are collectively and individually referred to in the *Anglo-Saxon Chronicle*'s entry for 942 which celebrates how King Edmund freed the Danes in the area from Norse tyranny, i.e. from the rule of York's Viking kings. The alliterative form of this entry makes it unlikely that it was altered after the annals for this period were finalised *c.* 955.[11] That this grouping was no mere device of the poet who composed the passage is shown by its appearance in other, slightly later sources, of which the earliest is the law-code of Æthelred II issued at Wantage in the period 978–1008.[12] It appears again in the *Anglo-Saxon Chronicle*'s entry for 1013, which was probably composed *c.* 1016–23;[13] here, a distinction is drawn between the various regions of the Danelaw, which include the Five Boroughs, Lindsey, Northumbria and other Danish settlers north of Watling Street (i.e. the south-east Danelaw and East Anglia). A phrase probably of related and inclusive meaning also occurs in the *Chronicle*'s account of

---

[6] J. Haslam, 'The Origin and Plan of Bedford', *Bedfordshire Archaeol.* 16 (1983) 28–36; 'The Ecclesiastical Topography of Early Medieval Bedford', *Bedfordshire Archaeol.* 19 (1986), 41–50; 'The Development and Topography of Saxon Cambridge', *Proc. of the Cambridge Ant. Soc.* 72 (1982–3), 13–29, esp. p. 26, n.3.

[7] See R.A. Hall, 'York 700–1050', *The Rebirth of Towns in the West AD 700–1050*, ed. B. Hobley and R. Hodges, CBA Research Report 68 (London, 1988), 125–32; and 'The Making of Domesday York', *Anglo-Saxon Settlements*, ed. D.M. Hooke (Oxford, 1988), pp. 233–47.

[8] T. Dyson and J. Schofield, 'Saxon London', *Anglo-Saxon Towns*, ed. J. Haslam (Chichester, 1984), pp. 249–84.

[9] F.M. Stenton, 'The Danes in England', *PBA* 13 (1927), 203–46, at 213.

[10] Events described in the *Anglo-Saxon Chronicle* are quoted by the year to which they are attributed in *The Anglo-Saxon Chronicle*, ed. D. Whitelock *et al.* (London, 1961).

[11] F.M. Stenton, *Anglo-Saxon England*, 3rd ed. (Oxford, 1971), p. 689.

[12] *English Historical Documents* c. *500–1042*, ed. D. Whitelock, Eng. Hist. Documents 1, 2nd ed. (London, 1979), no. 43.

[13] S.D. Keynes, 'The Declining Reputation of King Ethelred the Unready', *Ethelred the Unready*, ed. Hill, pp. 227–54, at 231.

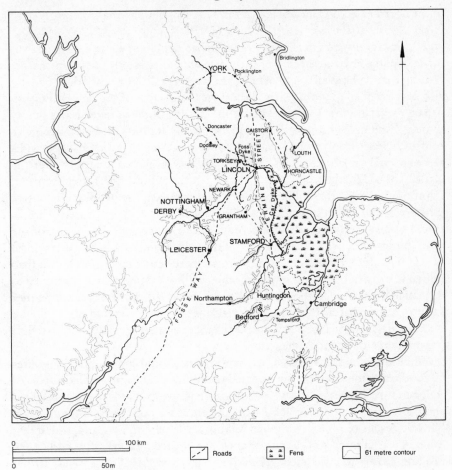

0   100 km

0   50m

Roads   Fens   61 metre contour

FIG. 3   The Five Boroughs and noteworthy contemporary sites in eastern England

Æthelred II's reign, *s.a.* 1015, where the Seven Boroughs are uniquely mentioned in connection with the death of the two thegns Sigeferth and Morcar. Both Whitelock and Stenton believed that this group included the Five Boroughs, and suggested, with varying degrees of assurance, that the other two were Torksey and York.[14] The issue is not clarified by the occurrence of the term Five Boroughs, also in connection with these two thegns, later in the same *Chronicle* entry, but the only likely alternative to the theory that the Seven Boroughs comprised the Five Boroughs and two others

---

[14] *Chronicle*, ed. Whitelock, *et al.*, p. 94, n. 1; Stenton, *Anglo-Saxon England*, p. 388, n. 2.

in the north-eastern Danelaw is that the Seven Boroughs was a name given to either a part or the whole of English Mercia.[15]

The desirability of a general survey of urban development in the Danelaw is made apparent by a gathering of the views and conclusions of commentators writing before the availability of new, archaeologically generated data, and has also been implied in more recent discussion. The views of the earliest English urban historians, that the boroughs of Domesday Book were relics of a purely military system,[16] and that they were essentially military and administrative centres,[17] were followed by Kendrick, who suggested that the Five Boroughs were specially fortified towns, established as Viking headquarters after the settlement of Mercia in 876, and that four southern boroughs (Northampton, Cambridge, Bedford and Huntingdon) were similarly created for a defensive purpose after Guthrum's settlement in 879; he also suggested that Alfred's policy of *burh*-building was imitative of these Danish *burhs*.[18] The use of the term 'town' to translate the meaning of the Old English *burh/burg* was typical of his day, and would seem to imply that these settlements were more than military bases; but nevertheless it was their military aspect which continued to dominate discussion, although Stephenson retreated slightly from his earlier view to allow that a handful of larger Danelaw towns, including York and Lincoln, had such a large Scandinavian element in their population as to reflect the existence of Scandinavian trade.[19]

While allowing that the siting of some *burhs* on good communication routes allowed trade to develop, Tait stressed the military and administrative role of the Scandinavian *burhs*, 'the well-chosen centres which the Danes had fortified and made district capitals';[20] and again the emphasis was purely military when Shetelig, in his Norwegian view of Viking settlement in England, stated that 'Mercia was allotted to other chieftains, as a confederation of five earls, each residing in his town, called "The Five Boroughs"'.[21] There is no further mention of a role played as a group by these settlements in later pre-Norman England.

Leading figures among the next generation of English historians had

[15] It has recently been suggested that the Seven Boroughs comprise the Five plus Doncaster and Manchester: see M.S. Parker, 'Some Notes on the Pre-Norman History of Doncaster', *Yorkshire Archaeol. Jnl* 59 (1987), 29–44, at 32–6.
[16] F.W. Maitland, 'The Origin of the Town', *EHR* 11 (1896), 13–19, at 13; *Domesday Book and Beyond* (Cambridge, 1897), pp. 172–219.
[17] C.W. Stephenson, 'The Anglo-Saxon Borough', *EHR* 45 (1930), 177–207, at 177.
[18] T.D. Kendrick, *A History of the Vikings* (London, 1930), pp. 236–41.
[19] C.W. Stephenson, *Borough and Town* (Cambridge, Mass., 1933), pp. 189–93.
[20] J. Tait, *The Medieval English Borough* (Manchester, 1936), p. 25.
[21] H. Shetelig, *Viking Antiquities in Great Britain and Ireland Part 1. An Introduction to the Viking History of Western Europe* (Oslo, 1940), p. 84.

nothing beyond historical précis to add on the subject of the Five Boroughs or, indeed, of York, and it is from this point that archaeologists have dominated the discussion of English urbanism in the pre-Conquest period. Biddle and Hill's thesis about planned towns in Wessex included the comment that 'the urban development of eastern and northern England in late Saxon times seems to have followed different lines, conditioned by other factors, not least the Danish occupation, the lack of a centralised authority, and commercial contacts with the continent'.[22] Yet the details of this Danelaw development remained enigmatic. As Biddle wrote:

> Even less [than very little] is currently known of the fortified centres established by the Danes in the eastern midlands . . . in none of them can the character and topography of the ninth-century Danish settlement be defined with any precision. In tracing the evolution of the pre-Conquest Town it clearly makes a great difference whether the Five Boroughs were urban foundations of the Danish period or whether their urban element was created by Edward the Elder in the early tenth century, in the aftermath of the construction of the Wessex *burhs*. Were the Danish fortifications fortresses or towns?[23]

This study will review the current state of knowledge of the Five Boroughs, drawing on the work of many excavators and excavation units: I am most grateful to those who have discussed their work with me.[24] For the most part, however, published sources or personal observation form the basis for the synthesis presented here, which is the author's sole responsibility.

DERBY
Origins

Apart from some evidence, sparse at present, for an Iron Age settlement in the vicinity of Derby Racecourse,[25] the earliest concentration of activity in the immediate vicinity of what is now central Derby was first-century Roman

---

[22] Biddle and Hill, 'Late Saxon Planned Towns', p.84.

[23] M. Biddle, 'Towns', *The Archaeology of Anglo-Saxon England*, ed. D.M. Wilson (Cambridge, 1976), pp. 99–150, at 122–3.

[24] I am indebted to archaeologists and historians studying this area for discussing their work with me, although I take full responsibility for the interpretations presented here. They include Christopher Green (Little Chester), Jean Mellor and Terry Pearce (Leicester), Michael Jones and John Wacher (Lincoln), Charles Young, Victoria Nailor and Christopher Drage (Nottingham), and Christine Mahany and David Roffe (Stamford). I have also benefited from Martin Biddle's editorial suggestions. David Patrick kindly drew the accompanying illustrations. The study was prepared for publication during a period of study leave granted by York Archaeological Trust, for which I am most grateful.

[25] J. Dool, 'Derby Racecourse: Excavations on the Roman Industrial Settlement, 1970', *Derbyshire Archaeol. Jnl* 105 (1985), 155–221, at 181.

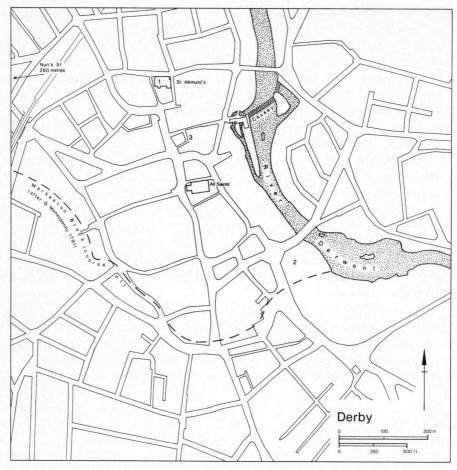

FIG. 4 Derby, showing the locations of sites referred to in the text

occupation 1km to the north-west of the medieval town at Strutt's Park, the probable site of a Neronian fort controlling access to the Peak District *via* the valley of the River Derwent.[26] Within decades this fort had been resited on the opposite bank of the River Derwent as Little Chester (Derventio), where the earliest recorded pottery is of the Flavian period.[27] The reason for this change of location is not clear. The fort, its *vicus* and a nearby industrial complex below

[26] M. Brassington, 'First-Century Roman Occupation at Strutt's Park, Derby', *Derbyshire Archaeol. Jnl* 90 (1970), 22–30, at 25.

[27] G. Webster, 'An Excavation on the Roman Site at Little Chester, Derby, 1960', *Derbyshire Archaeol. Jnl* 81 (1961), 85–110, at 109: H. Wheeler, 'Conclusion: the Development of Roman Derby', *Derbyshire Archaeol. Jnl* 105 (1985), 300–4, at 300.

the modern Derby Racecourse Fields were occupied into the mid fourth century.[28]

Early and mid-Saxon activity

There is no evidence for continuity of occupation in the fifth century, but Little Chester was again a focus for activity in the pagan Saxon period. An inhumation cemetery of seventeen graves attributed to the sixth century has been excavated by Green in and around a late Roman colonnaded structure outside the south-east defences of the fort.[29] No traces of contemporary occupation have been found, but this is not surprising in view of the small amount of excavation undertaken, particularly within the fort.

While there is no coherent historical narrative dealing with Derby's role in the mid-Saxon period, sporadic later literary references illuminate specific events. Æthelweard's *Chronicle*, composed at the end of the tenth century,[30] reports that in 871 the body of Æthelwulf, ealdorman of Berkshire, who had been killed in battle with the Danes at Reading, was carried away secretly into Mercia 'in loco qui Northworthige nuncupatur, iuxta autem Danaam linguam Deoraby'.[31] This passage does not, of course, imply that the Danes were taking any special interest in the site in 871; rather it demonstrates that the site exerted an attraction which led Æthelwulf's retinue to transport his body for a considerable distance.[32]

The name Northworthy, 'the northern enclosure', continues to puzzle, and a variety of explanations has been proposed. If Northworthy is equated with the area occupied by the town in 1066, around the churches of St Alkmund's and All Saints, its name cannot have been given to distinguish it from the Roman camp at Little Chester, which is to the north-east. Cameron has suggested that the name was given in relation to the River Trent;[33] Hart has suggested that it was the 'capital' of the kingdom of North Mercia mentioned by Bede (*HE* III. 24), and was so called to distinguish it from that of the South Mercians which, he suggests, was at Tamworth;[34] and Roffe has suggested that the name reflects the site's relation to Repton, a pre-Viking monastery and royal mausoleum subsequently turned into a fortified Viking winter encampment in 873–4.[35] None of these hypotheses seems completely convincing.

[28] Wheeler, 'Conclusion', p. 304.
[29] R. Birss and H. Wheeler, 'Introduction', *Derbyshire Archaeol. Jnl* 105 (1985), 7–14, at 11; Wheeler, 'Conclusion', p. 304.
[30] *The Chronicle of Æthelweard*, ed. A. Campbell (London, 1962), p. xiii, n. 2.
[31] 'to the place called Northworthy, but in the Danish language Derby'.
[32] 140km as the crow flies.
[33] K. Cameron, *The Place-Names of Derbyshire*, EPNS 28 (Cambridge, 1959), 446.
[34] C. Hart, 'The Kingdom of Mercia', *Mercian Studies*, ed. Dornier, pp. 43–62, at 53.
[35] D. Roffe, 'The Origins of Derbyshire', *Derbyshire Archaeol. Jnl* 106 (1986), 102–22, at 111.

Æthelwulf was a Mercian – he was already an ealdorman in 844 when the Mercian king Berhtwulf granted him land in Berkshire[36] – and this may explain his link with the locale, which could be a purely secular one. Northworthy/ Derby may have been his estate or residence: through an analysis of the parochial structure in the vicinity Roffe has identified a possible pre-Viking estate there.[37] This may have been associated with an important religious centre, a minster church, and such a centre is documented in the Old English *List of Saints' Resting Places*, which was compiled in its present form by *c.* 1031, although based on earlier, undated components.[38] This records that 'Ealhmund rests at Northworthy'. The background to this statement is known only through the compilations of later chroniclers. A set of northern annals for 732–802, incorporated in Byrhtferth of Ramsey's historical miscellany (a work subsequently embedded in the *Historia Regum* attributed to Simeon of Durham),[39] records *s.a.* 800: 'Alchmund, filius Alcredi regis, ut dicunt quidam, a tutoribus Eardulfi regis est apprehensus eiusque iussione cum suis profugis occisus est.'[40] According to still later tradition, Ealhmund was killed in the battle of Kempsford in 802, and was buried first at the White Monastery (Lilleshall, Shropshire) and then at Derby, 'in the north church built in his name.'[41] The Lilleshall reference may, however, stem from a Norman or later confusion,[42] and it is possible that he was never interred there.

In conjunction, the *List of Saints' Resting Places* and the *Historia Regum* indicate that Ealhmund was killed *c.* 800 and venerated at Derby before *c.* 1031. Even if the translation from Lilleshall to Derby is fictitious, the date by which Ealhmund's body reached Derby is uncertain. The use in the *List of Saints' Resting Places* of the name form Northworthy, rather than Derby, might suggest that it arrived before the Scandinavian take-over, but this is questionable since it is not known how long the older name remained current. Nonetheless, there is evidence for an early ninth-century religious presence on

---

[36] P.H. Sawyer, *Anglo-Saxon Charters: an Annotated List and Bibliography*, R. Hist. Soc. Guides and Handbooks 8 (London, 1968), no. 1271; *English Historical Documents*, ed. Whitelock, no. 87.

[37] D. Roffe, *The Derbyshire Domesday* (Matlock, 1986), pp. 23–5.

[38] D.W. Rollason, 'Lists of Saints' Resting-places in Anglo-Saxon England', *ASE* 7 (1978), 61–93, at 68.

[39] See M. Lapidge, 'Byrhtferth of Ramsey and the Early Sections of the *Historia Regum* Attributed to Simeon of Durham', *ASE* 10 (1982), 97–122; see also *English Historical Documents*, ed. Whitelock, p. 127, and no. 3 (a).

[40] 'Alhmund, son of King Alhred [of Northumbria] was seized, as some say by agents of King Eardwulf, and on his order was killed by his fellow exiles.'

[41] See D.W. Rollason, 'The Cults of Murdered Royal Saints in Anglo-Saxon England,' *ASE* 11 (1983), 1–22, at 4 n.13, and 5 n. 17, citing the *Vita Ælkmundi*; a similar story is reported by Ranulf Higden, in his *Polychronicon* (compiled in the middle of the fourteenth century).

[42] See Rollason, 'Cults of Murdered Royal Saints' p. 5 n. 17.

the site later known as St Alkmund's church (1),[43] on the north side of the medieval town of Derby, and this may have been the magnet which attracted the body of Ealdorman Æthelwulf.

Excavation of the site of the Victorian and medieval St Alkmund's church revealed that the earliest recognizable structure was a two-cell stone building, possibly with porticus to south and north.[44] The date of this structure is uncertain. The chancel wall incorporated two fragments of pre-Conquest sculpture, thought to be of ninth-century style, but the date of their use here as building rubble is unknown. It is, however, the recovery of these pieces and others, including an elaborately carved coffin of *c.* 800 which had been filled with rubble and buried in the south-east corner of the nave at an unknown date thought by the excavator to be in the twelfth century,[45] which suggests strongly that there was a church here from the ninth century, dedicated to St Alkmund, and therefore that this area is the Northworthy referred to by Æthelweard and in the *List of Saints' Resting Places*.

Anglo-Scandinavian Derby

Derby's earliest appearance in a contemporary source is in the Mercian Register section of the *Anglo-Saxon Chronicle*, for the year 917. At that date it was a centre of Danish resistance, captured by Æthelflæd after a battle in which four of her thegns were killed within the gates. The area's first serious visitation by the Scandinavians had probably been in 873, for the *Chronicle* records that in 874 the Viking army took up winter quarters at Repton, drove out the Mercian king Burgred, then conquered all Mercia.[46] Derby, already an important ecclesiastical site if nothing else, can hardly have failed to interest a Viking army based only 9.5 km away. After a two-year respite, the Viking army returned to Mercia in 877 and settled in its eastern part, which included Derby. Their interest in the site is not, however, explicitly mentioned until 917; in 942, when Derby is next recorded in the *Chronicle*, it is as one of the five *burhs* re-taken by King Edmund after the invasion of Olaf Guthfrithsson. The *Chronicle*'s only other pre-Conquest reference to the site is the report of an earthquake at Derby, Worcester and Droitwich in 1048.

Domesday Book records two churches at Derby in royal ownership with the status of *minster*, and although neither is named there, evidence in the cartulary of Darley Abbey, compiled *c.* 1275, indicates that one was St Alkmund's and

---

[43] Numbers in brackets within the text refer to the relevant town plan, where the site in question is indicated by this number.

[44] C.A.R. Radford, 'The Church of St Alkmund, Derby', *Derbyshire Archaeol. Jnl* 96 (1976), 26–61, at 31–2.   [45] *Ibid.* pp. 35–7.

[46] For a brief discussion of the correct dating of these annals see *Chronicle*, ed. Whitelock *et al.*, p. xxiv.

the other All Saints.[47] The foundation of St Alkmund's by *c.* 800, as implied by the sarcophagus found there, indicates that it was one of the earlier stratum of minster churches associated with royal or aristocratic estate centres.[48] As noted above, Æthelwulf's burial might suggest that it was an aristocratic foundation associated with his family; alternatively, the political ramifications of burying and venerating a Northumbrian prince suggest the hand of Mercian royalty and perhaps, by extension, that St Alkmund's was a royal foundation.

The other information contained in Domesday Book's reference to Derby as it was in 1066 has been described as 'only fragments of information which do not constitute an ordered survey'.[49] Two hundred and forty-three resident burgesses were recorded, forty-one of whom had shares in the twelve carucates of land belonging to the *burh*. In addition to St Alkmund's and All Saints churches, one of which had seven and the other six priests, at least four other churches seem to have been in existence by 1066, since in 1086 they had each had one previous owner. There were fourteen mills, and the town rendered £24 to the king.

These statistics are of little help in assessing the role which Derby played in the Anglo-Scandinavian period. The fact that in 1086 there were 143 burgesses and 103 waste tenements, equivalent to the number of burgesses in 1066, allows the equation of burgess with tenement to be made here with conviction, and thus indicates that in 1066 Derby was a settlement of at least 243 properties, with a population of perhaps 1,000–1,500. In size the town was then broadly comparable to other Danelaw centres with population or housing/tenement statistics recorded in Domesday Book's entries for 1066, such as Cambridge, Huntingdon, Leicester, Nottingham, Stamford and Torksey.

There have been few attemps to investigate Viking-age Derby by excavation. On the basis of a single penny of *c.* 900 struck at York, it seems possible that activity around the early ninth-century church of St Alkmund continued in the tenth century, although it has been suggested that the Viking Age saw neglect or destruction of the church.[50] Excavation in the south-east corner of the town at Full Street (2) demonstrated that occupation there commenced in the later eleventh century;[51] investigation in the car park of St

[47] *The Cartulary of Darley Abbey*, ed. R.R. Darlington (Derby, 1945), p. 164.

[48] J. Blair, 'Secular Minster Churches in Domesday Book', *Domesday Book: a Reassessment* ed. P. Sawyer (London, 1985), pp. 104–42, esp. 116.

[49] D. Holly, 'Derbyshire', *The Domesday Geography of Northern England*, ed. H.C. Darby and I.S. Maxwell (Cambridge, 1962), pp. 278–329, at 322.

[50] Radford, 'St Alkmunds', pp. 42 and 34.

[51] R.A. Hall and G. Coppack, 'Excavations at Full Street, Derby, 1972', *Derbyshire Archaeol. Jnl* 92 (1972), 29–77.

Michael's church (3) was thwarted by the total obliteration of all archaeological deposits by cellars and other features.[52]

This sparse archaeological record of the pre-Norman period is not credibly augmented by other chance finds in the vicinity. A fourth-to-seventh-century pilgrim's flask from the shrine of St Menas at Karm Abu Mina, on the edge of the Libyan desert, was found in Nuns Street in 1949; it could have entered England at any time from the late Roman period onwards, but in view of the proximity of the Benedictine nunnery of St Mary, founded *c.* 1160, it is most likely to be a post-Conquest importation.[53] The origins of the so-called 'Derby' runic inscribed bone mounting, ascribed to the period 700–1000, are equally nebulous – it has no firmer connection with the town than that it first came to general notice whilst in the possession of a former resident, and must therefore be discounted here.[54]

Only the identification of St Alkmund's and All Saints churches are of use in locating the area of the *burh* as it was in 1066. St Alkmund's, 'the north church' where Ealhmund was buried, may not have been on the north of the pre-Norman settlement, but was presumably within or close to the main concentration of occupation, as presumably was All Saints. Until the relocation of St Alkmund's in the late 1960s, both occupied a relatively elevated position with potential for defence. The River Derwent formed a barrier to the east; there is no evidence for a pre-Conquest bridge, and it is possible that the ford, known later as the Causey, may have been the crossing point in the pre-Norman period. Indeed the settlement shift from the Little Chester area to the All Saints/St Alkmund's area may have been inspired by the decay of the Roman bridge thought to have existed north of Little Chester[55] and the need for a defensible position controlling an alternative crossing point. Water may also have provided a natural barrier to the west and south, where the Markeaton Brook and its tributaries curve sharply to define a promontory before joining the Derwent. With or without the addition of a rampart, settlement here would be protected on three sides, and it would require only the erection of an earthwork across the neck of the promontory to defend it against assault from the north. To date, however, there is no archaeological evidence to substantiate these hypotheses.

In contrast with the paucity of pre-Conquest evidence from the area of the post-Conquest town, C.J.S. Green's excavations at Little Chester have

---

[52] C. Drage, pers. comm.

[53] R.S.M. O'Ferrall, 'A Pilgrim's Flask Found in Derby', *Jnl of the Derbyshire Archaeol. and Nat. Hist. Soc.* 71 (1951), 78–9; D. Knowles and R.N. Hadcock, *Medieval Religious Houses, England and Wales* (London, 1971), p. 258.

[54] J.M. Bately and V.I. Evison, 'The Derby Bone Piece', *MA* 5 (1961), 301–5.

[55] Brassington, 'Strutt's Park', p. 30.

unearthed evidence which may be interpreted as representing activity and possibly occupation in the Anglo-Scandinavian period. A cess-pit containing Stamford and St Neots ware was dug through the ruins of a Roman building outside the East Gate, and a rubble platform added to the south-east corner of the Roman walls sealed sherds of St Neots, Stamford and Thetford-type wares and may be contemporary with them. A narrow ditch immediately south of the platform, following the line of the defences, produced similar pottery.[56]

This evidence raises the question of the role of Little Chester at this time. Stukeley's illustration ostensibly shows that the stone defensive circuit was intact when he visited the site in 1721, and he records that the walls were being blown up during his second visit in 1725;[57] the surviving stonework may have been largely the rubble of the wall-core, for facing stones had earlier been used in the late medieval manor house. Nevertheless, with substantial lengths of the wall still in existence into the early eighteenth century, it is possible, if not probable, that the fortification could have been defensible in the ninth or tenth centuries. The only written evidence for Little Chester's pre-Norman role is Domesday Book's record that the parish of one of the two churches in royal ownership in Derby held two carucates freely at (Little) Chester, thus suggesting that the site had itself been in royal ownership in the pre-Norman period.

Archaeological evidence for activity *within* the fort at this time is minimal – the only discoveries which may possibly relate to this era are five human skeletons found close to the west wall in 1926.[58] Three adult males, one adult female and a child aged about six had been buried, each on an east–west alignment, their feet to the east. There is no record of any objects interred with the bodies, or of coffin fittings. These burials, which lay only 0.75m below the modern surface, could be dated to any period from the Roman onwards, but as there is no reference to a church or burial ground here in the post-Norman period, it is more likely that they pre-date the Norman conquest. Their orientation ostensibly suggests a Christian milieu, but a non-Christian Roman origin cannot be ruled out, as has been pointed out of other similar cemeteries.[59] Although they are perhaps related to settlement here after the conversion of Mercia in the late seventh century this cannot be proved, and Clews's claim for a mid-late Saxon date must be treated with reservation. Nonetheless, the evidence from Green's excavations points to secular activity at Little Chester in the Anglo-Scandinavian period; there are contemporary

---

[56] Birss and Wheeler, 'Introduction', p. 11.

[57] F. J. Haverfield, 'Romano-British Remains', *The Victoria History of the County of Derby* i, ed. W. Page (Oxford, 1905), 191–216, at 216.

[58] C. A. Clews, 'Human Remains, Little Chester', *Jnl of the Derbyshire Archaeol. and Nat. Hist. Soc.* 49 (1927), 376–7.   [59] P Rahtz, 'Grave Orientation', *ArchJ* 135 (1978), 1–14, at 6.

objects from Wheeler's 1979–80 excavations in the north-west sector of the fort;[60] and, as suggested above, Little Chester may well have been defensible at this time.

It is therefore worth considering the possibility that when in 917 Æthelflæd captured what the compiler of the Mercian Register called 'Derby', she was attacking the refurbished Roman fortification at Little Chester. The place-name Derby, synonymous with Northworthy by the late tenth century, if Æthelweard is taken at face value, was already current in the reign of Athelstan (924–39) when it appeared on his coinage in a variety of closely related forms.[61] It is not impossible that this new name of Scandinavian form, combining the elements *by*, 'settlement', and *djur*, 'animal' or 'deer',[62] was given initially by the Scandinavians to the vicinity of Little Chester, and then later transferred to the Anglian settlement of Northworthy, which is certainly to be equated with the Derby of Domesday Book and the modern town centre. In the absence of archaeological evidence this can be only speculation, but it emphasises the need for examination of post-Roman levels at Little Chester as well as the obvious requirement for further excavation within the medieval nucleus of Derby.

The reason for the complete change of name, unique among the late ninth-/ early tenth-century Viking strongholds, continues to puzzle place-name scholars. Jensen suggests, on the basis of onomastic evidence alone, that Derby's position towards the western outskirts of the Danelaw encouraged its Viking settlers to cluster for protection at the *burh* in a way not necessary at their other strong-points, and that this led to a change to a purely Scandinavian name-form. She also sees the striking lack of -*by* place-names around Derby as possible confirmation of this suggestion, although noting the possibility that this absence merely reflects the comparatively swift reconquest of Derbyshire by the English; as she has pointed out elsewhere, however, there is a similar thinning out of -*by* names around the other boroughs.[63] Given the uncertain-

---

60 E.g. a facetted-headed pin with ring and dot ornament (copper-alloy object no. 21), and fragments of bone/antler combs (bone and shale objects nos. 18 and 19); the pin and one of the comb fragments come from topsoil and therefore have no useful archaeological context. H. Wheeler, 'North-west Sector Excavations 1979–1980', *Derbyshire Archaeol. Jnl* 105 (1985), 38–153, at 145–6.

61 C.E. Blunt, 'The Coinage of Athelstan, King of England 924–39', *BNJ* 42 (1974), 35–160, at 94.

62 Cameron, *Place-Names of Derbyshire* p. 446; G.F. Jensen, *Scandinavian Settlement Names in the East Midlands* (Copenhagen, 1978), p. 44.

63 G.F. Jensen, 'Scandinavian Settlement in the Danelaw in the Light of the Place-Names of Denmark', *Proceedings of the Eighth Viking Congress*, ed. H. Bekker-Nielsen *et al.* (Odense, 1981), pp. 133–45, at 141–2; 'Place-Names and Settlements: Some Problems of Dating as Exemplified by Place-Names in -*by*', *Nomina* 8 (1984), 29–40, at 33; and *Scandinavian Settlement Names in the East Midlands*, p. 261.

ties of place-name evidence, notably the relatively late first record of most names and the problem of interpreting distribution patterns of various name types in political or ethnic terms, these remain possible but unverifiable hypotheses.

Once Northworthy/Derby had played out its role as a Scandinavian military centre, its function becomes more difficult to determine. The transfer of its name to the surrounding area (Derbyshire is first recorded in 1049) may merely reflect its early tenth-century role as the rallypoint of a particular group of Scandinavian settlers, but the volume of its coinage as early as the reign of Athelstan (924–39), when minting commenced there, in comparison with the output of contemporary mints in the region such as Nottingham, Tamworth and Leicester, shows that Derby predominated in the striking of coins.[64] It has been pointed out, however, that centres of high mint output were not necessarily an index of commercial activity or general prosperity,[65] and it may be that the reason for Derby's importance in this sphere was its proximity to the lead deposits in the Peak District, which may also have been a source of silver through the use of the cupellation process. The Peak lead deposits were worked in the pre-Viking period – that at Wirksworth was referred to in 835,[66] and in Domesday Book lead mines or renders are mentioned in connection with seven places in the Peak.[67] No archaeological or direct historical evidence exists to prove that cupellation was practised, but it remains a possible explanation of Derby's predominance over the mints of Nottingham, Tamworth and Leicester in the time of Athelstan, a supremacy which, however, virtually disappeared after Edgar's reform of the coinage.[68]

Its mint apart, there is nothing tangible to indicate Derby's economic, social or administrative function in the pre-Norman period, and Darby has commented that 'the salient features of the borough in 1066 may still have been military and agrarian'.[69] There is no direct evidence for industry or a market, although toll was rendered to the king, but this hardly counterbalances the rural aspect presented by references to fourteen mills, twelve carucates, meadowland, underwood and fishery (the last three mentioned in Domesday Book's return for 1086, but presumably equally applicable to the situation in 1066). The evidence at present suggests that Derby was a local centre for the

---

[64] Blunt, 'Coinage of Athelstan', pp. 93–7.
[65] D.M. Metcalf, 'The Ranking of the Boroughs: Numismatic Evidence from the Reign of Æthelred II', *Ethelred the Unready*, ed. Hill, pp. 159–212, at 162–3.
[66] S 1624.   [67] Holly, 'Derbyshire', p. 324.
[68] D.M. Metcalf, 'Continuity and Change in English Monetary History *c.* 973–1066. Part 2', *BNJ* 51 (1981), 52–90, at 75–6.
[69] H.C. Darby, *An Historical Geography of England before 1800* (Cambridge, 1961), p. 215.

shire, important for control of the Peak but for little more. Sited off the principal routes from north to south, it was apparently a political backwater in the tenth and eleventh centuries, unvisited by English kings who, when they ventured north, travelled via Nottingham where the *witan* met in 934 and in *c*. 973.[70] Its secondary importance is emphasized by the comparative neglect of Derby by William I – no Norman borough was established like the one at Nottingham, and no castle was built to overawe its inhabitants.

Derby remains as Stenton described it over sixty years ago, the unit of the Five Boroughs 'whose history is most obscure'.[71]

LEICESTER
Prehistoric activity

Leicester stands on the east bank of the River Soar, approximately 29km above its confluence with the Trent. The site has been of regional importance since at least the late Iron Age; Kenyon found pre-Roman pottery of both local and imported types at her Jewry Wall excavations, and, more recently, crouched inhumations dated to the immediately pre-Roman period and other features containing pottery of *c*. 10 BC–AD 40 have been found at Blackfriars Street; both imply a late Iron Age settlement on the east bank of the river.[72] In all, five sites in the western part of the Roman town have now produced Iron Age pottery, and its recovery alongside kilns at a further site approximately 1 km south of the Roman walls demonstrates that Iron Age activity was not confined within the Roman fortified area as earlier suggested.[73] Coins of the Corieltauvi have also been recovered within the town, and, since the first element of the Roman name for the site, *Ratae*, is derived from a Celtic word meaning 'ramparts', it has been suggested that this Iron Age site was defended, and perhaps an *oppidum*.[74] A more recent analysis, however, proposes that *Ratae* was a Celtic name for the defences of the Roman fort, and that the pre-Roman settlement was undefended.[75]

Roman occupation

The early history of Roman military activity at Leicester is not yet clear. Two apparently unrelated lengths of military ditch have been excavated, but their

---

[70] Stenton, *Anglo-Saxon England*, p. 350.

[71] F.M. Stenton, *Documents Illustrative of the Social and Economic History of the Danelaw* (London, 1920), p. cxviii.

[72] K.M. Kenyon, *Excavations at the Jewry Wall Site, Leicester* (London, 1948), pp. 124–5; R. Goodburn, *et al.*, 'Roman Britain in 1976', *Britannia* 8 (1977), 403–86, at 435.

[73] M. Todd, *The Coritani* (London, 1973), p. 3, J.B. Whitwell, *The Coritani: Some Aspects of the Iron Age Tribe and the Roman Civitas*, BAR Brit. ser. 99 (Oxford, 1982), 25.

[74] J. Wacher, *The Towns of Roman Britain* (Leicester, 1974), p. 335.

[75] A.L.F. Rivet and C. Smith, *The Place-Names of Roman Britain* (London, 1979), pp. 443–4.

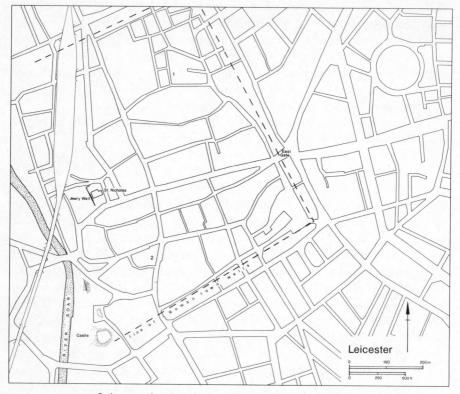

FIG. 5 Leicester, showing the locations of sites referred to in the text

precise dates and the layout of the forts to which they belong are unknown.[76] The forts lay on the Fosse Way, the Roman road running from north-east to south-west, and after the frontier was pushed northwards, the site was replanned as a civilian capital for the Corieltauvi, and ultimately defended by walls on the north, east and south sides, the line of which was followed in later medieval refortification.[77] The existence of a west wall in both the Roman and medieval periods has been doubted, with the River Soar suggested as a sufficient defence. Now, however, Lucas has assembled evidence which proves the existence of a medieval west wall, and suggests by implication that a Roman wall may also have existed here. The Roman street plan seems to have

[76] J. Mellor, 'Leicester', *Recent Archaeological Research in English Towns*, ed. Schofield and Palliser, p. 51.   [77] Wacher, *Towns of Roman Britain*, pp. 351–3.

exerted little influence on that of the later period as recorded in plans of *c.* 1600 and 1610,[78] and even the position of the Roman gateways is conjectural.[79]

Early and mid-Saxon activity

There is, too, little evidence for Leicester in the early and mid-Saxon periods, partly because later medieval disturbance has often destroyed the latest Roman and post-Roman levels. In the forum and basilica there is evidence for a fire which occurred after AD 364 and which may have finally ended occupation of parts of the building, but in one room there was some evidence for reconstruction or tidying up in the shape of a new floor above the destruction debris. A coin, pierced for re-use as a pendant, was found in the destruction level of another room, and might indicate that the destruction took place in the pagan Saxon period when such pendants were common, as opposed to the Roman period, when they were very uncommon, but either interpretation is possible.[80]

To the north of the forum and basilica, Wacher observed that the west range of the *macellum* (shopping precinct) had also been destroyed by fire, 'during' or perhaps after the last quarter of the fourth century; after a period of abandonment, a rough pebble floor had been laid, unfortunately without any datable objects on top of it.[81] Lucas has interpreted the thinning of archaeological deposits over the forum to indicate that it stood 'for some time' and was not rebuilt with a corresponding accumulation of debris, but this is essentially speculative.[82] The still upstanding Jewry Wall, the east side of the baths complex which occupied the *insula* immediately west of the forum, has been proposed as part of the fabric of an early (or mid-) Saxon building on or near the site of the late Saxon St Nicholas;[83] elsewhere the only hint that Roman structures continued to exert an influence on later development has come from Causeway Lane (1) where Roman and medieval pits have been shown to respect the same alignments.[84]

There are more early Anglo-Saxon objects from Leicester than from any other of the Five Boroughs, although some of the material previously assigned to this period has recently been re-attributed. For example, the bronze 'strap

---

[78] J.N. Lucas, 'The Town Walls of Leicester: Evidence for a West Wall', *Trans. of the Leicestershire Archaeol. and Hist. Soc.* 54 (1979), 61–6.   [79] Mellor, 'Leicester', p. 51.

[80] M. Hebditch and J. Mellor, 'The Forum and Basilica of Roman Leicester', *Britannia* 4 (1973), 1–83, at 42–3.   [81] Wacher, *Towns of Roman Britain*, p. 357.

[82] J.N. Lucas, 'The Debris of History: an Archaeological Topographic Survey of Leicester', *Trans of the Leicestershire Archaeol. and Hist. Soc.* 56 (1981), 1–9, at 6.

[83] Kenyon, *Jewry Wall Site*, p. 8.

[84] F.O. Grew *et al.*, 'Roman Britain in 1980', *Britannia* 12 (1981), 313–96, at 336.

end', a buckle loop assigned a mid-fifth-century date by Kendrick, may now be placed in the mid-fourth-century and is therefore not relevant to this discussion:[85] neither is the bronze belt plate of Hawkes and Dunning's Type IIA, also found unstratified at the Jewry Wall.[86] Other objects are only dubiously assigned to the early Anglo-Saxon period – there is a single 'possibly Saxon sherd' from the forum, and the possibly post-Roman coin pendant from the same site.[87] Unequivocal, however, are several items of jewellery, as well as pottery and miscellaneous objects, which point to activity among the Roman structures in the early Saxon period.[88] Two pagan Saxon cemeteries have been identified, at East Gate and Westcotes,[89] and the frequently destroyed or badly disturbed state of the relevant levels may account for the only possible cases of early Saxon occupation being those recorded above in relation to the forum, basilica and *macellum*, which are of uncertain date.

The start of the middle Anglo-Saxon period in the area may be taken as coincident with the conversion to Christianity of Peada, *princeps* of the Middle Angles, in 653, and the subsequent division, *c.* 680 of the extensive see of Mercia into a number of smaller bishoprics. There is no conclusive proof that Leicester itself was the Middle Anglian diocesan see before the eighth century, when the site is mentioned in a collection of Anglo-Saxon episcopal lists, but it is at least likely that the see was there from its institution in the late seventh century; and Bailey has suggested that this positioning was due not just to a nostalgia for the Roman origin of Leicester, but rather to the contemporary importance of the site as a focus of population in the early Anglo-Saxon period, as indicated by both archaeological and place-name evidence.[90] The relatively large quantity of early Saxon artifacts from Leicester supports this interpretation, but nothing else is certain, although it has provisionally been suggested that the earliest phase of Brixworth church, dated pre-750, includes building materials salvaged in part from Leicester, and indicating the destruction of

---

[85] Kenyon, *Jewry Wall Site*, p. 255; S. Hawkes, 'Some Recent Finds of Late Roman Buckles', *Britannia* 5 (1974), 386–93; G. Clarke, *The Roman Cemetery at Lankhills*, Winchester Stud. 3.2 (Oxford, 1979), 288–91.

[86] S.C. Hawkes and G.C. Dunning, 'Soldiers and Settlers in Britain, Fourth to Fifth century; with a Catalogue of Animal Ornamented Buckles and Related Belt-fittings', *MA* 5 (1961), 1–70, at 52.

[87] Mellor, 'Leicester', p. 51: Hebditch and Mellor, 'Forum and Basilica', pp. 42–3.

[88] R.A. Rutland, 'Gazetteer. Leicestershire other than Rutland', *Anglo-Saxon and Viking Leicestershire including Rutland*, ed. T.H. McK. Clough, *et al.* (Leicester, 1975), pp. 40–76, at 54–62.

[89] A. Meaney, *A Gazetteer of Early Anglo-Saxon Burial Sites* (London, 1964), pp. 146 and 150.

[90] R. Bailey, *The Early Christian Church in Leicester and its Region* (Leicester, 1980), p. 10.

Roman buildings; it is not clear if the site was more than just a convenient quarry at this time.[91]

As so little is known of the site in the mid-Anglo-Saxon period between the establishment of the church and the coming of the Vikings, 'it would certainly be most unwise to assume that Leicester was truly urban at this time.'[92]

The hypothetical building which may have preceded St Nicholas and which may have incorporated the Jewry Wall is most likely to have been a church, perhaps the bishops' seat; its position between two of the principal Roman municipal buildings, the baths and the forum, may offer a comparison with important early churches at York and Lincoln, for example, but since the post-Roman history of both buildings and of other Roman structures in Leicester is hardly known, the significance of this site is impossible to assess.

Anglo-Scandinavian occupation

Whatever the size of the bishop's establishment, and whatever other functions, if any, mid-Anglo-Saxon Leicester exercised, the site became one of the Vikings' strongholds in the late ninth or early tenth century, being recorded as an army base in the *Anglo-Saxon Chronicle*'s entries for 913 and 917. The bishopric apparently ceased to function some time after 872.[93] The *Chronicle* records the Leicester army's submission to Æthelflæd in 918. In 940, Leicester was occupied by Olaf Guthfrithsson and Archbishop Wulfstan, who were besieged within it by King Edmund but escaped; it was named in the *Chronicle*'s celebratory entry for 942. Nothing further is recorded of Leicester until Domesday Book's terse summary. In 1066 the town rendered £30 and fifteen sesters of honey, and supplied twelve burgesses or four horses in time of war. By 1086 the render had increased to £42.10.00, but it cannot be known if the 1086 figures of sixty-five burgesses, three hundred and twenty houses and six churches likewise reflect a forty per cent increase on the figures for 1066.

The numismatic evidence points to relatively small-scale minting at Leicester under Athelstan;[94] after the reform of Edgar, minting at a modest level is again attested, the scale being normally greater than at Derby or Nottingham, but less than at Stamford and Lincoln.[95]

---

[91] D.A. Sutherland and D. Parsons, 'The Petrological Contribution to the Survey of All Saints' Church Brixworth, Northamptonshire: an Interim Study', *JBAA* 137 (1984), 45–64, at 59–61.

[92] P. Liddle, *Leicestershire Archaeology: the Present State of Knowledge*, 11 *Anglo-Saxon and Medieval Periods* (Leicester, 1982), p. 9.   [93] Bailey, *Early Christian Church in Leicester*, p.3.

[94] Blunt, 'Coinage of Athelstan', pp. 96–7.

[95] Hill, 'Trends in the Development of Towns', pp. 216–17; Metcalf, 'Continuity and Change', pp. 75–6.

An archaeological *lacuna* marks the Anglo-Scandinavian period of Leicester's development. A small collection of miscellaneous and mostly unstratified artifacts of this period exists, but little else is known.[96] The defences within which Olaf Guthfrithsson and Archbishop Wulfstan were besieged are unidentified; the Roman walls may still have provided a defensible circuit, but this is hypothetical, and there could equally have been other, smaller enclosures as yet unlocated. Similarly, the development of the street plan remains enigmatic. It has been proposed, on the basis of the distribution of street names with a *gata* element, that the Anglo-Danish *burh* lay to the east and north-east of the Roman walled area, but this has been challenged by Buckley and Lucas, who speculate that grid-like elements in the street plan of Leicester, recorded on a seventeenth-century plan, may perhaps have originated in the pre-Conquest period.[97] As they admit, however, archaeological confirmation for this, and for any part of the Anglo-Scandinavian *burh* and its defences, is entirely lacking, and no trace has yet been found of any secular structure of this period.[98] Liddle's suggestions concerning the area occupied at this time, based as they are on the hypothetical identification of Domesday Book's churches and the tacit assumption that these were the only churches at this time and thus define an inhabited area, cannot be sustained.[99] Only St Nicholas, immediately east of Jewry Wall, can be identified as retaining pre-Conquest fabric.[100]

The one site which has produced intact levels of this period is the stoke pit of a pottery kiln at Southgate Street (2), tentatively dated by its excavator to the second half of the tenth century, on the basis of the form of its products, but assigned a wide bracket by other authorities.[101] Thus Leicester appears to follow the Anglo-Scandinavian urban tradition of town-based potteries, seen also at Lincoln, Stamford and Nottingham, and now suspected at York. The discovery supports the suggestion that Leicester, like the better understood centres such as York or Lincoln, was a manufacturing and commercial centre, but the size, layout and more precise role of the site remain enigmatic.

[96] Rutland, 'Gazetteer', pp. 54–62.
[97] R. Millward, 'Saxon and Danish Leicestershire', *Leicester and its Region*, ed. N. Pye (Leicester, 1972), pp. 218–34, at 233–4; R. Buckley and J. Lucas, *Leicester Town Defences* (Leicester, 1987), pp. 56–7.
[98] A. Dornier, 'An Introduction to the Archaeology of Leicestershire from the 5th to the 11th Centuries AD', *Anglo-Saxon and Viking Leicestershire* ed. Clough *et al*, 11–21, at 19: this was still true in 1987 (Mellor, pers. com.).   [99] Liddle, *Leicestershsire Archaeology*, p. 13.
[100] H.M. and J. Taylor, *Anglo-Saxon Architecture* 1 (Cambridge, 1965), 384–6.
[101] M. Hebditch, 'A Saxo-Norman Pottery Kiln Discovered in Southgate Street, Leicester, 1964', *Trans. of the Leicestershire Archaeol. and Hist. Soc.* 43 (1986), 4–9, at 9; J.G. Hurst, 'The Pottery', *The Archaeology of Anglo-Saxon England*, ed. D.M. Wilson (Cambridge, 1976), pp. 283–348, at 332.

LINCOLN
Origins

The Roman and medieval walled nucleus of Lincoln is sited where the belt of limestone known as the Jurassic Ridge is cut by the River Witham flowing towards the Wash, some 50km to the south-east. There had been Iron Age activity in the vicinity, evidenced by objects recovered from the river,[102] and a single structure demonstrating late prehistoric occupation has been discovered at 181–2 High Street, 150m south-west of Brayford Pool, the natural widening of the river where it curves abruptly eastwards to flow through the Lincoln Gap.[103]

Lincoln owes its historical importance to the Roman army. It is thought that a camp was built here in the Claudian period, but its location is uncertain; it may lie below the Neronian fortress or, alternatively, south of the River Witham, between it and the presumed junction of Ermine Street and Fosse Way.[104] In the Neronian period a *c.* 15ha fortress was constructed with its centre at the highest point on the Jurassic Ridge overlooking the Brayford Pool, which gave its name to the site; 'Lindon', the first recorded form, is cognate with Welsh *llyn*, 'a lake'.[105] Early in the second century, when a *colonia* was founded, the earth and timber legionary defences were replaced in stone, and after mid-/late second century additions these were rebuilt in the late third to fourth century.[106] In the late second or early third century the defended area was more than doubled by the erection of walls which joined the upper town at their north ends and extended down the steep slope to within 80m of the River Witham. These walls and their gateways were also remodelled in the second half of the fourth century.[107]

In addition to its role as *colonia*, Lincoln was a provincial capital from the early fourth century.[108] This administrative role was given to a settlement which by then extended south of the River Witham for nearly 1km along

---

[102] F.T. Baker, *Roman Lincoln* (Lincoln, 1938), p. 7.

[103] M.J. Jones, ed., 'Excavations at Lincoln. Third Interim Report', *AntJ* 61 (1981), 83–114, at 84.

[104] S.S. Frere, *Britannia*, revised ed. (London, 1978), p. 113, n. 16; J.R. Magilton and D.A. Stocker, 'St Mary's Guildhall', *Archaeology in Lincoln Tenth Annual Report 1981–1982*, ed. M.J. Jones (Lincoln, 1982), pp. 8–16, at p. 16.

[105] E. Ekwall, *The Concise Oxford dictionary of English Place-Names*, 4th ed. (Oxford, 1960), p. 298.

[106] M.J. Jones, *The Defences of the Upper Roman Enclosure*, CBA, Archaeol. of Lincoln 7.1 (London, 1980), 48–55.

[107] C. Colyer, 'Excavations at Lincoln 1970–1972: the Western Defences of the Lower Town', *AntJ* 55 (1975), 227–66, at 231–45.   [108] Frere, *Britannia*, pp. 241–2.

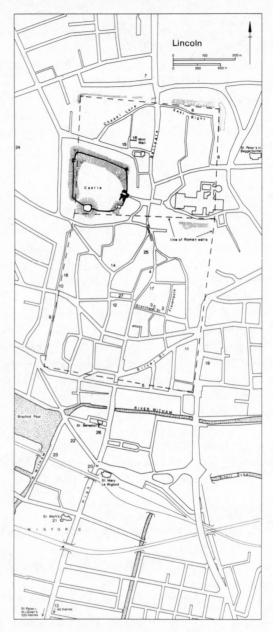

FIG. 6 Lincoln, showing the locations of sites referred to in the text

Ermine Street.[109] Settlement here was undefended, although Sincil Dyke, an arm of the Witham which encloses this area, may have existed in the Roman period. Two other dykes certainly originated at this time: Foss Dyke, a navigable waterway connecting the Witham with the Trent, and Car Dyke, partly a natural tributary of the Witham below Lincoln, which was extended in the Hadrianic period towards the Wash, and which acted as both drain and routeway.[110]

Although it was a defended settlement of considerable size and population, there is only a little evidence from Lincoln to indicate that the Roman city continued to function much beyond *c*. AD 400, although the virtual absence of fifth-century coinage from Britain and the paucity of other closely datable artifacts of the fifth and sixth centuries hamper analysis of the often ephemeral evidence for continuing occupation in Lincoln, as elsewhere. Nonetheless, in terms of institutions, the suggestion that a zoomorphic belt buckle fragment of Hawkes and Dunning type IIA, found at The Park, just outside the western defences of the lower city, in 1968, represents evidence for a continued military presence here into the fifth century can now be discounted: the type is now recognised as being earlier than previously believed, perhaps dating as early as *c*. AD 350.[111]

Recent excavations have uncovered a number of sites where, bearing in mind the difficulty over precise dating referred to above, there seems to have been a break in occupation or activity in the fourth or early fifth century, and Roman features were unknown or disregarded in later periods. At East Bight in the upper walled town (6) a Roman road was apparently disused by the end of the Roman period, buried by material which had, perhaps, washed down from the adjacent rampart.[112] At the Park (9) the west gateway to the lower walled town is believed to have become disused soon after the end of the Roman period; since, however, the antepenultimate surface incorporated a coin of Arcadius, probably of 388–92, disuse may not have come as swiftly as the excavator suggests.[113] Nonetheless, there was no evidence for continuity into the medieval period, and the gateway is not on the line of a modern or medieval street. Also in the lower walled town, Roman north–south streets discovered at Silver Street (11), and Saltergate (5) were both abandoned after the end of the Roman period; that at Silver Street was covered at one point by

[109] Magilton and Stocker, 'St Mary's Guildhall', pp. 13–16.
[110] B.B. Simmons, 'The Lincolnshire Car Dyke', *Britannia* 10 (1979), 183–96, at 196.
[111] Hawkes, 'Recent Finds of Late Roman Buckles', pp. 387–93; Clarke, *Lankhills*, pp. 288–91.
[112] M.J. Jones, *Lincoln Archaeological Trust Ninth Annual Report 1980–1981* (Lincoln, 1981), p. 12. [113] Colyer, 'Excavations at Lincoln 1970–1972', p. 245.

an Anglo-Scandinavian-period kiln.[114] At the corner of Hungate and St Martin's Lane (12), where a Roman building went out of use in the late fourth century, its walls collapsed and then other walls were constructed on top of the ruins.[115] Unfortunately there is no dating evidence associated with this phase, provisionally interpreted as an animal pen; it was subsequently covered by a 1– 1.5 m deep layer of dark earth, either hill wash or a deliberate dump, which may indicate horticulture or agriculture hereabouts at a date somewhere between the sixth and ninth centuries.

Equally clear evidence for the disregard of Roman features has come from Wigford, where St Mary's Guildhall (13) has been shown to lie over rubbish pits of the Anglo-Scandinavian period, which are themselves cut into Fosse Way, the main Roman road to Lincoln from the south-west.[116] Abandonment has also been recognized at St Mark's church, Wigford, built on land unoccupied from the early fifth to the early tenth century,[117] and at waterfront sites on Brayford Pool.[118] Also relevant as an indicator of the decay of the Roman layout is the alignment of Silver Street in the lower walled town, which runs from the Roman south gate at an angle of forty-five degrees towards the presumed site of an east gate. It seems unlikely that this alignment could belong to the Roman period, and presumably it indicates the ability to create easy access between the two adjacent gates at a time when Roman buildings here had collapsed or been cleared. Chapel Lane in the upper walled town may reflect a similar situation.

Yet despite this evidence for urban decay, there are hints, both historical and archaeological, that Lincoln was not totally abandoned in the period between the Roman withdrawal of *c.* AD 400 and the arrival of the missionary Paulinus in the early seventh century. Since the publication of Stenton's paper on 'Lindsey and its Kings' it has been accepted that in the early and mid-Anglo-Saxon periods, until the time of Offa, there was a distinct political kingdom, Lindsey, which took its name from, and therefore was in some way associated with, Lincoln.[119] Although its existence has been baldly denied,[120] the evidence

---

[114] C. Colyer and M. J. Jones, 'Excavations at Lincoln. Second Interim Report', *AntJ* 59 (1979), 50–91, at 83 and 86.

[115] K. Camidge, 'Hungate', *Archaeology in Lincolnshire 1985–1986*, ed. E. Nurser (Lincoln, 1986), p. 23.

[116] Magilton and Stocker, 'St Mary's Guildhall', pp. 12–13.

[117] B. J. J. Gilmour and D. A. Stocker, *St Mark's Church and Cemetery*, CBA, Archaeol. of Lincoln 13.1 (London, 1986), p. 14.

[118] See below, p. 183.

[119] F. M. Stenton, 'Lindsey and its Kings', *Essays in History Presented to Reginald Lane Poole* (Oxford, 1927), pp. 136–50.

[120] W. Davies and H. Vierck, 'The Contexts of Tribal Hidage: Social Aggregates and Settlement Patterns', *FS* 8 (1974), 223–93, at 237.

of Anglo-Saxon royal genealogies,[121] the *Tribal Hidage* and the *Chronicle*'s passage for 841, which refers to it in conjunction with other kingdoms, all encourage belief in it, as does the geography of the area, with its well-defined natural boundaries.

The fact that there was a separate bishopric of Lindsey from the later seventh century, albeit created in the aftermath of Ecgfrith of Northumbria's annexation of the area in 674, again suggests that there was a separate political entity here, for the bishopric survived the Mercian re-annexation of Lindsey in 678.[122] The bishopric's boundaries are not clear: as mapped by Hunter Blair or Hill they encompass the kingdom of Lindsey and more,[123] but it seems that Lincoln will have lain within the diocese. Nonetheless, there is no record that Lincoln was the bishops' seat; it is generally thought that the bishop of Lindsey was the *Syddensis civitatis episcopus* who attested a document from the Council of Clovesho in 803,[124] but the place in question has not been identified. The usage of *civitas* in the document supports an identification with a Roman centre, and it is possible that Lincoln may have had an alternative name to that which has survived; indeed, Campbell has pointed out an analogy here with reference to Bath.[125] Nonetheless, until some corroborating evidence is found, Lincoln cannot claim with certainty to have been a bishop's see in the pre-Viking period.

Although the historical sources are so tantalizingly uncertain, there is archaeological evidence for Lincoln after the Roman withdrawal. Excavation at the church of St Paul-in-the-Bail (1), at the heart of the upper city within the courtyard of the Roman forum, has revealed a sequence of buildings and cemeteries with their main axis running east–west, an alignment they share with the forum. All these features are thought to be Christian. Within the earliest structure, an apsidal stone building closely comparable in plan and dimension to the Kentish churches thought to be associated with the seventh-century Augustinian mission, was a grave containing a possibly seventh-century hanging bowl.[126] The date of this earliest church is called into question by the results of C-14 determinations on six skeletons from the earliest levels of the adjacent cemetery, determinations which fall between the late fourth and early seventh centuries.[127] That there was a Christian community in later

[121] D.N. Dumville, 'The Anglian Collection of Royal Genealogies and Regnal Lists', *ASE* 5 (1976), 23–50, at 31 and 46–7.   [122] Stenton, *Anglo-Saxon England*, p. 134.

[123] P. Hunter Blair, *An Introduction to Anglo-Saxon England*, 2nd ed. (Cambridge, 1977), p. 145; D. Hill, *An Atlas of Anglo-Saxon England* (Oxford, 1981), p. 148.   [124] BCS 312.

[125] J. Campbell, 'Bede's Words for Places', *Names, Words and Graves*, ed. P.H. Sawyer (Leeds, 1979), pp. 34–54, at 36, n. 5.

[126] B. Gilmour, 'The Anglo-Saxon Church at St Paul-in-the-Bail, Lincoln', *MA* 23 (1979), 214–17.

[127] M.J. Jones, 'Updating the Past', *PA* October 1982, 14–18.

Roman Lincoln is unquestioned – a bishop of Lincoln attended the Council of Arles in AD 314.[128] It is possible that the St Paul-in-the Bail cemetery is to be associated with this late Roman Christian community, and also possible that this community's sub-Roman descendants continued to live in the city in succeeding centuries and were the population represented by the excavated early phase burials. A possible analogue is provided by burials from Worcester Cathedral dated to the sixth century.[129]

This late fourth- to early-seventh-century community is of great interest when viewed against the evidence for Anglo-Saxon settlement in the vicinity of Lincoln. Cremation cemeteries of the sixth century have been noted at both Cherry Willingham and Middle Carlton, each only some 7km from Lincoln, indicating that there was no long-lasting, independent sub-Roman *territorium* or kingdom based on the city.[130] Furthermore, Bede's record of Paulinus's visit to Lincoln in 628 includes a reference to the city's *praefectus* Blæcca who, with his household, was the first Christian convert.[131] This man's status is uncertain, although it is likely that he was either of royal stock or a regally appointed official, and he was in a position of authority in Lincoln. It is conceivable that he was leader of the descendants of the Romano-British community, who may be represented by the St Paul-in-the-Bail burials; alternatively he may have been an Anglo-Saxon representative of the new political order. Yet neither his presence, nor the community represented by the fourth- to seventh-century burials at St Paul-in-the-Bail, is evidence that in these centuries Lincoln was anything other than largely deserted. Even in the generations after Blæcca's conversion there was evidently no viable Christian community to maintain the 'ecclesiam operis egregii de lapide' built by Paulinus, for it was in ruins in Bede's day.

A provisional interpretation of the St Paul-in-the-Bail sequence is that a Roman church continued as a focus for burial into the seventh century and beyond; burials with C-14 dates of as late as 900 below the second church, the simple rectangular structure, suggest that like others of its type (e.g. St Helen-on-the-Walls, York), it is of Anglo-Scandinavian date.[132] If this is so, where is the church built by Paulinus which Bede records? Did he indeed build a

---

128 Frere, *Britannia*, p. 375, n. 30.
129 P. A. Barker *et al.*, 'Two Burials under the Refectory of Worcester Cathedral', *MA* 18 (1974), 146–51; for speculation about other possible ecclesiastical/secular foci near the cathedral, see N. Baker, 'Churches, Parishes and Early Medieval topography', 'Medieval Worcester: an Archaeological Framework', ed. M.O.H. Carver, *Trans. of the Worcestershire Archaeol. Soc.* 3rd ser. 7 (1980), 31–8, at 35–7.
130 P. Everson, 'Pagan Saxon Pottery from Cherry Willingham and Middle Carlton Villages', *Lincolnshire Hist. and Archaeol.* 14 (1979), 79–80.   131 Bede, *HE* II.16.
132 J. Magilton, *The Church of St Helen-on-the-Walls, Aldwark*, CBA, Archaeol. of York 10.1 (London, 1980), 18.

church, or did he rather make use of an existing structure, St Pauls? If he did build a church, perhaps it is to the site of St Martin's that attention should be directed, for the St Martin coinage suggests that St Martin's church may have become the minster church of Lincoln.[133]

There is only a little other evidence for activity in Lincoln before the Viking takeover of 877. At Flaxengate (2) a Roman building which stood in part into the eighth or ninth century had a number of pits containing pre-Viking pottery, some attributed to the sixth century, cut through its floors, and the site also produced window and vessel glass of the seventh to ninth centuries. Other activity here included the construction of a dry-stone wall across the site, perhaps a property boundary, before the start of intensive Anglo-Scandinavian occupation.[134] No remains of domestic structures were recognised. At the corner of Grantham Place, 20m away (3), it is suggested that Roman buildings were dismantled in the sub/post-Roman period, before the ninth/tenth centuries, but there appears to be no evidence for occupation here until the eleventh century, and so the reason for the demolition is enigmatic.[135] Equally nebulous in their context are the pre-Viking sherds, found in residual contexts at 4–7 Steep Hill (4).[136] To this may be added more recent discoveries of eighth- to ninth-century pottery at The Lawn Hospital site (24), to the west of the upper walled city, which may suggest contemporary activity or even occupation.[137] Further excavation is, however, required before the significance of these discoveries can be properly assessed. The recovery of a seventh- to ninth-century *ansate* brooch of continental origin in a residual, thirteenth-century context at St Mark's church, Wigford, may also be relevant here,[138] although broadly similar brooches were found in Anglo-Scandinavian contexts at 16–22 Coppergate, York, suggesting that these items were in circulation for some time and are not exclusively indicators of seventh- to ninth-century activity.

Only excavation between Saltergate and Silver Street (5) has yielded what is ostensibly more clear-cut evidence for post-Roman but pre-Viking activity. Here the collapsed debris of part of a Roman building, sealing pottery which may itself be of post-Roman date, was cut into by four graves, one of which was dated to AD 780 ± 90 by a single C-14 analysis of the skeleton.[139] In the area

[133] R. Morris, 'Parish Churches', *Urban Archaeology in Britain*, ed. Schofield and Leech, pp. 177–91, at 188; see below, p. 182.

[134] Colyer and Jones, 'Second Interim Report', pp. 59–61; D. Perring, *Early Medieval Occupation at Flaxengate, Lincoln*, CBA, Archaeol. of Lincoln 9.1 (London, 1981), 5–6.

[135] Jones, 'Tenth Interim Report', pp. 6–8.

[136] Colyer and Jones, 'Second Interim Report', p. 79.

[137] S.M. Youngs *et al.* 'Medieval Britain in 1985', *MA* 30 (1986), 114–98, at 157.

[138] Gilmour and Stocker, *St Mark's Church*, p. 41.

[139] Colyer and Jones, 'Second Interim Report', pp. 84 and 88.

of an adjacent Roman room, there was a cobbled surface into which a series of post-holes had been dug; these may represent part of a sunken-floored structure, possibly contemporary with the burials. The reservation about this evidence is that the chronology is dependent upon one C-14 determination.

This archaeological evidence demonstrates that there was activity in widely spread parts of Lincoln in the fifth to ninth centuries, but is not sufficient for conclusions to be drawn about the site's status throughout this period. No certain domestic structure has been identified, and there is no evidence for craft/economic activity. The Wigford suburb south of the river, first recorded as *Wich(e)ford* in 1107,[140] contains in its name the element *wic*, which occurs in the name of several important pre-Viking trading centres such as *Hamwic*, *Lundenwic* and *Eoferwic*, but there is as yet nothing to demonstrate that such a centre existed at Lincoln. No finds of sceattas are reported;[141] there are no coin hoards to mark the Viking takeover, a notable contrast with York; and it has been commented that, judging by the rarity of silver coin finds of the period, the economy of Lindsey, and thus of Lincoln, was sadly depressed *c.* 825–75.[142]

Morris has emphasized the intermittent nature of urban activity in eighth-century Lincoln, which he sees as a place overwhelmingly dormant for much of the time until sparked into occasional life by the arrival of traders, or a peregrinating royal household, or an important festival.[143] Certainly there is no evidence yet from Lincoln to match that for an area of intense occupation and activity such as those recently discovered at York or London, that known longer at Hamwic (Southampton), or that suspected at Canterbury.[144]

The Anglo-Scandinavian period

Historical introduction

Lincoln's role in the Anglo-Scandinavian period is scarcely illuminated by historical sources. It was taken over during the Viking settlement of eastern Mercia in 877, but its sole mention in the *Anglo-Saxon Chronicle*'s record of the

---

[140] K. Cameron, *The Place-Names of Lincolnshire. Part 1: The Place-Names of the County of the City of Lincoln*, EPNS 58 (Cambridge, 1985), 45.

[141] S.E. Rigold and D.M. Metcalf, 'A Revised Check-List of English Finds of Sceattas', *Sceattas in England and on the Continent*, ed. D. Hill and D.M. Metcalf, BAR Brit. ser. 128 (Oxford, 1984), 245–68, at 254.

[142] M. Blackburn *et al.*, *Early Medieval Coins from Lincoln and its Shire c. 770–1100*, CBA, Archaeol. of Lincoln 6.1 (London, 1983), 9–11.

[143] Morris, 'Parish Churches', p. 190.

[144] R. Kemp, 'Anglian York – the Missing Link', *CA* 104 (1987), 259–63; M. Biddle, 'London on the Strand', *PA* 6.1 (July 1984), 23–7; A. Vince, 'The Aldwych: Mid-Saxon London Discovered?', *CA* 93 (1984), 310–12; P. Holdsworth, 'Saxon Southampton', *Anglo-Saxon Towns*, ed. J. Haslam (Chichester, 1984), pp. 331–44; T. Tatton-Brown, 'The Towns of Kent', *ibid.*, pp. 1–36, at 5–8.

period is in 942, when Edmund regained control of the Mercian Danelaw. By the early eleventh century at latest it had given its name to the surrounding shire – Lincolnshire is first recorded in the *Chronicle* in 1016. Domesday Book reports that there were 1,164 inhabited messuages in the city in 1066; of its statistics for 1086, the twelve and a half carucates in the fields outside the city, the one hundred acres of meadow, and the city's twelve lawmen all also echo the pre-Norman situation.

Defences

The Roman fortifications continued to define the defended area up to the Norman Conquest and beyond. The most systematic study has been that of the upper Roman enclosure, where the Roman stone wall was found to survive to considerable heights in several places: at East Bright (6) the North wall ran for 10m standing up to 5.5m above its plinth; at Cecil Street (7) a 25m length survived up to 3m in height; and at the Eastgate Hotel (8) 29m of the East wall were observed, standing in places nearly 7m above the Roman ground surface.[145] Nowhere is there any evidence for modification to the Roman defences before the Norman Conquest.

The lower Roman enclosure defences have also been investigated. On their western side at The Park (9) the Roman wall had stood on average at least 4.5m high above its foundations throughout the medieval period, but there were no surviving traces of post-Roman modification.[146] Approximately 50m to the north at Motherby Hill (10) the Roman wall survived up to a height of 3m; neither it nor the associated rampart showed any sign of later alterations except for the post-Norman insertion of a postern gate at one point – thus demonstrating that the Roman wall formed the nucleus of the late medieval defences.[147]

On the south of the lower Roman enclosure at Saltergate (5) the Roman wall was found surviving to a height of 2.25m, capped by an undated medieval stone wall. On the east of the lower Roman enclosure at Silver Street (11) the Roman stone wall had been largely robbed and there was no trace of what state the defences were in here in the Anglo-Scandinavian period.[148]

At present then, there is no evidence for Anglo-Saxon or Anglo-Scandinavian defences other than the likelihood that the Roman walls survived in a largely defensible state – certainly it was the Roman enceinte, with an extension to the south, which was defended in the later medieval period, and eighteenth-century antiquarians record and depict the enceinte as

---

[145] Jones, *Defences of the Upper Roman Enclosure*, pp. 17, 20 and 31–2.
[146] Colyer, 'Excavations at Lincoln 1970–1972', pp. 241–5.
[147] *Ibid.*, pp. 246–59.   [148] Colyer and Jones, 'Second Interim Report', pp. 81–6.

largely intact,[149] although some of the defences they described may be of the medieval period.

Nonetheless, in the absence of any indication of other fortifications, for example sub-dividing the Roman enclosures, it seems at present that if Lincoln was defended by walls, palisades or ditches in the pre-Norman period, these defences followed the Roman lines.

The later influences of Roman topography

The fact that Roman features survived at Lincoln until the Anglo-Scandinavian period has long been recognized, not only in relation to the defences but also with regard to an intra-mural structure, the Mint Wall, which still survives for a length of 22.5 m, stands up to 7.5 m above the present ground level and is now identified as the northern limit of a forum–basilica complex.[150] In addition to these visible structures, recent excavations have now added a considerable body of new information about the influence of other Roman features on the appearance and development of the city in subsequent centuries.

Few streets in Lincoln are known to have a Roman origin, although this may as much reflect the current absence of information on the Roman layout as post-Roman divergence from it. Bailgate connects the north and south gates of the upper walled town, and certainly has a Roman origin; East Bight might be thought to reflect the Roman intra-mural road, but such a feature could have been instituted at a later period, and the rapid covering of the Roman road at one point does not encourage a belief in continuity here. The insertion of Lincoln Castle and the cathedral into the upper walled town in the Norman period has also brought about changes in layout which the medieval street pattern reflects; the plan of the area in the Anglo-Scandinavian period is not known. In the lower walled town the principal north–south route, High Street/Steep Hill, is more or less on the line between the south gates of the upper and lower towns: on a site between Steep Hill and Michaelgate (25), close to where they converge just below the upper south gate, an imposing stepped Roman street has been located, which was obliterated after the Roman period. The renewal of a road here in the tenth century, parallel to but west of its Roman precursor, clearly reflects the need for a direct route to and from the adjacent gate rather than any form of continuity of use.[151] Elswhere there is no evidence that the later medieval street pattern reflects a Roman origin. Indeed,

---

[149] *Ibid.*, p. 91, n. 59.

[150] M. J. Jones and B. J. J. Gilmour, 'Lincoln, Principia and Forum', *Britannia* 11 (1980), 61–72, at 69–72.

[151] A. Snell, 'Michaelgate 1984–1985', *Archaeology in Lincolnshire 1984–1985. First Annual Report of the Trust for Lincolnshire Archaeology*, ed. E. Nurser (Lincoln, 1985), pp. 38–41, at 39.

the abandonment of several Roman streets has already been mentioned[152], and there is evidence which demonstrates that the establishment of streets on entirely new lines sometimes took place in the Anglo-Scandinavian period.

The evidence comes from the lower walled town at Flaxengate (2), previously assumed to reflect a Roman street; the excavation of 1972–6 has shown, however, that it was a creation of the early Anglo-Scandinavian period, perhaps *c.* 900, which was resurfaced, sporadically, up to the Norman Conquest and beyond.[153] Grantham Street, which runs east–west and intersects with Flaxengate, did not lie within the excavated area but formed its southern boundary. The earliest structures which apparently respect the alignment of Grantham Street were dated *c.* 970, and from this it might be inferred that the street dates from this time; if, however, the area excavated at Flaxengate was all one property, as has been suggested,[154] then the south boundary of the site, Grantham Street, may have been laid out at the same time as Flaxengate.

Although the weight of the newly excavated evidence favours the conclusion that, with the few principal exceptions noted above, the Roman street pattern of both lower and upper walled towns exerted relatively little influence on Anglo-Scandinavian developments, it has become increasingly clear that individual Roman structures sometimes played a significant role in later developments, although in other cases Roman buildings were demolished before redevelopment took place. An example of such clearance was discovered in the case of the Roman apsidal structure which occupied the western portion of the Flaxengate site. This building was apparently still standing, at least in part, into the ninth century, for when a layer of dark brown loam was deposited over the site at approximately this time, only the area defined by this structure was not covered by it. A further layer of loam, which then sealed the entire site and provided the horizon upon which the earliest Anglo-Scandinavian buildings were constructed, may be interpreted as being partly debris from the trenches excavated to rob the stone from the apsidal building, an activity which took place at approximately this time. The demolition of Roman structures at the adjacent Grantham Place site (3) may be interpreted as a contemporary event.[155]

It has been claimed that the east wall of the Flaxengate Roman building, which had previously also acted as a terrace revetment, influenced later developments through being perpetuated as the western boundary of the single unit of property envisaged here in the Anglo-Scandinavian and Norman periods, and also suspected in the later medieval period. This is not supported

[152] Above, p. 171.   [153] Perring, *Flaxengate*, p. 6, and *passim*.
[154] *Ibid.* p. 43.   [155] Magilton and Stocker, 'St Mary's Guildhall', p. 8.

by published plans and sections which show structures assigned to the Norman period traversing this line and also show no trace of a terrace here during the Anglo-Scandinavian phase;[156] any continuity can have been perpetuated only by features so ephemeral as to leave no recoverable trace. Indeed, it is only the fluidity characterizing the siting of Anglo-Scandinavian structures at Flaxengate which suggests that most of the excavated area was a single property – the negative evidence of lack of divisions within the site might alternatively reflect the ephemeral nature of such features rather than a true absence of divisions.

These sites at or near Flaxengate and another in the angle between Spring Hill and Michaelgate at the northern limit of the lower walled town (14) are the only ones which have produced evidence for clearance preceding Anglo-Scandinavian redevelopment[157] – elsewhere Roman structures survived to exert a positive influence, to attract activity or occupation, and in some cases to be incorporated into new Anglo-Scandinavian structures. Anglo-Scandinavian activity or occupation within Roman structures is known in the lower walled town from the Saltergate site (5), where sherds of this period were found on a floor sealed by the building's destruction levels.[158] The case of the possibly Roman building at St Paul-in-the-Bail in the upper town has already been discussed;[159] other possible instances of the re-use of Roman structures in this part of the town have been noted behind 2 West Bight (15) and north of Mint Wall (16) but in both cases the suggestion is based on negative evidence gleaned from small-scale work, and must be treated with caution until larger-scale excavations allow a clearer perspective to emerge.[160] The influence of other upstanding Roman features such as the Mint Wall in the upper town, or those Roman walls which were incorporated into twelfth- to fifteenth-century buildings at Danes Terrace 1 in the lower town (17) has not yet been elucidated.[161] Evidence for the incorporation of Roman structures into Anglo-Scandinavian structures has come from the St-Paul-in-the-Bail site (1) where sunken-featured structures of perhaps tenth-century date consisted in part of a Roman wall *in situ*.[162] At 4–7 Steep Hill (4) one wall of a Roman structure was

---

[156] Perring, *Flaxengate*, p. 43, and figs. 30 and 34, structures 24, 25 and 32.

[157] A. Snell, 'Spring Hill', *Archaeology in Lincoln 1983–1984. Twelfth and Final Annual Report of the Lincoln Archaeological Trust*, ed. M. J. Jones and E. Nurser (Lincoln, 1984), pp. 9–15, at 14.

[158] Colyer and Jones, 'Second Interim Report', p. 88.   [159] Above, pp. 173–4.

[160] M. J. Jones, *Lincoln Archaeological Trust Fifth Annual Report 1976–1977* (Lincoln, 1977), p. 8; M. J. Jones, *Lincoln Archaeological Trust Eighth Annual Report 1979–1980* (Lincoln, 1980), p. 14.   [161] Colyer and Jones, 'Second Interim Report', pp. 68–9.

[162] M. J. Jones, *Lincoln Archaeological Trust Seventh Annual Report 1978–1979* (Lincoln, 1979), p. 15.

also modified for re-use in the Saxo-Norman period, although it is not clear if this was before or after the Norman Conquest.[163]

Anglo-Scandinavian occupation and activity

Until the recent campaign of excavation by Lincoln Archaeological Trust, and other complementary work, the Vikings' occupation and settlement of Lincoln were known in archaeological terms through only a handful of objects, all of them chance finds.[164] Now, Anglo-Scandinavian activity and presumed occupation have been identified at sites widely spaced throughout Lincoln, mainly through the discovery of rubbish pits or layers containing recognizable artefacts. These sites include West Parade (18), Danes Terrace (17), Saltergate (5) and St Mary's Guildhall (13).

Domestic structures have been recorded in the upper city at St-Paul-in-the-Bail (1),[165] where a sunken-floored structure probably served a domestic/industrial function; in the lower city at Flaxengate (2),[166] on the corner of Grantham Place (3),[167] at Hungate, where among a series of ninth- to tenth-century buildings was a structure built on stone post-pads, with traces of internal partitions and small hearths (12),[168] and at nearby Michaelgate (25) where a tenth-century building had stone foundations;[169] immediately east of the lower city at Broadgate (19);[170] and south of the Witham, in Wigford, where at 181–2 High Street (20) a fragmentary structure dating from the mid-tenth century has been found.[171]

The St Paul-in-the-Bail cemetery, already established in the pre-Viking period, seems to have been in use in the Anglo-Scandinavian period, although the tentative phasing of superimposed churches initially proposed may have to be revised in the light of the unexpectedly early C-14 determinations from the earliest inhumations.[172] More immediately comprehensible are the results of excavations at St Mark's church in Wigford (21), where in the mid-tenth century a timber church was erected on what had previously been marginal or agricultural land. It was built within a graveyard defined to one side by a ditch and fence; fourteen decorated stone monuments from the site date to the mid/late tenth to late eleventh century, and imply parochial status from the outset.

The pattern of parish boundaries in Wigford suggests that the parish was

---

[163] C. Colyer, *Lincoln Archaeological Trust Third Annual Report 1974–1975* (Lincoln, 1975), p. 20.
[164] A. Bjørn and H. Shetelig, *Viking Antiquities in England*, Viking Antiquities in Great Britain and Ireland 4, ed. H. Shetelig (Oslo, 1940), 7–99, at 99.
[165] Jones, *Seventh Annual Report*, p. 15.   [166] Perring, *Flaxengate, passim*
[167] Magilton and Stocker, 'St Mary's Guildhall', p. 8.
[168] Youngs *et al.*, 'Medieval Britain in 1985', at p. 157.   [169] *Ibid.*
[170] Jones, 'Third Interim Report', p. 104.   [171] *Ibid.* pp. 87–8.
[172] Gilmour, 'St Paul-in-the-Bail', *passim*; Jones, 'Updating the Past', p. 18.

founded relatively late in comparison with those around it, and this implies a burgeoning in Lincoln's prosperity and population in the preceding decades; the rebuilding of St Mark's in stone in the mid-eleventh century testifies to continuing success in the parish,[173] a characteristic of the city as a whole, as demonstrated by its mint output.[174] The position of the church, 450m south of the walled city, together with the eleventh-century churches of St Mary-le-Wigford, St Peter-at-Gowts and possibly St Benedict,[175] complements the evidence from 181–2 High Street (20) and from the Dickinson's Mill (22) St Benedict's Square and Brayford Wharf East (23) sites, that the Wigford suburb was revived in the Anglo-Scandinavian period after a decline which, starting in the late Roman period, led to its disappearance in the Anglo-Saxon era.

The position of St Martin's at the centre of the lower walled city, mirroring that of St Paul-in-the-Bail in the upper, is perhaps an additional pointer to its being an early foundation; however, the most plausible indicator of its early origin is the appearance of the name of St Martin on the series of coins minted at Lincoln *c.* 920.[176] Analogous to the York St Peter issue, where the dedication is taken to refer to the cathedral church, the series suggests that St Martin was an important figure and St Martin's an important church in the pre-Norman town.

Domesday Book's entry for Lincoln does not, of course, clearly state the number of churches, and its ecclesiastical references may be interpreted in a number of ways. Darby, for example, adopted a minimalist position, counting five churches within the city as well as two built outside in the period 1066–86 on land previously undeveloped; Morris, on the other hand, calculates that eleven churches are referred to in the city and its suburbs. Yet by 1100 there is evidence of one sort or another for at least thirty-two and perhaps as many as thirty-seven churches, i.e. two-thirds to three-quarters of the city's medieval maximum.[177]

Apart from St Mark's, St Paul-in-the-Bail and perhaps St Martin's, there is no evidence to enable the others to be identified. Of the two new suburban churches there are strong historical grounds for believing that one is likely to have been the now demolished St Peter in Baggerholme on the east of the upper walled city.[178] This is of interest not for the church itself, which as a

[173] Gilmour and Stocker, *St Mark's*, pp. 17–18.
[174] Below, p. 186.   [175] Taylor and Taylor, *Anglo-Saxon Architecture* I, 390–8.
[176] B.H.I.H. Stewart, 'The St Martin Coins of Lincoln', *BNJ* 36 (1967), 46–54.
[177] H.C. Darby, *The Domesday Geography of Eastern England*, 3rd ed. (Cambridge, 1971), p. 79; R. Morris, 'Parish Churches', p. 180.
[178] J.W.F. Hill, *Medieval Lincoln* (Cambridge, 1948), pp. 133–4 and 161.

Norman construction is not relevant here, but because it points to an area not built up in the Anglo-Scandinavian period.

Turning from the churches to the commercially important area of the waterfront, investigation on the banks of the Witham has shown that attention was paid to the riverside in the tenth century, after a period of neglect. At Dickinson's Mill, on the east side of Brayford Pool (22), the area was found to have been reclaimed from a waterlogged or at least extremely marshy state in the tenth century, when limestone metalling was laid above a sequence of silt and peat deposits.[179] A similar picture was seen at the nearby St Benedict's Square excavation (26) where the site of a Roman building, demolished in the mid-fourth century, was encroached upon by the Brayford Pool which deposited layers of silt and peat until wattle fences were inserted at the water's edge in the tenth century.[180] Provisionally interpreted by the excavator as the setting for fish-farming, one of his discarded hypotheses, that they were erected to stabilize or protect the shore-line, seems preferable. The land was reclaimed with soil dumps in the eleventh century, when the waterfront was advanced by 35m.[181]

Approximately 150m to the south, the Brayford Wharf East excavation of 1982 (23) showed that in the tenth century the river, which had been virtually stagnant here since the late Roman period, was cleared, and started to flow freely, and soon afterwards, probably before the Norman Conquest, fish-traps were laid in the shallows.[182] These three sites clearly demonstrate the resurgence of activity in Lincoln after the Scandinavian take-over, and combine with the structural and artifactual evidence outlined above to indicate a marked contrast with the preceding four centuries.

Crafts and industry

Evidence for the economy of Anglo-Scandinavian Lincoln is all but restricted to one site, on the corner of Flaxengate and Grantham Street in the lower walled city, and even here interpretation is hampered by problems of residuality, considerable uncertainty over dating, and the lack of recorded associations between finds, or between finds and structures. In addition, the likelihood of contamination and the regular shifting of earth and debris make it impossible to determine whether particular crafts were confined to individual structures or were practised in all the buildings in a given phase of

---

[179] Jones, 'Third Interim Report', p. 90.
[180] C. J. Guy, 'St Benedict's Square', *Archaeology in Lincolnshire 1985–1986. Second Annual Report of the Trust for Lincolnshire Archaeology*, ed. E. Nurser (Lincoln, 1986), pp. 23–5.
[181] Youngs *et al.*, 'Medieval Britain in 1985', pp. 157–8.
[182] B. Gilmour 'Brayford Wharf East', *Tenth Annual Report*, ed. M. J. Jones, pp. 20–4, at 24.

occupation.[183] Furthermore, there is as yet no detailed study of the metal and glassworking evidence reported from the site. It is possible, therefore, only to generalize about the material from Flaxengate.

Manufacturing on a commercial scale is clearly evident in phases IV–VI of the site's occupation, broadly dated c. 970–1060/70. Finger-rings and perhaps beads of high-lead glass were produced, and copper-alloy working also took place, with hooked-tags being common finds; silver-working may also have occurred.[184] There was much waste antler, particularly in the late ninth- to tenth-century contexts, and rather fewer bone offcuts which, however, maintained a steady level throughout the tenth and eleventh centuries. Composite combs and cases may have been made, but with a total representation of only eight apparently unfinished pieces (albeit from a total comb population of twenty-nine fragments), such production may have been either domestic or carried out by an itinerant worker.[185] Another craft, often considered a specialist's preserve, is jet-working; this is represented in an eleventh-century context by five fragmentary finger-rings in addition to jet flakes and chips. The other craft represented, textile production, was probably a broadly based domestic industry. As demonstrating a suite of crafts, this Flaxengate evidence is very similar to that from four Anglo-Scandinavian tenements excavated under the writer's direction at 16–22 Coppergate, York.

Other evidence for manufacturing in Lincoln is severely limited, and what there is cannot yet be interpreted satisfactorily. At 181–2 High Street in Wigford (20) evidence for small-scale industrial activity in the vicinity has been found in layers dated only broadly to the mid-tenth to early twelfth centuries. It includes crucible fragments for copper-alloy and glassworking, and a small amount of smithing slag.[186] More firmly dated to the pre-Norman period are the crucible fragments for copper-alloy working, found in association with an early eleventh-century timber structure at St Paul-in-the-Bail.[187] The scale and purpose of these operations is not yet clear, but they suggest a further example of the widespread appearance of evidence for industrial activities noted in York. There are also pointers that pottery manufacture was taking place in Lincoln in the Anglo-Scandinavian period; cooking pot wasters were found on the Flaxengate site in levels of this period,

---

[183] J. Mann, *Early Medieval Finds from Flaxengate 1: Objects of Antler, Bone, Stone, Horn, Ivory, Amber and Jet*, CBA, Archaeol. of Lincoln 14.1 (London, 1982), 4 and 43.

[184] Perring, *Flaxengate*, p. 41.

[185] Mann, *Early Medieval Finds*, pp. 4–8 and 44; A. Christophersen, 'Raw Material, Resources and Production Capacity in Early Medieval Comb-Manufacture in Lund', *Meddelanden fran Lunds Universitets historiska museum* 3 (1980), 150–65.

[186] Jones, 'Third Interim Report', p. 88.   [187] Jones, *Seventh Annual Report*, p. 15.

and a kiln excavated at Silver Street (11) produced shelly wares of contemporary date.[188]

Trade

The Flaxengate site, with the coin evidence, is also the principal source of evidence for Lincoln's inter-regional and international contacts. Within Britain there was evidently contact with the Derbyshire/Yorkshire Pennine area which accounts for millstone grit items; with the jet sources in North Yorkshire, perhaps via York; with the Wealden area for Kentish rag honestones; and into the Bristol/Forest of Dean area for Coalmeasures sandstone hones. Pottery includes Thetford, Grimston, St Neots and Ipswich wares from East Anglia; Stamford and Torksey wares from Lincolnshire; one sherd of York ware and two sherds of Winchester ware.[189] The wide range of contact areas around England, even if contacted at several removes, is also attested in the pre-Conquest coin finds from the site which include issues from Northampton/East Anglia, Rochester, the West Midlands (?Chester), Hertford, Hereford and York.[190] International contacts are demonstrated by four soapstone vessel sherds, walrus ivory and amber, all of which probably originated in Scandinavia; by a Slavonic-type urn from the Baltic area; by Niedermendig lava quern fragments (although these may be residual material) and by Badorf ware sherds, both of which originate in the Rhineland – the latter found in contexts pre-dating the earliest timber buildings; and by early continental glazed sherds, probably from the Low Countries and Spain or from France, found in early tenth-century contexts. Badorf ware has also been found at 181–2 High Street (20) and West Parade (18).[191]

More remarkable are the six sherds of an early ninth-century Islamic vessel, provisionally attributed to North Syria, and the rim of a Chinese stoneware Yüeh bowl of the eight to ninth centuries, both found in layers pre-dating the earliest timber buildings at Flaxengate.[192] The attempt to place the construction of this earliest phase of buildings in the decade *c.* 870/80, that is, to coincide with the Scandinavian settlement of Lincolnshire in 877, is not wholly convincing; the evidence could as well support a date of *c.* 900 or even slightly later.[193] In conjunction with the virtual absence of evidence for Anglo-Saxon

---

[188] Colyer and Jones, 'Second Interim Report', p. 84; *The Vikings in England*, ed. E. Roesdahl *et al.* (London, 1981), p. 101.   [189] Mann, *Early Medieval Finds, passim.*

[190] Blackburn *et al., Early Medieval Coins from Lincoln, passim.*

[191] *Vikings in England*, ed. Roesdahl, pp. 101–2; *Lincoln. 21 Centuries of Living History*, ed. M. J. Jones and E. Nurser (Lincoln, 1984), p. 39.

[192] L. Adams, 'Early Islamic Pottery from Flaxengate, Lincoln', *MA* 23 (1979), 218–19; Perring, *Flaxengate*, p. 33; Mann, *Early Medieval Finds*, p. 47.

[193] *pace* Perring, *Flaxengate*, pp. 33 and 36.

activity on the site, this suggests that it is as likely that the foreign material found in the immediately pre-building levels reached Lincoln in the decades between the Scandinavian take-over and the start of redevelopment on the site as that these items were brought to Lincoln in the pre-Viking period. The volume of Lincoln's emission of coinage in the Anglo-Scandinavian period, combined with the evidence for manufacturing and trade found at Flaxengate, demonstrates the regional pre-eminence of Lincoln in that era.

The earliest and apparently sparse coinage of Lincoln is the series imitating King Alfred's London monogram issue of c. 886;[194] this was superseded by the exiguous St Martin coinage c. 925,[195] perhaps also by a coinage of Sihtric I of York struck late in his reign (921–6),[196] and then probably by either the North-Eastern II or North-Eastern III group of unsigned coins of Athelstan as isolated by Blunt.[197] From the time when mint signatures appear regularly on the coinage until the Norman Conquest, Lincoln's output was on a scale surpassed only by London, and approximately equivalent to that of York.[198]

Lincoln's importance in tenth- to eleventh-century economics is further illustrated by its role as a die-cutting centre. There was some local die-cutting throughout the reign of Æthelred II, and for part of Cnut's reign Lincoln supplied dies to Nottingham, Derby, and Ipswich, and was also connected with the export of dies for Cnut's Danish coinage.[199]

The scale of minting and the die-cutting activities place Lincoln in the category of larger towns which overshadow all others in use of coinage, despite having no obvious extra administrative functions as regional centres, and which may therefore have owed their prosperity largely to overseas trade.[200] The late Saxon monetary policy of not permitting foreign coins to circulate has, it is generally assumed, lessened the amount of evidence for overseas trade by requiring foreign coins to be re-minted. Two Scandinavian coins have, however, been found in Lincoln. The first is a Danish coin of c. 1045 found at West Parade (18); the second a Norwegian coin struck at Trondheim early in the reign of King Olay Kyrre (1067–93);[201] they may be

---

194 R.H.M. Dolley and C.E. Blunt, 'The Chronology of the Coins of Ælfred the Great 871–99', *Anglo-Saxon Coins*, ed. R.H.M. Dolley (London, 1961), pp. 77–95, at 90.

195 Stewart, 'St Martin Coins'.

196 B.H.I.H. Stewart, 'The Anonymous Anglo-Viking Issue with Sword and Hammer Types and the Coinage of Sihtric I', *BNJ* 52 (1982), 108–16, at 114.

197 Blunt, 'Coinage of Athelstan', p. 88.

198 H.R. Mossop, *The Lincoln Mint c. 890–1279* (Newcastle upon Tyne, 1970), *passim*; Hill, 'Trends in the Development of Towns', fig 9.1; Metcalf, 'Continuity and Change', pp. 72–8.

199 C.S.S. Lyon, 'Analysis of the Material', in Mossop, *Lincoln Mint*, pp. 11–9, at 12.

200 Metcalf, 'Ranking of the Boroughs', p. 194.

201 M. Blackburn and M. Dolley, 'Two Scandinavian Coins Found in Lincoln', *Tenth Annual Report*, ed. Jones, pp. 33–5.

interpreted as further indications that international trade did indeed play a part in Lincoln's prosperity.

NOTTINGHAM

Origins

Nottingham occupies a defensible eminence by the River Leen, a tributary of the navigable Trent system, at a point where the river was fordable. The commanding but spatially limited vantage now occupied by the castle is separated from the less elevated area of the medieval town by a shallow valley. It has been suggested that the castle crag may have been fortified in the Iron Age, but no traces of Iron Age occupation or defences have been discovered in excavations there to date.[202] Evidence for Iron Age activity is, however, present below the medieval town north of Fishergate and at Halifax Place.[203] On both sites there was evidence for farmsteads of the late Iron Age, with occupation at Fishergate continuing into the third century AD. With the exception of a small quantity of Roman sherds, there is, however, no evidence for a Roman or Romanized presence at Nottingham; the main Roman presence in the area was 11km north-east at Margidunum (Castle Hill), East Bridgeford, a small walled town enclosing some 2.5 ha. Todd has suggested that this was essentially an administrative centre, and as such would have withered after the breakdown of the Roman administration.[204]

Early and mid-Saxon occupation

The name Nottingham, first recorded in the *Anglo-Saxon Chronicle* for 868 as *Snotengaham* meaning 'the village of Snot's followers', is an *ingaham* place-name, a type now generally believed to belong to a secondary stratum of Anglo-Saxon settlement names, perhaps of the sixth and seventh centuries.[205] At present there is no archaeological evidence from the town for pagan Anglian settlement, the nearest pagan cemeteries being at Holme Pierrepoint and Cotgrave, 5km and 10km respectively to the south-east:[206] a shield boss and a cruciform brooch have been dredged from the River Trent at Clifton,

---

202 M. Barley and I.F. Straw, 'Nottingham', *Atlas of Historic Towns* I ed. M.D. Lobel (London, 1969), 1; C. Drage, 'Nottingham Castle', *Chateau Gaillard: Études de castellologie médiévale* 11 (Caen, 1983), 117–27.

203 C.S.B. Young, 'Excavations in Nottingham', *Trans. of the Thoroton Soc. of Nottinghamshire* 75 (1971), 1–2; C.S.B. Young, *Discovering rescue archaeology in Nottingham* (Nottingham, 1981).

204 M. Todd, 'The Small Towns of Roman Britain', *Britannia* 1 (1970), 114–30, at 120.

205 B. Cox, 'The Significance of English Place-Names in *ham* in the Midlands and East Anglia', *Place-Name Evidence for the Anglo-Saxon Invasion and Scandinavian Settlements*, ed. K. Cameron (Nottingham, 1975), pp. 55–98, at 72 and 79.   206 Meaney, *Gazeteer* pp. 200–1.

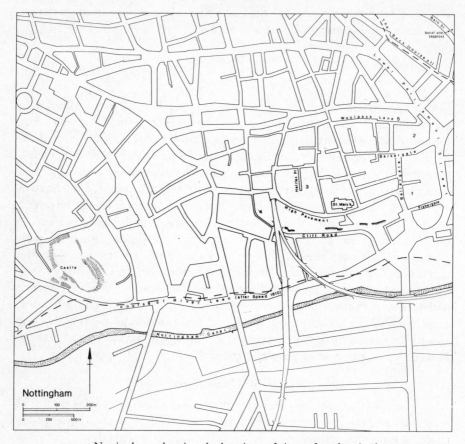

FIG. 7 Nottingham, showing the locations of sites referred to in the text

some 5 km upstream (south-west).[207] Although pagan finds from Margidunum are few, it may be that the Roman precedence which that site enjoyed continued into the fifth to seventh centuries.[208] Before the mid-Saxon period, however, there is little evidence that Nottingham and its vicinity were a focus for occupation in the way that Northampton and its surrounds were.[209]

Asser, writing in the late ninth century, records a British name 'Tig Guocobauc', literally meaning 'cavey house', the first reference to caves at Nottingham. Caves formed an important element in the storage facilities of

[207] C.W. Phillips, 'Some Recent Finds from the Trent near Nottingham', *AntJ* 21 (1941), 133–43, at 142.
[208] M. Todd, 'The Roman Settlement at Margidunum: the Excavations of 1966–8', *Trans. of the Thoroton Soc. of Nottinghamshire* 73 (1969), 7–104, at 78.
[209] Williams, 'Late Saxon Urban Origins', *passim*.

medieval Nottingham, being easily and safely dug from the sandstone, but there is no evidence that either man-made or natural caves were occupied in Asser's day, and it has been suggested that the name was of Asser's invention rather than being current in Wales.[210] Even so, it demonstrates that Asser had some knowledge of the area and its characteristic geology.

Traces of a possible mid-Saxon enclosure which pre-dates the Viking takeover recorded by the *Chronicle* in 868 have been found at the eastern side of the medieval town. North of Fishergate (1) a *c.* 50m length of ditch, *c.* 5m wide and up to 1.5m deep, running east–west, has been located, and approximately 150m to the north, between Woolpack Lane and Barkergate (2) a parallel and similar ditch has been traced for approximately 15m.[211] Both these lengths of ditch are dated to the mid-Saxon period on the basis of pottery found in their backfill.

There is no indication of the eastern boundary of this enclosure, which could have extended to The Beck watercourse; alternatively, medieval defensive ditches below Lower Parliament Street could have removed all traces of an earlier cutting there. As for its west side, an observation just west of the Fishergate excavation failed to record the ditch continuing on its alignment there, and so, unless there was an interruption of the feature at that point, for example for a gateway, the ditch may be presumed to have turned northwards some 10–20m east of Bellar Gate. It is to the east of this line that all but a handful of the approximately two hundred sherds of mid-Saxon pottery known from Nottingham have come, a fact which supports this hypothetical layout of the mid-Saxon defence. Nevertheless, there are other, undated lengths of defensive work which could have extended this mid-Saxon enclosure to the west. On the Halifax Place site (3), some 250m further west, the earliest feature recognized was an undated defensive ditch running east–west across the excavated area.[212] There is also evidence for an undated ditch at Drury Hill (4), preceding the firmly dated late Saxon one,[213] but this earlier phase may itself be late Saxon. At neither Halifax Place nor Drury Hill can the undated, early ditches be linked by their form with the wide, shallow ditches recognized at Woolpack Lane/Barkergate and north of Fishergate, and in the absence of such a link and given the distribution of mid-Saxon pottery, it seems wisest at present to suggest that the mid-Saxon enclosure was limited to the east end of the medieval town. The putative area enclosed there is not in the

[210] S. Keynes and M. Lapidge, *Alfred the Great* (Harmondsworth, 1983), p. 241, n. 59.
[211] Young, 'Excavations in Nottingham', 1–2; C.S.B. Young, 'Excavations in Nottingham', *Trans. of the Thoroton Soc. of Nottinghamshire* 76 (1972), 1–3, at 2.
[212] C.S.B. Young, pers. com.
[213] C.S.B. Young, 'Excavations in Nottingham', *Trans. of the Thoroton Soc. of Nottinghamshire* 74 (1970), 2–3.

best defensive position, since it is overlooked to the west, and it may therefore not have been primarily of military importance. As yet the nature of activity within it is unknown, for no structures or features contemporary with the ditches have been located, and there is no evidence for an early church there – St Mary's, the mother-church of the Anglo-Scandinavian *burh*, lies outside this earlier enclosure.[214]

Anglo-Scandinavian Nottingham

Introduction

The *Anglo-Saxon Chronicle*'s entry for 868 describes the Viking army wintering in a fortress at Nottingham, and being besieged there by the English; Asser adds that the English could not break down the wall. From the *Chronicle* we know that in 918 Edward captured the borough and repaired it, and that in 920 he returned to Nottingham and built a second borough on the south bank of the river opposite the earlier one, connecting the two with a bridge. Little else is recorded of pre-Norman Nottingham: its standing as one of the Five Boroughs is recorded in the *Chronicle* for 942, and the *witan* is known to have met in Nottingham at least twice, in 934 and *c*. 973.[215] *Domesday Book*'s record of Nottingham at the Conquest provides meagre details of one hundred and seventy-three burgesses, two moneyers, nineteen villeins and perhaps a further thirty-eight burgesses in the town, accounting for a maximum of two hundred and thirty-two inhabitants. There is mention of a church and, most interestingly, the importance of both the Fosse Way, the road to York, and the River Trent is stressed. A reference in Domesday's Derby entry confirms that there was a shire court in Nottingham.

Defences

The best understood element of Anglo-Scandinavian Nottingham is its defences north of the river, although even here there is still uncertainty. It is not clear if the mid-Saxon enclosure recognized at the east end of the medieval town was still functioning when the Viking army arrived in 868, and was the site of the English siege of that year. Alternatively, the Vikings may have fortified a new position, as yet unlocated. Either or both of the undated ditches found at Halifax Place (3) and Drury Hill (4) could perhaps be associated with such an enclosure, or it could have been defined by the ditches discovered to the north between Woolpack Lane and Hockley (5) and to the west at Drury

---

[214] A. Rogers, 'Parish Boundaries and Urban History', *JBAA*, 3rd ser. 35 (1972), 46–64, at 51–6.   [215] Stenton, *Anglo-Saxon England*, p. 350.

Hill (4).[216] This enclosure presumably had its southern boundary north of the cliff line which runs between High Pavement and Narrow Marsh (now Cliff Road). The eastern limit is uncertain, although there were indications of a possible north-east corner at the Woolpack Lane site (5), and a later, medieval ditch below Lower Parliament Street may have removed traces of an earlier eastern boundary. Such a fortification, positioned to embrace the most readily defended area east of the castle crag, would enclose an area of approximately 13.75 hectares. This work was refurbished at least once in the pre-Norman period, with evidence for a re-cutting of the ditch from a flattened U-shaped profile to a flattened V-shape with a deeper central channel at both Woolpack Lane/Hockley (5) and Drury Hill (4).[217]

Precise dates for the two phases of defence identified on both these sites cannot be determined; indeed, the Woolpack Lane/Hockley site contained no dating evidence whatsoever in either phase, and is attributed to the Anglo-Scandinavian period only by analogy with Drury Hill. There the recut ditch contained quantities of eleventh-century Stamford ware in its backfill, above which was a building dated to the mid-eleventh century, and perhaps to be equated with one of those erected in the city ditch to which Domesday Book refers. A sunken-featured structure beyond the ditch contained Stamford ware of the eleventh century, identical to sherds recovered from the ditch, but the relationship of ditch to structure was unclear, thanks to a modern intrusion. This evidence, together with the presumption that this circuit must pre-date the enlarged Norman circuit which incorporated the castle to the west, seems to place at least the later of the two phases in the Anglo-Scandinavian period, but no further refinement is possible, and the various refurbishments cannot be attributed either to the original Viking army, to Edward the Elder, to the brief period of domination by the York Viking Olaf Guthfrithsson *c.* 940, or to any other hypothetical late Saxon strengthening. Further investigation to recover more dating evidence is therefore required, as is the location of the southern *burh*.

Topography

The defensive ditches, cut relatively deeply into the Bunter sandstone, have largely survived later intrusions except in the case of direct recuttings, but widespread medieval disturbance of the ground, notably the creation of undercrofts, cellars and caves, coupled with Victorian and more recent rebuilding, has severely limited the survival of pre-Norman deposits. Additional archaeological problems are created by the well-drained subsoil, probably the

---

[216] Young, 'Excavations in Nottingham' (1970), p. 2.   [217] *Ibid.*

principal factor in the generally poor condition of surviving artifacts, and the apparent lack of rubbish or occupation deposits associated with the buildings that have been recognized.

In ecclesiastical terms, there is documentary evidence for only one church in Domesday Book, and the inter-relationships of parish boundaries suggest that St Mary's, which seems originally to have encompassed the whole *burh*, was the primary and principal church.[218] It retains no pre-Conquest fabric, however, and no archaeological trace of the Anglo-Scandinavian church has been found.

Secular structures assignable to this period are known from the south frontage of Woolpack Lane (2), where a late ninth- to early tenth-century date is inferred on the grounds of relative stratigraphy for a slight building of wattle and daub construction, and at Fishergate (1), outside the mid-Saxon ditch, where a bow-sided structure thought to be of similar date is reported. The sunken-featured structure cut by the ditch system at Drury Hill (4) may also belong to this period: and a sequence of three building phases uncovered at Halifax Place (3) is thought to pre-date *c.* 1000, although the earliest structure is not closely dated and might pre-date the Viking arrival. At none of these sites is there evidence that the Anglo-Scandinavian layout exerted a long-lasting influence on the tenurial pattern in the vicinity; indeed at Halifax Place, there is evidence for clearance of the structures *c.* 1000, and wholesale re-organization of the area *c.* 1100.[219]

Crafts, industry and the economy

Evidence for manufacturing is restricted to a group of pottery wasters and kiln material excavated at Halifax Place.[220] The forms are of cooking pots/jars, bowls and possible storage vessels; the cooking pots/jars were thrown on a fast wheel. None of this pottery has been identified on other excavated sites in Nottingham, but it is clearly in the late Saxon tradition, and the kiln equates with those known in other East Mercian Danelaw towns such as Lincoln, Stamford, Torksey, and further afield at Thetford.

The only other clue to Nottingham's role in the economy of the area is the Nottingham mint. This was in existence from the reign of Athelstan, but only two moneyers were recorded in Domesday Book, a reflection of its limited output in the Anglo-Scandinavian period, when it can have been only of local

[218] Rogers, 'Parish Boundaries', pp. 51–3.
[219] Young, *Rescue Archaeology in Nottingham*, passim.
[220] A.V. Nailor, 'A Preliminary Note on a Late Saxon Ware from Nottingham', *Med. Ceramics* 8 (1984), 59–64.

significance; for most of the period 973–1066 it was the least important minting centre among the Five Boroughs.[221] .

Conclusion

At present, if the documentary evidence is left aside, it is principally the evolution and growth of its defences which demonstrate the importance of Nottingham in the later pre-Conquest period. Were it not for two Viking graves discovered on the south side of Bath Street in 1851,[222] the presence of a Scandinavian army or settlement would not be deduced through the known artifacts. The documents attest the political and social importance of Nottingham as a shire centre with corresponding judicial functions, but there is no archaeological indication of a substantial commercial or mercantile presence in the town.

STAMFORD

Origins

Stamford is sited on the line of the prehistoric route, the Jurassic Way, on either bank of the River Welland, less than 1km downstream from where the Roman Ermine Street crossed the river at a ford.[223] Hoskins has suggested that a ford just east (downstream) of the present bridge was the eponymous ford of the place-name, the site of the earliest post-Roman river crossing, and in this he has been followed by Perrott.[224] Alternatively, it has been suggested that there was an early ford approximately 180m upstream of the present bridge, where the twin branches of the river, flowing through water meadow, are now crossed by the Lammas and George Bridges.[225] This latter hypothesis gains support from Stamford's street plan – the sharply curving course of the existing main through-route across the river has the appearance of being an alteration to a more direct route leading from the south via Pinfold Lane and Wothorpe Road to this second suggested ford and then via Castle Dyke and Mallory Lane to Scotgate. The date when these streets were established has

---

[221] Blunt, 'Coinage of Athelstan', pp. 95–6; Hill, 'Trends in the Development of Towns', p. 216; Metcalf, 'Continuity and Change', pp. 76–7.   [222] *ArchJ* 1851, 425–6.

[223] W.F. Grimes, 'The Archaeology of the Stamford Region', *The Making of Stamford*, ed. A. Rogers (Leicester, 1964), pp. 1–14, at 2–7; C. Mahany and D. Roffe, 'Stamford: the Development of an Anglo-Scandinavian Borough', *Anglo-Norman Studies* V, ed. R.A. Brown (Woodbridge, 1983), 197–219, at 197.

[224] W.G. Hoskins, *Local History in England* (London, 1972), pp. 98–9; A.M.J. Perrott, 'The Place-Name Stamford', *Stamford Historian* 2 (1978), 38–40.

[225] Royal Commission on Historical Monuments England, *The Town of Stamford* (London, 1977), pp. xxxviii–xxxix.

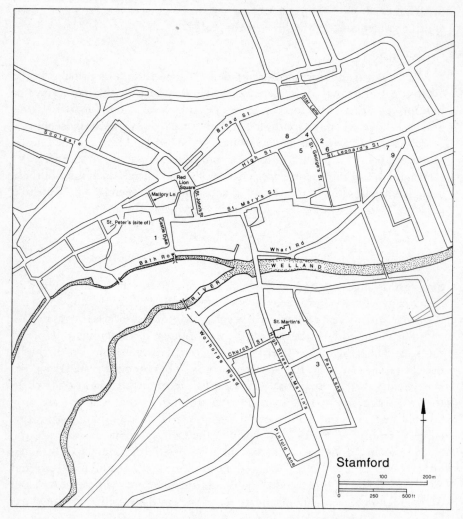

FIG. 8 Stamford, showing the locations of sites referred to in the text

not, however, been investigated, and a third derivation of the place-name sees it originating from the Roman ford 1km further upstream.[226]

The principal settlement at Stamford seems always to have been on the north bank, where the limestone plateau overlooking the river is traversed by the Scotgate valley.[227] The bridge at Stamford is at a point where the Welland's course narrows markedly in contrast to the wide area of water-meadow to both

[226] Mahany and Roffe, 'Stamford', p. 197.   [227] Royal Commission, *Stamford*, p. xxxv.

east and west; the river passage from the North Sea could be cut here, with river crossing and, if necessary, river blocking, controlled from positions of some strength on the limestone ridges which ran steeply down to the river.

There is no evidence for prehistoric occupation where the medieval town stands, while such Roman structures and objects as are known suggest that at that time there was only very limited occupation in the vicinity.[228] There are one or two poorly documented pagan Saxon funerary urns which may have come from Stamford,[229] and it has been suggested that the site fits neatly into a series of quite regularly spaced early or mid-Saxon settlements situated on the north bank of the Welland.[230] There is as yet an absence of features which could be attributed without question to such a pre-Viking phase of Stamford's existence, although a defended enclosure, discussed below, could possibly belong to the immediately pre-Viking period.

Between Bath Row and Castle Dyke (1), below the bailey of the Norman castle, three concentric ditches were traced over a total length of approximately 33m.[231] The relatively slight, innermost cut is interpreted as a palisade trench. The other two ditches were both at least 1.4–1.5m in depth, the uncertainty being caused by later features which may have cut away their tops; their widths at the extant top varied between 1.8m and 2.75m. The central ditch at least was V-shaped, and ran some 3m inside the outermost.[232] The outermost ditch is possibly later than the inner two,[233] although there is no direct stratigraphical evidence for their sequence, and this distinction is suggested on the basis of a difference in the material backfilling them. The feature seems too substantial merely to mark a property boundary, and is better interpreted as a defended enclosure. Since even the short length investigated does not form a true arc, the continuation of the ditches' line and the area they enclose are both difficult to estimate; nonetheless, it has been suggested that these works could have encircled the knoll upon which the castle was later built, thus enclosing an area of approximately 1.1ha. This is the same size as the seventh-century and earlier ditched and palisaded 'Great Enclosure' at the Northumbrian palace site of Yeavering, which, although interpreted by its excavator as a cattle corral, may have served the function of a *burh*,[234] and is almost three times as large as the earliest ringwork of *c.* AD 850–

228 *Ibid.*   229 Meaney, *Gazeteer*, p. 164.   230 Royal Commission, *Stamford*, p. xxxvi.

231 C. Mahany, 'Excavations at Stamford Castle 1971–1976', *Chateau Gaillard: Études de castellologie médiévale* 8 (Caen, 1977), 223–45, at 237 and fig. 6.

232 *Ibid.*; Mahany and Roffe, 'Stamford', p. 203 and n. 21.

233 K. Kilmurry, *The Pottery Industry of Stamford, Lincs., c. AD 850–1250*, BAR Brit. ser. 84 (Oxford, 1980), 32.

234 B. Hope-Taylor, *Yeavering: an Anglo-British Centre of Early Northumbria* (London, 1977), pp. 789 and 157.

940 at Goltho, Lincolnshire, a defensible domestic and presumably aristocratic site where, by the early eleventh century, the refurbished bank and ditch enclosed approximately one hectare.[235]

Dating evidence for the Stamford ditch system is varied in its form. The cuts appear to have been backfilled after a short period with their own upcast, a clean pink clay. In the fill of the centre ditch was found a coin of Alfred, most probably lost *c.* 890–925. Pottery wasters were also found here. The outer ditch cut a layer containing red-painted Stamford ware, and this layer also pre-dated a pottery kiln which has yielded an archaeomagnetic determination of AD 850 ± 50. Together, these strands of evidence suggest a date of *c.* 850–900 for the defences.[236]

This date is sufficiently uncertain to allow various interpretations of the defensive work, which might be pre-Viking, Viking, or even Edwardian English in origin. If, however, the causeway across the river opposite the castle is the earliest crossing point at Stamford, and if the secondary bridge site downstream can be attributed to the Edwardian period, a pre-Viking or Viking origin would be suggested for these defences. Furthermore, as Mahany and Roffe have argued, St Peter's Church, which is sited either immediately adjacent to or within these defences, may have been the 'mother' church of Stamford and may itself be of pre-Viking origin – it was a 'royal' church in the hands of Queen Edith in 1066, and associated with an estate or manor which was tenurially distinct from the borough at the time of Domesday Book.[237] There are, in sum, several pointers which suggest that the defended enclosure at Stamford Castle may be a mid-Saxon, pre-Viking, aristocratic manor or estate nucleus, although the form this took and the function it fulfilled are unknown. Alternatively, this area may have been the nucleus of a newly founded, Viking, aristocratic stronghold, although this seems a less likely milieu for an early church.

Anglo-Scandinavian occupation

Historical introduction

Although referred to in passing by the late tenth-century chronicler Æthelweard in connection with events of *c.* 894, Stamford is not mentioned in

[235] G. Beresford, 'Goltho Manor, Lincolnshire: the Buildings and their Surrounding Defences', *Proc. of the Battle Conference on Anglo-Norman Studies IV. 1981* ed. R. A. Brown (Woodbridge, 1982), 13–36, at 20–2.

[236] Two C-14 determinations calibrated at AD 678 ± 83 and AD 837 ± 77 (Kilmurry, *Pottery Industry of Stamford*, p. 32), based on charred wood found in the kiln's stokehole, may be disregarded, as the wood may be considerably older than the use of the kiln.

[237] Mahany and Roffe, 'Stamford', pp. 201–6; see also Williams, 'Late Saxon Urban Origins', p. 29.

any contemporary historical source until 918, when the *Anglo-Saxon Chronicle* records the submission of the [Vikings in the] northern borough and the construction of a second *burh* on the south bank. Stamford next appears in the *Chronicle*'s list of Five Boroughs in 942; the *Chronicle* later records that in 1016 Cnut passed through Stamford. Between 942 and 1016 minting activity commenced at Stamford, the earliest coins yet known being of Edgar's Reform issue of *c.* 973.[238] Domesday Book's record of the borough in 1066 is typically short, referring only to sub-division into six wards, five in Lincolnshire and one in Northamptonshire. The five Lincolnshire wards contained one hundred and forty one messuages at that date. Mahany and Roffe have presented evidence supporting the thesis that St Peter's was one of the four churches mentioned in the Domesday entry;[239] the significance of this is discussed below.

Defences

Whatever attribution is given to the pre-Conquest defences at the castle, they cannot be linked with the other defended enclosure which has been recognized north of the Welland. Topographical analysis has suggested that the pre-Conquest *burh* was bounded by Broad Street to the north, St Mary's Street to the south, Star Lane and George Street to the east and St John's Street/Red Lion Square to the west.[240] The only site yet excavated on this putative defensive line is to the north-east, to the north of 4 St George's Street (2). Here an undated series of post-holes and slots was recorded in association with a possible turf rampart, and compared to the more readily comprehensible remains of defences discovered at Tamworth.[241] It is possible, however, that this supposed defence may have been part of a timber building, for its remains were encountered only at the extreme western edge of a small trench, and the complete feature was not uncovered. Furthermore, traces of ninth- to tenth-century occupation and activity, including iron-working slags, underlay the slots and post-holes,[242] indicating that even if the feature is interpreted as a defence it was not a primary feature of occupation here, and may be a product of the Edwardian or an even later pre-Conquest period. The area enclosed within the putative defences is approximately six hectares.

South of the river, the rectangle enclosed by Park Lane, Pinfold Lane and

---

238 R.H.M. Dolley and D.M. Metcalf, 'The Reform of the English Coinage under Eadgar', *Anglo-Saxon Coins*, ed. Dolley, pp. 136–68, at 145.

239 Mahany and Roffe, 'Stamford', p. 201.

240 C. Mahany, *Stamford: Castle and Town (South Lincolnshire Archaeol.* 2 (1978)), 8; Royal Commission, *Stamford*, p. xxxviii.   241 Mahany, *Castle and Town*, p. 10.

242 C. Mahany, A. Burchard and G. Simpson, *Excavations in Stamford Lincolnshire 1963–1969* (London, 1982), p. 10.

Church Street, with High Street St Martin's running axially through the centre, seems the most likely area for the southern *burh* built by Edward in 918. An excavation at the rear of 24 and 24A High Street St Martin's (3) located a ditch running north-south which is at present the only possible vestige of the southern enclosure, which would encompass approximately 3.75 hectares.[243] The study of parish boundaries is unhelpful on both sides of the river because of later medieval parish amalgamations.[244]

Topography

Within the hypothetical defended area north of the river, High Street appears to be a centrally positioned east-west route. High Street, however, has been shown to overlie iron-working residues which are presumed to be *in situ*, although there is a possibility that they were brought in from elsewhere as road make-up. Similar residues have been discovered at several intra-mural sites including High Street (4), High Street/Maiden Lane (5), St Leonard's Street/St George's Street (6), St Leonard's Street (7) and 32-4 High Street (8). Pottery associated with the deposits at 32-4 High Street has been dated to before the mid-eleventh century, and by comparison with this assemblage the iron-working at High Street/Maiden Lane has been placed in the early tenth to early eleventh century.[245] These dates should not, however, be extrapolated to suggest when the residues below High Street were laid down or when High Street was created; and they are in any case too vague to be of much value in that respect. Since, however, timber structures which may be as early as the late ninth century preceded the iron-working at High Street/Maiden Lane and apparently respected the line of High Street, it may have been created before AD 900, although this event has been placed considerably later in the pre-Conquest period.[246] Across the river, High Street St Martin's likewise takes a central course through the presumed south *burh*, but the date of its creation has not been tested in excavation. Suburban settlement has been suggested, on the basis of documentary evidence,[247] but has not been recoverd in excavation.

Structures

With the exception of the timber remains excavated at 4 St George's Street (2) and interpreted as parts of a defensive line, the only pre-Conquest building remains investigated at Stamford are those at High Street/Maiden Lane (5). These structures, the earliest features on the site, appear to have been demolished to make way for iron-working dated broadly to the early tenth to

[243] *Ibid.* p. 10.   [244] Rogers, 'Parish Boundaries', pp. 62-3.
[245] Mahany, Burchard and Simpson, *Stamford*, pp. 10 and 119.
[246] *Ibid.* p. 9.   [247] Mahany and Roffe, 'Stamford', p. 215.

early eleventh century on the basis of ceramic evidence.[248] It is possible that the underlying buildings may therefore date as early as the later ninth century, and may reflect the occupation of the *burh* by the Danish army inferred from the *Chronicle*.

The remains themselves were so limited in extent as to be virtually uninterpretable, although it has been suggested that two buildings and a dividing fence were represented, and that at least one of the structures was perhaps a substantial hall or barn.[249] Most striking is the apparent rectilinearity of their layout, closely spaced and with gable ends on to High Street, the nearest point of which lay some 6–7m north of the visible part of the structure. This may imply that the High Street was already in existence before the iron-working residues were placed on its line.

Industry and economy

Archaeologically, the economy of Anglo-Scandinavian Stamford is domi-nated by two industries, pottery and iron-working, both the product of local geology. A range of clays suitable for pottery production occurs in the area, although the precise source of those used has not been determined.[250] Ironstone formations also occur, specifically of Northampton sand ironstone, which outcrops immediately south of the river and west of the putative south *burh*, and also at other sites in the immediate vicinity.[251]

The Stamford ware pottery industry, represented in its pre-Conquest phase by kilns at the castle (1) and Wharf Road (9) which both lie outside the area thought to be the Anglo-Scandinavian *burh*, is well known through its distinctive glazed forms, and has been more fully studied than any other pre-Conquest ware. It also appears to be more generally and widely distributed than other contemporary wares, with a distribution network extending over a 200km radius from Stamford. The types traded included fine table wares and some culinary wares, as well as storage vessels, the contents of which were perhaps more important than the pottery itself, and crucibles, for which, it is suggested, there was relatively little competition from other suitable wares.[252]

It has been shown that manufacture of Stamford ware started at an early date; kiln debris and wasters are associated with the concentric ditched defence discovered at the castle, which itself may date *c.* AD 900.[253] These wasters include red-painted sherds, which seem to indicate contact with and inspiration from continental production centres. Such contacts would also

---

[248] Mahany, Burchard and Simpson, *Stamford*, p. 24. [249] *Ibid.* p. 21.
[250] Kilmurry, *Pottery Industry of Stamford*, pp. 63ff.
[251] Mahany, Burchard and Simpson, *Stamford*, p. 136.
[252] Kilmurry, *Pottery Industry of Stamford*, pp. 156, 162 and 166–8.
[253] Mahany and Roffe, 'Stamford', p. 203.

have initiated the use of glaze and the fast wheel, and the growth of the industry has been tentatively linked to the disruption of the north French potteries caused by Viking raids in the mid-ninth century and the consequent migration, enforced or otherwise, of a French potter or potters.[254] Although stress has been placed on the relative unimportance of the potters's contribution to Stamford's economy,[255] the town was nonetheless a principal ceramic production centre of the pre-Conquest period.

As with pottery production, evidence for iron-working has come from sites quite widely spread throughout Stamford both inside and outside the northern *burh*. Hearths for roasting iron ore and dumps of slag and waste 'fines' dated to the tenth and early eleventh centuries were found at High Street/Maiden Lane (5) and an area used in the later tenth to early eleventh centuries for roasting, smelting and secondary working is known from 32–4 High Street (8).[256] The near absence of metal objects on these sites indicates that only the mass-production of wrought iron was carried out here, with the forging/ manufacture of objects taking place elsewhere. Watching briefs have recorded further evidence for iron-working below the St Leonard's Street/St George's Street junction, where a bowl furnace was revealed (6), slag in the centre of St Leonard's Street (7), ore residues in the centre of High Street (4) and slag below the timber features east of St George's Street (2).[257] The material from these watching briefs cannot be closely dated, and neither can the dated, excavated sites be used as an indication of the date of material recorded elsewhere. The various iron-working locations need not be contemporary, and might represent quite widely spaced chronological stages in this industry. Its prevalence in Stamford's Anglo-Scandinavian archaeological record seems marked at present but there is no reason to believe that the industry was more than of local/regional significance.[258]

Conclusion

With the notable exception of its pottery industry and now, to a lesser extent, its iron-working, Anglo-Scandinavian Stamford remains little known. Settlement appears to have developed *c.* AD 850–900, perhaps from the basis of a mid-Saxon estate centre, an interpretation based on the discoveries at the castle site. The only evidence for occupation within what can be recognized as the defended *burh* north of the river is the vestigial and imprecisely dated structures from High Street/Maiden Lane; and nothing is yet known of

[254] Kilmurry, *Pottery Industry of Stamford*, pp. 193–5.   [255] *Ibid.* p. 152.
[256] Mahany, Burchard and Simpson, *Stamford*, pp. 23–4 and 106–7.   [257] *Ibid.* p. 10.
[258] Cf. J. Hassall, 'Excavations in Bedford 1977 and 1978', *Bedfordshire Archaeol.* 16 (1983), 37–64, at 48 and 50; E. Baker, 'Three Excavations in Bedford, 1979–1984', *Bedfordshire Archaeol.* 17 (1986), 51–71, at 53.

activity south of the Welland. Only the Viking and Kufic coins found in a hoard dated *c.* 895,[259] and a hitherto overlooked ringed pin from the castle, found in a thirteenth-century context, may be interpreted as tangible proof of a Scandinavian presence.

The fortress aspect of the Vikings' *burh*, recognizable in the Anglo-Saxon *Chronicle*, has recently been suggested as a continuing *raison d'être* for the site in the mid- and late tenth-century, controlling part of a buffer zone against the Vikings of York, linked closely with and supporting Lincoln, and commanding the route between Scandinavian colonies in Northumbria and East Anglia.[260] There must, however, have been more to Stamford's role than this, for its mint ranks among the top ten most prolific coining centres in late Saxon England, out-done by Lincoln and York, but clearly busier than other centres in the north-eastern Danelaw.[261] This may be an extension of an earlier commercial importance, hinted at in the coin hoard noted above, in which Metcalf detects both a monetary dependence on south-east England and an east-west trade that was by-passing the south-east.[262] Perhaps, as Sawyer suggested,[263] wool exports were already important in the late Saxon economy, and Stamford already enjoyed the eminence in this branch of archaeologically invisible exports which it is known to have had in later centuries.

SUMMARY

Important new information about the sites known collectively as the Five Boroughs has become available during the last decade or so of increased excavation, but ignorance of many vital topics is still total or nearly total. Many of the conclusions which may now be drawn are argued on the basis of negative evidence, and they may be overturned by future discoveries.

The settlements have in common positions on navigable rivers, with important prehistoric or Roman land-routes either passing through them or nearby. Their origins, however, are diverse: Derby, Leicester, Lincoln and Nottingham were all occupied to an unknown extent in the Iron Age, but prehistoric activity has yet to be found at Stamford. In the Roman era, Leicester and Lincoln both eventually became substantial walled towns, and there were also fortifications at Little Chester, 1km from Derby, but the sites of

---

[259] R.H.M. Dolley, *The Hiberno-Norse Coins in the British Museum* (London, 1966), p. 49.

[260] Mahany and Roffe, 'Stamford', pp. 214–15.

[261] Hill, 'Trends in the Development of Towns', p. 216; Metcalf, 'Continuity and Change', pp. 76–7.

[262] D.M. Metcalf, 'The Monetary History of England in the Tenth Century Viewed in the Perspective of the Eleventh Century', *Anglo-Saxon Monetary History*, ed. M.A.S. Blackburn (Leicester, 1986), pp. 133–58, at 138.

[263] P.H. Sawyer, 'The Wealth of England in the Eleventh Century', *TRHS* 5th ser. 15 (1965), 145–64, at 161–4.

Nottingham and Stamford were apparently not occupied. This pattern seemingly continued into the succeeding centuries, with pagan Saxon cemeteries at Little Chester and just outside Leicester, and the late fourth- to seventh-century cemetery, perhaps continuously Christian, at St Paul-in-the-Bail, Lincoln. Derby itself has not produced pagan Saxon material, and there are no other finds from Lincoln, but at Leicester objects of this period have been found in limited quantities throughout the Roman area. Nottingham's name suggests a sixth- to seventh-century origin, but there is no archaeological confirmation of this, while Stamford has only a dubious pagan cemetery, represented by ill-provenanced pottery vessels.

All these sites have, however, produced evidence which, with varying degrees of certainty, points to occupation in the mid-Saxon period. From Derby and Leicester the evidence is ecclesiastical. St Alkmund's, Derby, has produced sculpture of the ninth century which, unless it was transported to the site, indicates a contemporary Christian site; and Northworthy/Derby was the burial place for a Mercian aristocrat in 871. Leicester was a bishop's seat certainly from 737, and perhaps earlier, and the upstanding Roman fabric of the Jewry Wall may have been incorporated into a mid-Saxon church. Nothing else of the seventh to ninth centuries is known from these two places.

At Nottingham and Stamford there is evidence for a defended enclosure which probably belongs to this period. At Stamford it is approximately 1.1ha in area, with a putative mid-Saxon church within or immediately adjacent; at Nottingham the area may be 1.5–3ha, not in the strongest defensible position, and without any indication of an associated church. Both may represent the secular focal point of their hinterland.

At Lincoln, where the presumption is that the Roman defences continued to define at least an outer boundary, there is evidence for activity in the lower walled town at Flaxengate, more ambiguous data from elsewhere, and the suggestion that, to the south of the River Witham, Wigford represents an important trading settlement.

In spite of the limited and varied nature of the evidence, it may be suggested that each of these sites was, in the seventh to ninth centuries, a secular and ecclesiastical centre for its région, a focus of power and wealth requiring the provision of services, including the fabrication of objects, and attracting visitors, including inter-regional and perhaps even occasionally international merchants. Lincoln, for a mixture of geographical and historical reasons, perhaps saw more mercantile activity than the others, but on the present evidence, none of these sites should be described as towns before the Vikings' arrival.[264]

---

[264] Cf. Williams, 'Late Saxon Urban Origins', pp. 27–9.

Thus it seems that at all five the Vikings found a pre-existing centre of occupation which had natural potential for development; but what, if any, development they underwent in the four decades between their takeover (if this happened as soon as the Vikings settled the area) and their recapture by the Anglo-Saxons is mostly unclear. The pottery kiln at Stamford Castle can be assigned to this phase with some confidence, but this apart the only clear evidence is from Flaxengate, Lincoln, where occupation was resumed perhaps *c.* 900 on a site largely deserted since the Roman period. The two 'pagan' Viking burials from Nottingham do not contribute to this study of settlement development, and indeed, by analogy with those from St Mary Bishophill Junior, York, could date to after the English recapture.[265] The assumption remains that at this time these places were principally defensive centres for surrounding immigrant landowners, but defences which can be definitely assigned to this phase are unknown, and although the Roman works at Leicester, Lincoln and Little Chester near Derby may all have continued to function, they would perhaps have been too large to be easily defended by a segment of the Viking army which, when a single unit, required only 1.4ha for its fortification at Repton.

The number of Viking settlers at any of these sites is impossible to assess, and the only indication of their population comes in Domesday Book, which gives what is likely to be an underestimate. Only the proportion of moneyers' names of Scandinavian derivation gives some insight into the degree of Viking settlement in the *burhs*, and this is a source available only from the late tenth century to the Norman Conquest, and one which may be biased by the social position of the moneyers and the name-giving habits of this successful class. Study of the coinage of 973–1016 has shown that at Lincoln almost 50 per cent of moneyers' names were Scandinavian and at Stamford the figure is 14 per cent. The percentages for Derby, Leicester and Nottingham are based on very small numbers of recorded moneyers, and do not have much statistical weight; the figures are 50, 22 and 50 per cent respectively.[266] This superficially suggests a higher proportion of Scandinavian settlers or a more enduring Scandinavian culture north of the Trent, but the nature of evidence does not allow conclusions to be drawn with confidence.

From the recapture to the Norman Conquest there is a little more archaeological evidence at some of the Five Boroughs, although Derby and Leicester remain particularly enigmatic. The extent of Anglo-Scandinavian

[265] L.P. Wenham and R.A. Hall, 'Excavation to the North of St. Mary Bishophill Junior, 1961–3 and 1967', *St. Mary Bishophill Junior and St. Mary Castlegate*, Archaeology of York 8.2, ed. P.V. Addyman (London, 1987), 75–83.

[266] V.J. Smart, 'Moneyers of the Late Anglo-Saxon Coinage 973–1016', *Commentationes de nummis saeculorum IX–XI in Suecia repertis* 2 (1986), 193–276, at 240–1.

Leicester is unknown, although if the Roman defences continued to form a boundary, some 35ha were enclosed. To estimate Derby's size, several assumptions must be made. If the peninsula enclosed by the River Trent and the Markeaton Brook is taken as the likely area of the *burh*, and the peninsula's neck was defended just above the Causey ford, then an area of approximately 29ha was enclosed.

Nottingham and Stamford were both established as double *burhs* by Edward the Elder, although it is not known how actively this provision was later maintained. At Nottingham a northern defensive enclosure of 13.75ha has been identified, but the southern *burh* is unknown; at Stamford the putative north *burh* is 6ha in extent, and the southern one 3.75ha. At Lincoln, if the Roman walls were maintained and extended to the waterfront, an area of some 38ha was defended, and there was a further 59ha enclosed between the River Witham and the Sincil Dyke in the Wigford suburb.

The defensible nuclei of the Five Boroughs thus varied considerably in size, although the extent to which the enclosures were built up is not yet known. In area they may be compared with the re-used Roman fortifications of some Wessex *burhs* such as Winchester with 58ha, or with the *de novo* Wessex earthworks such as Cricklade with 29ha;[267] in the south-east Danelaw, tenth-to eleventh-century Northampton covered 24 ha;[268] in East Anglia, settlement at Norwich before *c.* 900 was restricted to no more than 20ha, but had doubled in area by *c.* 1000;[269] and in western Mercia, the defences of Tamworth enclosed some 20ha.[270] The sizes of many of the West Midlands shire centres are not certain, and it is therefore not possible to make all the comparisons required, but it does appear that Derby, Nottingham and Stamford were small to medium-sized *burhs*.

The development of internal layout can be discerned only at Lincoln, with the laying out of Flaxengate perhaps *c.* 900, and other indications that the Roman plan was largely disregarded, although individual Roman structures exerted an influence, as Jewry Wall possibly did at Leicester.

With the exception of coins struck at their mints, which were not prolific, pottery kilns at Southgate Street, Leicester and at Nottingham are the sole remains of manufacturing known from either place, and Derby has produced no evidence for industry apart from its coins. Stamford's pottery and iron-working industries are better represented, but they do not convincingly account for the quite substantial output of its mint which, as a reflection of the *burh's* size, is exceptional; the silver flowing into Stamford presumably reflects

[267] Biddle, 'Towns', p. 126.　　[268] Williams, 'From "Palace" to "Town"', p. 133.
[269] A. Carter, 'The Anglo-Saxon Origins of Norwich: the Problems and Approaches', *ASE* 7 (1978), 175–204, at 201.　　[270] Biddle, 'Towns', p. 135.

trading activities, and in addition to its glazed pottery, wool may also have been exported.

A single excavation in Lincoln at Flaxengate accounts for most of the available information on manufacturing and trade there, but the range from here and elsewhere in the town is impressive, an additional index of Lincoln's position as the most important of the Five Boroughs in terms of size and wealth. This reflects in part a larger and perhaps wealthier hinterland than those which the others of the Five Boroughs serviced, and perhaps too the export of wool via either the Foss Dyke/Trent or the Witham/Wash. The Flaxengate manufacturing evidence comes from layers dated *c.* 970 onwards, but Lincoln's long-distance international contacts were present from the late ninth to the early tenth century, although their scale is unknown. Simultaneously, coin-minting began at Lincoln, and this was to grow in volume until by the later tenth century the city was one of the major mints in England.

Thus, even from an early stage after the Viking take-over, Lincoln started to develop markedly, in a range of ways and on a scale not detected in the other four East Midland boroughs, and it is clear that by the late tenth to early eleventh century the term 'Five Boroughs' embraced a series of places varied in their size, economy, and perhaps in other ways yet to be detected. Whether the term 'the Five Boroughs' originated in the late ninth- to early tenth-century phase of their existence, when the Scandinavian armies centred on each were presumably in very close contact, or whether it was coined by the English after Olaf Guthfrithsson's southern campaign of 940–1, when they may have attempted to cement an East Midlands confederacy against Anglo-Scandinavian Northumbria,[271] it is the diversity rather than the uniformity of the five components that is at present striking when the available details of the archaeological record are studied. Nonetheless, their broadly comparable development in the pre-Viking phase is becoming clearer, as is the difficulty of identifying much that is tangibly Viking or Scandinavian in their subsequent evolution. For the confirmation of these ideas and their fuller development, however, there is an obvious requirement for a broader data-base of excavated evidence; the archaeological work of the past decades has illustrated the range of information potentially available, and it will be to the lasting detriment of Anglo-Saxon studies if this source of knowledge is not fully exploited as opportunities occur.

ADDENDUM

Among the more important works which have appeared since this paper was submitted for publication, J. Haslam has surmised an Offan instigation for these *burhs* ('Market and fortress in England in the reign of Offa', *World Archaeology* 19.1 (1987), 76–93; he

---

[271] Roffe, 'Origins of Derbyshire', p. 115.

has also suggested a location for 'The second *burh* of Nottingham' (*Landscape History* 9 (1987), 45–52). Investigations of the Lincoln waterside at St Benedict's Square and Waterside North have both shown evidence for renewed activity in the ninth to eleventh centuries (*Second/Fourth Annual Report of the Trust for Lincolnshire Archaeology*). L. A. Gilmour has published *Early Medieval Pottery from Flaxengate, Lincoln*, CBA Archaeol. of Lincoln 17.2 (1988), with minor refinements to the Period dating offered by Perring.[272]

[272] In *Flaxengate*.

The lost cartulary of Abbotsbury

SIMON KEYNES

The buildings and lands of Abbotsbury abbey in Dorset were acquired by Sir Giles Strangways soon after the dissolution of the abbey in 1539, and various records pertaining to the abbey's estates seem to have passed into Sir Giles' possession at about the same time. Among these records was a cartulary, which is known to have belonged to Sir Giles' descendant, Sir John Strangways, in the seventeenth century, but which is said to have been destroyed when parliamentary forces set fire to Sir John's house at Abbotsbury during the Civil War. It is possible, however, to reconstruct something of the nature and contents of the lost cartulary from the writings of certain seventeenth-century antiquaries, and in the process to recover parts of the texts of six Anglo-Saxon charters whose existence has not previously been recorded.[1]

ABBOTSBURY ABBEY

At an unknown point in his reign, King Edmund (939–46) gave five hides of land at *Abbedesburi* to his thegn Sigewulf.[2] The charter recording this act does not itself survive, but a copy of it was seen in a Glastonbury cartulary by William of Malmesbury, who believed that Sigewulf had in turn given the land to Glastonbury abbey.[3] If the reference is to Abbotsbury in Dorset, it would follow that the place had been an abbot's property in the earlier tenth century, or perhaps some time before then; and since there is no reason to believe that William had particular evidence of Sigewulf's grant to Glastonbury, beyond

---

[1] I am indebted to Sarah Bridges, Senior Assistant Archivist in the Dorset County Record Office at Dorchester, for her invaluable help in the gathering of material from the Fox-Strangways (Ilchester) archive; to Laurence Keen, for much guidance on matters to do with Dorset; to Susan Kelly for chasing hares in the Bodleian Library; and to Robin Fleming and Katie Mack for their constructive comments.

[2] S 1727. In references to Anglo-Saxon charters, S = P.H. Sawyer, *Anglo-Saxon Charters: an Annotated List and Bibliography*, R. Hist. Soc. Guides and Handbooks 8 (London, 1968), followed by the number of the document; BCS = W. de G. Birch, *Cartularium Saxonicum*, 3 vols. (London, 1885–93); KCD = J.M. Kemble, *Codex Diplomaticus Aevi Saxonici*, 6 vols. (London 1839–48); and *OSFacs.* = W.B. Sanders, *Facsimiles of Anglo-Saxon Manuscripts*, 3 vols. (Ordnance Survey, Southampton, 1878–84).

[3] See J. Scott, *The Early History of Glastonbury: an Edition, Translation and Study of William of Malmesbury's 'De Antiquitate Glastonie Ecclesie'* (Woodbridge, 1981), pp. 116 and 142.

the presence of the charter in the Glastonbury archive, it is quite possible that the land in question was actually in secular hands throughout the later tenth century and into the eleventh.[4]

In the early years of the reign of King Cnut, a certain Orc (or Urki) settled in the vicinity of Abbotsbury with his wife Tola. Orc is known to have acquired land at Portesham (immediately to the east of Abbotsbury) in 1024,[5] and is found among the thegns attesting two charters of King Cnut, in 1033 and 1035, both of which concern estates in Dorset.[6] He attested a charter of Harthacnut in 1042,[7] acquired land at (Abbotts) Wootton (in Whitchurch Canonicorum, Dorset) from Edward the Confessor in 1044,[8] and attested two of Edward's charters, in 1043 and 1045.[9] It would appear that Orc and Tola found an existing church at Abbotsbury, manned by a single priest and his wife; but presently they established a monastery there, and, not having any children of their own, enriched it with various estates which they acquired in the county.[10] In a writ issued some time between 1053 and 1058, King Edward declares that Orc (Urk), his housecarl, 'is to have his shore, all that is over against his own land, everywhere completely and freely, up from the sea and out into the sea, and all that is driven to his shore, by my full command';[11] and it was Orc himself who organized and endowed the guild at Abbotsbury, laying down a detailed set of regulations to govern its operation for the mutual benefit of the guild-brothers and to the advantage of the minster.[12] Orc died probably in the late 1050s or early 1060s; and in another writ, issued between 1058 and 1066, King Edward declares that Tola, his 'man', Orc's widow, has his permission 'to bequeath her land and possessions to St Peter's at Abbotsbury as best pleases her, with my full consent, as fully and completely as it was arranged by the agreements previously made, that it should after the death of both of them – her death and that of Orc her lord – pass into the possession of the holy

4 See S. Keynes, *The 'Liber Terrarum' of Glastonbury Abbey*, Stud. in Anglo-Saxon Hist. (Woodbridge, forthcoming).   5 S 961 (KCD 741): *OSFacs.* ii. Ilchester 2.

6 S 969 (grant by Cnut of land at Horton to Bovi, his thegn) and S 975 (grant by Cnut of land at Corscombe to Sherborne abbey); see *Charters of Sherborne*, ed. M.A. O'Donovan, AS Charters 3 (London, 1988), nos. 20 and 16 respectively.

7 S 993 (KCD 762), concerning land in Berkshire.

8 S 1004 (KCD 772): *OSFacs.* ii. Ilchester 3.

9 S 999 (KCD 767) and 1010 (KCD 778), both concerning land in Wiltshire. Cf. F. Barlow, *Edward the Confessor* (London, 1970). p. 75.   10 See further below, pp. 222 and 236.

11 S 1063 (F.E. Harmer, *Anglo-Saxon Writs* (Manchester, 1957), no.1).

12 *OSFacs.* ii. Ilchester 4 (facsimile, text and translation); KCD 942 (text); B. Thorpe, *Diplomatarium Anglicum Ævi Saxonici* (London, 1865), pp. 605–8 (text and translation); *English Historical Documents c. 500–1042*, ed. D. Whitelock, 2nd ed. (London, 1979), no. 139 (translation). See also G. Rosser, 'The Anglo-Saxon Gilds', *Minsters and Parish Churches: the Local Church in Transition 950–1200*, ed. J. Blair (Oxford, 1988), pp. 31–4.

monastery for [the benefit of] their souls', adding that he would be 'protector and guardian over it and over the property that belongs to it.'[13] For what it is worth, it can be shown that Orc's death was commemorated at Abbotsbury on 21 November, and Tola's on 26 June.[14] By the end of the Anglo-Saxon period the endowment of Abbotsbury, as recorded in Domesday Book, comprised twenty-one hides at Abbotsbury itself,[15] eighteen hides at Tolpuddle, eighteen hides at Hilton, twelve hides at Portesham,[16] five virgates at Shilvinghampton (in Portesham), two and a half hides at Abbotts Wootton (in Whitchurch Canonicorum), half a hide in Burcombe (in North Poorton), and two hides in Atrim (in Netherbury);[17] in addition, the abbey is said to have had interests at Waddon[18] and at (Little) Cheselbourne.[19] It was a fairly substantial endowment under the circumstances,[20] and in its own way affords striking testimony of how one of Cnut's Scandinavian followers had melted into the Anglo-Saxon landscape, assuming the role appropriate to one of his standing and taking an interest in the welfare of the local population.[21]

Abbotsbury abbey maintained an existence throughout the Middle Ages, attracting confirmations of its lands and privileges from kings, as well as

---

[13] S 1064 (Harmer, *Writs*, no. 2)

[14] See London, British Library, Cotton Cleopatra B. ix (a late-thirteenth-century manuscript from Abbotsbury, with a calendar), 59v and 57r. The dedication of the church itself was commemorated on 12 October (59r).

[15] A further hide at Abbotsbury, said to have been *ad uictum monachorum* TRE, had been appropriated by Hugh fitz Grip, sheriff of Dorset, and was still held by Hugh's wife at the time of the Survey.

[16] A further virgate at Portesham, said to have been *ad uictum monachorum* TRE, had similarly been appropriated by Hugh fitz Grip, and was held by Hugh's wife at the time of the Survey.

[17] DB i. 78rv (*A History of the County of Dorset*, Victoria Hist. of the Counties of Eng. [hereafter VCH *Dorset*] III (London, 1968), 79–81).

[18] DB i. 79r. The estate was held by three thegns TRE, but owed renders to Abbotsbury; it passed into the hands of Hugh fitz Grip, who never paid the renders, and who (or whose wife) gave the land itself to St Mary's, Montivilliers (for which grant, see *Gallia Christiana* XI (Paris, 1759), Appendix, cols. 329–30).

[19] DB i. 83v. An estate of two hides at Little Cheselbourne was held by two thegns TRE, and by the wife of Hugh fitz Grip TRW; Hugh's men said that he had held the land from the abbot of Abbotsbury, though the abbot denied it. This is likely to mean the land was the abbey's property (perhaps leased to the thegns), and that although Hugh's men claimed that he had held it with the abbot's permission, in fact he had taken control of it against the abbot's will. A tenth-century charter which is apparently a title-deed for this estate was preserved in the Abbotsbury archive (below, p. 220).

[20] Of course it is uncertain exactly which estates constituted the founders' endowment. In 1212 the abbot is recorded as holding Abbotsbury, Portesham, Hilton, Tolpuddle and Wootton, 'que data fuerunt per Orc et Tolam uxorem suam' (*The Book of Fees commonly called Testa de Nevill*, 3 vols. (London, 1920–31) I, 92).

[21] There may, however, have been more to Orc than meets the eye: see below, pp. 230–1.

patronage from the local landowning classes.[22] In a vernacular writ issued probably in the late 1060s, King William declares that the abbot of Abbotsbury, the monks, the land, men and everything belonging to St Peter's minster, are under his own guardianship and protection, as fully as in the days of King Edward.[23] It is apparent from Domesday Book that the Norman sheriff of Dorset, Hugh fitz Grip, was able nevertheless to appropriate some land from the abbey,[24] and it may be that his actions underlie the two further writs which the abbey secured from King William: in one, the king confirms the abbey's title to its lands and privileges as enjoyed in the reign of King Edward,[25] and in the other he reiterates the abbot's rights with specific reference to a ship which had been wrecked on his land;[26] but even so, Hugh's wife retained possession of at least part of the appropriated lands at the time of the Domesday survey in 1086. Further general confirmations of the abbey's lands and privileges were issued by Henry I in 1106,[27] by Stephen between

---

[22] For accounts of Abbotsbury abbey, see J. Hutchins, *The History and Antiquities of the County of Dorset*, 2 vols. (London, 1774) I, 532–41 (3rd ed., ed. W. Shipp and J.W. Hodson, 4 vols. (London, 1861–74) II, 714–37); H.J. Moule, 'Abbotsbury Abbey', *Proc. of the Dorset Natural Hist. and Antiq. Field Club* 8 (1886), 38–48; VCH *Dorset* II (London, 1908), 48–53; W.S. Moule, *Abbotsbury: the Parish Church, the Abbey and Other Points of Interest*, 4th ed. (Abbotsbury, 1965); Royal Commission on Historical Monuments, *An Inventory of the Historical Monuments in the County of Dorset* I (London, 1952), 1–11; and L. Keen, in *ArchJ* 140 (1983), 21–4. Translations and transcripts of a series of documents relating to Abbotsbury's history from the eleventh century to the sixteenth (and beyond) were printed by the fifth earl of Ilchester in 1888, in connection with a lawsuit against some local fishermen: see *The Earl of Ilchester* v. *Raishley and Others: Plaintiff's Documents of Title*, High Court of Justice, Chancery Division, no. 1–56 (1888), and E.H. Tindal Atkinson, 'Some Abbotsbury Records', *Proc. of the Dorset Natural Hist. and Antiq. Field Club* 48 (1927), 70–85. The majority of the documents were derived from Lord Ilchester's own muniments, and these are now in the Dorset County Record Office at Dorchester (Fox-Strangways (Ilchester) Archive [D.124]); others were derived from the Public Record Office.

[23] *Regesta Regum Anglo-Normannorum 1066–1154* I, ed. H.W.C. Davis (Oxford, 1913), no. 108; see also Harmer, *Writs*, pp. 119–20. For William I's vernacular writs, see S. Keynes, 'Regenbald the Chancellor (*sic*)', *Anglo-Norman Studies X*, ed. R.A. Brown (Woodbridge, 1988), pp. 185–222, at 217; a date for the writ early in the Conqueror's reign is suggested by the fact that its addressees include two English thegns, Brihtwig and Scewine, apparently representing local authority before the appointment of Hugh fitz Grip. See further below, p. 219, n. 68.

[24] For Hugh fitz Grip's activities in Dorset, see A. Williams, 'Introduction to the Dorset Domesday', VCH *Dorset* III, 1–60, at 6–7 and 37.

[25] *Regesta* I, no. 109, issued (in Latin) between 1066 and 1078, and addressed to Bishop Hermann and Hugh fitz Grip.

[26] *Regesta* I, no. 203, issued (in Latin) between 1078 and 1084, and addressed to Bishop Osmund and Hugh fitz Grip.

[27] *Regesta Regum Anglo-Normannorum 1066–1154* II, ed. C. Johnson and H.A. Cronne (Oxford, 1956), no. 754.

1149 and 1154,[28] and by Henry II between 1154 and 1158;[29] and from time to time the abbots submitted their charters to the authorities for confirmation. Thus, in 1269 King Henry III inspected and confirmed the two Latin writs of William the Conqueror, and the writs of Kings Henry I, Stephen, and Henry II;[30] and in 1315 King Edward II inspected and confirmed the two (vernacular) writs of Edward the Confessor, the vernacular writ of William the Conqueror, and the Inspeximus charter of Henry III.[31] In 1356 the abbey pleaded its charters *coram baronibus*, and a 'Saxon charter' was among those placed before them.[32] In 1475 Richard, duke of Gloucester, in his capacity as Admiral of England, inspected and confirmed the Inspeximus charter of Edward II,[33] and the same Inspeximus of Edward II (together with another charter issued in favour of the abbey by Henry III) was again inspected and confirmed by Henry VII in 1493;[34] further Inspeximus charters were issued by Henry VIII in 1516,[35] and by John Woodhall, Commissary of the Admiralty, in 1524.[36] It is not known when the charters which accumulated in the abbey's archive were copied in a cartulary, and it need not have been until the fifteenth or early sixteenth century. The antiquary John Leland listed six books which he found

---

[28] *Regesta Regum Anglo-Normannorum 1066–1154* III, ed. H.A. Cronne and R.H.C. Davis (Oxford, 1968), no. 1.

[29] See *Calendar of the Charter Rolls* II (London, 1906), 132. The original writ of Henry II is in the Strangways archive (*Ilchester* v. *Raishley*, no. 4a); it is not recorded in T.A.M. Bishop, *Scriptores Regis* (Oxford, 1961), or in *Acta of Henry II and Richard I*, ed. J.C. Holt and R. Mortimer, List & Index Soc., Special Ser. 21 (1986). I am grateful to Professor Tom Keefe for guidance on the apparent date of the writ.

[30] The original Inspeximus charter of Henry III is in the Strangways archive (*Ilchester* v. *Raishley*, no. 6b; ptd Hutchins, *History of Dorset* (3rd ed.) II, 733–4). There is a copy in London, Public Record Office, Charter Rolls, 54 Henry III (c53/59), membrane 14: *Calendar of the Charter Rolls* II, 131–2 (omitting the witnesses who are named in the original).

[31] PRO, Charter Rolls, 8 Edward II (c53/101), membrane 3, no. 5: *Calendar of the Charter Rolls* III (London, 1908), 274–5; translated, from the PRO text, in *Ilchester* v.*Raishley*, no. 10a.

[32] See Hutchins, *History of Dorset* (3rd ed.) II, 717, citing PRO, Originalia Rolls, 30 Edw. III (E371/115), rot. 64.

[33] The original Inspeximus charter of the Duke of Gloucester is in the Strangways archive (*Ilchester* v. *Raishley*, no. 17a). It was issued at Abbotsbury itself, and was presumably based on the (lost) original of Edward II's Inspeximus charter (of which, however, it gives only an abbreviated text).

[34] PRO, Confirmation Roll, 6–10 Henry VII (c56/23), no. 1; translated, from the PRO text, in *Ilchester* v. *Raishley* no. 19a. For the charter of Henry III, see *Calendar of the Charter Rolls* II, 181.

[35] The original of this Inspeximus was apparently preserved in the Strangways archive in the early seventeenth century; see further below, p.219, n.68.

[36] The original Inspeximus charter of John Woodhall is in the Strangways archive (*Ilchester* v. *Raishley*, no. 20a). It was issued at Abbotsbury; but it does not cite any of the earlier texts directly.

at Abbotsbury during the course of his library-tour in the 1530s (including 'Pars veteris testamenti Saxonice'), but if he also saw a cartulary there, he did not bother to mention it.[37]

THE STRANGWAYS OF MELBURY AND ABBOTSBURY

Abbotsbury abbey was dissolved by Henry VIII in 1539.[38] Two years later, in 1541, Henry leased the buildings and lands to Sir Giles Strangways (the Elder), of Melbury Sampford in Dorset, whose family had patronised the abbey since the early sixteenth century;[39] and by charter issued on 29 July 1543, the king granted the buildings and lands to Sir Giles outright, in consideration of his payment of over £1,900.[40] There does not appear to have been any ill-will between the last abbot of Abbotsbury and its new lord, for the abbot himself became vicar of the parish church of St Nicholas (which had been built in the early fourteenth century, immediately to the north of the abbey), and is soon to be found writing to Sir Giles apprising him of the fishery rights enjoyed by the abbots his predecessors (and sending him 'titlez and olde confirmacions' in a box).[41] In these circumstances, therefore, the ancient charters and records of Abbotsbury abbey were acquired by the Strangways family, and the abbey itself, once converted by Sir Giles to domestic use, became a place of residence for its new owners.[42]

---

[37] *Joannis Lelandi Antiquarii De Rebus Britannicis Collectanea*, ed. T. Hearne, 6 vols., 2nd ed. (London, 1774) IV, 149–50. For a list of surviving books from the abbey, see N.R. Ker, *Medieval Libraries of Great Britain*, R. Hist. Soc. Guides and Handbooks 3, 2nd ed. (London, 1964), 1; one is described by C.M. Kauffmann, *Romanesque Manuscripts 1066–1190* (London, 1975), pp. 112–13 (no. 87).

[38] PRO, Deeds of Surrender, no. 1 (E322/1). The charter is sealed with an impression made from a much earlier seal-matrix, depicting an ecclesiastical building (illustrated in Hutchins, *History of Dorset* (3rd ed.) II, 719); R.H. Ellis, *Catalogue of Seals in the Public Record Office: Monastic Seals* I (London, 1986), 1 (M005), and W. de G. Birch, *Catalogue of Seals in the Department of Manuscripts in the British Museum*, 6 vols. (London, 1887–1900) I, 422 (no. 2539). Dr Sandy Heslop advises me that the matrix would appear to date from the late eleventh or early twelfth century. For an account of the abbey's holdings at the Dissolution, see *Valor Ecclesiasticus Temp. Henr. VIII. Auctoritate Regia Institutus*, 6 vols. (London, 1810–34) I, 227–30; its total income was just over £400.

[39] A Strangways chantry was established at Abbotsbury in 1505 (see below, p. 235).

[40] See *Ilchester* v. *Raishley*, nos. 21a–24a, for (translations of) the documents pertaining to Sir Giles' acquisition of Abbotsbury. Leland visited Sir Giles at Melbury, *c.* 1540; but there is no evidence that he went to Abbotsbury on this occasion. See *The Itinerary of John Leland* I, ed. L. Toulmin Smith (London, 1907), 247–8.

[41] The original letter is in the Strangways archive (*Ilchester* v. *Raishley*, no. 25a).

[42] The contents of rooms in the houses at Melbury and Abbotsbury are itemized in great detail in the inventory of Sir Giles' personal estate drawn up (shortly after his death) in 1547; see S.E. B[ridges], 'Inventory of Sir Giles Strangways 1547', Dorset County Record Office (Dorchester, 1986). There is no reference to muniments in either house; but perhaps they were not considered part of the personal estate.

The descendants of Sir Giles Strangways maintained a close interest in their formerly monastic property;[43] and it is apparent that they were also assiduous in the care of the documents in what had become their family archive. Sir Giles died in 1546, and was succeeded by his grandson Sir Giles Strangways the Younger, who died in 1562; whereupon the inheritance passed to John Strangways I (son of Sir Giles the Younger). John died in 1593, and was himself succeeded by his eldest son, another Giles, who died in 1596 while still a minor in the custody of Queen Elizabeth I. John's younger son, John Strangways II, was aged ten on his elder brother's death, and also a ward of the Crown. He was brought up by Lady (Katherine) Newton, his late brother's mother-in-law, and in March 1604 (when John was eighteen) Lady Newton formally relinquished custody of the family archive:

Memorandum that on the xxix[th] of Marche, 1604, Roberte Langridge gent for and in the behalfe of the Ladye Katherine Newton widowe late comittie of the bodye and landes of John Strangwayes Esquier the king's Majesties warde, did deliver vnto the same John Strangways the charters evidences and wrytings concerninge the mannors and landes of the same John Strangwayes hereafter following, viz:

Inprimis in the turrett or evidence howse one longe great Chest of tymber close barred with broade iron barres, and havinge to yt one great locke (but unlocked) and two Iron hapses (but all open, and there were conteyned in this Cheste sixe and thirtie Boxes of Evidences and two tylls of wrytings and evidence as followeth; viz:

1. One longe boxe entituled Abbotsburye Conteyninge in yt two Lettres Pattents under the great seale, namelye the Lettres Pattents of the graunte of the Mannor of Abbotsburye by king Henrye the eighte vnto Sir Gyles Strangwayes knight grandfather[44] of the above named John Strangewayes and his heires, the other beinge an inspeximus of diverse auncient records,[45] also seven Evidences sealed, two vnsealed, one loose seale, and one paper booke, All Concerninge the Mannor of Abbotsburye.

There follow similar descriptions of the contents of each of the remaining boxes kept in the 'great Chest of tymber', and of the two tills (or drawers) in the chest itself. Some of the boxes contained family papers, and others contained documents relating to particular (named) estates in the family's possession; but in a few cases we are given no more than a statement that the box contained (for example) 'eight auncient charters under the great seale'. Three of the boxes in

---

43 For the Strangways family in the sixteenth and seventeenth centuries, see the documents of the period assembled in *Ilchester* v. *Raishley*; see also Hutchins, *History of Dorset* 1, 506–16 (3rd ed., 11, 656–82), and the earl of Ilchester, 'The Abbotsbury Swannery', *Proc. of the Dorset Nat. Hist. and Archaeol. Soc.* 55 (1933), 154–64, at 156–62.

44 *Recte* great-great-grandfather.

45 Perhaps the Inspeximus of 8 Henry VIII (1516); see below, p.219, n.68.

the 'great Chest of tymber', besides the first, are said to have contained documents relating to Abbotsbury:

6. One longe drawinge boxe entitled Abotsburye contayninge in yt ten Charters vnder the greate seale, one exemplification vnder the seale of the common place, 33 auncient deedes sealed, one Indenture of a fyne and 23 auncient wrytings vnsealed all concerninge Abbotsburye.

7. One boxe entitled Abbotsburye contayninge in yt 43 deedes sealed, and 16 escripts and wrytings vnsealed concerninge Abbotsburye, Stockingwaye and Melburye.

8. One longe broade drawinge boxe entitled Abotsburye contayninge in yt 50 deedes sealed, and 4 vnsealed all Concerninge Abbotsburye.

The memorandum continues with a description of various other containers which were apparently distinct from the 'great Chest of tymber', including:

37. One Iron bounde truncke Chest, havinge in yt verye manye of Courteroles accompts and other things without nomber concerninge Abbotsburye Mannor for the most parte, with two baggs of wrytings, and an instruement of parchement verye longe, concerninge the Bishopp of Sarum and the abbott of Abbotsburye.

38. One other verye olde Iron bounde truncke chest havinge in yt olde Accompts Courtrolles, and other paper bookes and escripts, which Chest was vnlockte, and the Cover thereof broken.

There was also 'One deske havinge in yt 6 boxes', of which the second was 'intituled Abbotsbury conteyninge 23 counterparts and deedes'; and 'att large in the sayd deske' were several other documents, including 'The Confirmation of the Crest in Armes of the Strangwayes, by two kings of heraults, with the pedigree of this house with manye papers and letters'. The memorandum concludes with descriptions of the contents of two further chests; and it is signed, finally, by George Trenchard (John Strangways' father-in-law), John Strangways himself, and John Strode.[46] One is left aghast at the sheer bulk of what would appear at this stage to have been an intact archive; and if one might pause to wish that it were possible to distinguish the Anglo-Saxon charters from the mass of later medieval records, one cannot but fail to be impressed by the general picture which the memorandum creates of chests piled high in the 'turrett or evidence howse', presumably the muniment room in the tower at Melbury.[47]

---

[46] The memorandum is preserved in the Strangways archive (D.124/Box 233); endorsed 'A note of Evydences delyvered by Mr Robert Langryshe unto Sir Georg Trenchard for Jo: Strangwayes Esquire', and dated 29 March 1604.

[47] For an account of the Muniment Room at Melbury House, see RCHM, *Inventory* I, 164–7, at 167.

John Strangways II (1585–1666) attained the age of twenty-one in 1606, and duly succeeded to his inheritance, including the site and estates of 'the late Monastery of Abbotsbury'.[48] It was apparently at about this time that the Devonshire antiquary, Sir William Pole (1561–1635), consulted the Abbotsbury records in Strangways' possession; for Pole's so-called 'Book of Evidences' contains a copy of a late thirteenth-century private charter, which is said to be 'Out of the Liedger of th'abbay of Abbodesbury remayning with Mr. John Strangways'.[49] In 1619 Strangways had occasion to draw up a list of 'Thevydences Fitt to be vsed and shewed for the Libertyes of Abbottesbury whervpon the Quo Warranto is to be brought for the Renewinge and Confirming of the same Libertyes'.[50] The list comprises eleven items, of which the first is the 'letters patents of Kinge Henrye theight' (either the Inspeximus of 1516, or Henry's grant to Sir Giles Strangways), the second 'The Saxon charter' (perhaps a reference to the Abbotsbury guild statutes), and the third 'The Admyrall charter' (presumably the Inspeximus of Richard, duke of Gloucester). The ninth item is 'The Lidger Boocke which proveth the Libertyes', perhaps the 'paper booke' from the main box of Abbotsbury records, and (in the light of Pole's reference to the 'Liedger' of Abbotsbury) clearly to be identified as the abbey's cartulary. Other antiquaries are known to have seen and used the cartulary in the 1620s and 1630s;[51] and John Strangways' own interest in his muniments is further attested by a hint that in 1636 he was sorting through the material.[52]

Sir John Strangways was a staunch supporter of King Charles I during the Civil War, but his loyalty to the royalist cause cost him dear. In April 1643, his house at Abbotsbury was occupied by a detachment of parliamentary troops under the command of Major Hercules Langrishe, and its contents ransacked (in the absence of any defenders) when Sir John's wife, Grace, refused to co-

---

[48] *Ilchester* v. *Raishley*, no. 34a.

[49] Sir William Pole's 'Book of Evidences' remains in the possession of Col. Sir John Carew Pole, Bt, at Antony House, Torpoint, Cornwall (and is accessible through the Cornwall Record Office). The Abbotsbury document (dated 1279, and concerning Nicholas de la Strode and the manor of Tolpuddle) occurs in Oxford, The Queen's College, MS. 152 (said to be a copy of Pole's book made in 1608 by Ralph Brooke, York Herald), 223r; on this manuscript, see H.O. Coxe, *Catalogus Codicum MSS. qui in Collegiis Aulisque Oxoniensibus Hodie Adservantur*, 2 vols. (Oxford, 1852) I, [The Queen's College] 29–30, and J. Batten, 'Arms of De Mandeville of Coker – Sir William Pole's MSS.', *Notes & Queries for Somerset and Dorset* 4 (1894–5), 170–3.

[50] Paper preserved in the Strangways archive (*Ilchester* v. *Raishley*, no. 37a (but not printed there)); endorsed 'A Note of Evidence to be shewne for the liberties of Abbottesbury 1619'.

[51] See further, below, pp. 221–34.

[52] A scrap of paper in the Strangways archive (below, p. 217, n. 59) is headed 'A Note of the writings in this Box the 11th of February 1636. JS.' Some of Strangways' endorsements on the single-sheet charters in his archive may date from this period.

operate.[53] Parliamentary forces returned to Abbotsbury in November 1644; but the house was then in the care of Sir John's son, Colonel James Strangways, who was evidently not minded to give up without a fight. The ensuing action is graphically described by a member of the attacking force, in a letter to a parliamentary chronicler:

Sir, etc. Wee marched from *Dorchester* to *Abothbury*, where Colonell *James Strangewayes* and all his Regiment were in Garrison, they held both the House and the Church which joyned to the House; It was night before wee summoned it, and they in a scorn refused the summons of Sir *Anthony Ashley-Cooper*, a very active and noble Gentleman, our Commander in cheif, whereupon hee sent his Major Generall with a considerable party against the Church, who presently assaulting it took it, and all the men in it prisoners, without the losse of one man of ours. After this wee summoned them in writing, the second time, to yeild on fair quarter, or else to expect no mercy, if they forced us to storm them. To this also they disdained to return an Answer; upon which denyall wee fell on, and after as hot a storm as ever I heard of, for six houres together, it pleased God, at length to give us the place, when by no other means wee could get it, wee found a way by desperately flinging in fired turf-fagots into the windowes; and the fight, thus, grew so hot, that our said Commander in cheif (who to his perpetuall renown behaved himself most gallantly in this service) was forced to bring up his men within Pistoll shot of the House, and could hardly, then, get them to stay and stand the brunt, yet in all this time (God bee praised) wee lost but 3 men, and some few wounded. Now, when as by the foresaid hot assault, half of the house was on a light fire, and not to bee quenched, then at length, Colonell *James Strangewayes* called out for quarter, which our Commander in cheif was resolved no man in the House should have, in regard they had so desperately and disdainfully scorned his summons, and also in regard that the Cavaliers custome was observed to bee to keep such paltry houses and pilfring Garrisons against any of our Armies, that they might thereby bee sure to doe us mischeif, and (by reason of our observed clemency) to have their lives at last granted to them; But some of our Commanders upon one side of the House, contrary to the minde of our said Commander in cheif, and against the opinion of all the Officers, in his absence, had given them quarter, which being granted them, wee instantly rushed into the House, which being of a light fire, and their Magazine in it (I beleive rather accidentally, than as some reported, purposely and trecherously) it set on fire 4 or 5 barrels of Gunpowder, and blew up between 30 and 40 of our men, yet the Lord bee blessed, my self and the rest were even miraculously preserved. Wee took prisoners, Colonell *James Strangewayes*, Sir *John Strangewayes* his Son, Governour of this Garrison, his Major, and 3 Captains; and not 3 of his whole Regiment, but were either killed or taken, and the House was wholly burnt down to the ground, and wee thereby freed of a pestilent and pernicious neighbour. Colonell *Bruen* and Mr. *Crompton*, behaved themselves very worthily in this action, and Captain *Starre* incomparably bravely.[54]

---

[53] See A.R. Bayley, *The Great Civil War in Dorset 1642–1660* (Taunton, 1910), pp. 70–1.

[54] J. Vicars, *The Burning-Bush Not Consumed, or, the Fourth and Last Part of the Parliamentarie-Chronicle* (London, 1646), pp. 67–8; see also Bayley, *Civil War in Dorset*, pp. 227–9.

Sir Anthony Ashley Cooper (1621–83), leader of the parliamentary forces, gave his own account of the action in a report to the Committee for the Parliament in Dorsetshire, acknowledging the gallantry of the defenders in initially admitting of no treaty, but justifying his own order to press home the attack when the defenders eventually cried out for quarter; and it emerges that those attackers who 'fell into the house to plunder' did so against their commanders' better judgement, suffering the consequences when the powder magazine exploded.[55] Sir John Strangways was taken prisoner at Sherborne Castle in 1645, and was committed to the Tower of London;[56] he was presently able to buy back his freedom and his sequestered estates, and on release from captivity in 1648 retired to his house at Melbury Sampford, and to the cares of managing his property.[57]

It has been assumed in the past that the records of Abbotsbury abbey were kept in the Strangways' house at Abbotsbury itself, and that many of them must have been destroyed when the house was 'wholly burnt down to the ground' in 1644.[58] It is certainly difficult to imagine how anything could have survived the conflagration; and it is worth bearing in mind, therefore, that the Abbotsbury and Strangways archives seem actually to have been kept in the 'evidence howse' at Melbury. And while the house at Melbury was itself 'plundered' in 1644,[59] there is no reason to believe that it suffered any fate worse than that. Moreover, a quantity of the Abbotsbury records survived in Sir John Strangways' possession, and it is apparent that he still took interest in the material, whether for antiquarian or for more practical purposes. In the

55 *Memoirs, Letters, and Speeches of Anthony Ashley Cooper, First Earl of Shaftesbury, Lord Chancellor*, ed. W.D. Christie (London, 1859), pp. 97–100, and W.D. Christie, *A Life of Anthony Ashley Cooper, First Earl of Shaftesbury 1621–1683*, 2 vols. (London, 1871) I, 62–4. See also K.H.D. Haley, *The First Earl of Shaftesbury* (Oxford, 1968), pp. 51–3.

56 See Bayley, *Civil War in Dorset*, pp. 30–1, 291, 295, 400 and 417. Sir John's elder son, Giles, was imprisoned with him; but James, the younger son, seems to have escaped, writing to his mother in January 1647 excusing his secret departure to avoid arrest, and again, from La Rochelle in July 1647, requesting an increase in his allowance; both letters are preserved in the Strangways archive.

57 At Melbury, Strangways wrote a perambulatory poem about his various estates (including Abbotsbury), which reveals that after his release he was not allowed to go beyond five miles from his house. The poem, dated 1 May 1650, is printed in the *Proc. of the Dorset Nat. Hist. and Archaeol. Soc.* 54 (1932), lvii–lxiv; on reading it to the Society in 1932, the then Lord Ilchester 'felt that perhaps his ancestor was considering more the quantity of his property than the quantities of his verses'.   58 See further below, p. 237, n. 150.

59 A copy of an Inquisition, dated 13 October 1427, finding that the abbot of Abbotsbury was entitled to the water known as the Fleet (i.e. the water behind Chesil Beach), is preserved in the Strangways archive (*Ilchester* v. *Raishley*, no. 15a); preserved with it is the scrap of paper which was to be used as a box-list in 1636 (above, p. 215, n. 52), and which is endorsed 'The Seales of the Inquisition for the Fleet weare Torne off when my howse was plundred att Melbury in the yeare 1644. J. Strangways 1644'.

early 1650s he gave what help he could to Sir William Dugdale, who was compiling an account of Abbotsbury abbey for the *Monasticon Anglicanum*.[60] Ten years later, when the Lord High Admiral of England contested Sir John's right to certain wreckage cast up on the shore by West Bexington farm (three miles west along the coast from Abbotsbury), on the grounds that West Bexington was not part of Abbotsbury manor, Strangways himself responded with a vigorous assertion of his rights, citing King Henry VIII's grant of the manor and monastery to Sir Giles, and claiming to be entitled thereby to the marine jurisdiction formerly enjoyed by the abbots of Abbotsbury and their predecessors.[61] In this connection Strangways began to search through his surviving muniments for records pertinent to his case, and arranged for copies and translations to be made of other documents preserved among the public records in the Tower of London. In June 1662 he wrote to the judge in the Admiralty Court, requesting a delay in the hearing of the suit to give him 'convenient tyme to searche amongst my broken deeds':

After my greate sufferinges by the worst of men (to whome my person and estate became a prey for some years) and then repurchaseing both could never obteyne the tyth of my evidences, soe that what formerly was easie is now difficult, unlesse prescription and 60 or 70 yeares enjoyment may serve for a title, wherein I must be advised by my Councell. In the great shippwrack of my deeds some few broken scripps came to hand conducing much, as I hope, to the mayntayneing of that just right which I am now enforced to contend for in that high and honorable Court where you sitt to doe all men equalle justice . . . And since my coming home have with some trouble lighted on a few auncient papers and have hopes to find more, and Michaelmas Terme shall indeavour to satisfye the Court therein makeing noe doubt but that his Highnes the Lord Admirall or his Councell shall see that my clayme is just and noe more than what my auncestors and those under whome I clayme have for some hundreds of yeares enjoyed without dispute.[62]

The gathering of evidence was still in hand in November, when Strangways sent a copy of an Inspeximus issued during the reign of Henry VIII to his lawyer, Henry Bestland;[63] and in January 1663 Bestland wrote to tell Sir John that the judge wished to have the 'Saxon deeds' translated, and that 'the doeing whereof will take upp some tyme'.[64] A sheet of paper headed 'A note of deeds

---

[60] See further below, pp. 235–8.   [61] See *Ilchester* v. *Raishley*, nos. 49–53.

[62] Draft of letter from Strangways to Dr Exton, in the Strangways archive (*Ilchester* v. *Raishley*, no. 54a).

[63] Letter from Strangways to Bestland, in the Strangways archive (*Ilchester* v. *Raishley*, no. 55a); the Inspeximus was that of John Woodhall (*Ilchester* v. *Raishley*, no. 20a).

[64] Letter from Bestland to Strangways, in the Strangways archive; it would appear that Bestland intended to seek help in this connection from 'Mr Dugdale', but in the event did not do so. Bestland reported again in February 1663 (*Ilchester* v. *Raishley*, no. 56a).

and writeings which are in the hands of Henry Bestland that concerne Sir John Strangways' lists the several documents which Strangways had managed to assemble.[65] The first is 'An old deed of King Cnuts attested by the Bishopps and Lords';[66] the second, 'An old Saxon deed which is written on the outside by Sir John Strangwayes with his owne hand';[67] and the seventh, 'A paper translateing 3 Saxon Charters in English'.[68] Altogether, Sir John submitted ten of his own deeds and six 'paper records' (copied from documents in the Tower and elsewhere);[69] but the 'Liedger Book' of Abbotsbury is conspicuous only by its absence. The various records were handed over to the Register of the Admiralty Court in December 1663, and the case assigned for hearing at the first opportunity thereafter;[70] yet litigation was still in progress in 1665–6, and since no outcome is recorded it seems that the suit was eventually dropped.[71] Strangways himself died on 30 December 1666, in his eighty-second year, and is commemorated to this day by a monument in the parish church at Melbury.[72]

---

[65] The original document is in the Strangways archive (*Ilchester* v. *Raishley*, no. 56b); drawn up by Bestland himself, who adds at the bottom, 'I doe acknowledge that theis Deeds and Copies are in my handes'.

[66] Presumably Cnut's charter granting Portesham to Orc (S 961), supplied *faute de mieux*; but see also below, p. 242, n. 165.

[67] Presumably the Abbotsbury guild statutes (*OSFacs*. ii. Ilchester 4), which are endorsed 'An old Saxon Deed concerning Abbotsbury. 11', in what appears to be Sir John Strangways' hand.

[68] This paper is preserved in the Strangways archive. It is a translation, evidently by Sir Henry Spelman, of the three vernacular writs concerning Abbotsbury (Harmer, *Writs*, nos. 1–2, and *Regesta* 1, no. 108), headed 'The English of the Saxon Charters confirmed by Inspeximus to the Abbot of Abbotesbury An. 8 Hen 8'. The original Inspeximus does not survive, and there seems to be no sign of a copy in the only surviving Confirmation Roll for 8 Hen. VIII (PRO, c56/53). That the translation is Spelman's is indicated by the hand (which appears to be his), and by the direction given for further explication of legal terms to 'my Glossarie' (published in 1626). It seems possible that Henry VIII's Inspeximus took its text of the writs from a source other than the Inspeximus of Edward II (or Henry VII); for in place of the garbled 'swa hit þeder in furð Orc leg' (*Regesta* 1, no. 108; cf. Harmer, *Writs*, p. 120, n. 1), Spelman's translation reads 'as they were hither disposed by Urks widowe', which makes good sense.

[69] The paper records included 'The copie of a Record in the Tower for confirmation of the Saxon and other Charters conteyning 12 sheets', and 'Another Copie out of the Tower translateing the Saxon Deeds, conteyning 6 sheets'. Both documents survive in the Strangways archive, and are derived from the Inspeximus of Edward II.

[70] Bestland's list (*Ilchester* v. *Raishley*, no. 56b) is endorsed (by an different hand): 'The 11th December 1663. Delivered Mr. Charles Moore the Register of the Admiralty Court, 10 Deeds of Sir John Strangways in a Box, and six Paper Records out of the Tower and att the Rolls and out of Mr. Fawconbridge's office. And the Cause assigned for heareing the first Court day in next Terme.'   [71] See *Ilchester* v. *Raishley*, no. 53.

[72] Hutchins, *History of Dorset* 1, 515 (3rd ed., 11, 679).

THE ANGLO-SAXON CHARTERS OF ABBOTSBURY

The muniments of the Strangways family passed by descent to the earls of Ilchester, who proved no less assiduous in their custody; and in 1959 the archive began to be transferred from Melbury to the Dorset County Record Office at Dorchester, where it remains on deposit.[73] Among the records are five Anglo-Saxon charters on single sheets of parchment, being the only pre-Conquest documents known to survive, in their original form, from the Abbotsbury archive. Three are royal diplomas, in Latin, with boundary clauses in the vernacular: King Edgar's grant of three *virgae* at (? Little) Cheselbourne in Dorset to Wulfheard, his faithful man, dated 965;[74] King Cnut's grant of seven hides at Portesham in Dorset to Orc, his thegn, dated 1024;[75] and King Edward the Confessor's grant of five *perticae* at (Abbotts) Wootton, in Whitchurch Canonicorum, Dorset, to Orc, his thegn, dated 1044.[76] The two remaining Anglo-Saxon documents were both written in the second quarter of the eleventh century, and are in the vernacular throughout. One is the exceptionally important text of the Abbotsbury guild statutes, as established by Orc himself;[77] and the other is a fragment of the lower part of a chirograph, which seems to relate to the acquisition by a woman (presumably Tola) of land at '[.]*eadan dune*' from a certain Sæwine, and its transfer to St Peter's minster at Abbotsbury.[78] In addition to the Anglo-Saxon charters there are, of course, large numbers of post-Conquest documents in the archive,

[73] Fox-Strangways (Ilchester) Archive [D.124]. See contributions by Laurence Keen and others in *The Archives of Dorset: a Catalogue of an Exhibition to Mark the First 30 Years of the Dorset Record Office* (Dorchester, 1986).

[74] S736 (BCS 1165): *OSFacs*. ii. Ilchester 1 (facsimile, text and translation). For discussion of the bounds, see G.B. Grundy, 'Saxon Charters of Dorset', *Proc. of the Dorset Nat. Hist. & Archaeol. Soc.* 56 (1934), 110–30, at 129–30; see also A. Fagersten, *The Place-Names of Dorset* (Uppsala, 1933), p. 177. The charter may relate to the two hides at (Little) Cheselbourne (in Puddletown), in which Abbotsbury had some interest (above, p. 209, n. 19); the other Cheselbourne in Dorset was a Shaftesbury estate.

[75] S961 (KCD 741): *OSFacs*. ii. Ilchester 2 (facsimile, text and translation); *Ilchester v. Raishley*, no. 1a (translation). See G.B. Grundy, 'Saxon Charters of Dorset', *Proc. of the Dorset Nat. Hist. & Archaeol. Soc.* 59 (1937), 95–118, at 113–18.

[76] S1004 (KCD 772): *OSFacs*. ii. Ilchester 3 (facsimile, text and translation). See C. Hart, 'Some Dorset Charter Boundaries', *Proc. of the Dorset Nat. Hist. & Archaeol. Soc.* 86 (1964), 158–63, at 161–3. Hart states that Kemble printed the charter 'from the lost Abbotsbury cartulary then in the possession of the Earl of Ilchester'; but Kemble himself states that he used Lord Ilchester's single sheets (KCD vi, xxiv).

[77] *OSFacs*. ii. Ilchester 4 (facsimile, text and translation); *Ilchester v. Raishley*, no. 2a (translation).

[78] *OSFacs*. ii. Ilchester 5 (facsimile, text and translation); *Ilchester v. Raishley*, no. 3a (translation, by John Mitchell Kemble). See further below, pp. 228–9.

including an original writ of Henry II (unrecorded in this form), and the original of Henry III's Inspeximus charter; but unfortunately there is no trace of the missing cartulary.

For knowledge of the cartulary we are dependent, therefore, on such references to it as we may find in the works of early modern antiquaries. When Leland visited Abbotsbury in the 1530s, he was given reason to believe that the abbey had been founded by Orc: 'Orkus, oeconomus Canuti regis, expulsis canonicis secularibus, introduxit monachos. Sepultus est ibidem cum Thola conjuge.'[79] Of course there is no means of knowing on what kind of evidence this statement was based, and it need have been nothing more substantial than local hearsay. A similarly inscrutable reference to Abbotsbury occurs in the *Apostolatus Benedictinorum in Anglia*, published by Clement Reyner in 1626:[80] 'Est autem Abbotesberiæ Abbatia in agro Dorsetensi S. Petro Apostolo dicata, fundata ab Orkingo, oeconomo palatii regis sub Canuto, circa annum Domini 1026.'[81] The reference to Orc as Cnut's *oeconomus*[82] might be taken to suggest that the compilers of the *Apostolatus* derived at least part of their information from Leland's own collections; but it seems rather more likely that their account is independent of his, and that it was based on a document or text from the Abbotsbury archive. As we shall see, the missing cartulary is known to have contained a 'story of the foundation',[83] and it may have been this text which provided the information (and suggested the date).

Thomas Gerard's 'Survey of Dorsetshire'

A more detailed account of Abbotsbury abbey occurs in the survey of Dorsetshire written by Thomas Gerard in the early 1620s. Gerard lived at Trent (near Sherborne), on the border between Dorset and Somerset, and produced surveys of both counties: his survey of Dorset was first published in

---

[79] *Collectanea*, ed. Hearne, IV, 149 (and cf. I, 66).

[80] For an account of the genesis of this work, see M.D. Knowles, in M. Powicke *et al.*, 'The Value of Sixteenth- and Seventeenth-Century Scholarship to Modern Historical Research', *English Historical Scholarship in the Sixteenth and Seventeenth Centuries*, ed. L. Fox (London, 1956), pp. 115–27, at 119–23. The *Apostolatus* is based on the collections of Augustine (David) Baker (1575–1641), which are now on deposit at the Bodleian Library; see Coxe, *Catalogus Codicum MSS.* II, [Jesus College] 25–30. There is no obvious sign of any Abbotsbury material.

[81] C. Reyner, *Apostolatus Benedictinorum in Anglia, sive disceptatio historica de antiquitate ordinis monachorum nigrorum S. Benedicti in regno Angliæ* (Douai, 1626), tract. 2, sect. 6, memb. 3 (p. 132).

[82] The word *economus* is glossed *stiward* in an eleventh-century glossary (N.R. Ker, *Catalogue of Manuscripts Containing Anglo-Saxon* (Oxford, 1957), no. 2, art.d).

[83] See below, p. 237, n. 148.

1732 (mistakenly attributed to John Coker), but that of Somerset was not published until 1900.[84] Gerard was a man of substance both in his own right and by virtue of his marriage to Anne, daughter of Robert Coker of Mappowder; he thus moved easily in the circles of the landed gentry, and enjoyed access to various private archives. He knew Sir John Strangways well, and refers in various contexts to the documents which he saw in Sir John's possession, presumably at Melbury.[85] Gerard's account of Abbotsbury is explicitly derived from information he found in the abbey's cartulary:

The next place wee meet withall of any Note is Abotsbury, where if you wilbeleeve a relacion in the Register, of that Monesterie, was built, in the very Infancy of christianity amongst the Britayns a Church to St. Petter, by Bertufus an holy Prest unto whom the same Saint had often appeared, and amongst other thinges gave him a Charter written with his owne hand, which wilbee needlesse for mee to examplefy; Onlie in it St. Peter, professeth, to have consecrated the Church himselfe, and to have given it to name, Abodesbyry, but to leave this, Abodesbyry, after, as it seemes became a retireing place for the West Saxons, Kings who beinge afterwards vanquished by the Danes, Kinge Canute gave to Sir Orc, his Houscarle this Abodesbyry, as also Portsham and Helton, all which the said Orc and Dame Thole his wife haveing noe issue gave unto the church of St. Peter at Abotsbury longe before built, but then decayed and forsaken by reason the Rovers from the Sea often infested it, here afterward the said Orc : with the consent of St. Edward the Kinge whose Steward hee was[86] in the yeare of our salvation 1044 : built a faire Monestery, and stored it with benedictan Monks from Cermill Abby,[87] which guift of his was confirmed, by the Charter of St. Edward, Will the first, Will the seconde and divers succeedinge Kings

---

[84] For Gerard's survey of Dorset, see J. Coker, *A Survey of Dorsetshire* (London, 1732); his authorship of the work was established by J. Batten, 'Who Wrote Coker's Survey of Dorsetshire?', *Notes & Queries for Somerset and Dorset* 5 (1896–7), 97–102. For his survey of Somerset, see *The Particular Description of the County of Somerset, Drawn up by Thomas Gerard of Trent, 1633*, ed. E.H. Bates, Somerset Record Soc. 15 (1900). See also E.H. Bates, 'Thomas Gerard of Trent, his Family and his Writings', *Proc. of the Dorset Nat. Hist. & Antiq. Field Club* 35 (1914), 55–70; A. Sandison, *Trent in Dorset* (Dorchester, 1969), pp. 35–42; *Coker's Survey of Dorsetshire*, with an Afterword by R. Legg (Milborne Port, 1980), pp. 171–5; and Q.E. Deakin, 'The Early County Historians of Wales and Western England, *c.* 1570–1656', unpublished Ph.D. dissertation (Univ. of Wales, 1981), pp. 301–20. There is a mid-seventeenth-century fair copy of the survey of Dorset in the Bodleian Library (MS. Top. Dorset c.1 (SC 30701)); the text published in 1732 was printed from another seventeenth-century copy, now in the Dorset County Record Office (Bond family archive [D.413]).

[85] See *Description of Somerset*, ed. Bates, pp. 83, 84 and 86. Most interestingly, in connection with Chiselborough, Somerset, Gerard remarks: 'my worthy friend Sir John Strangwayes now Lord of it hath an old Saxon deede of it, in which it is written *Cealsberge*' (p. 86); this charter is not otherwise recorded. For Gerard at Melbury, see Coker, *Survey of Dorsetshire*, p. 58.

[86] Cf. the references (in Leland's *Collectanea* and Reyner's *Apostolatus*) to Orc as Cnut's *oeconomus*.

[87] 'Cermill Abby' is Cerne Abbas, Dorset; see Fagersten, *Place-Names of Dorset*, pp. 196–7.

and popes likewise granted them many Immunityes, as freedom from my Lord Admirall, wreck of the Sea; neither were the Gentry of those tymes any thinge behind, in giveing large revenues unto them, soe that they grew very rich.[88]

But although the abbey had prospered, 'yet was it not able to beare that fatall blow, which Henry the Eight gave to all religious houses'. Gerard adds that 'the bones of the founder Orc, inclosed in a dainty Marble Coffin, which I have often seene, were removed to the adioyneing Parish Church'.[89] Abbotsbury itself was purchased by Sir Giles Strangways; 'and in place of the Abbie a faire Mansion House built, nowe descended to Sir John Strangwayes'.

It is uncertain whether Gerard's source was the 'story of the foundation' which he would have read in the cartulary, or whether he constructed his own account on the basis of the charters themselves. Whatever the case, the basis of his remark that Abbotsbury became a 'retiring place' for the West Saxon kings was perhaps no more than a charter showing that in the ninth or tenth century the place had been in a king's gift; and it seems likely that the cartulary also contained separate charters of Cnut granting Abbotsbury, Portesham and Hilton to Orc, and Edward the Confessor's charter confirming the foundation of the monastery. Gerard's statement elsewhere in the survey, that Tol, wife of Orc, gave Tolpuddle to Abbotsbury,[90] is perhaps a further reflection of his knowledge of the contents of the cartulary (if it is not simply a natural deduction from the name); and of course it is clear from Gerard's account that the cartulary contained copies of various post-Conquest charters. Needless to say, it is much to be regretted that Gerard did not provide a more detailed description of the book which he calls the 'Register of that Monesterie'.

Sir Henry Spelman's extracts from the Abbotsbury cartulary

Another antiquary who can be shown to have used material from the lost cartulary of Abbotsbury abbey was Sir Henry Spelman (*c.* 1564–1641).

---

[88] Printed here from the manuscript in the Dorset County Record Office, Bond family archive [D.413], pp. 18–19; see also Coker, *Survey of Dorsetshire*, pp. 30–1.

[89] The coffin is further described by Hutchins (in his account of the parish church): 'On the N. side of the altar, was a very ancient coffin of coarse black marble, with a cover of the same. It is supposed to have contained the bones of the founder of the abbey and his wife, and to have been removed hither at the Dissolution out of the conventual church, but, as present tradition says, out of the vicarage house. It was four feet and a half long, one foot and a half deep, and two feet broad, and in 1750, was deposited under ground, near the place where it once stood, there being no convenient place to receive it.' (Hutchins, *History of Dorset* I, 539–40 (3rd ed., II, 728).) The coffin would perhaps have borne comparison in certain respects with the mid-twelfth-century (inscribed and decorated) tombstone of Gundrada, from the Priory of St Pancras, Lewes, Sussex (*English Romanesque Art 1066–1200*, ed. G. Zarnecki, *et al.*, Exhibition Catalogue (London, 1984), no. 145), which is made of Tournai marble; I owe this reference to Laurence Keen.   [90] Coker, *Survey of Dorsetshire*, p. 82.

Spelman is chiefly renowned for his 'Glossary' (published in 1626) and for his *Concilia* (published in 1639);[91] but he also made significant contributions to the early development of Anglo-Saxon studies in several of his shorter tracts, most of which were published posthumously.[92] Among these tracts are two in which Spelman expounded his views on the technicalities of Anglo-Saxon law and diplomatic.[93] In 'Of Antient Deeds and Charters', he discusses the constituent parts of pre- and post-Conquest documents (with frequent reference to texts in the chronicle-cartulary of Ramsey abbey, then in his possession), whilst regretting that in his day Anglo-Saxon charters were 'so rare, as though I have seen diverse, yet could I never obtein one Originall'.[94] His most sustained discussion of charters is, however, to be found in his tract on 'Feuds and Tenures by Knight-Service in England', written in 1639 in response to those who had criticized his view (expressed in the 'Glossary') that 'Feuds' were introduced at the time of the Norman Conquest.[95] Spelman was thus concerned to demonstrate that the system of feudal tenure had not existed in Anglo-Saxon England: 'It appeareth also by many charters of the Saxon kings that thane-lands were not feodal, and that the military expedition made no tenure by knight-service. Give me leave therefore to produce some of them, that you may see thereby the use of those times, and what the kings themselves conceiv'd therein.' He proceeds to quote quite extensive extracts from the dispositive sections of seven Anglo-Saxon charters, in order to illustrate the condition of tenure. Two of the charters are derived from the chronicle-cartulary of Hyde Abbey (i.e. the New Minster, Winchester).[96] A third, however, is cited from a 'MS. de Abbotsb.', and it can be shown that the same manuscript was the source for the remaining charters.

Spelman's extracts from this 'MS. de Abbotsb.' are edited below from the available manuscripts and printed editions of his tract on 'Feuds and

---

91 See E.N. Adams, *Old English Scholarship in England from 1566 to 1800*, Yale Stud. in Eng. 55 (New Haven, 1917), 47–55.

92 See E. Gibson, *Reliquiæ Spelmannianæ: the Posthumous Works of Sir Henry Spelman Kt. Relating to the Laws and Antiquities of England* (Oxford, 1698); re-issued (re-set and corrected), with some additional material, in *The English Works of Sir Henry Spelman, Kt, Published in his Lifetime; together with his Posthumous Works, Relating to the Laws and Antiquities of England* (London, 1723).

93 For the wider context of Spelman's work, see H.A. Cronne, 'The Study and Use of Charters by English Scholars in the Seventeenth Century: Sir Henry Spelman and Sir William Dugdale', *English Historical Scholarship*, ed. Fox, pp. 72–91.

94 'Of Antient Deeds and Charters', first published in *The English Works of Sir Henry Spelman*, pt 2, pp. 233–56, at 236.

95 'The Original, Growth, Propagation and Condition of Feuds and Tenures by Knight-Service, in England', first published in Gibson, *Reliquiæ Spelmannianæ*, pp. 1–46; reprinted, with some alterations, in *The English Works of Sir Henry Spelman*, pt 2, pp. 1–46.

96 For Spelman's use of this manuscript, see *Liber Monasterii de Hyda*, ed. E. Edwards, RS (London, 1866), pp. lxxxiv–lxxxv. The extracts are from S 865 (*ibid.* pp. 231–2) and 746 (*ibid.* pp. 202–3), and are accurately transcribed.

Tenures': a manuscript in the Harvard Law School (designated H), which appears to be Spelman's working draft (and which differs in many significant respects from the text as printed);[97] the fair copy of the tract in the Bodleian Library (designated Bod.);[98] and the editions published in 1698 (designated RS[1]) and 1723 (designated RS[2]).[99] In the early editions the Latin text is printed in italics, and roman type is reserved for proper names, for those parts of the text to which Spelman wished to draw attention (notably the reservation clauses), and for his own interpolated comments. For present purposes the whole text is given in roman type, capitalisation (more prevalent in RS[2] than in RS[1]) has been normalized, and '&' silently expanded to 'et'; Spelman's interpolations are given in italics. The texts of the charters in H and Bod. are derived independently from Spelman's source (and of the two, Bod. is usually the fuller); some of the minor differences between these manuscripts and the two editions of RS reveal that attempts were made to 'correct' certain readings. Only the more significant variations are given in the apparatus.

1. *King Eadwig grants two and a half hides at Shilvinghampton, in Portesham, Dorset, to Ælfwine, his thegn.* [A.D. 955 × 957]

Ego Eadwigh monarchiam totius Britanniæ insulæ cum superno iuvamine optinens[a], cuidam meo fideli ministro, vocitato nomine Ælfwine, duas mansas et dimidiam tribuo perhenniter[b] illic ubi antiquorum hominum relatu nominatur at Schylfhinghatune, habeat quamdiu vivat, et post se[c] cui voluerit impertiat, cum his rebus quæ sibi rite pertinent tam in magnis quam in minimis. Sit hæc donatio immunis a servitute mundana, excepto illo labore, qui communis omni populo videtur esse (*not naming 'expeditione', etc, but concluding*) Si quis augeat, augeatur. Si quis minuat, careat præmio æterno, *etc. So that here he was freed 'a servitute mundana' both great and small, that was incident or inherent to the land by way of Tenure, and yet he was chargeable to military Expedition, and to the repairing of Bridges, Castles, Burroughs, and Fortifications, but that not otherwise than as all the land of the Kingdom was charg'd, (as before we have shew'd).*

a H, Bod.; obtinens RS   *b* H, Bod.; perenniter RS   *c* H; *om.* Bod., RS

97 Harvard Law School, MS. 2062 (at 211v–212v); acquired by Harvard in 1936 at the sale of books from the library of Hudson Gurney (see below, p. 234), in whose collection it was part of MS. 34 (pp. 182–244). I am grateful to Professor J.H. Baker for his assistance in locating this manuscript, and to Robin Fleming for obtaining copies of the relevant pages.

98 Oxford, Bodleian Library, e. Mus. 79 (SC 3694), at pp. 47–53; sold to the University of Oxford by Spelman's grandson, Charles, in 1672 (see *The Reports of Sir John Spelman*, 2 vols., ed. J.H. Baker, Selden Soc. 93–4 (London, 1977–8) I, xxi).

99 Gibson, *Reliquiæ Spelmannianæ*, at pp. 19–20, and *The English Works of Sir Henry Spelman*, pt 2, at pp. 19–20. Gibson printed the text in 1698 from what he describes in the Preface as 'a fair Copy in the Bodleian Library, corrected with Sir Henry Spelman's own hand', evidently e. Mus. 79. The account of Spelman in the *Dictionary of National Biography* states that the tract was the last work which he published in his lifetime (London, 1641); but I can find no trace of this edition.

There is nothing particularly distinctive about the formulation of this extract, and equally there is nothing which would be exceptionable in the context of mid-tenth-century diplomatic. The royal style ('monarchiam totius Britanniæ insulæ cum superno iuvamine optinens') implies an extent of authority which would not have been appropriate for Eadwig after Edgar's accession to the kingdom of Mercia and Northumbria,[100] and it is likely, therefore, that the charter was issued some time between Eadwig's accession in 955 and the division of the kingdom in 957.[101] Abbotsbury abbey held five virgates at Shilvinghampton at the time of the Domesday survey, and this charter is evidently a title-deed in respect of that land. Shilvinghampton came to be part of Portesham;[102] but it was not included in Cnut's grant of land at Portesham to Orc,[103] and one imagines that Orc (or Tola) acquired it separately.

2. *King Edgar grants land in Dorset, and three* perticae *at Lonk (? Looke (Farm), in Puncknowle, Dorset), to 'Alur.', his thegn, for his own life and for that of one heir.* A.D. '958'.

Regnante in perpetuum domino nostro, *etc.* Ego Eadgarus rex Anglorum, cæterarumque gentium in circuitu persistentium gubernator et rector, cuidam fideli meo ministro vocato nomine Alur. modicam muniminis mei partem terræ, *i.e. in Dorset.* et tres perticas in illo loco, ubi Anglica appellatione dicitur at Lonk, ut habeat ac possideat quamdiu vivat, et post se unum hæredem, quicunque sibi placuerit, derelinquat. Sit hoc prædictum rus liberum ab omni malorum obstaculo cum omnibus ad rus rite pertinentibus, campis, pascuis, pratis, sylvis; excepto communi labore, expeditione, pontis et arcis constructione. Si quis vero hominum hanc meam donationem cum stultitiæ temeritate iactando infringere tentaverit, sit ipse gravibus per colla depressus*a* catenis inter flammivomas*b* tetrorum dæmonum catervas, nisi prius ad satisfactionem emendare voluerit.*c* Istis terminis hæc tellus ambita videtur. Đis is þe landgemark at Lonk, *etc.* Hæc charta scripta est anno dominicæ incarnationis, *958*.

a RS²; depressis Bod., RS¹   *b* RS²; flammivomes Bod., flamivomes RS¹   *c* maluerit Bod., *which is the verb usually found in this context*

---

100 It is used of Edgar himself in S 736 (BCS 1165), dated 965. This charter is one of the surviving single sheets from the Abbotsbury archive; but its relationship with Eadwig's charter is slight, and by no means necessarily direct.

101 See S. Keynes, *The Diplomas of King Æthelred 'the Unready' 978–1016: a Study in their Use as Historical Evidence* (Cambridge, 1980), p. 69, n. 135.

102 See Fagersten, *Place-Names of Dorset*, pp. 248–50, citing no form for Shilvinghampton earlier than Domesday Book.

103 See Grundy, 'Saxon Charters of Dorset (1937)', pp. 113–18.

The formulation of this charter is entirely acceptable for the central decades of the tenth century, though parts have become garbled in transmission. It appears to have been a grant to a certain 'Alur' (? Alfred, or Ælfric) of an estate said to be in Dorset, the name of which has dropped out; to which were added the three *perticae* at 'Lonk'. Unusually, the terms of the grant stipulate that it is to be for the beneficiary's lifetime, and then for one heir of his choosing; but it is not clear what was intended to happen thereafter. The anathema ('Si quis . . . voluerit') is one of the standard types current in the tenth century, first appearing in a charter dated 949 and recurring several times in the 950s, 960s and 970s.[104] Two difficulties remain. In the first place, the date of the charter is given as '958', at which time Edgar was in no position to grant land in Dorset, since his brother Eadwig was still in control of England south of the Thames; moreover, the royal style is appropriate to the period after the reunification of the kingdom in 959. It would appear, therefore, that the date has been miscopied. Secondly, 'Lonk' is not a plausible place-name, and is probably corrupt; but if one infers from the context of its preservation that the charter is most likely to be another Abbotsbury title-deed, one possibility would be that 'Lonk' is a misreading of 'Louk', with reference to land at Looke (Farm), in Puncknowle, to the west of Abbotsbury.[105] Looke is not separately assessed in Domesday Book, and was probably in lay hands;[106] but it certainly belonged to the abbey in the later Middle Ages, and did so at the Dissolution.[107] In other words, it would appear that the land was not part of the original endowment; and while we remain ignorant of the charter's exact status as a title-deed (since the main estate concerned is not named in the extract), it may be that the charter itself was similarly a later arrival in the abbey's archive.

3. *King Æthelred grants five hides at Rodden, near Abbotsbury, Dorset, to 'Sealwyne', his thegn.* A.D. 1014.

So King Ethelred in the Charter to his Thane Sealwyne, granteth five cassatos *in* Readdn, cum omnibus, *etc.* cuicunque sibi libuerit cleronomo derelinquat*ᵃ* hereditate, *etc.* Sit autem istud præfatum rus liberrimum ab omni mundiali*ᵇ* obstaculo in magnis ac modicis, campis, pascuis, pratis; tribus tantummodo rationabiliter rebus exceptis quæ*ᶜ* usuali

---

104 See Keynes, *Diplomas*, p. 65, n. 120.

105 For Look(e) in Puncknowle, see Fagersten, *Place-Names of Dorset*, pp. 251–2.

106 It may have been assessed under Bexington (held by Ailmar, TRE, and by Roger Arundel, TRW), or under Puncknowle (held by Alward, TRE, and by the wife of Hugh fitz Grip, TRW).

107 For Looke's connection with Abbotsbury, see a charter dated 1336 (10 Edw. III, no. 41), in *Calendar of Charter Rolls* IV (London, 1912), 357; see also Hutchins, *History of Dorset* (3rd ed.) II, 717 and 726.

ritu observantur, id est cum glomerata sibi expeditioni compulerit populari commilitonum confligere castra, atque cum sua petunt*[d]* pontis titubantia muniri vada: ac cum concivium*[e]* turma urbium indigent muniri stabiliter septa, *etc.* Dat. anno dominicæ incarnat. *1014*. indict. *12*.

[a] H, Bod.; direlinquat RS¹; darelinquat RS²   *[b]* mundali H, Bod., RS¹; munduali RS²   *[c]* Sic Ed. Conf. in chart. fact. Orco Minist. 7 *note in* H, Bod., RS   *[d]* petivit H, Bod., RS, *evidently a misreading of a sequence of minims*   *[e]* concinni H, Bod., RS, *evidently a misreading of a sequence of minims* (conciuiū)

This extract comprises little more than a rather verbose reservation clause, but it is nevertheless of considerable interest. The formula in question would appear to have become current in the 980s, to judge from the fact that a variation of it occurs in a charter (dated 988) by which King Æthelred granted land in Sussex to Æthelgar, bishop of Selsey, and from its occurrence in a charter by which King Æthelred granted land in Hampshire to his thegn Æthelweard, dated 990 and preserved in the archive of the Old Minster, Winchester.[108] The same formula also occurs in Edward the Confessor's charter for Orc,[109] though it is uncertain whether this indicates that the draftsmen of Edward's charter had access to Æthelred's, or that both were ultimately (and independently) dependent on a common source.[110]

The beneficiary of Æthelred's charter is named by Spelman as 'Sealwyne', which is not in itself a credible form, but which might represent 'Selewine', 'Seolwine', or (at the risk of stretching too far a copyist's capacity to introduce error) 'Sæwine'.[111] 'Readdn', on the other hand, evidently stands for *Read dun* ('red hill'), and can be identified as Rodden in Dorset, a hamlet which lies between Abbotsbury and Shilvinghampton; the soil there is said to be 'a rich red clay'.[112] The fact that King Æthelred granted five hides at Rodden to his thegn 'Sealwyne', or conceivably Sæwine, in 1014, throws light on the fragment of a chirograph preserved in the Abbotsbury archive.[113] Only the right-hand third of the document survives, giving the ends of each of the eight lines of the text:

[108] S 869 (*Liber Monasteria de Hyda*, ed. Edwards, pp. 238–42) and 874 (KCD 673); see Keynes, *Diplomas*, pp. 92–4.

[109] S 1004 (KCD 772).

[110] Edward's charter shares one reading (*alternatim*) with S 874, against Æthelred's charter; but of course it is possible that the word has dropped out of the latter in the course of transmission.

[111] See O. von Feilitzen, *The Pre-Conquest Personal Names of Domesday Book*, Nomina Germanica 3 (Uppsala, 1937), 357 (for Selewine) and 354–5 (for Sæwine). It should be noted that the Sæwine who held Northleigh, Devon, TRE (DB i. 104v) is named as 'Salwinus' in Exon Domesday, 217r.

[112] Hutchins, *History of Dorset* (3rd ed.) II, 726. For Rodden, see Fagersten, *Place-Names of Dorset*, p. 245 (citing no form earlier than the thirteenth century).

[113] *OSFacs.* ii. Ilchester 5 (*Ilchester* v. *Raishley*, no. 3a); not printed by Kemble, and not included in Sawyer's catalogue.

```
....................P      H      U      M :
.................... [r]eadan dune ðe heo earnode æt Sæwine
....................e Petres mynstre æt Abbodes byrig.
....................e gan ealle feower þa hyda to gædere
.................... 7 for ð[. .] cyncges þe nyt us bocian
.................... gewittnysse Brihtwine . b . 7 Godwine
.................... red æt Abbodes byrig 7 Ælfstan æt bors
.................... r 7 Wada Ægelgeðe sunu 7 Ælfric æt
....................s 7 sce Petres
```

The feminine personal pronoun in the first line indicates that the document involved a woman, who held or 'earned' a parcel of land at Rodden from a certain Sæwine.[114] The second line suggests that St Peter's minster at Abbotsbury was also involved in some way, perhaps as a prospective beneficiary. The third line might be taken to imply that all four hides at a certain place (presumably Rodden), comprising what had once been separate holdings, were henceforth to be treated as a whole. And the fourth line could be part of a statement to the effect that a grant or arrangement was made for the good of the souls of two people, and for the king's; and that the king had agreed to grant (by charter) the enjoyment of some land or privileges to the two people in question, perhaps for the duration of their lifetimes. The occurrence among the witnesses of Brihtwine (II), bishop of Sherborne (1023–45), places the document during the lifetimes of both Orc and Tola, and although neither is named in the fragment it would seem natural to suppose that the document was concerned with some part of their arrangements for the endowment of their newly founded monastery.

4. *King Cnut grants seventeen hides at Abbotsbury, Dorset, to Orc, his thegn.* [A.D. 1016 × 1035]

[a] In nomine dei almi et agiæ sophiæ, *etc*. Idcirco ego Cnute rex, Anglorum gubernator et rector, quandam ruris portionem, decem et septem, *viz*. terræ mansas, illo in loco ubi jamdudum solicolæ illius regionis nomen imposuerunt at Abbodesburi, meo fideli ministro, quem noti[b] affines Orc appellare solent, in perpetuam confirmo hereditatem quatenus ille bene perfruatur ac perpetualiter possideat quamdiu Deus per suam ineffabilem misericordiam vitam illi et vitalem spiritum concedere voluerit, deinde namque sibi succedenti cuicunque libuerit[c] cleronomi[d] jure hereditario derelinquat, ceu supra diximus in æternam hereditatem. Maneat igitur hoc nostrum donum immobile eterna libertate iocundum cum universis quæ ad eundem locum pertinere dinoscuntur tam in magnis quam in modicis rebus, in campis, pascuis, pratis, rivulis,

---

[114] The implications of *earnode* are unclear; but see *Anglo-Saxon Wills*, ed. D. Whitelock (Cambridge, 1930), p. 178, for discussion of the verb in other contexts.

silvis, aquarumque cursibus. Excepto communi labore quod omnibus liquide patet, *viz.* expeditione, pontis constructione, arcisue munitione. Si quis autem, *etc.*

^a MS. de Abbotsb. Chart. 2 *note in* Bod., RS   ^bRS²; notis Bod., RS¹   ^c H; voluerit Bod., RS ^d H, Bod., RS¹; cleronomo RS²

The formulas employed in the dispositive section of this extract originated in the central decades of the tenth century, and recur frequently in later tenth- and eleventh-century charters. It is perhaps more significant that the formulation of the Abbotsbury charter as a whole is closely related to that of King Cnut's charter granting land at Horton, in Dorset, to Bovi, dated 1033.[115] This may simply indicate that the draftsmen of the charters used similar texts as their model, and it need not follow that the charters were drawn up at the same time, by one and the same agency; but while Orc was already established in the vicinity of Abbotsbury in 1024 (when he received Portesham from the king), and could have acquired Abbotsbury itself at any time between 1016 and 1035, one is certainly tempted to infer that his charter might have been drawn up, like Bovi's, in 1033. It should be noted that the assessment of the land given to Orc was seventeen hides; with the five hides at Rodden, this would presumably account for the abbey's holding of twenty-two hides at Abbotsbury (including the one held by the wife of Hugh fitz Grip) at the time of the Domesday survey.

The similarities between Cnut's charters for Orc and Bovi raise a matter of wider historical interest. A number of Cnut's Scandinavian followers appear to have been established by the king in the south-west, and may have been expected in some way to represent his interests in the area;[116] and although one imagines that they were regularly present at gatherings of the king and his councillors held in various parts of the kingdom, there seems to have been a tendency (though by no means a rule) only to include them among the witnesses to a charter if the charter in question concerned the area in which they were based. In 1019 a certain Agemund (clearly the Scandinavian name Aghmund or Ogmundr, rather than a corrupt form of OE Æthelmund) received a grant of sixteen hides at Cheselbourne, in Dorset;[117] the land was subsequently acquired by Shaftesbury abbey, appropriated by Earl Harold, and then restored to the abbey by Edward the Confessor.[118] Agemund attested Cnut's charter granting Portesham to Orc,[119] and otherwise occurs in two

---

[115] S 969 (*Charters of Sherborne*, ed. O'Donovan, no. 20).

[116] For the settlements of Cnut's followers in England, see F.M. Stenton, *The First Century of English Feudalism 1066–1166*, 2nd ed. (Oxford, 1961), pp. 120–2, and *Anglo-Saxon England*, 3rd ed. (Oxford, 1971), pp. 413–14; see also J. Insley, 'Some Scandinavian Personal Names from South-West England', *Namn och Bygd* 70 (1982), 77–93, and 'Some Scandinavian Personal Names in South-West England from Post-Conquest Records', *Studia Anthroponymica Scandinavica* 3 (1985), 23–58.

[117] S 955 (KCD 730).   [118] DB i. 78v.   [119] S 961 (KCD 741).

charters of Kentish interest.[120] Bovi, on the other hand, seems to occur only in 'Dorset' contexts: he is found among the group of Scandinavian thegns who attested Agemund's charter in 1019, and otherwise attested Orc's Portesham charter in 1024 and a charter for Sherborne abbey dated 1035;[121] and having received Horton in 1033, he was possibly instrumental in the founding of a monastery there.[122] Orc himself occurs among the witnesses to Bovi's Horton charter (1033) and to the charter for Sherborne abbey (1035); and it was not until the reigns of Harthacnut and Edward the Confessor that he was included in the witness-lists of a few charters dealing with estates further afield.[123] The facts are few, and one might well doubt their significance; but they do appear to suggest that Agemund, Bovi and Orc were recognised by their contemporaries as specifically 'Dorset' thegns, perhaps with specifically 'Dorset' interests. Of course, we happen to be able to locate these three Scandinavians in Dorset because their properties came to form part of the endowments of religious houses, leading to the preservation of the charters which had formerly constituted their own title-deeds. There were doubtless others like them, presumably to be found among the number of 'housecarls' established in the vicinity:[124] whatever its exact significance, the term is applied to both Bovi and Orc,[125] and they and their kind would have been the beneficiaries of the renders *ad opus huscarlium* levied before the Conquest from the four Dorset boroughs of Dorchester, Bridport, Wareham and Shaftesbury.[126] King Cnut would have been among friends whenever he visited Dorset; and of course it was at Shaftesbury that he died.[127]

---

[120] S 959 (KCD 737) and 981 (*Anglo-Saxon Charters*, ed. A.J. Robertson, 2nd ed. (Cambridge, 1956), no. 85).

[121] S 975 (*Charters of Sherborne*, ed. O'Donovan, no. 16).

[122] That Bovi founded Horton abbey was taken for granted by Stenton (*Anglo-Saxon England*, p. 414); but the situation is complicated by evidence that the place was patronized (if not necessarily founded) by Ordulf, son of Ordgar (see *Charters of Sherborne*, ed. O'Donovan, pp.lx–lxi).

[123] S 993 (KCD 762), 999 (KCD 767) and 1010 (KCD 778).

[124] For the incidence of 'housecarls' in England as a whole, see K. Mack, 'Changing Thegns: Cnut's Conquest and the English Aristocracy', *Albion* 16 (1984), 375–87, at 376, n. 5, and N. Hooper, 'The Housecarls in England in the Eleventh Century', *Anglo-Norman Studies VII*, ed. R.A. Brown (Woodbridge, 1985), pp. 161–76, at 172–3.

[125] Bovi is styled *minister* in the body of the text of the Horton charter (S 969: *Charters of Sherborne*, ed. O'Donovan, no. 20), but is called Cnut's *huskarl* in the rubric (evidently derived from the contemporary endorsement on the original single sheet). The same may have applied to Orc's Abbotsbury charter; and he is styled *huskarl* in Edward the Confessor's writ (S 1063: Harmer, *Writs*, no. 1)

[126] DB i. 75r. See Hooper, 'Housecarls', p. 170, and Williams, 'Introduction to the Dorset Domesday', p. 26.

[127] I do not mean to imply that Dorset was a Danish stronghold, for similar arrangements perhaps obtained elsewhere in the kingdom. It is true that the cult of St Olaf the Martyr (who

5. *King Cnut grants land to Bovi, his thegn.* [A.D. 1016 × 1035]

And in his Charter to his Thane Bouy he saith: Quod omnibus communiter indictum est, expeditione pontis arcisue constructione.

This admittedly pitiful extract occurs only in the Harvard manuscript of Spelman's tract, following the extract from Cnut's charter for Orc; on his second thoughts, Spelman evidently decided to omit it altogether. One might have imagined that the text was derived from the Sherborne cartulary, in which Cnut's charter granting land at Horton to Bovi is preserved; but the equivalent passage in that charter reads 'quod omnibus liquide patet . uidelicet expeditione pontis constructione . arcisue munitione', so it is clearly a different charter which is here in question. Needless to say, one should like to know more about the circumstances in which a charter for Bovi ended up in the Abbotsbury archive; but the fact that one did suggests that Orc and Bovi had dealings of some kind with each other.

6. *King Edward grants two and a half hides at Abbotts Wootton, in Whitchurch Canonicorum, Dorset, to Tola, widow of Orc.* [A.D. 1053 × 1066]

[a] And King Edward the Confessor granting duas mansas et dimidiam in Wudeton, *etc. to* Thola (*widow of the foresaid Orc, whom in a Saxon charter he calleth his Man, that is his Thane*) *saith thus*: In æternam hereditatem concedo quatenus illa habeat et perpetualiter possideat hanc meam regalem donationem quamdiu vivat, et post obitum suum cuicunque voluerit hæredi relinquat. Sit autem præfatum rus liberum ab omni seculari gravedine tam in magnis quam in modicis rebus, in campis, pascuis, pratis, siluis, aquarumque decursibus; tribus exceptis quæ omnibus hominibus communia sunt, *viz.* expeditione, pontis, arcisue restauratione.

[a] Lib. Abotsb. Chart. 8 *marginal note in* H

In terms of its diplomatic, this extract is unexceptionable; parallels could be cited from any number of charters issued between the mid-tenth and the mid-eleventh century. Tola was apparently a widow when the charter was drawn up, and since her husband was still alive in 1053 (when Earl Harold, who is addressed in Edward the Confessor's writ for Orc, was appointed earl of Wessex), it follows that the charter must have been issued some time between 1053 and Edward's death in 1066. Orc himself had received five *perticae* at Wootton from Edward in 1044, and one would guess that the two and a half hides here given to his widow supplemented that small holding; but it may be

died in 1030) made an early impression at Sherborne (and Exeter; see B. Dickins, 'The Cult of S. Olave in the British Isles', *SBVS* 12 (1937–45), 53–80, at 56–7 and 69), and there is an entry for him in the Abbotsbury calendar (cited above, p. 209, n. 14); but the popularity of the cult was widespread.

that Orc and Tola had accumulated land at Wootton bit by bit, and that the present charter represents the (re-) booking to Tola of the consolidated whole. The abbey held two and a half hides at Wootton at the time of the Domesday survey.

Apart from a single footnote citing Cnut's grant of Abbotsbury to Orc as 'MS. de Abbotsb. Chart. 2', there is no reference in the printed text of Spelman's tract to the source from which he derived his extracts. It is especially interesting, therefore, to find that in the Harvard manuscript of the tract, each extract is given a marginal reference: in the order in which Spelman cites them (which differs from the order he finally adopted), Edward the Confessor's charter for Tola is 'Lib. Abotsb. Chart. 8'; Cnut's charter for Orc is 'Chart. 2' (as in the printed text); Cnut's charter for Bovi is 'Chart. 11'; Æthelred's charter for Sealwyne is 'Chart. 6'; and Eadwig's charter for Ælfwine is 'Chart. 13'.[128] Moreover, in the Harvard manuscript there are marginal cross-references, against parts of the text of Edward the Confessor's charter for Tola, to 'Chart. 9' (which Spelman does not otherwise cite); and in all versions of the tract there is a cross-reference, against a passage in Æthelred's charter for Sealwyne, to Edward the Confessor's 'Chart. fact. Orco Minist. 7', indicating that this (surviving) charter had been copied in the same book as the others. In other words, it is abundantly clear that Spelman was working from a source which contained copies of at least thirteen charters (not in chronological order), and there is every reason to believe that all were derived from one and the same Abbotsbury book, which must have been the abbey's cartulary. At no point, however, does Spelman say that he had seen any charters at Melbury, or that he had been in contact with Sir John Strangways; and this makes one wonder whether he might have been working from a transcript of some or all of the cartulary's contents made by another person. It is no less interesting, therefore, to notice the presence in the Strangways archive of a sheet of paper bearing translations of the three known vernacular writs for Abbotsbury, apparently derived from an original Inspeximus charter of Henry VIII and written by none other than Sir Henry Spelman himself;[129] for it suggests that Spelman had indeed visited Melbury, and that Strangways had taken the opportunity to ask him to provide a translation of the writs for his own records.[130] A reference, in the tract, to Tola as 'widow of the foresaid Orc,

---

[128] Edgar's charter is not cited in the Harvard manuscript.

[129] See above, p. 219, n. 68.

[130] Also preserved in the Strangways archive is a hand-written book, bearing the title: 'Archaismus Graphicus ab Henrico Spelmanno conscriptus in usum filiorum suorum. Anno Domini 1606.' It contains accounts of letter-forms, and lists of abbreviations arranged alphabetically; one would like to think that Spelman inadvertently left it at Melbury, or that he presented it to Sir John Strangways.

whom in a Saxon charter he calleth his man, that is his thane', confirms that Spelman had seen a text of Edward the Confessor's writ in which the king describes Tola as 'my *mann*';[131] but it remains uncertain whether Spelman had seen a copy of the writ in the cartulary, or whether he cited it from his knowledge of Henry VIII's Inspeximus.

While we should be grateful to Spelman for the information which he does provide, we may regret that it was not germane to his purpose to give complete texts of the Abbotsbury charters. It seems reasonable to assume, however, that Spelman had copied the texts in their entirety, and that he did not make the selection of passages until the need arose; so it is possible that fuller texts of the Abbotsbury charters are awaiting 'discovery' in Spelman's surviving papers. Parts of Spelman's library were sold at auction in the early eighteenth century;[132] but the bulk of his manuscript collections remained intact, and passed eventually into the hands of the Suffolk antiquary Dr Cox Macro (who died in 1767). On the sale of the Macro library in 1820 those of predominantly historical, legal and antiquarian interest were acquired by Hudson Gurney, and the rest by Dawson Turner.[133] The Spelman papers described and catalogued in the libraries of these two men are now widely dispersed;[134] some may have perished, and the present locations of others are for the time being known to their owners alone. Of those which can be traced, several contain copies of charters made by Spelman and others;[135] but if anything from the Abbotsbury cartulary survives, it has so far proved elusive.

---

[131] S 1063 (Harmer, *Writs*, no. 1). Elsewhere in the tract, Spelman refers to the contents of the writ in more detail: see Gibson, *Reliquiæ Spelmannianæ*, p. 34.

[132] See *List of Catalogues of English Book Sales 1676–1900 now in the British Museum* (London, 1915), pp. 27–8.

[133] The Spelman–Gurney manuscripts are described (in detail) by W.D. Macray, 'The Manuscripts of the late John Henry Gurney, Esq, of Keswick Hall, Norfolk', *The Manuscripts of the Duke of Beaufort, K.G., the Earl of Donoughmore, and Others*, Hist. Manuscripts Commission, 12th Report, Appendix, pt 9 (London, 1891), 116–64. The Spelman–Turner manuscripts are described (in detail) in *Catalogue of the Manuscript Library of the late Dawson Turner, Esq.*, Puttick and Simpson sale catalogue, 6–10 June 1859 (London, 1859); they include three volumes of Spelman's correspondence with antiquaries (Lot 442), now BL Add. 34599–34601.

[134] The Spelman–Gurney manuscripts were sold at Sotheby's on 30–1 March 1936 (and many were broken up into three or four lots); I am indebted to Richard Linenthal, of Quaritch's, for his help in elucidating their fate at the sale. For information on the present whereabouts of some of these manuscripts, see Royal Commission on Historical Manuscripts, *Guide to the Location of Collections Described in the Reports and Calendars Series 1870–1980*, Guides to Sources for Brit. Hist. 3 (London, 1982), 28; the annotated copy of the RCHM report on the Gurney manuscripts, in the National Register of Archives, Quality Court, London, is less accessible, but more helpful.

[135] For example, Norwich, Norfolk Record Office, MS. 7198 (T.139F) [formerly Gurney MS. 22, pt 1 (fols. 1–131)] and MS. 7197 (T.139F) [formerly Gurney MS. 28, fols. 195–358];

Dugdale, Strangways, and the 'Monasticon'

Towards the end of his life Spelman met William Dugdale (1605–86), and encouraged him to collaborate with Roger Dodsworth in the collection of materials for the history of the religious houses of England.[136] It was quite possibly Spelman himself who apprised Dugdale of the existence of an Abbotsbury cartulary in the possession of Sir John Strangways;[137] and when Dugdale came to write his account of the abbey, it was naturally to Strangways that he turned for information. The account, incorporated in the first volume of the *Monasticon Anglicanum* (1655),[138] begins with details of the abbey's foundation and early endowment, given on Strangways' authority:

Hæc autem ex relatione viri quidem cui credatur longe dignissimi, domini *Johannis Strangeways*, ordinis sui, equestris scilicet, magni sane ornamenti, ac ædium istarum nunc domini nuper accepimus, una cum duabus chartis . . . Chartæ vero, quas ex ipsissimis descripsimus autographis, nobis a nobilissimo equite, pro sua erga nos humanitate et benevolentia, atque operis istius promovendi et exornandi studio, nuper, ut diximus, libentissime transmissis, sequuntur.[139]

It would appear that Dugdale had been in touch with Strangways in the early 1650s, for later on in his account Dugdale prints a third document which he had been lent (on the ordination of the Strangways Chantry, 1505), declaring his text to be derived 'ex autographo penes D. Johannem Strangways mil. an. 1652'.[140] It should be noted, therefore, that Strangways provided his information about the abbey's foundation several years after the burning of

---

Oxford, Bodleian Library, Eng. hist. c. 241 [formerly Gurney MS. 30, fols. 1–75]; Manchester, John Rylands Library, English 880 [formerly Gurney MS. 32]; and Ipswich, Suffolk Record Office, MS. HD695/3 [formerly Gurney MS. 22, pt 3 (fols. 218–65)]. The last of these incorporates (253r–255v) a list of the contents of a three-volume set of transcripts made from various cartularies, by various people, in the 1630s and 1640s; but there is no reference to anything from Abbotsbury.

[136] See *The Life, Diary, and Correspondence of Sir William Dugdale*, ed. W. Hamper (London, 1827), pp. 9–11.

[137] See Dugdale's list of cartularies, in Oxford, Bodleian Library, Dugdale MS. 48 (SC 6536), fols. 54–64, at 56r: 'Abbotsbury – Johannes Strangways de eadem miles.'

[138] W. Dugdale, *Monasticon Anglicanum*, 3 vols. (London, 1655–73) I, 276–82; new ed., 6 vols., ed. J. Caley, H. Ellis and B. Bandinel (London, 1817–30) III, 52–61. See further D.C. Douglas, 'The Grand Plagiary', in his *English Scholars* (London, 1939), pp. 31–59, at 40–2.

[139] *Monasticon* I, 276. 'I received this information recently, from the account of a certain most worthy man, in whom one may trust implicitly – Sir John Strangways, a truly great ornament of his order, namely of knighthood, and now the owner of these buildings – together with two charters . . . And the charters follow, which I have transcribed from the very originals recently and most generously sent to me, as I have said, by the most noble knight, in his courtesy and kindness towards me, and in his enthusiasm for the encouragement and embellishment of this work.' [140] *Monasticon* I, 280.

Abbotsbury and the plundering of Melbury: if he did not have access to the cartulary itself, he could have perused such single-sheet charters as were still in his possession, or he could have used notes taken from the cartulary some time in the past, or he could have relied on his own memory of its contents.

Dugdale's account of the foundation, based on the information provided by Strangways, is as follows:

Quidam *Orcus*, vir suo tempore præpotens, & *Canuto Anglo Danorum* regi, eximie charus, simul cum Heroina quadam, *Tola* nomine, conjuge sua, *Rothomagi* in *Normannia* oriunda, coenobium istud fundavit. Quæ quidem *Tola* villam quandam, tunc Piddle, hodie vero Tole-Piddle, nuncupatam, in agro *Dorsetensi*, pretio emit, quam cum villis istis, Abbottesbury, Portesham, Helton, & Anstie, vulgo nominatis, & in eodem agro sitis, ipsa simul cum viro, coenobio suo dono dedit. De cuius fundationis quam ita vocant charta, hæc (inter alia) olim excerpta: – – – *Et cum ea (Tola* scil.) *diu vixit* (idem *Orcus*) *non sine spe, sed sine possibilitate procreandæ prolis.* Ubi etiam, de ecclesiastico loci officio hæc: – – – *Et ecclesiam raro servitio, ibidem ministratam invenit ab uno presbytero suam uxorem habente.*[141]

Strangways perhaps derived much of this information from the foundation charter, and it would appear that he had notes of some kind in front of him. We may have some confidence, therefore, in the interesting detail that Tola came from Rouen in Normandy;[142] that the initial endowment of the abbey comprised Abbotsbury, Portesham, Hilton, and *Anstie*;[143] that Orc and Tola had lived for a long time 'not without hope but without any possibility of having children';[144] and that Orc had found the church (at Abbotsbury) served by just one priest with his wife.[145]

Following these general remarks on the foundation of Abbotsbury,

---

[141] *Monasticon* I, 276. 'A certain Orc (a powerful man in his time and especially dear to Cnut, king of the Anglo-Danes), together with a certain noble woman called Tola, his wife (from Rouen in Normandy), founded this monastery. This Tola, indeed, bought for a price a certain estate in Dorset then called Piddle, today called Tolepiddle; which she, together with her husband, gave by gift to their monastery, with the estates commonly called Abbotsbury, Portesham, Hilton and Ansty. These things, among others, were formerly excerpted from the charter of its so-called foundation, to wl. ch they refer as follows: "And he (the same Orc) lived for a long time with her (namely Tola) not without hope but without possibility of having children." These remarks concerning the ecclesiastical office of the place are also found there: "And he found the church there supplied with infrequent service, by one priest who had his wife with him."'

[142] It is conceivable that Tola came to England in the retinue of Emma, daughter of Duke Richard of Normandy (and former wife of King Æthelred the Unready), who married Cnut in 1017.

[143] Ansty, a hamlet attached to Hilton; see Fagersten, *Place-Names of Dorset*, p. 189.

[144] Cf. Gerard's remark (above, p. 222) to the effect that Orc and Tola had no issue.

[145] Cf. Leland's remark (above, p. 221) to the effect that secular canons were expelled, and replaced by monks.

Dugdale supplies the texts of the two Anglo-Saxon charters lent to him by
Strangways: the first is Cnut's grant of seven hides at Portesham to Orc, dated
1024,[146] and the second is the document relating to the establishment and
constitution of Orc's guild at Abbotsbury.[147] He then mentions the cartulary
for the first time:

Præter hæc, monumenta quidem haud vulgaria, superius exhibita, pauca alia a nobis,
saltem ad præsens expectanda; quandoquidem veterem coenobii librum ms.
(Registrum vulgo vocant) in quem & fundationis historia, & donationum omnium
tabulæ, cætæraque loci monumenta literaria, superioris ævi cura, relata fuerant, ab
eodem equite ornatissimo, ejus domino, in nupera rerum *Anglicarum* adeo funesta,
vere scelesta commotione, aut sublesta manu surreptum, aut hostium igne
consumptum, magno cum suo ipsius & rei antiquæ dispendio, periisse juste
doleamus.[148]

It is difficult to penetrate the nuances of Dugdale's prose, but one gets the
impression that in telling him about the cartulary Strangways had said that it
had been missing since the time of the civil wars, and that he was uncertain
whether it had been burnt, or looted; and if Dugdale had any expectation of
receiving more charters, it may be that Strangways had not given up all hope of
its recovery.[149] Certainly, there is no justification here for taking Dugdale's
account as evidence that the cartulary was actually destroyed in the burning of
Abbotsbury house.[150]

Dugdale otherwise cites Leland's brief reference to the foundation of

[146] S 961: *OSFacs.* ii. Ilchester 2.   [147] *OSFacs.* ii. Ilchester 4; see above, p. 208, n. 12.

[148] *Monasticon* I, 278. 'Apart from these (charters) given above – records by no means common –
few others are to be expected by us, at least for the present. For indeed we may justly lament
the loss of an old manuscript book of the monastery (they commonly call it a "register") –
into which both the story of its foundation and lists of all donations and other written
records of the place had been entered through the care of a preceding age – (a loss) suffered
by the same distinguished knight, its owner, in the recent quite deadly, nay abominable,
turmoil of English affairs, whether snatched by a stealthy hand or consumed by enemy fire,
with great loss to himself and to antiquity.'

[149] Correspondence between Dugdale (or Dodsworth) and Strangways would clarify the issue;
but I have not yet traced any. For Dugdale's papers, see *The Life, Diary and Correspondence of
Sir William Dugdale*, ed. Hamper, and F. Maddan *et al.*, *A Summary Catalogue of Western
Manuscripts in the Bodleian Library at Oxford* II.ii (Oxford, 1937), pp. 1068–92. There does not
appear to be anything of this sort among the papers of Sir John Strangways in the Dorset
County Record Office.

[150] Hutchins, *History of Dorset* I, 533: 'This register, or chartulary, which Sir William Dugdale
says was in the possession of Sir John Strangways (but destroyed in the civil wars, when his
house was burnt)...'. VCH *Dorset* II, 48: the register was 'unfortunately destroyed with the
mansion-house of the Strangeways at Abbotsbury in the civil wars of Charles I'. Harmer,
Writs, p. 119, n. 1: 'The only register of the monastery known to have existed is said to have
been destroyed with the house of the Strangeways in the Civil War.'

Abbotsbury abbey, and prints the vernacular writs of Edward the Confessor and William the Conqueror, deriving his text of the writs from the Inspeximus charter of King Edward II; and of course it was Dugdale's account which provided the basis for subsequent writing on Abbotsbury.[151]

CONCLUSION

Perhaps the most interesting (if unintended) result of this exercise has been the emergence into the limelight of Sir John Strangways of Melbury and Abbotsbury, in his capacity as the custodian of an ancient monastic archive: for there cannot be many better illustrations of how a member of the landed gentry in the seventeenth century might regard the ancient charters in his possession, whether as title-deeds to be brought forward for the purposes of litigation in his own time, or as historical documents to be shared with the growing band of antiquaries. We are also reminded of the awe-inspiring industry of the antiquaries themselves, and of the fact that they enjoyed access to manuscripts which have since been lost or destroyed; and while it may be difficult to track down their collections and then to sort the wheat from the chaff, there can be no doubt that the task is thoroughly worthwhile, both for the light it throws on their own work, and for the prospect it brings of finding material of special interest in a quite different connection.

The Abbotsbury cartulary itself emerges from the exercise as something rather more substantial than just another of the many manuscripts which fell victim to indignities of various kinds, whether at the time of the Dissolution of the Monasteries, in the Civil Wars, in the Cotton fire of 1731, or in any other circumstances.[152] It contained a charter of St Peter in favour of the mysterious priest Bertufus, of which Gerard was sceptical and doubtless with very good reason; but such outrageous texts are not uncommon in monastic cartularies, and St Peter's charter need not in itself cast too long a shadow over the character of the cartulary as a whole. It contained a group of tenth- and eleventh-century title-deeds relating to estates which came into the possession of the abbey, including charters of King Eadwig, King Edgar and King Æthelred the Unready; and it is of some interest that charters up to one

---

151 Later on in the seventeenth century, Thomas Tanner said of Abbotsbury: 'A.D. 1026. Orcus and Tola his wife built an Abby for Black Monks to the honour of St Peter.' See T. Tanner, *Notitia Monastica* (Oxford, 1695), p. 53, citing Dugdale. This was expanded in later editions: 'Orcius, or Orking, steward to K. Canute, about the year 1026 instituted a society of Secular canons here, who by him or his widow named Tola (temp. Ed. Confes.) changed into a monastery of the Benedictine order, and dedicated to St Peter' (*Notitia Monastica* (London, 1744), p. 105). This is perhaps no more than an attempt to reconcile statements in Leland, Reyner and Dugdale.

152 See C.E. Wright, 'The Dispersal of the Monastic Libraries and the Beginning of Anglo-Saxon Studies: Matthew Parker and his Circle. A Preliminary Study', *Trans. of the Cambridge Bibliog. Soc.* 1 (1949–53), 208–37.

hundred years old were still serving their intended purpose in the mid-eleventh century. It contained a series of charters in favour of Orc, including King Cnut's original grant of Abbotsbury, and Edward the Confessor's grant of Abbotts Wootton; and to judge from Gerard's account, there may have been a copy of Cnut's grant of Portesham, and perhaps a copy of a charter by which Cnut granted him the estate at Hilton. It contained a charter of King Edward the Confessor confirming the foundation of Abbotsbury abbey, apparently dated 1044; the charter seems to have given an account of the circumstances of the foundation (supplying among other things the information that the monks were brought in from Cerne, in Dorset), and it listed the estates with which Orc and Tola endowed the place, including Tolpuddle, Abbotsbury, Portesham, Hilton and Ansty. It contained at least one charter in favour of Tola, by which King Edward the Confessor granted her land at Abbotts Wootton, some time after her husband's death (and there may have been a separate charter in respect of her purchase of land at (Tol)puddle); and, most remarkably, it appears to have contained a charter for Orc's fellow housecarl, Bovi of Horton. It may also have contained a copy of the writ by which King Edward granted Tola permission to bequeath her property to the abbey in accordance with arrangements made during Orc's lifetime, and copies of other vernacular documents of the same kind; in which case, the cartulary would be one of the (surprisingly) few to contain vernacular writs as well as Latin diplomas. In addition to all of these pre-Conquest texts, the cartulary contained various later charters, as well as a story of the foundation, lists of benefactions, and other 'written records' connected with the abbey.

It has also emerged that the Abbotsbury cartulary had been kept with the other archives of the Strangways family at Melbury, and that there is accordingly no good reason to believe that it was destroyed by fire in 1644. The cartulary would appear, however, to have been mislaid during the 'great shippwrack' of Sir John Strangways' deeds which occured at the same time, and it cannot be traced in the family archives thereafter. The cartulary was mentioned in a list of monastic cartularies published in 1834, and was said (citing Dugdale) to have been 'destroyed in the civil wars'; but it was noted that 'there are excerpts from it in Dodsworth's Collection'.[153] Corrigenda to

---

[153] T. Phillipps and F. Maddan, 'List of Monastic Cartularies at present existing, or which are known to have existed since the Dissolution of Religious Houses', *Collectanea Topographica et Genealogica* i (1834), 73–9, 197–208 and 399–404, at 74. For Dodsworth's collection (including various extracts from cartularies, made in connection with the *Monasticon*), see J. Hunter, *Three Catalogues* (London, 1838), pp. 57–249, and Maddan *et al.*, *Summary Catalogue* ii.ii, 865–961; but the material has been well studied and indexed, and there is no obvious sign of extracts from the Abbotsbury cartulary (beyond the statement, in Oxford, Bodleian Library, Dodsworth 24, fol. iii, that 'Sir John Strangways hath the coucher of Abbotsbury').

this list were published in the following year, and include, under Abbotsbury, a tantalizing statement to the effect that 'the cartulary supposed to have been lost, has been lately discovered in the archives of the Earl of Ilchester', presumably at Melbury.[154] Perhaps there was some confusion, for otherwise it would be difficult to understand how Kemble, and later Birch, missed it: both acknowledge only single-sheet copies from the collection of the earl of Ilchester, and those which they print are those which still survive in the Dorset County Record Office.[155] It may also be significant that when the fifth earl of Ilchester put together his comprehensive collection of title-deeds for Abbotsbury in 1888, for the purposes of a lawsuit against some local fishermen, he would appear not to have known of the existence of any cartulary, for the only Anglo-Saxon documents cited from his own muniments are three of the single-sheet charters.[156] It is just conceivable that the cartulary remained at Melbury somehow forgotten and unrecognized, and that it lurked among the books which were dispersed when the contents of the library were auctioned in the early 1960s;[157] but it has to be said that the cartulary could not be found there in the 1950s,[158] and certainly, it is not known to exist at Melbury today.[159]

In all these circumstances it is startling to find evidence, among the papers in the Fox-Strangways (Ilchester) archive, of the existence of a 'Chartulary of Abbotsbury' in the second half of the nineteenth century. A page from what is apparently a rough list of manuscripts at Melbury includes the following items:[160]

17   Compositions in the Tower – Sir J. Strangways
45 & 6 Alvacado Arte of living well – 2 vols
86   Chartulary of Abbotsbury

---

[154] *Collectanea Topographica et Genealogica* 2 (1835), 400.

[155] Kemble's presence at Melbury is reflected by his providing a 'restored' translation of the fragmentary chirograph to the then Lord Ilchester (*Ilchester* v. *Raishley*, no. 3a); Birch, on the other hand, would have been able to rely on the published facsimiles of the Ilchester charters.

[156] *Ilchester* v. *Raishley*, nos. 1a (S 961), 2a (the Abbotsbury guild statutes), and 3a (the fragment of a chirograph).

[157] Unfortunately, I have not been able to establish how, or even precisely when, the library at Melbury was sold. It is worth adding, however, that a vast quantity of the papers of the Ilchester family, from their home at Holland House, were sold to the British Museum in 1960, and are now BL Add. 51318–52254; among them are the papers of Dr John Allen, including correspondence with J.M. Kemble (Add. 52184) and B. Thorpe (Add. 52185–6), and several volumes of notes on Anglo-Saxon laws, etc. (Add. 52222–30). Books and manuscripts from Holland House were sold at Sotheby's between July 1962 and July 1964.

[158] See G.R.C. Davis, *Medieval Cartularies of Great Britain* (London, 1958), no. 1.

[159] I am most grateful to the late Lady Teresa Agnew for authorizing another search; and to Mr Waine, Steward at Melbury House, and Mr Green, agent for the Strangways Estate, for apprising me of the result.   [160] Dorset County Record Office, D.124/Box 261.

100	Commonplace Book – 1600 –
38	Bellum Trojanum cir. 1400 –
– –	Chartulary of Bruton – 1400 –
91	Ledger – *Sir* J. Strangways 1625

This list was probably drawn up in about 1860, apparently in connection with the preparation of a report on the library at Melbury written by a person who had been charged with the task of making recommendations about its organization and upkeep. The report itself, headed 'Melbury Library' and dated 1861,[161] incorporates a fuller account of the manuscripts at Melbury, beginning: 'Tho' not very numerous these comprehend some curious things. They may be divided into two classes: those of General, & those of merely local or Family interest.' Under those of general interest, the writer of the report makes a further distinction between those 'on parchment or vellum', including 'The Chartulary of Bruton Abbey', and those 'on paper', including the 'Chartulary (so called) of Abbotsbury'. The Bruton cartulary survives, and is indeed a manuscript on parchment;[162] but the writer of the report implies a distinction in kind between it and the 'Chartulary (so called) of Abbotsbury', which was written on paper. A wishful thinker would have to be forgiven for imagining that the manuscript seen in 1861 was none other than the cartulary whose rediscovery was reported in 1835, itself identified as the one which went missing in the Civil Wars, and which had previously been used by Thomas Gerard and Sir Henry Spelman; but the devil's advocate would respond that the reference in 1861 (and perhaps in 1835) could have been to a different book, which at some time and for some reason had been mistaken for the missing cartulary. In fact the 'Chartulary (so called) of Abbotsbury' survives to this day among the records which remain at Melbury House:[163] it proves to be a 'Book of Tenures of Lands in the County of Dorset', compiled by a certain Richard Swayne in the first half of the seventeenth century, and although of considerable interest in its own right, it is unfortunately not the cartulary seen by Gerard and Spelman.

Among the manuscripts of family interest mentioned by the writer of the report on the library at Melbury are several associated with Sir John Strangways himself, comprising his account books, 'Meditations in the

---

161 Dorset County Record Office, D.124/Box 261, written in the same hand as the list.

162 Davis, *Medieval Cartularies*, no. 83: see *Two Cartularies of the Augustinian Priory of Bruton and the Cluniac Priory of Montacute in the County of Somerset*, ed. H.C. Maxwell Lyte *et al.*, Somerset Record Soc. 8 (1894). The Bruton cartulary was sold by Lord Ilchester to the British Museum in 1962, and is now BL Egerton 3772.

163 It is a leather-bound volume (comprising 193 folios of text), with 'Chartulary of Abbotsbury' tooled in gold on the spine; the number '86' is written inside, on the earl of Ilchester's bookplate.

Tower', 'Diaries of H. of Commons', 'Survey in fol. on vellum' (with another, marked J.S.), and a 'Rental in copybook'. The writer of the report also gives an account of 'Other MSS.' in the library, including 'The Saxon Charters' (at this stage kept, with translations, 'in a Portfolio by themselves'), 'The Papal Bull' (of Pope Eugenius III),[164] and 'Old Family Deeds & Documents (the latter in various tin boxes, sorted & labelled according to places, persons & families ...)'. He considered the most interesting of these records to be those relating to Abbotsbury, and remarks in this connection that 'a catalogue & analysis of these has been attempted, having been made necessary by legal proceedings relating to the Fleet'. It would appear, therefore, that members of the Strangways family continued to make good use of their archive in connection with the lawsuits about wreck, fishing rights and related matters in which they so frequently became embroiled; indeed, the practice of putting together collections of documents which were, in effect, their own cartularies was adopted on more than one occasion in the nineteenth century,[165] and the collection produced in 1888 thus takes its place as the last of a most interesting series.[166]

The recovery of extracts from six previously unrecorded Anglo-Saxon charters is as much as can be achieved for the time being; but further information about the charters of Abbotsbury abbey may yet be forthcoming. There are several stories of the discovery in modern times of medieval charters, cartularies and books,[167] and there can be little doubt that more will

---

164 This document survives in the Strangways archive. It is a confirmation of properties to the bishop and church of Exeter, and corresponds to the text printed, from a fourteenth-century manuscript at Exeter, by W. Holtzmann, *Papsturkunden in England* II, Abhandlungen der Gesellschaft der Wissenschaften zu Gottingen, Phil.-Hist. Klasse, 3rd ser. 14–15 (Berlin, 1935–6), no. 78. The Exeter copy lacks the witnesses and date; and (unaware of the original's existence) Holtzmann suggested that the bull was issued on the same occasion as another papal privilege for Exeter, dated 14 March 1153 (*ibid.* no. 77). In fact the original is dated 7 February '1145', in the ninth indiction (for 1146), and was evidently issued on the same occasion as Pope Eugenius's privileges for Lincoln (*ibid.* nos. 48–9).

165 One such collection, compiled in the early nineteenth century, survives at Melbury House. The existence of another is demonstrated by a paper preserved among a bundle of documents relating to a lawsuit in 1852 (Fox-Strangways (Ilchester) Archive, D.124/Box 333), summarising the contents of a book apparently produced for the purposes of that lawsuit. The first item (said to have been copied on pp. 1–4) was 'A Charter from K. Canute to Orc founding & endowing the Monastery of Abbotsbury', dated 1023. I should like to believe that this is an unrecorded text, but I suspect it would turn out to be a copy of S 961 (Cnut's grant of Portesham to Orc, dated 1024). The book also contained copies of various later documents, ranging in date from the reign of Henry II to 1634.

166 See *Ilchester* v. *Raishley* (above, p. 210, n. 22). The case must represent one of the more recent instances of the citation of Anglo-Saxon charters as evidence in legal proceedings; it was heard before Mr Justice Kekewich, and there is a hand-written copy of his judgement in the Dorset County Record Office.

167 See Davis, *Medieval Cartularies*, p. xvi, and R.M. Wilson, *The Lost Literature of Medieval England*, 2nd ed. (London, 1970), pp. 237–8.

be found, especially in the form of late paper manuscripts of unprepossessing appearance, whether works in their own right, or early modern transcripts of manuscripts now lost. An original tenth-century will of exceptional importance was found in the 1960s;[168] an early-modern transcript of a previously unknown charter of King Edgar was discovered in 1983;[169] and a sixteenth-century cartulary containing copies of eleven unrecorded Anglo-Saxon charters was brought to light in 1985.[170] The Abbotsbury cartulary is not the Holy Grail, but nor is it likely to be wholly uninteresting; and while there is a good chance that further transcripts of its contents await identification in the papers of those who saw and used the book in the seventeenth century, there is perhaps as good a chance that the real thing will be rediscovered in due course, and will then be allowed to speak for itself.

---

[168] S 1497: D. Whitelock *et al.*, *The Will of Æthelgifu* (Oxford, 1968).

[169] See N. Brooks *et al.*, 'A New Charter of King Edgar', *ASE* 13 (1984), 137–55.

[170] For a preliminary account of this most remarkable discovery, see K. Bascombe, 'Two Charters of King Suebred of Essex', *An Essex Tribute*, ed. K. Neale (London, 1987), pp. 85–96, at 85. The charters are derived from the archives of Barking abbey, and are being edited by Dr C.R. Hart for the series published under the auspices of the British Academy – Royal Historical Society Joint Committee on Anglo-Saxon Charters.

Bibliography for 1988

CARL T. BERKHOUT, MARTIN BIDDLE,
MARK BLACKBURN, SARAH FOOT,
SIMON KEYNES and ALEXANDER RUMBLE

This bibliography is meant to include all books, articles and significant reviews published in any branch of Anglo-Saxon studies during 1988. It excludes reprints unless they contain new material. It will be continued annually. The year of publication of a book or article is 1988 unless otherwise stated. The arrangement and the pages on which the sections begin are as follows:

Carl Berkhout has been mainly responsible for sections 2, 3 and 4, Alexander Rumble for sections 6 and 9, Sarah Foot for section 7, Mark Blackburn for section 8 and Martin Biddle for section 10. Section 5 has been compiled on the basis of information supplied by Don Scragg; Section 10 has been compiled with help from Birthe Kjølbye-Biddle. References to publications in Japan have been supplied by Professor Yoshio Terasawa. Simon Keynes has been responsible for co-ordination.

The following abbreviations occur where relevant (not only in the bibliography but also throughout the volume):

A Ae   *Archaeologia Aeliana*
AB   *Analecta Bollandiana*

Bibliography for 1988

AC	*Archæologia Cantiana*
AHR	*American Historical Review*
AIUON	*Annali, Istituto Universitario Orientale di Napoli: sezione germanica*
AntJ	*Antiquaries Journal*
ArchJ	*Archaeological Journal*
ASE	*Anglo-Saxon England*
ASNSL	*Archiv für das Studium der neueren Sprachen und Literaturen*
ASSAH	*Anglo-Saxon Studies in Archaeology and History*
BAR	British Archaeological Reports
BBCS	*Bulletin of the Board of Celtic Studies*
BGDSL	*Beiträge zur Geschichte der deutschen Sprache und Literatur*
BIAL	*Bulletin of the Institute of Archaeology* (London)
BN	*Beiträge zur Namenforschung*
BNJ	*British Numismatic Journal*
CA	*Current Archaeology*
CBA	Council for British Archaeology
CCM	*Cahiers de civilisation médiévale*
CMCS	*Cambridge Medieval Celtic Studies*
DAEM	*Deutsches Archiv für Erforschung des Mittelalters*
EA	*Études anglaises*
EconHR	*Economic History Review*
EEMF	Early English Manuscripts in Facsimile
EETS	Early English Text Society
EHR	*English Historical Review*
ELN	*English Language Notes*
EPNS	English Place-Name Society
ES	*English Studies*
FS	*Frühmittelalterliche Studien*
HZ	*Historische Zeitschrift*
IF	*Indogermanische Forschungen*
JBAA	*Journal of the British Archaeological Association*
JEGP	*Journal of English and Germanic Philology*
JEH	*Journal of Ecclesiastical History*
JMH	*Journal of Medieval History*
JTS	*Journal of Theological Studies*
LH	*The Local Historian*
MA	*Medieval Archaeology*
MÆ	*Medium Ævum*
MLR	*Modern Language Review*
MP	*Modern Philology*
MS	*Mediaeval Studies*
MScand	*Mediaeval Scandinavia*
N&Q	*Notes and Queries*
NChron	*Numismatic Chronicle*
NCirc	*Numismatic Circular*

NH	*Northern History*
NM	*Neuphilologische Mitteilungen*
OEN	*Old English Newsletter*
PA	*Popular Archaeology*
PBA	*Proceedings of the British Academy*
PMLA	*Publications of the Modern Language Association of America*
PQ	*Philological Quarterly*
RB	*Revue bénédictine*
RES	*Review of English Studies*
SBVS	*Saga-Book of the Viking Society for Northern Research*
SCBI	Sylloge of Coins of the British Isles
SCMB	*Seaby's Coin and Medal Bulletin*
SettSpol	*Settimane di studio del Centro italiano di studi sull'alto medioevo* (Spoleto)
SM	*Studi Medievali*
SN	*Studia Neophilologica*
SP	*Studies in Philology*
TLS	*Times Literary Supplement*
TPS	*Transactions of the Philological Society*
TRHS	*Transactions of the Royal Historical Society*
YES	*Yearbook of English Studies*
ZAA	*Zeitschrift für Anglistik und Amerikanistik*
ZDA	*Zeitschrift für deutsches Altertum und deutsche Literatur*
ZVS	*Zeitschrift für vergleichende Sprachforschung*

1. GENERAL AND MISCELLANEOUS

Berkhout, Carl T., 'Old English Bibliography 1987', *OEN* 21.2, 43–70

Berkhout, Carl T., Martin Biddle, Mark Blackburn, C. R. E. Coutts, David N. Dumville, Sarah Foot and Simon Keynes, 'Bibliography for 1987', *ASE* 17, 283–335

Blair, John, ed., *Minsters and Parish Churches: the Local Church in Transition 950–1200*, Oxford Univ. Committee for Archaeol. Monograph 17 (Oxford)

Bond, James, 'Rabbits: the Case for their Medieval Introduction into Britain', *LH* 18, 53–7

Calder, Daniel G., and T. Craig Christy, ed., *Germania: Comparative Studies in the Old Germanic Languages and Literatures* (Wolfeboro, NH, and Woodbridge)

Cameron, Kenneth, 'C. E. Blunt, OBE, FBA', *Jnl of the EPNS* 20 (1987–8), 48

Cameron, M. L., 'Anglo-Saxon Medicine and Magic', *ASE* 17, 191–215

Clement, Richard W., 'Short-Title Catalogue of the Clubb Anglo-Saxon Collection', *OEN* 21.2, B1–B25

Conner, Patrick W., 'Oxford Text Archive', *OEN* 21.2, 29

Crépin, André, 'Medieval English Studies in France', *Med. Eng. Stud. Newsletter* (Tokyo) 18, 1–3

Ford, Boris, ed., *The Cambridge Guide to the Arts in Britain I: Prehistoric, Roman and Early Medieval* (Cambridge)

Frank, Roberta, 'Medieval English Studies at the University of Toronto', *Med. Eng. Stud. Newsletter* (Tokyo) 19, 3–6

Gardner, Philip, '"Make Me an Offa": Geoffrey Hill and *Mercian Hymns*', *Dalhousie Rev.* 67, 202–16

Gray, Douglas, 'Medieval English Studies at Oxford', *Med. Eng. Stud. Newsletter* (Tokyo) 19, 1–3

Herendeen, W. H., 'William Camden: Historian, Herald, and Antiquary', *SP* 85, 192–210

Hill, Joyce, 'Third Progress Report: *Fontes Anglo-Saxonici*', *OEN* 21.2, 24–5

Knapp, Peggy A., 'Alienated Majesty: *Grendel* and its Pretexts', *Centennial Rev.* 32, 1–18

Kubouchi, Tadao, William Schipper and Hiroshi Ogawa, ed., *Old English Studies from Japan 1941–81*, OEN Subsidia 14 (Binghamton)

Lapidge, Michael, *Abbreviations for Sources and Specification of Standard Editions for Sources, Compiled for 'Fontes Anglo-Saxonici' and 'Sources of Anglo-Saxon Literary Culture'* (Binghamton)

Lapidge, Michael, and Roberta Frank, 'Record of the Third Conference of the International Society of Anglo-Saxonists, at Toronto, 20–3 April 1987', *ASE* 17, 1–3

Lester, Geoffrey, comp., *Handbook of Teachers of Medieval English Language and Literature in Great Britain and Ireland* (Sheffield, 1987)

Lutz, Angelika, 'Zur Entstehungsgeschichte von William Somners *Dictionarium Saxonico-Latino-Anglicum*', *Anglia* 106, 1–25

Marples, N. J., and O. D. Macrae-Gibson, *A Critical Discography of Readings in Old English* (Kalamazoo)

Methven, Patricia J., 'Obituary: Thomas Julian Brown, 1923–1987', *Jnl of the Soc. of Archivists* 9, 59–60

Mitchell, Bruce, *On Old English: Selected Papers* (Oxford and New York)

Oshitari, Kinshiro, *et al.*, ed., *Philologia Anglica: Essays Presented to Professor Yoshio Terasawa on the Occasion of His Sixtieth Birthday* (Tokyo)

Overing, Gillian R., 'Reinventing Beowulf's Voyage to Denmark', *OEN* 21.2, 30–9

Page, Christopher, 'Music', *The Cambridge Guide to the Arts in Britain I*, ed. Ford, pp. 246–53

Page, R. I., 'A Little Liberal, or else a Little Conservator?' *OEN* 22.1, 20–8

Piggott, Stuart, 'Sir Thomas Browne and Antiquity', *Oxford Jnl of Archaeol.* 7, 257–69

Pulsiano, Phillip, *An Annotated Bibliography of North American Doctoral Dissertations on Old English Language and Literature*, Med. Texts and Stud. 3 (East Lansing, MI, and Woodbridge)

Robinson, Fred C., 'Medieval English Studies at Yale University', *Med. Eng. Stud. Newsletter* (Tokyo) 18, 4–6

Robinson, Fred C., Larry D. Benson and George Kane, 'Morton Wilfred Bloomfield', *Speculum* 63, 756–8

Salmon, Vivien, 'Anglo-Dutch Linguistic Scholarship: a Survey of Seventeenth-Century Achievements', *Historiographia Linguistica* 15, 129–53

Schichler, Robert L., ed., 'Abstracts of Papers in Anglo-Saxon Studies', *OEN* 21.2, A1-A34

Simmons, Clare A., 'The Historical Sources of Sir Richard Blackmore's *Alfred*', *ELN* 26.2, 18–23

Stewart, Ian, 'Obituary: C. E. Blunt 1904–1987', *BNJ* 57 (1987), 157–60, with a supplement listing C.E.B.'s publications 1983–7 compiled by R. H. Thompson, pp. 160–1

Szarmach, Paul E., ed., *Old English Newsletter* 21.1–2 (Binghamton, 1987–8)

Trahern, Joseph B., Jr, ed., 'Year's Work in Old English Studies 1987', *OEN* 22.1, 33–178

Tricomi, Albert H., 'R. Kirkham's *Alfred, or Right Re-enthroned*', *OEN* 22.1, 30–1

2. OLD ENGLISH LANGUAGE

Amodio, Mark C., 'Laȝamon's Anglo-Saxon Lexicon and Diction', *Poetica* (Tokyo) 27, 48–59

Amos, Ashley Crandell, Antonette diPaolo Healey *et al.*, ed., *Dictionary of Old English: C* (Toronto)

Anderson, John M., 'Old English Ablaut Again: the Essentially Concrete Character of Dependency Phonology', *On Language: Rhetorica, Phonologica, Syntactica*, ed. Caroline Duncan-Rose and Theo Vennemann (London and New York), pp. 161–82

'The Status of Voiced Fricatives in Old English', *Edinburgh Studies in the English Language*, ed. John M. Anderson and Norman Macleod (Edinburgh), pp. 90–112

'The Type of Old English Impersonals', *Edinburgh Studies in the English Language*, ed. John M. Anderson and Norman Macleod (Edinburgh), pp. 1–32

Arngart, O., 'Old English *a* from *ō*', *SN* 60, 145–8

Bammesberger, Alfred, 'Der indogermanische Aorist und das germanische Präteritum', *Languages and Cultures: Studies in Honor of Edgar C. Polomé*, ed. Mohammad Ali Jazayery and Werner Winter, Trends in Ling., Stud. and Monographs 36 (Berlin, New York and Amsterdam), 55–62

Bately, Janet, 'On Some Aspects of the Vocabulary of the West Midlands in the Early Middle Ages: the Language of the Katherine Group', *Medieval English Studies Presented to George Kane*, ed. Edward Donald Kennedy *et al.* (Wolfeboro, NH, and Woodbridge), pp. 55–77

Beekes, R. S. P., 'The Pronominal Genitive Singular in·Germanic and Proto-Indo-European', *BGDSL* (Tübingen) 110, 1–5

Blockley, Mary, 'Constraints on Negative Contraction with the Finite Verb and the Syntax of Old English Poetry', *SP* 85, 428–50

Bremmer, Rolf H., Jr, 'The Old Frisian Component in Holthausen's *Altenglisches etymologisches Wörterbuch*', *ASE* 17, 5–13

Brinton, Laurel J., *The Development of English Aspectual Systems: Aspectualizers and Post-Verbal Particles*, Cambridge Stud. in Ling. 49 (Cambridge)

Bubennikova, O. A., 'Razvitie sistemy lichnykh mestoimennī 3-go litsa v dialektakh angliĭskogo iazyka', *Vestnik Moskovskogo Universiteta* 1988, seriia 9.2, 37–46 [development of 3rd-person pronouns in English dialects]

Bublitz, Wolfram, and Jürgen Strauss, '*Heah cyning* vs. *heahcyning*: Time-Stability in Old English Compounding', *Perspectives on Language in Performance*, ed. Wolfgang Lörscher and Rainer Schulze, Tübinger Beiträge zur Linguistik 317 (Tübingen, 1987), 88–99

Bynon, Theodora, 'Syntactic Change and the Lexicon', *Papers from the 7th International Conference on Historical Linguistics*, ed. Anna Giacalone Ramat *et al.*, Current Issues in Ling. Theory 48 (Amsterdam and Philadelphia, 1987), 123–36

Cameron, M. L., 'On *peor* and *peoradl*', *Anglia* 106, 124–9

Coates, Richard, 'Middle English *badde* and Related Puzzles', *North-Western European Lang. Evolution* 11, 91–104

Collins, Janet Duthie, 'The Word Order of Old English Poetry', *The Thirteenth LACUS Forum 1986*, ed. Ilah Fleming (Lake Bluff, IL, 1987), pp. 570–80

Colman, Fran, 'Heavy Arguments in Old English', *Edinburgh Studies in the English Language*, ed. John M. Anderson and Norman Macleod (Edinburgh), pp. 33–89

D'Aronco, Maria Amalia, see sect. 3*c* [botanical terms]

Davenport, P. E., *A Student's History of English* (Tokyo)

Dekeyser, Xavier, 'Relative Clause Formation in the Anglo-Saxon Chronicle', *Folia Linguistica Historica* 7 (1987), 351–61

Denison, David, 'A Note on t/d Deletion', *Folia Linguistica Historica* 7 (1987), 415–18

Dietz, Klaus, 'The Late Old English Type *leinten* "Lent"', *On Language: Rhetorica, Phonologica, Syntactica*, ed. Caroline Duncan-Rose and Theo Vennemann (London and New York), pp. 183–94

Ebbinghaus, E. A., 'Addendum to the Foregoing Note on OE. *teagor*', *General Ling.* 28, 120–1 [see Peeters below]

Elliott, Ralph W. V., 'Runes and Their Uses (1)', *Rising Generation* (Tokyo) 134.9, 486–9

Enkvist, Nils Erik, and Brita Wårvik, 'Old English *þa*, Temporal Claims, and Narrative Structure', *Papers from the 7th International Conference on Historical Linguistics*, ed. Anna Giacalone Ramat *et al.*, Current Issues in Ling. Theory 48 (Amsterdam and Philadelphia, 1987), 221–37

Fisiak, Jacek, *A Bibliography of Writings for the History of the English Language*, 2nd ed. (Berlin, New York and Amsterdam, 1987)

'Old East Anglian: a Problem in Old English Dialectology', *AUMLA* 70, 336–65

Fraser, Thomas, 'The Establishment of "by" to Denote Agency in English Passive Constructions', *Papers from the 7th International Conference on Historical Linguistics*, ed. Anna Giacalone Ramat *et al.*, Current Issues in Ling. Theory 48 (Amsterdam and Philadelphia, 1987), 239–49

Fujiwara, Hiroshi, 'The VSO Construction in *Beowulf*', *Philologia Anglica*, ed. Oshitari *et al.*, pp. 60–70

Fujiwara, Yasuaki, 'On the Function of Alliteration', *English Linguistics* (Tokyo) 5, 204–25

Görlach, Manfred, 'Lexical Loss and Lexical Survival: the Case of Scots and English', *Scottish Lang.* 6 (1987), 1–20

Goossens, Louis, 'The Auxiliarization of the English Modals: a Functional Grammar View', *Historical Development of Auxiliaries*, ed. Martin Harris and Paolo Ramat,

Trends in Ling., Stud. and Monographs 53 (Berlin, New York and Amsterdam, 1987), 111–43

Hamp, Eric P., 'Old English *hæst*', *North-Western European Lang. Evolution* 11, 89
'On Criteria for Northwest Germanic', *Lingua Posnaniensis* 27 (1985 for 1984), 7–11
'On Indo-European Marriage in Old English', *Jnl of Indo-European Stud.* 16, 183–4

Hasenfratz, Robert, see sect. 3*c*

Hess, H. Harwood, 'Old English Skewing', *The Thirteenth LACUS Forum 1986*, ed. Ilah Fleming (Lake Bluff, IL, 1987), pp. 581–90

Hoad, T. F., 'Old English *dwellan* and *dwelian*', *Philologia Anglica*, ed. Oshitari *et al.*, pp. 13–28

Hofmann, Dietrich, 'Altfriesisch *pellef/palef thredda* "Seidenstoff als dritter", nicht *palef-thred* "Seidenfaden"', *Us Wurk* 37, 45–51

Hofstetter, Walter, 'Winchester and the Standardization of Old English Vocabulary', *ASE* 17, 139–61

Hogg, Richard M., 'Snuck: the Development of Irregular Preterite Forms', *An Historic Tongue: Studies in English Linguistics in Memory of Barbara Strang*, ed. Graham Nixon and John Honey (London and New York), pp. 31–40

Hopper, Paul, and Janice Martin, 'Structuralism and Diachrony: the Development of the Indefinite Article in English', *Papers from the 7th International Conference on Historical Linguistics*, ed. Anna Giacalone Ramat *et al.*, Current Issues in Ling. Theory 48 (Amsterdam and Philadelphia, 1987), 295–304

Howell, Robert B., 'Tracing the Origin of Uvular *r* in the Germanic Languages', *Folia Linguistica Historica* 7 (1987), 317–49

Ikegami, Yoshihiko, '*Se* and *he* in Personal Reference in Old English: a Text-Linguistic Approach', *Philologia Anglica*, ed. Oshitari *et al.*, pp. 43–52

Jack, George, 'The Origins of the English Gerund', *North-Western European Lang. Evolution* 12, 15–75
'Relative Pronouns in Laȝamon's *Brut*', *Leeds Stud. in Eng.* 19, 31–66

Jankowsky, Kurt R., 'Old English *mæl* and *sæl* in the All-Germanic Environment: a Comparative Study', *Germania*, ed. Calder and Christy, pp. 67–84

Jones, Charles, *Grammatical Gender in English: 950 to 1250* (London, New York and Sydney)
'A Dependency Approach to Some Well-Known Features of Historical English Phonology', *Dependency and Non-Linear Phonology*, ed. Jacques Durand (London, Sydney and Dover, NH, 1986), pp. 257–67

Karakida, Shigeaki, 'A Note on Syntax and Style in the *Vices and Virtues*', *Philologia Anglica*, ed. Oshitari *et al.*, pp. 126–39 [influence of OE prose]

Kemenade, Ans van, *Syntactic Case and Morphological Case in the History of English* (Dordrecht and Providence, RI, 1987)

Kitson, Peter, 'Two Old English Plant-Names and Related Matters', *ES* 69, 97–112 [*cex, æðelferðingwyrt*]

Kmiezsa, Veronika, 'Accents and Digraphs in the Peterborough Chronicle', *Studia Anglica Poznaniensia* 21, 15–23

Kojima, Kenichi and Kiyoshi Mikawa, 'Prepositions in the West-Saxon gospels (2)', *Eng.-Lit.* (Waseda Univ.) 64, 1–18 [in Japanese]

Kubouchi, Tadao, 'Manuscript Punctuation, Prose Rhythm and S . . . V Element Order in Late Old English Orally-Delivered Prose', *Philologia Anglica*, ed. Oshitari *et al.*, pp. 71–87

'One Aspect of ON Loanwords in the Danelaw as reflected in Wulfstan's Vocabulary', *Aspects of English Vocabulary*, ed. Y. Terasawa and S. Takebayashi (Tokyo), pp. 113–33 [in Japanese]

Kurahashi, Hidehiro, 'Some notes on late OE word-order with special reference to the *Peterborough Chronicle* from 1122 to 1154', *Bull. of Dept. of Liberal Arts, Numazu Tokai Univ.* 15, 53–63

Lass, Roger, 'The "Akzentumsprung" of Old English *ēo*', *On Language: Rhetorica, Phonologica, Syntactica*, ed. Caroline Duncan-Rose and Theo Vennemann (London and New York), pp. 221–32

Lehmann, Winfred P., *Workbook for Historical Linguistics*, Summer Inst. of Ling., Publ. in Ling. 71 (Dallas and Arlington, TX, 1984)

Liberman, Anatoly, 'The Etymology of Modern English *heifer*', *General Ling.* 28, 163–75

'Two German Dialectal Words for "pig"', *General Ling.* 28, 104–18

Liberman, Anatoly, and Lawrence Mitchell, 'A New Etymological Dictionary of the English Language', *General Ling.* 28, 176–82 ['heifer' as sample entry]

Manabe, Kazumi, 'Alfredian Finite and Non-Finite Clauses', *Stud. in Eng. Lang. and Lit.* (Kyushu Univ.) 38, 87–107

Markey, T. L., 'English -*s* vs. -*th* in the Third Person Singular: Historical Contrasts and Cross Language Argumentation', *Studia Anglica Poznaniensia* 21, 3–13

Markus, Manfred, 'Zur altenglischen Worttrennung und Silbenstruktur', *IF* 93, 197–209

Matsui, Noriko, 'On the Semantic Limitation of "gecynd" in the King Alfred's OE Version of Boethius' *De Consolatione Philosophiae*', *Philologia Anglica*, ed. Oshitari *et al.*, pp. 106–25

Mimura, Eri, 'The Syntax and Semantics of *Gāst* and *Sāwol* in Old English Poetry', *Ann. Collection of Essays and Studies* (Faculty of Letters, Gakushuin Univ.) 34, 201–45 [in Japanese]

Minkova, Donka, 'The Prosodic Character of Early Schwa Deletion in English', *Papers from the 7th International Conference on Historical Linguistics*, ed. Anna Giacalone Ramat *et al.*, Current Issues in Ling. Theory 48 (Amsterdam and Philadelphia, 1987), 445–57

Mitchell, Bruce, see sect. 3*bii*

Molencki, Rafał, 'Some Observations on Relative Clauses in the Old English Version of Bede's *Historia Ecclesiastica Gentis Anglorum*', *Studia Anglica Poznaniensia* 20 (1987), 83–99

Morris, Richard L., 'An Analysis of the Future Tense in the Early Germanic Languages as a Modal Category', *The Thirteenth LACUS Forum 1986*, ed. Ilah Fleming (Lake Bluff, IL, 1987), pp. 600–7

Nakamura, Mayumi, 'The Pleonastic Reflexive Dative in Old English', *Kobe Eibei Ronso* (Kobe Univ.) 1, 7–21

Nakamura, Yuji, 'Agentive Prepositions in *The Blickling Homilies*', *Chofu Gakuen Women's Junior Coll.* 21, 49–62

Ogawa, Hiroshi, 'OE **sculan/willan* in Dependent Requests: a Note', *Philologia Anglica*, ed. Oshitari *et al.*, pp. 53–9

Ogura, Michiko, 'Direct or Indirect? – *þæt* as a Quotation Indicator', *Philologia Anglica*, ed. Oshitari *et al.*, pp. 88–105

'*Him self, him selfe*, and *him selfa*: a Reflexive Pronoun + Uninflected or Nominative *self*', *SN* 60, 149–57

'*Ne ondræd þu* and *nelle þu ondrædan* for *noli timere*', *Stud. in Eng. Lit.* (Tokyo) 1988 Eng. Number, pp. 87–101

Ono, Shigeru, 'A Note on the Old English Equivalents of Latin *possidere*', *Philologia Anglica*, ed. Oshitari *et al.*, pp. 35–42

'The Verb of Knowing in OE and its Historical Background', *Aspects of English Vocabulary*, ed. Y. Terasawa and S. Takebayashi (Tokyo), pp. 135–57 [in Japanese]

Ono, Shoko, 'Some Notes on the Relative Pronouns in Old English Interlinear Glosses to the Latin Psalters (Pt 1)', *Essays and Stud. in Brit. and Am. Lit.* (Tokyo Woman's Christian Univ.) 34, 1–22

Pasicki, Adam, *Temporal Adverbials in Old and Middle English* (Lublin, 1987)

Peeters, Christian L., 'Etymological Notes', *General Ling.* 28, 119 [*teagor*]

Penzl, Herbert, 'The Horn of Gallehus and the Subgrouping of the Germanic Languages', *Languages and Cultures: Studies in Honor of Edgar C. Polomé*, ed. Mohammad Ali Jazayery and Werner Winter, Trends in Ling., Stud. and Monographs 36 (Berlin, New York and Amsterdam), 489–508

Polomé, Edgar C., 'The Non-Indo-European Component of the Germanic Lexicon', *O-o-pe-ro-si: Festschrift für Ernst Risch zum 75. Geburtstag*, ed. Annemarie Etter (Berlin and New York, 1986), pp. 661–72

Poussa, Patricia, 'The Relative WHAT: Two Kinds of Evidence', *Historical Dialectology, Regional and Social*, ed. Jacek Fisiak, Trends in Ling., Stud. and Monographs 37 (Berlin, New York and Amsterdam), 443–74

Roberts, Jane, 'Old English Thesaurus: Report', *OEN* 21.2, 21–3

Samuels, M. L., C. J. Kay and I. A. W. Wotherspoon, 'Historical Thesaurus of English: Annual Report, 1987/88', *OEN* 22.1, 16–19

Schabram, Hans, 'The Latin and Old English Glosses to *electrum* in the Harley Glossary', *Philologia Anglica*, ed. Oshitari *et al.*, pp. 29–34

Shields, Kenneth, 'The Indo-European Origins of the Germanic Third Weak Class', *Leuvense Bijdragen* 77, 43–56

Stanley, E. G., 'The Difficulty of Establishing Borrowings between Old English and the Continental West Germanic Languages', *An Historic Tongue: Studies in English Linguistics in Memory of Barbara Strang*, ed. Graham Nixon and John Honey (London and New York), pp. 3–16

'The Meaning of Old English *corþer, corþor*, *N&Q* 35, 292–4

Stiles, Patrick V., 'Gothic Nominative Singular *brōþar* "brother" and the Reflexes of Indo-European Long Vowels in the Final Syllables of Germanic Polysyllables', *TPS* 86, 115–43

Suphi, Menekse, 'Old English Stress Alignment', *Lingua* 75, 171–202

Suzuki, Seiichi, 'Old Germanic Metrics in the Light of I-E Metrics and Accent Typology', *English Linguistics* (Tokyo) 5, 226–44

'On the 1 Sg. Pres. Ind. Ending -*u* and High Vowel Deletion in Anglian and Other West Germanic Languages', *IF* 93, 210–24

Tajima, Matsuji, *Old and Middle English Language Studies: a Classified Bibliography 1923–1985*, Lib. and Information Sources in Ling. 13 (Amsterdam and Philadelphia)

Vigil, Julián Josué, *An Anglo-Saxon Vocabulary Based on the Glossary to Sweet's 'Anglo-Saxon Primer'* (Guadalupita, NM)

Voss, Manfred, 'Old English Glossaries and Dialectology', *Historical Dialectology, Regional and Social*, ed. Jacek Fisiak, Trends in Ling., Stud. and Monographs 37 (Berlin, New York and Amsterdam), 601–8

Voyles, Joseph B., 'Early Germanic Changes in Unstressed Word-Final Syllables', *Lingua* 76, 63–90

Wakelin, Martyn, *The Archaeology of English* (London)

Yamakawa, Kikuo, 'OE Clausal Idiom "*swa he betst mæge*" and its Related Constructions (Pt 1)', *Stud. in Humanities* (Fukuoka Univ.) 20.3, 597–641

3. OLD ENGLISH LITERATURE

a. General

Alexander, Michael, 'Old English Literature', *The Cambridge Guide to the Arts in Britain* 1, ed. Ford, 179–93

Baker, Peter S., 'English Literature: the Old English Period, the Early Middle English Period', *The New Encyclopaedia Britannica*, 15th ed. (Chicago 1987) XVIII, 570–3

Hall, Thomas N., 'The Ages of Christ and Mary in the Hyde Register and in Old English Literature', *N&Q* 35, 4–11

Hill, Joyce, 'Old English Literature [1985]', *Year's Work in Eng. Stud.* 66, 112–35

Hill, Thomas D., see sect. 7

Koike, Kazuo, 'The Figure of Ælfric in the *Encyclopaedia Britannica*', *Obirin Stud. in Eng. Lang. and Lit.* (Obirin Univ.) 28, 105–12

Millett, Bella, 'The Saints' Lives of the Katherine Group and the Alliterative Tradition', *JEGP* 87, 16–34

Robinson, Fred C., 'The Prescient Woman in Old English Literature', *Philologia Anglica*, ed. Oshitari *et al.*, pp. 241–50

Russom, Geoffrey, 'The Drink of Death in Old English and Germanic Literature', *Germania*, ed. Calder and Christy, pp. 175–89

b. Poetry

i. General

Bernárdez, Enrique, 'El lenguaje de la poesía anglosajona', *Estudios literarios ingleses: edad media*, ed. J. F. Galván Reula (Madrid, 1985), pp. 69–83

Blockley, Mary, see sect. 2

Duggan, Hoyt N., 'The Evidential Basis for Old English Metrics', *SP* 85, 145–63
'Final -*e* and the Rhythmic Structure of the B-Verse in Middle English Alliterative Poetry', *MP* 86, 119–45

Etchells, Ruth, *A Selection of Poems by Early English Poets: Caedmon to Thomas More* (Tring, Herts., Batavia, IL, and Sydney) [extracts from previously published translations]

Foley, John Miles, *The Theory of Oral Composition: History and Methodology* (Bloomington, IN, and Indianapolis)

Fry, Donald K., 'The Cliff of Death in Old English Poetry', *Comparative Research on Oral Traditions*, ed. John Miles Foley (Columbus, OH, 1987), pp. 213–33

García Tortosa, Francisco, 'La estructura temática de las elegías anglosajonas', *Estudios literarios ingleses: edad media*, ed. J. F. Galván Reula (Madrid, 1985), pp. 43–67

Garde, Judith N., and Bernard J. Muir, 'Patristic Influence and the Poetic Intention in Old English Religious Verse', *Lit. and Theol.* 2, 49–68

Hansen, Elaine Tuttle, *The Solomon Complex: Reading Wisdom in Old English Poetry*, McMaster OE Stud. and Texts 5 (Toronto, Buffalo and London)

Hieatt, Constance B., 'On Envelope Patterns (Ancient and – Relatively – Modern) and Nonce Formulas', *Comparative Research on Oral Traditions*, ed. John Miles Foley (Columbus, OH, 1987), pp. 245–58

Hollowell, Ida Masters, 'On Old English Verse-Rhythm: Further Considerations', *ES* 69, 193–204

Lass, Roger, 'Cyn(e)wulf Revisited: the Problem of the Runic Signatures', *An Historic Tongue: Studies in English Linguistics in Memory of Barbara Strang*, ed. Graham Nixon and John Honey (London and New York), pp. 17–30

Minkova, Donka, see sect. 2

Olsen, Alexandra Hennessey, 'Oral-Formulaic Research in Old English Studies, II', *Oral Tradition* 3.1–2, 138–90

Renoir, Alain, *A Key to Old Poems: the Oral-Formulaic Approach to the Interpretation of West-Germanic Verse* (University Park, PA, and London)
'Oral-Formulaic Rhetoric and the Interpretation of Written Texts', *Oral Tradition in Literature*, ed. John Miles Foley (Columbia, MO, 1986), pp. 103–35
'Oral-Formulaic Tradition and the Affective Interpretation of Early Germanic Verse', *Germania*, ed. Calder and Christy, pp. 113–26
'Repetition, Oral-Formulaic Style, and Affective Impact in Mediaeval Poetry: a Tentative Illustration', *Comparative Research on Oral Traditions*, ed. John Miles Foley (Columbus, OH, 1987), pp. 533–48

Savage, Anne, 'The Place of Old English Poetry in the English Meditative Tradition', *The Medieval Mystical Tradition in England: Exeter Symposium IV*, ed. Marion Glasscoe (Woodbridge and Wolfeboro, NH, 1987), pp. 91–110

Shaw, Patricia, 'Elementos humoristicos en la literatura medieval inglesa, 800–1400', *Estudios literarios ingleses: edad media*, ed. J. F. Galván Reula (Madrid, 1985), pp. 85–106

Stanley, E. G., 'Parody in Early English Literature', *Poetica* (Tokyo) 27, 1–69

'Rhymes in English Medieval Verse: from Old English to Middle English', *Medieval English Studies Presented to George Kane*, ed. Edward Donald Kennedy *et al.* (Wolfeboro, NH, and Woodbridge), pp. 19–54

Suphi, Menekse, see sect. 2

Suzuki, Seiichi, 'The Indo-European Basis of Germanic Alliterative Verse', *Lingua* 75, 1–24

ii. *'Beowulf'*

Creed, Robert P., *'Beowulf* on the Brink: Information Theory as Key to the Origins of the Poem', *Comparative Research on Oral Traditions*, ed. John Miles Foley (Columbus, OH, 1987), pp. 139–60

'The Remaking of *Beowulf*', *Oral tradition in Literature*, ed. John Miles Foley (Columbia, MO, 1986), pp. 136–46

Dahlberg, Charles, 'The Kingdom of Unlikeness: *Beowulf*', in his *The Literature of Unlikeness* (Hanover, NH, and London), pp. 26–54

Dumville, David N., see sect. 6

Enright, Michael J., see sect. 7

Florey, Kenneth, 'Grendel, Evil, "Allegory," and Dramatic Development in *Beowulf*', *Essays in Arts and Sciences* 17, 83–95

Fujiwara, Hiroshi, 'Struggles between Paganism and Christianity in *Beowulf* – A Lexical Study', *Bull. of the Lang. Inst. of Gakushuin Univ.* 10, 108–21 [in Japanese] see also sect. 2

Gerritsen, Johan, see sect. 6

Haarder, Andreas, 'The Seven *Beowulf* Reviewers: Latest or Last Identifications', *ES* 69, 289–92

Handelman, Anita F., 'Wulfgar at the Door: *Beowulf*, 11. 389b–90a', *Neophilologus* 72, 475–7

Harris, A. Leslie, 'Litotes and Superlative in *Beowulf*', *ES* 69, 1–11

Heinemann, Fredrik J., *'Beowulf* 665b–738: a Mock Approach-to-Battle Type Scene', *Perspectives on Language in Performance*, ed. Wolfgang Lörscher and Rainer Schulze, Tübinger Beiträge zur Linguistik 317 (Tübingen, 1987), 677–94

Hengen, Shannon, 'A Note on the Existential Coloring of *Beowulf*', *NM* 89, 171–3

Irving, Edward B., Jr, 'What to Do with Old Kings', *Comparative Research on Oral Traditions*, ed. John Miles Foley (Columbus, OH, 1987), pp. 259–68

Lehmann, Ruth P. M., *'Beowulf': an Imitative Translation* (Austin, TX)

'Some Problems in the Translation of *Beowulf*', *Languages and Cultures: Studies in Honor of Edgar C. Polomé*, ed. Mohammad Ali Jazayery and Werner Winter, Trends in Ling., Stud. and Monographs 36 (Berlin, New York and Amsterdam), 365–71

Mazzuoli Porru, Giulia, *'Beowulf*, v. 33: *īsig ond ūtfus*', *Studi linguistici e filologici per Carlo Alberto Mastrelli* (Pisa, 1985), pp. 263–74

Miletich, John S., 'Muslim Oral Epic and Medieval Epic', *MLR* 83, 911–24

Mitchell, Bruce, 'Relative and Personal Pronouns in *Beowulf*: Eight Notes', *Philologia Anglica*, ed. Oshitari *et al.*, pp. 3–12

Müller, Wolfgang G., 'Syntaktisch-semasiologische Analyse des Grendel-Kampfes im *Beowulf*', *Literaturwissenschaftliches Jahrbuch* 29, 9–22

Noguchi, Shunichi, 'Beowulf and "sothfæstra dom"', *Philologia Anglica*, ed. Oshitari *et al.*, pp. 251–8

Onega, Susana, 'Poesía épica anglosajona: *Beowulf*', *Estudios literarios ingleses: edad media*, ed. J. F. Galván Reula (Madrid, 1985), pp. 17–41

Oshitari, Kinshiro, 'A Japanese Analogue of *Beowulf*', *Philologia Anglica*, ed. Oshitari *et al.*, pp. 259–69

Overing, Gillian R., 'The Object as Index: a Peircean Approach to *Beowulf*', *Semiotics 1985*, ed. John Deely (Lanham, MD, 1986), pp. 569–83

Parks, Ward, 'Ring Structure and Narrative Embedding in Homer and *Beowulf*', *NM* 89, 237–51

Pope, John C., 'The Irregular Anacrusis in *Beowulf* 9 and 402: Two Hitherto Untried Remedies, with Help from Cynewulf', *Speculum* 63, 104–13

Russom, Geoffrey, 'Verse Translations and the Question of Literacy in *Beowulf*', *Comparative Research on Oral Traditions*, ed. John Miles Foley (Columbus, OH, 1987), pp. 567–80

Tripp, Raymond P., Jr, 'The Restoration of *Beowulf* 1051b: *brimlēade*, "sea-lead"', *MP* 86, 191–5

Vickrey, John F., 'On *Beowulf* 997–1002', *ASNSL* 225, 339–42

'*Un[h]litme* "voluntarily" in *Beowulf* Line 1097', *JEGP* 87, 315–28

Watanabe, Hideki, 'Monsters Creep?: the Meaning of the Verb *Scriðan* in *Beowulf*', *Stud. in Lang. and Culture* (Osaka Univ.) 14, 107–20

Wieland, Gernot, '*Manna mildost*: Moses and Beowulf', *Pacific Coast Philol*, 23, 86–93

Wrenn, C. L., and W. F. Bolton, ed., '*Beowulf*' *with the Finnsburg Fragment* (Exeter) [reprint of 1973 edition, with supplementary bibliography]

iii. Other poems

Ajiro, Atsushi, 'Blackburn's Edition of Old English *Exodus*', *Daito Bunka Review* (Daito Bunka Univ.) 19, 58–76 [in Japanese]

Anderson, Earl R., 'Cynewulf's *Elene* 1115b–24, the Conversion of the Jews: Figurative or Literal?' *ELN* 25.3, 1–3

Bethel, Patricia, 'Anacrusis in the Psalms of the Paris Psalter', *NM* 89, 33–43

Biggs, Frederick M., 'The Passion of Andreas: *Andreas* 1398–1491', *SP* 85, 413–27

Biggs, Frederick M., and Sandra McEntire, 'Spiritual Blindness in the Old English *Maxims I*, Part 1', *N&Q* 35, 11

Brzezinski, Monica, 'The Harrowing of Hell, the Last Judgment, and *The Dream of the Rood*', *NM* 89, 252–65

Butcher, John W., 'Formulaic Invention in the Genealogies of the Old English *Genesis A*', *Comparative Research on Oral Traditions*, ed. John Miles Foley (Columbus, OH, 1987), pp. 73–92

Dale, Simon, 'Britain's Lost City', *Brit. Archaeol. Monthly* 1 (1987), 7–9 [uses *The Ruin* in a search for Camelot]

Donoghue, Daniel, 'On the Old English *Metres of Boethius* xxix, lines 82–3', *N&Q* 35, 3–4

Fiocco, Teresa, 'Il viaggio della nave nell'enigma 32 dell'Exeter Book', *Blue Guitar* 7–8 (1984–7), 80–9

Frank, Roberta, 'Hand Tools and Power Tools in Eilífr's *Thorsdrapa*', *The Sixth International Saga Conference, 28.7.–2.8.1985: Workshop Papers* 1 [Copenhagen, 1986], 347–72 [*Exodus*]

'What Kind of Poetry Is *Exodus*?' *Germania*, ed. Calder and Christy, pp. 191–205

Fujiwara, Yasuaki, 'Old English *Genesis A*: a Translation (1)', *Stud. in Lang. and Cultures* (Tsukuba Univ.) 26, 151–62 [in Japanese]

Galloway, Andrew, '1 Peter and *The Seafarer*', *ELN* 25.4, 1–10

Garde, Judith N., and Bernard J. Muir, see sect. *3bi* [esp. *Exodus*]

Gay, David E., 'Anglo-Saxon Metrical Charm 3 against a Dwarf: a Charm against Witch-Riding?' *Folklore* 99, 174–7

Hauer, Stanley R., 'The *segl* in the Old English *Exodus*', *ASNSL* 225, 334–9

Heffernan, Carol Falvo, *The Phoenix at the Fountain: Images of Woman and Eternity in Lactantius's 'Carmen de Ave Phoenice' and the Old English 'Phoenix'* (Newark, DE, London and Toronto)

Hill, Thomas D., 'Saturn's Time Riddle: an Insular Latin Analogue for *Solomon and Saturn II* lines 282–291', *RES* 39, 273–6

see also sect. *3c* [*Solomon and Saturn*]

Jacobs, Nicolas, 'The Old English "Book-moth" Riddle Reconsidered', *N&Q* 35, 290–2

Jager, Eric, 'Tempter as Rhetoric Teacher: the Fall of Language in the Old English *Genesis B*', *Neophilologus* 72, 434–48

Jember, Gregory K., 'Literal and Metaphorical: Clues to Reading the Old English Riddles', *Stud. in Eng. Lit.* (Tokyo) 65, 47–56

Jonassen, Frederick B., 'The Pater Noster Letters in the Poetic *Solomon and Saturn*', *MLR* 83, 1–9 [also *Rune Poem*]

Kendall, Calvin B., 'Let Us Now Praise a Famous City: Wordplay in the OE *Durham* and the Cult of St Cuthbert', *JEGP* 87, 507–21

Klegraf, Josef, ed. and trans., *Die altenglische 'Judith': eine Ausgabe für den akademischen Unterricht*, Ausgewählte Texte aus der Geschichte der christlichen Kirche 3 (Stuttgart, 1987)

Kleiner, Yu. A., see sect. 4 [*Cædmon's Hymn*]

Klinck, Anne L., '*The Riming Poem*: Design and Interpretation', *NM* 89, 266–79

Leslie, R. F., ed., *Three Old English Elegies: 'The Wife's Lament', 'The Husband's Message', 'The Ruin'* (Exeter) [reprint of 1961 edition, with supplementary bibliography]

Liuzza, Roy Michael, 'The Texts of the Old English *Riddle 30*', *JEGP* 87, 1–15

Locherbie-Cameron, M. A. L., 'Byrhtnoth, His Noble Companion and His Sister's Son', *MÆ* 57, 159–71

'Wisdom as a Key to Heroism in *Judith*', *Poetica* (Tokyo) 27, 70–5

Lucas, Peter J., 'Some Aspects of *Genesis B* as Old English Verse', *Proc. of the R. Irish Acad.* 88C, 143–78

Nelson, Marie, 'Plus Animate: Two Possible Transformations of Riddles by

Symphosius', *Germanic Notes* 18 (1987), 46–8 [Riddles 9 and 37]

'The Sacrifice of Isaac: a Humanistic Interpretation', *NM* 89, 286–94 [*Genesis A* and Ælfric]

O'Neill, Patrick P., 'Another Fragment of the Metrical Psalms in the Eadwine Psalter', *N&Q* 35, 434–6

Porter, Nancy A., '"Wrestling with Loan-Words: Poetic Use of "engel", "seraphim", and "cherubim" in *Andreas* and *Elene*', *NM* 89, 155–70

Remley, Paul G., 'The Latin Textual Basis of *Genesis A*', *ASE* 17, 163–89

Richardson, John, 'The Hero at the Wall in *The Wanderer*', *NM* 89, 280–5

Roberts, Jane, '*Guthlac A*: Sources and Source Hunting', *Medieval English Studies Presented to George Kane*, ed. Edward Donald Kennedy *et al.* (Wolfeboro, NH, and Woodbridge), pp. 1–18

Smith, Margaret M., 'Thomas Percy, William Shenstone, *Five Pieces of Runic Poetry*, and the *Reliques*', *Bodleian Lib. Record* 12, 471–7

Squires, Ann, ed., *The Old English Physiologus*, Durham Med. Texts 5 (Durham)

Stevick, Robert D., 'The Manuscript Divisions of *Andreas*', *Philologia Anglica*, ed. Oshitari *et al.*, pp. 225–40

Surles, Robert L., *Roots and Branches: Germanic Epic/Romanic Legend*, Amer. Univ. Stud., Germanic Lang. and Lit. 58 (New York, 1987) [*Waldere*]

Viereck, Wolfgang, see sect. 6 [*Bede's Death Song*]

Viljoen, Leonie, 'The Old English *Exodus*: Paraphrase or Homily?' *Unisa Eng. Stud.* 26.1, 1–7

Waterhouse, Ruth, 'Self-Reflexivity and "wraetlic word" in *Bleak House* and *Andreas*', *Jnl of Narrative Technique* 18, 211–25

Wieland, Gernot, see sect. 3*bii* [*Exodus*]

c. Prose

Ajiro, Atsushi, 'The Recapitulation-Construction in the West-Saxon Gospel of St John', *Gogaku Kyoiku Kenkyu Ronso* (Daito Bunka Univ.) 5, 1–20 [in Japanese]

Barker, Katherine, see sect. 7

Bately, Janet M., 'Old English Prose before and during the Reign of Alfred', *ASE* 17, 93–138

see also sect. 6

Cameron, M. L., see sect. 1

D'Aronco, Maria Amalia, 'The Botanical Lexicon of the Old English *Herbarium*', *ASE* 17, 15–33

Dean, Paul, 'Three Episodes in Bede's *History*', *Durham Univ. Jnl* 81, 81–5

Enkvist, Nils Erik, and Brita Wårvik, see sect. 2

Farmer, D. H., see sect. 7 [Ælfric]

Guerrieri, Anna Maria, ed. and trans., '*Ewangelium De uirginibus*' in *CCCC 303* (Naples)

Hasenfratz, Robert, 'A Curious Etymology: Ælfric's Derivation of *rex*', *PQ* 67, 256–61

Hill, Joyce, 'Ælfric and the Name of Simon Peter', *N&Q* 35, 157–8

'Ælfric's Use of Etymologies', *ASE* 17, 35–44

Hill, Thomas D., 'The Devil's Forms and the Pater Noster's Powers: "The Prose Solomon and Saturn *Pater Noster* Dialogue" and the Motif of Transformation Combat', *SP* 85, 164–76

Kubouchi, Tadao, see sect. 2

Lebecq, Stéphane, 'Ohthere et Wulfstan: deux marchands-navigateurs dans le Nord-Ouest européen à la fin du IX⁰ siècle', *Horizons marins, itinéraires spirituels (V⁰–XVIII⁰ siècles)*, ed. Henri Dubois *et al.* (Paris, 1987) II, 167–81

Lees, Clare A., 'The Blickling Palm Sunday Homily and its Revised Version', *Leeds Stud. in Eng.* 19, 1–30

'Theme and Echo in an Anonymous Old English Homily for Easter', *Traditio* 42 (1986), 115–42

Lindström, Bengt, 'The Old English Translation of Alcuin's *Liber de Virtutibus et Vitiis*', *SN* 60, 23–35

McEntire, Sandra, 'The Doctrine of Compunction from Bede to Margery Kempe', *The Medieval Mystical Tradition in England: Exeter Symposium IV*, ed. Marion Glasscoe (Woodbridge and Wolfeboro, NH, 1987), pp. 77–90

Matsui, Noriko, see sect. 2

Molencki, Rafał, see sect. 2

Moores, Jane, '*Rex Omnipotens*: a Sequence Used in an Old English Ascension Day Homily', *Anglia* 106, 138–44

Nelson, Marie, see sect. 3*biii* [Ælfric]

Olsen, Alexandra Hennessey, 'Literary Artistry and the Oral-Formulaic Tradition: the Case of Gower's *Appolinus of Tyre*', *Comparative Research on Oral Traditions*, ed. John Miles Foley (Columbus, OH, 1987), pp. 493–509 [comparative remarks on OE version]

Pfaff, Richard W., 'Some Anglo-Saxon Sources for the "Theological Windows" at Canterbury Cathedral', *Mediaevalia* 10, 49–62

Stanley, E. G., 'King Alfred's Prefaces', *RES* 39, 349–64

Thomas, Rebecca, 'The Binding Force of Friendship in King Alfred's *Consolation* and *Soliloquies*', *Ball State Univ. Forum* 29.1, 5–20

Wright, Charles D., 'Blickling Homily III on the Temptations in the Desert', *Anglia* 106, 130–7

4. ANGLO-LATIN, LITURGY AND OTHER LATIN ECCLESIASTICAL TEXTS

Berry, Mary, 'What the Saxon Monks Sang: Music in Winchester in the Late Tenth Century', *Bishop Æthelwold*, ed. Yorke, pp. 149–60

Bischoff, Bernhard, *et al.*, see sect. 6

Bodden, Mary Catherine, 'Evidence for Knowledge of Greek in Anglo-Saxon England', *ASE* 17, 217–46

Borst, Arno, 'Computus: Zeit und Zahl im Mittelalter', *DAEM* 44, 1–82

Braidotti, Cecilia, 'Gildas fra Roma e i barbari', *Romanobarbarica* 9 (1986–7), 25–45

Breen, Aidan, see sect. 6

Clark, Francis, *The Pseudo-Gregorian Dialogues*, Stud. in the Hist. of Christian Thought 37–8 (Leiden, 1987), 2 vols.

Dean, Paul, see sect. 3*c*

Dolbeau, François, 'Le *Breuiloquium de omnibus sanctis*: un poème inconnu de Wulfstan chantre de Winchester', *AB* 106, 35–98

Dronke, Peter, 'Towards the Interpretation of the Leiden Love-Spell', *CMCS* 16, 61–75

Dungey, Kevin R., 'Faith in the Darkness: Allegorical Theory and Aldhelm's Obscurity', *Allegoresis: the Craft of Allegory in Medieval Literature*, ed. J. Stephen Russell (New York and London), pp. 3–26

Dwyer, M. E., see sect. 6

Godman, Peter, *Poets and Emperors: Frankish Politics and Carolingian Poetry* (Oxford, 1987)

Goffart, Walter, see sect. 7

Herren, Michael W., 'The Stress Systems in Insular Latin Octosyllabic Verse', *CMCS* 15, 63–84

Hine, Harry M., 'Seneca and Anaxagoras in Pseudo-Bede's *De mundi celestis terrestrisque constitutione*', *Viator* 19, 111–27

Ireland, C. A., 'Boisil: an Irishman Hidden in the Works of Bede', *Peritia* 5 (1986), 400–3

Kleiner, Yu. A., 'The Singer and the Interpreter: Caedmon and Bede', *Germanic Notes* 19, 2–6

Lapidge, Michael, 'Æthelwold as Scholar and Teacher', *Bishop Æthelwold*, ed. Yorke, pp. 89–117

'A Frankish Scholar in Tenth-Century England: Frithegod of Canterbury/ Fredegaud of Brioude', *ASE* 17, 45–65

Law, Vivien, 'When Is Donatus Not Donatus? Versions, Variants and New Texts', *Peritia* 5 (1986), 235–61

Lindström, Bengt, see sect. 3*c*

Löfstedt, Bengt, 'Zu Bedas Predigten', *Arctos* 22, 95–8

Meyvaert, Paul, 'The Enigma of Gregory the Great's *Dialogues*: a Response to Francis Clark', *JEH* 39, 335–81

Muir, Bernard James, ed., *A Pre-Conquest English Prayer-Book (BL MSS Cotton Galba A.xiv and Nero A.ii (ff. 3–13))*, Henry Bradshaw Soc. 103 (Woodbridge)

Muzzarelli, Maria Giuseppina, 'Il valore della vita nell'alto medioevo: la testimonianza dei libri penitenziali', *Aevum* 62, 171–85

Parabiaghi, Mario, 'Pitture ed apparato di culto nelle opere del Venerabile Beda', *Ecclesia Orans* 4 (1987), 203–34

Pavlovskis, Zoja, 'The Riddler's Microcosm: from Symphosius to St Boniface', *Classica et Mediaevalia* 39, 219–51

Piacente, Luigi, 'Un nuovo frammento ciceroniano in Beda', *Romanobarbarica* 9 (1986–7), 229–45

Powell, Susan, 'An Accident-Prone Anglo-Saxon', *N&Q* 35, 154–7

Prescott, Andrew, 'The Text of the Benedictional of St Æthelwold', *Bishop Æthelwold*, ed. Yorke, pp. 119–47

Rollason, D. W., *Two Anglo-Saxon Rituals: Church Dedication and the Judicial Ordeal*, Vaughan Paper 33, Fifth Brixworth Lecture (Leicester)

Thompson, Pauline, and Elizabeth Stevens, 'Gregory of Ely's Verse Life and Miracles of St Æthelthryth', *AB* 106, 333–90

Thomson, Ron B., 'Further Astronomical Material of Abbo of Fleury', *MS* 50, 671–3

Vogüé, Adalbert de, 'Grégoire le Grand et ses *Dialogues* d'après deux ouvrages récents', *Revue d'Histoire Ecclésiastique* 83, 281–348

Voigts, Linda Ehrsam, see sect. 6

Wallace-Hadrill, J. M., see sect. 7

Wright, Neil, 'Imitation of the Poems of Paulinus of Nola in Early Anglo-Latin Verse: a Postscript', *Peritia* 5 (1986), 392–6

5. FONTES ANGLO-SAXONICI

A Database Register of Written Sources used by Authors in Anglo-Saxon England,
ed. D. G. Scragg and M. Lapidge (Univ. of Manchester)

Godden, M. R., 'The Sources of Ælfric's Catholic Homilies I.xxvii', 19 entries: nos. C.B.1.1.29.001–019

'The Sources of Ælfric's Catholic Homilies I.xxviii', 42 entries: nos. C.B.1.1.30.001–042

'The Sources of Ælfric's Catholic Homilies II.xxiii', 18 entries: nos. C.B.1.2.29/30.001–018

Roberts, Jane, 'The Sources of the Anonymous Life of Paulinus', 7 entries: nos. C.B.3.3.31.001–007

Wilcox, J., 'The Sources of the Anonymous Napier homily xlvi', 7 entries: nos. C.B.3.4.37.001–007

6. PALAEOGRAPHY, DIPLOMATIC AND ILLUMINATION

Alexander, J. J. G., T. J. Brown, and Joan Gibbs, ed., *Francis Wormald: Collected Writings*, II, *Studies in English and Continental Art of the Later Middle Ages* (London)

Bately, Janet M., 'Manuscript Layout and the Anglo-Saxon Chronicle', *Bull. of the John Rylands Univ. Lib. of Manchester* 70.1, 21–43

Bischoff, Bernhard, Mildred Budny, Geoffrey Harlow, M. B. Parkes and J. D. Pheifer, *The Épinal, Erfurt, Werden, and Corpus Glossaries*, EEMF 22 (Copenhagen and Baltimore)

Bonner, Gerald, and Roger Norris, *Saint Cuthbert and his Heritage: an Exhibition of Manuscripts Brought Together at Durham to Celebrate the Saint's 1300th Anniversary and the Work of His Early Community*, ed. Ronald Coppin (Durham, 1987)

Breen, Aidan, 'A New Irish Fragment of the *Continuatio* to Rufinus–Eusebius *Historia Ecclesiastica*', *Scriptorium* 41 (1987), 185–204

Budny, Mildred, 'The Visual Arts and Crafts', *The Cambridge Guide to the Arts in Britain* I, ed. Ford, 122–78

Crick, Julia, see sect. 7

Deshman, Robert, '*Benedictus Monarcha et Monachus*: Early Medieval Ruler Theology and the Anglo-Saxon Reform', *FS* 22, 204–40

Dumville, David N., 'Beowulf Come Lately: Some Notes on the Palaeography of the Nowell Codex', *ASNSL* 225, 49–63

Dwyer, M. E., 'An Unstudied Redaction of the *Visio Pauli*', *Manuscripta* 32, 121–38 [Codex Vaticanus latinus 220, 56r–60r]

Edwards, Heather, *The Charters of the Early West Saxon Kingdom*, BAR Brit. ser. 198 (Oxford)

Forde, Helen, 'Domesday Bound: 1066–1986', *Book Collector* 36 (1987), 201–6

Gerritsen, Johan, 'British Library MS Cotton Vitellius A.xv – a Supplementary Description', *ES* 69, 293–302

Henderson, Isabel, 'The Arts of Late Celtic Britain (AD 600–900)', *The Cambridge Guide to the Arts in Britain* I, ed. Ford, 206–19

Hill, Joyce, 'The Exeter Book and Lambeth Palace Library MS 149: the Monasterium of Sancta Maria', *Amer. N&Q* ns 1, 4–9

Hutter, Irmgard, and Hans Holländer, *Kunst des Frühen Mittelalters*, Neue Belser Stilgeschichte 3 (Stuttgart and Zürich, 1987)

Kerscher, Gottfried, 'QVADRIGA TEMPORVM. Studien zur Sol-Ikonographie in mittelalterlichen Handschriften und in der Architekturdekoration (mit einem Exkurs zum Codex 146 der Stiftsbibliothek Gottweig)', *Mitteilungen des Kunsthistorischen Institutes in Florenz* 22, 1–76 [British Library, Cotton Tiberius B.v and C.i, Harley 647, etc.]

Keynes, Simon, see sect. 7

Kleinschmidt, Harald, 'Die Titulaturen englischer Könige im 10. und 11. Jahrhundert', *Intitulatio III. Lateinische Herrschertitel und Herrschertitulaturen vom 7. bis zum 13. Jahrhundert*, ed. Herwig Wolfram and Anton Scharer, Mitteilungen des Instituts für österreichische Geschichtsforschung, suppl. 29 (Vienna, Cologne and Graz), 75–130

Lapidge, Michael, see sect. 4

Lewis, Suzanne, *The Art of Matthew Paris in the 'Chronica Majora'* (London, 1987) [pictures of Anglo-Saxon kings]

Liuzza, Roy Michael, 'The Yale Fragments of the West Saxon Gospels', *ASE* 17, 67–82

Morrish, Jennifer, 'Dated and Datable Manuscripts Copied in England during the Ninth Century: a Preliminary List', *MS* 50, 512–38

O'Donovan, M. A., ed., *Charters of Sherborne*, AS Charters 3 (Oxford)

Pulsiano, Phillip, 'BL Cotton MS Tiberius A.iii: Fulgentius, Injunction', *Amer. N&Q* ns 1, 43–4

Richards, Mary P., *Texts and their Traditions in the Medieval Library of Rochester Cathedral Priory*, Trans. of the Amer. Philosophical Soc. 78.3 (Philadelphia)

Robinson, P. R., *Catalogue of Dated and Datable Manuscripts c. 737–1600 in Cambridge Libraries*, 2 vols. (Cambridge)

Scharer, Anton, 'Die Intitulationes der angelsächsischen Könige im 7. und 8. Jahrhundert', *Intitulatio III. Lateinische Herrschertitel und Herrschertitulaturen vom 7. bis zum 13. Jahrhundert*, ed. Herwig Wolfram and Anton Scharer, Mitteilungen des Instituts für österreichische Geschichtsforschung, suppl. 29 (Vienna, Cologne and Graz), 9–74

Sims-Williams, Patrick, 'St Wilfrid and Two Charters Dated AD 676 and 680', *JEH* 39, 163–83 [Sawyer nos. 51 and 52]

Stevenson, Janet H., ed., *The Edington Cartulary*, Wiltshire Record Soc. 42 (1986) [includes three charters of King Edgar (Sawyer nos. 727, 765 and 812)]

Stevick, Robert D., 'The Echternach Gospels' Evangelist-Symbol Pages: Forms from "The Two True Measures of Geometry"', *Peritia* 5 (1986), 284–308

Turville Petre, Joan, 'Illustrations of Woden and his Sons in English Genealogical Manuscripts', *N&Q* 35, 158–9

Viereck, Wolfgang, 'Beda in Bamberg', *Einheit in der Vielfalt: Festschrift für Peter Lang zum 60. Geburtstag*, ed. Gisela Quast (Bern), pp. 556–67

Voigts, Linda Ehrsam, 'A Fragment of an Anglo-Saxon Liturgical Manuscript at the University of Missouri', *ASE* 17, 83–92

Witney, K. P., see sect. 7

7. HISTORY

Abels, Richard P., *Lordship and Military Obligation in Anglo-Saxon England* (Berkeley, Los Angeles and London)

Alcock, Leslie, *Bede, Eddius, and the Forts of the North Britons*, Jarrow Lecture 1988 (Jarrow)

Alonso-Núñez, J. M., 'Jordanes and Procopius on Northern Europe', *Nottingham Med. Stud.* 31 (1987), 1–16

[Anon.] 'The Image of Saint Dunstan', *Archaeol. Today* 9.2, 33

Bachrach, Bernard S., 'Gildas, Vortigern and Constitutionality in Sub-Roman Britain', *Nottingham Med. Stud.* 32, 126–40

Bailey, Keith, 'East Saxon Kings – Some Further Observations', *Essex Jnl* 23.2 (Summer), 34–40

Bailey, Richard, 'The Cultural and Social Setting', *The Cambridge Guide to the Arts in Britain* 1, ed. Ford, 100–20

Baines, Arnold H. J., 'The Origin of the Borough of Newport Pagnell', *Records of Buckinghamshire* 28 (1986), 128–37

Barker, Katherine, 'Aelfric the Mass-Priest and the Anglo-Saxon Estates of Cerne Abbey', *The Cerne Abbey Millennium Lectures*, ed. Barker, pp. 27–42

   ed., *The Cerne Abbey Millennium Lectures* (Cerne Abbas)

Batcock, Neil, 'The Parish Church in Norfolk in the 11th and 12th Centuries', *Minsters and Parish Churches*, ed. Blair, pp. 179–90

Blair, John, 'Introduction: from Minster to Parish Church', *Minsters and Parish Churches*, ed. Blair, pp. 1–19

'Minster Churches in the Landscape', *Anglo-Saxon Settlements*, ed. Hooke, pp. 35–58

ed., *Saint Frideswide, Patron of Oxford: the Earliest Texts* (Oxford)

[Boccaccio, Arthur Austin] 'Concepts of Anglo-Saxon Law', *Tournaments Illuminated* 86, 15–18

Bond, C. J., 'Church and Parish in Norman Worcestershire', *Minsters and Parish Churches*, ed. Blair, pp. 119–58

Bonner, Gerald, 'St Cuthbert – Soul Friend', *Cuthbert: Saint and Patron*, ed. Rollason, pp. 23–44

Bradbury, J., 'An Introduction to the Buckinghamshire Domesday', *Buckinghamshire Domesday*, ed. Williams and Erskine, pp. 1–36

Brown, R. Allen, ed., *Anglo-Norman Studies X: Proceedings of the Battle Conference 1987* (Woodbridge)

Cleary, Simon Esmonde, 'The End of Roman Britain', *Hist. Today* 38 (December), 35–40

Cottle, Basil, 'Cults of the Saints in Medieval Bristol and Gloucestershire', *Trans. of the Bristol and Gloucestershire Archaeol. Soc.* 106, 5–18

Cowdrey, H. E. J., 'Towards an Interpretation of the Bayeaux Tapestry', *Anglo-Norman Studies X*, ed. Brown, pp. 49–65

Crick, Julia, 'Church, Land and Local Nobility in Early Ninth-Century Kent: the Case of Ealdorman Oswulf', *Hist. Research* 61, 251–69

Croom, Jane, 'The Fragmentation of the Minster *Parochiae* of South-East Shropshire', *Minsters and Parish Churches*, ed. Blair, pp. 67–81

Dales, Douglas, *Dunstan: Saint and Statesman* (Cambridge)

Davis, R. H. C., 'The Warhorses of the Normans', *Anglo-Norman Studies X*, ed. Brown, pp. 67–82

Delaney, Frank, *A Walk in the Dark Ages* (London)

Deshman, Robert, see sect. 6

Drewett, Peter, David Rudling, and Mark Gardiner, *The South East to AD 1000* (London and New York)

Driscoll, S. T., and M. R. Nieke, ed., *Power and Politics in Early Medieval Britain and Ireland* (Edinburgh)

Dutton, L. S., 'King Alfred at Shaftesbury: the Location of Egbert's Stone', *Proc. of the Dorset Nat. Hist. and Archaeol. Soc.* 109 (1987), 141–2

Dymond, David, and Edward Martin, ed., *An Historical Atlas of Suffolk* (Ipswich) [Anglo-Saxon Suffolk, pp. 36–9, 140]

Edwards, Heather, see sect. 6

Enright, Michael J., 'Lady with a Mead-Cup: Ritual, Group Cohesion and Hierarchy in the Germanic Warband', *FS* 22, 170–203

Everson, Paul, see sect. 10c

Farmer, D. H., 'The Monastic Reform of the 10th Century and Cerne Abbas', *The Cerne Abbey Millennium Lectures*, ed. Barker, pp. 1–10

Fuchs, Rüdiger, *Das Domesday Book und sein Umfeld: zur ethnischen und sozialen Aussagekraft einer Landesbeschreibung im England des 11. Jahrhunderts*, Historische Forschungen 13 (Stuttgart, 1987)

Gelsinger, Bruce E., 'The Battle of Stamford Bridge and the Battle of Jaffa: a Case of

Confused Identity?' *Scandinavian Stud.* 60, 13–29

Goffart, Walter, *The Narrators of Barbarian History (A.D. 550–800): Jordanes, Gregory of Tours, Bede, and Paul the Deacon* (Princeton)

Gransden, Antonia, '1066 and All That Revised', *Hist. Today* 38 (September), 47–52

Hagerty, R. P., 'The Buckinghamshire Saints Reconsidered 2: St Osyth and St Edith of Aylesbury', *Records of Buckinghamshire* 29 (1987), 125–32

Hall, David, 'The Late Saxon Countryside: Villages and their Fields', *Anglo-Saxon Settlements*, ed. Hooke, pp. 99–122

Hase, P. H., 'The Mother Churches of Hampshire', *Minsters and Parish Churches*, ed. Blair, pp. 45–66

Haslam, Jeremy, 'Parishes, Churches, Wards and Gates in Eastern London', *Minsters and Parish Churches*, ed. Blair, pp. 35–43

Hayward, John, 'Hereward the Outlaw', *JMH* 14, 293–304

Herbert, Máire, *Iona, Kells, and Derry: the History and Hagiography of the Monastic* Familia *of Columba* (Oxford)

Heywood, Stephen, 'The Round Towers of East Anglia', *Minsters and Parish Churches*, ed. Blair, pp. 169–77

Higham, N. J., 'The Cheshire Landholdings of Earl Morcar in 1066', *Trans. of the Historic Soc. of Lancashire and Cheshire* 137 (1987), 139–47

Hill, Thomas D., 'Woden as "Ninth Father": Numerical Patterning in Some Old English Royal Genealogies', *Germania*, ed. Calder and Christy, pp. 161–74

Hodges, Richard, 'Anglo-Saxon England and the Origins of the Modern World Economy', *Anglo-Saxon Settlements*, ed. Hooke, pp. 291–304

Hooke, Della, 'Introduction: Later Anglo-Saxon England', *Anglo-Saxon Settlements*, ed. Hooke, pp. 1–8

'Regional Variation in Southern and Central England in the Anglo-Saxon Period and its Relationship to Land Units and Settlement', *Anglo-Saxon Settlements*, ed. Hooke, pp. 123–51

ed., *Anglo-Saxon Settlements* (Oxford)

Hooper, N. A., 'An Introduction to the Berkshire Domesday', *Berkshire Domesday*, ed. Williams and Erskine, pp. 1–28

Hughes, Shaun F. D., 'The Battle of Stamford Bridge and the Battle of Bouvines', *Scandinavian Stud.* 60, 30–76

Johnson, Douglas, '"Lichfield" and "St Amphibalus": the Story of a Legend', *South Staffordshire Archaeol. and Hist. Soc. Trans.* 28 (1986–7), 1–13

Jones, Anthea, and Jane Grenville, 'Some New Suggestions about the Pre-Conquest History of Tewkesbury and Tewkesbury Church', *Southern Hist.* 9 (1987), 9–33

Jones, Michael E., 'The Appeal to Aetius in Gildas', *Nottingham Med. Stud.* 32, 141–55

Jones, Michael E., and John Casey, 'The Gallic Chronicle Restored: a Chronology for the Anglo-Saxon Invasions and the End of Roman Britain', *Britannia* 19, 367–98

Keynes, Simon, 'Regenbald the Chancellor (*sic*)', *Anglo-Norman Studies X*, ed. Brown, pp. 185–222

Klaniczay, Gábor, 'From Sacral Kingship to Self-Representation: Hungarian and European Royal Saints in the 11th–13th Centuries', *Continuity and Change*, ed.

Elisabeth Vestergaard (Odense, 1986), pp. 61–86

Kleinschmidt, Harald, see sect. 6

Kristensen, Anne K. G., 'Free Peasants in the Early Middle Ages: Freeholders, Freedmen or What?' *MScand* 12, 76–106

Lapidge, Michael, see sect. 4

Leaver, R. A., 'Five Hides in Ten Counties: a Contribution to the Domesday Regression Debate', *EconHR* 41, 525–42

Lewis, C. P., 'An Introduction to the Herefordshire Domesday', *Herefordshire Domesday*, ed. Williams and Erskine, pp. 1–22

Locherbie-Cameron, M. A. L., see sect. 3*biii*

Loyn, Henry, 'Anglo-Saxon England', *The Historian* 19 (Summer), 10–12

McDonnell, J., 'The Role of Transhumance in Northern England', *Northern Hist.* 24, 1–17

Merdrignac, Bernard, 'Saint Guénolé et les monachismes insulaires et continentals au haut Moyen Age', *Annales de Bretagne et des Pays de L'Ouest* 95, 15–33

Metcalf, D. M., see sect. 8

Moore, John S., 'The Gloucestershire Section of Domesday Book: Geographical Problems of the Text: Part 1', *Trans. of the Bristol and Gloucestershire Archaeol. Soc.* 105 (1987), 109–32

Morris, Richard K., see sect. 10*e*

O'Donovan, M. A., see sect. 6

Orme, Nicholas, 'St Michael and his Mound', *Jnl of the R. Inst. of Cornwall* 10.1 (1986–7), 32–43

Peirce, Ian, 'Arms, Armour and Warfare in the Eleventh Century', *Anglo-Norman Studies X*, ed. Brown, pp. 237–57

Ramsey, Nigel, and Margaret Sparks, *The Image of St Dunstan* (Canterbury)

Richter, Michael, 'Die Kelten im Mittelalter', *HZ* 246, 265–95

Ridyard, Susan J., *The Royal Saints of Anglo-Saxon England: a Study of West Saxon and East Anglian Cults*, Cambridge Stud. in Med. Life and Thought, 4th ser. 9 (Cambridge)

Rollason, D. W., 'The Wanderings of St Cuthbert', *Cuthbert: Saint and Patron*, ed. Rollason, pp. 45–59

'Why was St Cuthbert so Popular?', *Cuthbert: Saint and Patron*, pp. 9–22

ed., *Cuthbert: Saint and Patron* (Durham, 1987)

Rosser, Gervase, 'The Anglo-Saxon Gilds', *Minsters and Parish Churches*, ed. Blair, pp. 31–4

Scharer, Anton, see sect. 6

Sims-Williams, Patrick, see sect. 6

Soulsby, I. N., 'An Introduction to the Cornwall Domesday', *Cornwall Domesday*, ed. Williams and Erskine, pp. 1–17

Squibb, G. D., 'The Foundation of Cerne Abbey', *The Cerne Abbey Millennium Lectures*, ed. Barker, pp. 11–14

Stevens, Clifford, 'Saint Cuthbert: the Early Years', *Cistercian Stud.* 23, 3–13

Tatton-Brown, Tim, 'The Churches of Canterbury Diocese in the 11th Century',

Minsters and Parish Churches, ed. Blair, pp. 105–18

'Images of St Dunstan', *Hist. Today* 38 (April), 36–9

see also sect. 10*b*

Thacker, Alan, 'Æthelwold and Abingdon', *Bishop Æthelwold*, ed. Yorke, pp. 43–64

Thorn, F. R., 'Hundreds and Wapentakes', *Berkshire Domesday*, ed. Williams and Erskine, pp. 29–33

'Hundreds and Wapentakes', *Buckinghamshire Domesday*, ed. Williams and Erskine, pp. 37–46

'Hundreds and Wapentakes', *Cornwall Domesday*, ed. Williams and Erskine, pp. 18–25

'Hundreds and Wapentakes', *Herefordshire Domesday*, ed. Williams and Erskine, pp. 23–30

'Hundreds and Wapentakes', *Worcestershire Domesday*, ed. Williams and Erskine, pp. 32–7

Thorpe, David A., 'The Enigma of Horsa and his Tomb', *Brit. Archaeol.* 6, 26–7

Unwin, Tim, 'Towards a Model of Anglo-Scandinavian Rural Settlement in England', *Anglo-Saxon Settlements*, ed. Hooke, pp. 77–98

van Houts, Elisabeth M. C., 'The Ship List of William the Conqueror', *Anglo-Norman Studies X*, ed. Brown, pp. 159–83

Wallace-Hadrill, J. M., *Bede's 'Ecclesiastical History of the English People': a Historical Commentary* (Oxford)

Warner, Peter, 'Pre-Conquest Territorial and Administrative Organization in East Suffolk', *Anglo-Saxon Settlements*, ed. Hooke, pp. 9–34

Whittock, M., 'Domesday Keynsham: a Retrospective Examination of an Old English Royal Estate', *Bristol and Avon Archaeol.* 6 (1987), 5–10

Williams, A., 'An Introduction to the Worcestershire Domesday', *Worcestershire Domesday*, ed. Williams and Erskine, pp. 1–31

Williams, A., and R. W. H. Erskine, ed., *The Berkshire Domesday*, 2 vols. (London)

ed., *The Buckinghamshire Domesday*, 2 vols. (London)

ed., *The Cornwall Domesday* (London)

ed., *The Herefordshire Domesday* (London)

ed., *The Worcestershire Domesday* (London)

Williamson, Tom, 'Settlement Chronology and Regional Landscapes: the Evidence from the Claylands of East Anglia and Essex', *Anglo-Saxon Settlements*, ed. Hooke, pp. 153–75

Witney, K. P., 'The Period of Mercian Rule in Kent, and a Charter of A.D. 811', *AC* 104 (1987), 87–113

Wood, I. N., 'Early Cheshire', *NH* 24, 227–31

Wormald, Patrick, 'Æthelwold and his Continental Counterparts: Contact, Comparison, Contrast', *Bishop Æthelwold*, ed. Yorke, pp. 13–42

'A Handlist of Anglo-Saxon Lawsuits', *ASE* 17, 247–81

Yorke, Barbara, 'Æthelmær: the Foundation of the Abbey at Cerne and the Politics of the Tenth Century', *The Cerne Abbey Millennium Lectures*, ed. Barker, pp. 15–26

'Æthelwold and the Politics of the Tenth Century', *Bishop Æthelwold*, ed. Yorke, pp. 65–88

'Introduction', *Bishop Æthelwold*, ed. Yorke, pp. 1–12
ed., *Bishop Æthelwold: his Career and Influence* (Woodbridge)

8. NUMISMATICS

Alstertun, Rolf, 'Ett intressant vikingamynt i Örebro Läns Museum eller Vad kraxar korpen?', *Svensk Numismatisk Tidskrift* 1988, 244–6 [penny of Anlaf Guthfrithsson, York mint]

Andrews, P., ed., *Southampton Finds* I: *the Coins and Pottery from Hamwic*, Southampton Archaeol. Monographs 4 (Southampton)

Archibald, Marion M., 'English Medieval Coins as Dating Evidence', *Coins and the Archaeologist*, ed. Casey and Reece, pp. 264–301 [revised version of 1974 paper]
'A Viking Copy of an Alfred London-Monogram Penny from Doncaster', *Yorkshire Numismatist* 1, 9–11

Archibald, M. M., and M. R. Cowell, 'The Fineness of Northumbrian Sceattas', *Metallurgy in Numismatics* II, ed. W. A. Oddy, R. Numismatic Soc., Special Pub. 19 (London), 55–64

Archibald, M. M., *et al.*, 'Coin Register', *BNJ* 57 (1987), 122–52 [includes 137 single-finds of the Anglo-Saxon period]

Bendixen, Kirsten, 'Nyere danske fund av merovingiske, karolingiska og ældre danske mønter', *Commentationes numismaticae 1988*, ed. Berghaus *et al.*, pp. 37–50

Berghaus, Peter, *et al.*, *Commentationes numismaticae 1988. Festgabe für Gert und Vera Hatz zum 4. Januar 1988 dargebracht* (Hamburg)

Blackburn, Mark, 'Three Silver Coins in the Names of Valentinian III (425–55) and Anthemius (467–72) from Chatham Lines, Kent', *NChron* 148, 169–74

Blackburn, M. A. S., and M. J. Bonser, 'The "Porcupine" Sceattas of Metcalf's Variety G', *BNJ* 57 (1987), 99–103

Blackburn, Mark, and David Haigh, 'A Penny of Eadgar from Castle Hill, Cambridge', *Proc. of the Cambridge Ant. Soc.* 75 (1986), 61–2

Casey, John, and Richard Reece, ed., *Coins and the Archaeologist*, 2nd ed. (London)

Challis, C. E., and B. J. Cook, comp., 'Coin Register', *BNJ* 57 (1987), 122–52 [Merovingian coins, sceattas, and later Anglo-Saxon coins, pp. 126–41]

Chown, John, 'A Cnut Short Cross from Denmark', *NCirc* 1988, 175
'A Parcel of Coins from an 11th Century Polish Hoard?', *NCirc* 1988, 111–12

Dolley, Michael, and Ivar Leimus, 'Unikaalne Anglonormanni Penn Maidla Aardes [A Unique Anglo-Norman Penny from the Maidla Hoard]', *Eesti NSV Teaduste Akadeemia Toimetised* 35 (1986), 314–16 [mule between William I, type i and Edward the Confessor's *Hammer Cross* type]

Frandsen, Lene B., and Stig Jensen, 'Pre-Viking and Early Viking Age Ribe. Excavations at Nicolajgade 8, 1985–86', *Journal of Danish Archaeology* 6 (1987), 175–89 [finds include 34 sceattas, 29 of the Wodan/monster type]

Harris, E. J., 'An Index of Articles Dealing with Early and Hammered Coins in the British Numismatic Journal Vols. 41–50', *SCMB* 1988, 68–72

Jonsson, Kenneth, 'Grantham – a New Anglo-Saxon Mint in Lincolnshire', *BNJ* 57 (1987), 104–5 [Æthelred II]

Kenny, M., 'English Viking and Anglo-Saxon Coins in the Stacpoole Collection', *NCirc* 1988, 207–9
'A Small Hoard of Pennies of Æthelraed II (978–1016) from Ireland', *BNJ* 57 (1987), 106–7
King, Michael D., 'Roman Coins from Early Anglo-Saxon Contexts', *Coins and the Archaeologist*, ed. Casey and Reece, pp. 224–9
Lowe, Barbara J., *et al.*, see sect. 10*e*
Malmer, Brita, 'Kilka skandynawskich nasladownict w typu Long Cross/Quatrefoil (Some Scandinavian Long Cross/Quatrefoil Imitations)', *Prace i Materiały. Muzeum Archeologicznego i Etnograficznego w Łodzi: Seria Numizmatyczna i Konserwatorska* 7 (1987), 11–19
'Zwei Stempelketten skandinavischer Long-Cross-Nachahmungen', *Commentationes numismaticae 1988*, ed. Berghaus *et al.*, pp. 81–8
Metcalf, D. M., 'A Coin of Edward the Elder', in H. R. Hurst, *Gloucester: the Roman and Later Defences*, Gloucester Archaeol. Reports 2 (Gloucester, 1986), 38–9
'The Coins', *Southampton Finds* I: *the Coins and Pottery from Hamwic*, ed. P. Andrews, Southampton Archaeol. Monographs 4 (Southampton), 17–59
'The Currency of the Kingdom of East Anglia in the First Half of the Eighth Century', *Commentationes numismaticae 1988*, ed. Berghaus *et al.*, pp. 19–27
'Monetary Expansion and Recession: Interpreting the Distribution-Patterns of Seventh and Eighth-Century Coins', *Coins and the Archaeologist*, ed. Casey and Reece, pp. 230–53 [revised version of 1974 paper]
'Were Ealdormen Exercising Independent Control over the Coinage in Mid-Tenth-Century England?', *BNJ* 57 (1987), 24–33
Metcalf, D. M., and J. P. Northover, 'Carolingian and Viking Coins from the Cuerdale Hoard: an Interpretation and Comparison of their Metal Contents', *NChron* 148, 97–116
Östergren, Majvor, 'Vikingatida silverskatt från Sälle i Fröjel socken, Gotland', *Svensk Numismatisk Tidskrift* 1988, 18–19 [deposited *c*.1016, includes *c*.315 Anglo-Saxon coins]
Pagan, H. E., 'The Imitative Louis the Pious Solidus from Southampton and Finds of Other Related Coins in the British Isles', *Southampton Finds* I: *the Coins and Pottery from Hamwic*, ed. P. Andrews, Southampton Archaeol. Monographs 4 (Southampton), 71–2
'The Older Finds of Anglo-Saxon Coins from Southampton', *Southampton Finds* I: *the Coins and Pottery from Hamwic*, ed. P. Andrews, Southampton Archaeol. Monographs 4 (Southampton), 60–70
Pirie, E. J. E., 'Early Northumbrian Orthography and a Problem of Convention', *Yorkshire Numismatist* 1, 1–8
Rudling, David, see sect. 10*h*
Seaby, W. A., and M. Kenny, 'The Stacpoole Collection of Hiberno-Norse Coins in the National Museum of Ireland', *NCirc* 1988, 75–8
Spufford, Peter, *Money and its Use in Medieval Europe*, (Cambridge)
Stewart, Ian, 'English Coinage from Athelstan to Edgar', *NChron* 148, 192–214
'Ministri and Monetarii', *Revue Numismatique*, 6th ser. 30, 166–75

'Winoth, a New Moneyer for Coenwulf, *NCirc* 1988, 147

Sugden, K., 'A Rare North-West Coin of Cnut', *NCirc* 1988, 315 [single-find from Drigg, near Whitehaven, Cumbria]

Talvio, Tuukka, 'Angelsächsischer Einfluss auf norddeutschen Münzen des späten 10. und frühen 11. Jahrhunderts', *Commentationes numismaticae 1988*, ed. Berghaus *et al.*, pp. 89–93

Thompson, R. H., 'Publications and Papers of Christopher Evelyn Blunt. Supplement', *BNJ* 57 (1987), 160–1

9. ONOMASTICS

Arngart, O., 'A Couple of English Hundred-Names', *Jnl of the EPNS* 20 (1987–8), 10–13

Baines, Arnold H. J., '*Wyrttruma* and *Wyrtwala*', *South Midlands Archaeol.* 17 (1987), 102–10

Bateson, M., and C. Clark, 'Bibliography', *Nomina* 11 (1987), 186–203

Bleach, John, and Richard Coates, 'Three More Walcots', *Jnl of the EPNS* 19 (1986–7), 56–63

Bourne, Jill, 'Kingston Place-Names: an Interim Report', *Jnl of the EPNS* 20 (1987–8), 13–37

Cameron, Kenneth, 'Bynames of Location in Lincolnshire Subsidy Rolls', *Nottingham Med. Stud.* 32, 156–64

Clark, Cecily, '*Willelmus Rex? vel alius Willelmus?*' *Nomina* 11 (1987), 7–33

Coates, Richard, *A Bibliography of Place-Names in Hampshire and the Isle of Wight, with a Section on Hampshire Dialect* (Brighton)

    A Classified Bibliography on Sussex Place-Names, 1586–1987, with an Essay on the State of the Art (Brighton, 1987)

    Toponymic Topics: Essays on the Early Toponymy of the British Isles (Brighton)

    see also sect. 2

Cole, Ann, 'The Distribution and Usage of the OE Place-Name *Cealc*', *Jnl of the EPNS* 19 (1986–7), 45–55

    'The Distribution and Usage of the Place-Name Elements *botm*, *bytme*, and *botn*', *Jnl of the EPNS* 20 (1987–8), 38–46

Colman, Fran, 'What *is* in a Name?' *Historical Dialectology, Regional and Social*, ed. Jacek Fisiak, Trends in Ling., Stud. and Monographs 37 (Berlin, New York and Amsterdam), 111–37

Copley, Gordon, *Early Place-Names of the Anglian Regions of England*, BAR, Brit. ser. 185 (Oxford)

Cox, Barrie, 'Furze, Gorse and Whin: an Aside on Rutland in the Danelaw', *Jnl of the EPNS* 20 (1987–8), 3–9

Dornier, Ann, 'Place-Names in *-wich*: a Preliminary Linguistic Survey', *Nomina* 11 (1987), 87–98

English Place-Name Society, 'Select Bibliography, 1980–87', *Jnl of the EPNS* 20 (1987–8), 50–71

Everson, Paul, see sect. 10*c*

Fellows-Jensen, Gillian, 'To Divide the Danes from the Norwegians: On Scandinavian Settlement in the British Isles', *Nomina* 11 (1987), 35–60

'Scandinavian Place-Names and Viking Settlement in Normandy: a Review', *Namn och Bygd* 76, 113–37 [with bibliography]

Gelling, Margaret, *Signposts to the Past: Place-Names and the History of England*, 2nd ed. (Chichester)

'Towards a Chronology for English Place-Names', *Anglo-Saxon Settlements*, ed. Hooke, pp. 59–76

Gerchow, Jan, *Die Gedenküberlieferung der Angelsachsen, mit einem Katalog der* Libri Vitae *und Necrologien*, Arbeiten zur Frühmittelalterforschung 20 (Berlin)

Hodgkinson, Jeremy S., and Michael J. Leppard, 'The Evolution of Warlege', *Sussex Archaeol. Collections* 126, 248

Kennett, D. H., 'Scandinavian Settlement in East Anglia: 1. Place-Names in North-East Suffolk', *Yarmouth Archaeol.* 2 (1987), 121–9

Kristensson, Gillis, 'The Place-Name Yelvertoft (Northamptonshire)', *N&Q* 35, 2–3

Ó Máille, T. S., '*Venta, Gwenta, Finn, Guen*', *Nomina* 11 (1987), 145–51

Owen, Hywel Wyn, 'English Place-Names and Welsh Stress Patterns', *Nomina* 11 (1987), 99–114

Padel, O. J., *A Popular Dictionary of Cornish Place-Names* (Penzance)

Peterson, Lena, 'Mono- and Dithematic Personal Names in Old Germanic', *Probleme der Namenbildung*, ed. Thorsten Andersson, Nomina Germanica 18 (Uppsala), 121–30

Piroth, Walter, 'Thüringer unter den Angelsachsen', *BN* 23, 114–30

Sandred, Karl Inge, 'Nominal Inflection in the Old English of the Anglo-Saxon Land Charters: Reduction of Medial *an* in Toponymical Composition. A Case for Socio-Historical Linguistics', *Probleme der Namenbildung*, ed. Thorsten Andersson, Nomina Germanica 18 (Uppsala), 131–53

'The Scandinavians in Norfolk: Some Observations on the Place-Names in *-by*', *Jnl of the EPNS* 19 (1986–7), 5–28

'Some Reflexes of Old Anglian and Viking Settlement in Norfolk Place-Names', *Norfolk Research Committee Bull.* 38 (1987), 10–12

Watts, V. E., 'Some Northumbrian Fishery Names III', *Durham Archaeol. Jnl* 4, 53–9

Waugh, Doreen, 'The Scandinavian Element *staðir* in Caithness, Orkney and Shetland', *Nomina* 11 (1987), 61–74

10. ARCHAEOLOGY

a. General

Abramson, Philip, ed., 'The Yorkshire Archaeological Register: 1987', *Yorkshire Archaeol. Jnl* 60, 181–7

Allen, David, 'Excavations in Bierton, 1979', *Records of Buckinghamshire* 28 (1986), 1–120 [includes early Anglo-Saxon finds]

Bibliography for 1988

[Anon.] 'Dorset Archaeology in 1987', *Proc. of the Dorset Nat. Hist. and Archaeol. Soc.* 109 (1987), 123–39

[Anon.] 'Researches and Discoveries in Kent', *AC* 104 (1987), 333–86 [Anglo-Saxon finds and a note on Reculver Church]

Arnold, C. J., *An Archaeology of the Early Anglo-Saxon Kingdoms* (London and New York)

'Territories and Leadership: Frameworks for the Study of Emergent Polities in Early Anglo-Saxon Southern England', *Power and Politics*, ed. Driscoll and Nieke, pp. 111–27

Beagrie, Neil, and David Gurney, 'The Norfolk Excavations Index', *Norfolk Archaeol.* 40.2, 185–93

Biddle, Martin, 'Authority and Continuity', *First Millennium Papers*, ed. Jones *et al.*, pp. 257–8

Bird, D. G., Glenys Crocker, and J. S. McCracken, comp., 'Archaeology in Surrey 1985–6', *Surrey Archaeol. Collections* 78 (1987), 133–48

CBA, *Archaeology in Britain 1987* [short reports on work of official, national, regional and local bodies relating to all periods]

CBA, *Brit. Archaeol. Abstracts* 21.1 [articles on all periods published between 1 July and 30 Dec. 1987]

CBA, Group 1 (Scottish Regional Group), *Discovery and Excavation in Scotland 1988* [annual summary of archaeological discoveries, excavations, surveys and publications]

CBA, Group 3, *News Bulletin* 3.9–10 (Jan. and Sept.) [reviews work on all periods in Cleveland, Cumbria, Durham, Northumberland, Tyne and Wear]

CBA, Group 6, *Bulletin* 30 (1985), 31 (1986), 32 (1987) [reviews work on all periods in Norfolk and Suffolk, 1984–6]

CBA, Group 8, *West Midlands Archaeol.* 30 (1987) [reviews work on all periods in Hereford and Worcester, Shropshire, Staffordshire, Warwickshire, and West Midlands]

CBA, Group 9, *South Midlands Archaeol.* 18 [reviews work on all periods in Bedfordshire, Buckinghamshire, Northamptonshire, Oxfordshire]

CBA, Group 12, *Newsletter* (April and Oct.) [reviews work on all periods in Berkshire, Channel Islands, Dorset, Hampshire, Isle of Wight, Wiltshire]

Cramp, Rosemary, 'Northumbria: the Archaeological Evidence', *Power and Politics*, ed. Driscoll and Nieke, pp. 69–78

Deegan, Marilyn, and Stanley Rubin, 'Written in Bones: Palaeopathology and Anglo-Saxon Remedies', *Archaeol. Today* 9.1, 40–5

Dennison, E., ed., 'Somerset Archaeology 1987', *Proc. of the Somerset Archaeol. and Nat. Hist. Soc.* 131 (1987), 203–31

Dix, Brian, 'Archaeology in Northamptonshire 1985–6', *Northamptonshire Archaeol.* 21 (1986–7), 153–9

Farley, Michael, 'Archaeological Notes from Buckinghamshire County Museum', *Records of Buckinghamshire* 28 (1986), 211–14

'Archaeological Notes from Buckinghamshire County Museum', *Records of Buckinghamshire* 29 (1987), 226–9

Faull, Margaret L., 'From Anglo-Saxon to Norman Yorkshire', *First Millenium Papers*, ed. Jones *et al.*, pp. 273–9

Fisher, Genevieve, 'Style and Sociopolitical Organisation: a Preliminary Study from Early Anglo-Saxon England', *Power and Politics*, ed. Driscoll and Nieke, pp. 128–44

Foard, Glenn, 'A Framework for Saxon Evidence from Northamptonshire', *First Millennium Papers*, ed. Jones *et al.*, pp. 259–71

Girardon, Sheila, and Jenni Heathcote, 'Excavation Round-up 1987: part 2, London Boroughs', *London Archaeologist* 5.15, 410–15

Hayes, P. P., 'Roman to Saxon in the South Lincolnshire Fens', *Antiquity* 62, 321–6

Herrman, Bernd, 'Parasitologisch-Epidemiologische Auswertungen Mittelalterliche Kloaken', *Zeitschrift für Archäologie des Mittelalters* 13 (1985), 131–61 [survey, including material from England]

Hodges, Richard, and John Moreland, 'Power and Exchange in Middle Saxon England', *Power and Politics*, ed. Driscoll and Nieke, pp. 79–95

Huggett, J. W., 'Imported Grave Goods and the Early Anglo-Saxon Economy', *MA* 32, 63–96

Johnson, A. M., 'Wisbech and West Walton Highway Bypass: an Archaeological Survey', *Proc. of the Cambridge Antiq. Soc.* 75 (1986), 43–60

Jones, R. F. J., J. H. F. Bloemers, S. L. Dyson and M. Biddle, ed., *First Millennium Papers. Western Europe in the First Millennium AD*, BAR International ser. 401 (Oxford)

Jope, E. M., 'Celtic Art: Expressiveness and Communication through 2500 Years', *PBA* 73 (1987), 97–124 [Celtic elements in Anglo-Saxon art, pp. 112–16]

Kruse, Susan E., 'Ingots and Weight Units in Viking Age Silver Hoards', *World Archaeol.* 20, 285–301

Lane, T., and P. P. Hayes, ed., 'Fieldwork and Excavation in the Fens of Eastern England 1986–87', *Fenland Research* 4 (1986–7)

Martin, Edward, Judith Plouviez, and Hilary Feldman, comp., 'Archaeology in Suffolk 1987', *Proc. of the Suffolk Inst. of Archaeol. and Hist.* 36.4, 309–20

Myres, J. N. L., and Philip H. Dixon, 'A Ninth-century *Grubenhaus* on Bucklebury Common, Berkshire', *AntJ* 68, 115–22

Nordic Archaeological Abstracts 1986 [pp. 117–62 abstract many items of Anglo-Saxon importance, incl. finds in both Scandinavia and the British Isles]

Poulton, Rob, 'Saxon Surrey', *The Archaeology of Surrey to 1540*, ed. Joanna Bird and D. G. Bird (Guildford, 1987), pp. 197–222

Priddy, Deborah, ed., 'Work of the Essex County Council Archaeology Section 1986' and 'Excavations in Essex 1986', *Essex Archaeol. and Hist.* 18 (1987), 88–113

ed., 'The Work of the Essex County Council Archaeology Section 1987', and 'Excavations in Essex 1987', *Essex Archaeol. and Hist.* 19, 240–71

Trust for Lincolnshire Archaeology, *Archaeology in Lincolnshire 1985–1986*, Second Annual Report (Lincoln, 1986)

Archaeology in Lincolnshire 1986–1987, Third Annual Report (Lincoln, 1987)

Archaeology in Lincolnshire 1987–1988, Fourth Annual Report (Lincoln)

Walton, Penelope, 'A Tangled Web', *Interim: Archaeol. in York* 13.3, 32–8 [discusses Anglo-Saxon and Viking weaving]

Youngs, Susan M., John Clark, David R. M. Gaimster and Terry Barry, 'Medieval Britain and Ireland in 1987', *MA* 32, 225–314

b. Towns and other major settlements

Atkin, Malcolm, 'The Kingsholm Dig', *Brit. Archaeol.* 5, 6–9 [Gloucester]

Atkin, Malcolm, and A. P. Garrod, 'Archaeology in Gloucester 1986', *Trans. of the Bristol and Gloucestershire Archaeol. Soc.* 105 (1987), 233–42

'Archaeology in Gloucester 1987', *Trans. of the Bristol and Gloucestershire Archaeol. Soc.* 106, 208–16

Ayers, Brian, 'Excavations at St Martin-at-Palace Plain, Norwich, 1981', *East Anglian Archaeol.* 37 (1987)

Bennet, Paul, 'Interim Report on Work Carried Out in 1986 by the Canterbury Archaeological Trust', *AC* 103 (1986), 191–234

Bennet, Paul, *et al.*, 'Rescue Excavations in the Outer Court of St Augustine's Abbey, 1983–84', *AC* 103 (1986), 79–117

Biddle, Martin, 'Winchester: the Rise of an Early Capital', *The Cambridge Guide to the Arts in Britain* 1, ed. Ford, 194–205

Blockley, Paul, *et al.*, 'Interim Report on Work Carried Out in 1987 by the Canterbury Archaeological Trust', *AC* 104 (1987), 291–332

Bourdillon, Jennifer, 'Countryside and Town: the Animal Resources of Saxon Southampton', *Anglo-Saxon Settlements*, ed. Hooke, pp. 177–95

Brinklow, David, 'The Lengths We Go To . . .', *Interim: Archaeol. in York* 13.1, 3–9 [Anglian finds]

Brisbane, Mark, 'Hamwic (Saxon Southampton): an 8th Century Port and Production Centre', *Rebirth of Towns in the West AD 750–1050*, ed. Hodges and Hobley, pp. 101–8

Brooks, Dodie A., 'The Case for Continuity in Fifth-Century Canterbury Re-examined', *Oxford Jnl of Archaeol.* 7, 99–114

Buckley, Richard, and John Lucas, *Leicester Town Defences. Excavations 1958–1974* (Leicester, 1987) [pre-Conquest, pp. 56–7]

Burl, Aubrey, ed., *From Roman Town to Norman Castle: Essays in Honour of Philip Barker* (Birmingham)

Canterbury Archaeological Trust, *Annual Report 1985–86* (Canterbury, n.d.) [includes Anglo-Saxon]

Darvill, Timothy, 'Excavations on the Site of the Early Norman Castle at Gloucester 1983–84', *MA* 32, 1–49

Dixon, Philip, 'Life after Wroxeter. A Medievalist's View of the Roman Town', *From Roman Town to Norman Castle*, ed. Burl, pp. 30–9

Green, Charles, Ida Green, and Carolyn Dallas, 'Excavations at Castor, Cambridgeshire, in 1957–8 and 1973', *Northamptonshire Archaeol.* 21 (1986–7), 109–48

Hall, Richard, 'The Making of Domesday York', *Anglo-Saxon Settlements*, ed. Hooke, pp. 233–47

'York 700–1050', *Rebirth of Towns in the West AD 750–1050*, ed. Hodges and Hobley, pp. 125–32

Haslam, Jeremy, 'The Second Burh of Nottingham', *Landscape Hist.* 9 (1987), 45–52

Heathcote, Jenny, 'Excavation Round-up 1987, Part 1: City of London', *London Archaeol.* 5.14, 382–7

Hill, David, 'Towns as Structures and Functioning Communities through Time: the Development of Central Places from 600–1066', *Anglo-Saxon Settlements*, ed. Hooke, pp. 197–212

Hobley, Brian, 'Lundenwic and Lundenburh: Two Cities Rediscovered', *Rebirth of Towns in the West AD 750–1050*, ed. Hodges and Hobley, pp. 69–82

Hodges, Richard, 'The Rebirth of Towns in the Early Middle Ages', *Rebirth of Towns in the West AD 750–1050*, ed. Hodges and Hobley, pp. 1–7

Hodges, Richard, *Primitive and Peasant Markets* (Oxford) [contains much discussion of Anglo-Saxon markets]

Hodges, Richard, and Brian Hobley, ed., *The Rebirth of Towns in the West AD 700–1050*, CBA Research Report 68 (London)

Horsman, V., C. Milne, and G. Milne, *Aspects of Saxo-Norman London, 1: Building and Street Development near Billingsgate and Cheapside*, London and Middlesex Archaeol. Soc., Special Paper 11 (London)

Hurst, H. R., *Gloucester: the Roman and Later Defences*, Gloucester Archaeol. Reports 2 (Gloucester, 1986) [contains discussion of the late Saxon defences, pp. 129–32]

James, T. B., 'The Population Size of Winchester over 2,000 Years: a Survey', *Hampshire Field Club and Archaeol. Soc. Section Newsletters*, ns 9 (Spring), 1–3

Jones, G. D. B., and D. C. A. Shotter, *Roman Lancaster: Rescue Archaeology in an Historic City 1970–71* (Manchester) [includes Anglo-Saxon Lancaster]

Nicholson, Rebecca A., and Jennifer Hillam, 'A Dendrochronological Analysis of Oak Timbers from the Early Medieval Site Dundas Wharf, Bristol', *Trans. of the Bristol and Gloucestershire Archaeol. Soc.* 105 (1987), 133–45

O'Connor, T. P., *Bones from the General Accident Extension Site*, Archaeol. of York 15/2 (London) [includes Anglo-Scandinavian]

'The Case of the Absent Rat', *Interim: Archaeol. in York* 13.4, 39–45 [Anglian York]

Ordnance Survey, *Roman and Anglian York. Historical Map and Guide* (Southampton)

Ordnance Survey, *Viking and Medieval York. Historical Map and Guide* (Southampton)

Ottaway, Patrick, 'Queen's Hotel: Excavations', *Interim: Archaeol. in York* 13.4, 5–22

'Stakis Hotel Site', *Interim: Archaeol. in York* 13.3, 3–11

Parker, M. S., 'Some Notes on the Pre-Norman History of Doncaster', *Yorkshire Archaeol. Jnl* 59 (1987), 29–43

Rady, Jonathan, *et al.*, 'Excavations at St Martin's Hill, Canterbury, 1984–85', *AC* 104 (1987), 123–218

[Selkirk, Andrew] 'Wic found at Norwich', *CA* 110 (July), 68

Strickland, T. J., 'The Roman Heritage of Chester: the Survival of the Buildings of *Deva* after the Roman Period', *Rebirth of Towns in the West AD 750–1050*, ed. Hodges and Hobley, pp. 109–18

Bibliography for 1988

Tatton-Brown, Tim, 'The Anglo-Saxon Towns of Kent', *Anglo-Saxon Settlements*, ed. Hooke, pp. 213–32

Teague, S. C., 'Excavations at Market Street, Winchester, 1987–88', *Hampshire Field Club and Archaeol. Soc. Section Newsletters*, ns 10 (Autumn), 19–22

Thacker, A. T., 'Early Medieval Chester: the Historical Background', *Rebirth of Towns in the West AD 750–1050*, ed. Hodges and Hobley, pp. 119–24

Vince, Alan, 'The Economic Basis of Anglo-Saxon London', *Rebirth of Towns in the West AD 750–1050*, ed. Hodges and Hobley, pp. 83–92

Wade, Keith, 'Ipswich', *Rebirth of Towns in the West AD 750–1050*, ed. Hodges and Hobley, pp. 93–100

Ward, S., *12 Watergate Street 1985: Roman Headquarters Building to Medieval Row*, Excavations at Chester 5 (Chester)

Weddell, Peter J., 'Excavations within the Anglo-Saxon Enclosure at Berry Meadow, Kingsteignton, in 1985', *Proc. of the Devon Archaeol Soc.* 45 (1987), 75–96

Winchester Archaeological Rescue Group, *Find* 39 (May 1986) – 43 (Sept. 1987)

Woodward, Peter J., and Roland J. C. Smith, 'Survey and Excavation Along the Route of the Southern Dorchester By-pass, 1986–1987 – an Interim Note', *Proc. of the Dorset Nat. Hist. and Archaeol. Soc.* 109 (1987), 79–89 [includes post-Roman structures]

York Archaeological Trust, *The Waterfronts of York. Prospects for Archaeological Research* (York)

c. Rural settlements, agriculture and the countryside

[Anon.] 'Dorchester', *CA* 112 (Dec.), 169–73 [early medieval (= Saxon?) timber halls similar to Chalton and Cowdery's Down]

Aston, Michael, 'Land Use and Field Systems', *Aspects of the Mediaeval Landscape of Somerset*, ed. Aston, pp. 83–97

'Settlement Patterns and Forms', *Aspects of the Mediaeval Landscape of Somerset*, ed. Aston, pp. 67–81

ed., *Aspects of the Mediaeval Landscape of Somerset* (Somerset County Council)

Blair, John, 'The Bampton Research Project: Second Report 1986–8', *South Midlands Archaeol.* 18, 89–93

Buckley, David G., and John D. Hedges, *The Bronze Age and Saxon Settlements at Springfield Lyons, Essex: an Interim Report* (Chelmsford)

Carr, R. D., A. Tester and P. Murphy, 'The Middle-Saxon Settlement at Staunch Meadow, Brandon', *Antiquity* 62, 371–7

Challis, C. E., and B. J. Cook, see sect. 8

Costen, Michael, 'The Late Saxon Landscape', *Aspects of the Mediaeval Landscape of Somerset*, ed. Aston, pp. 33–47

Dix, Brian, 'The Raunds Area Project: Second Interim Report', *Northamptonshire Archaeol.* 21 (1986–7), 3–29

Everson, Paul, 'What's in a Name? "Goltho", Goltho and Bullington', *Lincolnshire Hist. and Archaeol.* 23, 93–9 [review article, on Guy Beresford, *Goltho: the Development of an Early Medieval Manor* (London, 1987)]

Bibliography for 1988

Fasham, P. J., 'Archaeological Investigations at Ipsley, 1968 and 1969', *Trans. of the Worcestershire Archaeol. Soc.* 3rd ser. 11, 7–22

Field, Naomi, 'Nettleton Top Anglo-Saxon Settlement', *Lincolnshire Hist. and Archaeol.* 23, 85

Gardiner, Mark, *et al.*, 'Excavations at Testers, White Horse Square, Steyning, 1985', *Sussex Archaeol. Collections* 126, 53–76

Gates, T., and C. F. O'Brien, 'Cropmarks at Milfield and New Berwick and the Recognition of Grubenhaüser in Northumberland', *AAe* 16, 1–9

Griffith, F. M., 'Salvage Observations at the Dark Age Site at Bantham Ham, Thurlestone, in 1982', *Proc. of the Devon Archaeol. Soc.* 44 (1986), 39–58

Hall, David, 'The Late Saxon Countryside: Villages and their Fields', *Anglo-Saxon Settlements*, ed. Hooke, pp. 99–122

Hamerow, Helena, 'Mucking: the Anglo-Saxon Settlement', *CA* 111 (Sept.), 128–31

Higham, Nick, 'Landscape and Land Use in Northern England: a Survey of Agricultural Potential, *c.* 500 BC–AD 1000', *Landscape Hist.* 9 (1987), 35–44

Huggins, P. J., 'Excavations in the Market Place, Waltham Abbey, Essex, 1981: the Moot Hall and Romano-British Occupation', *Essex Archaeol. and Hist.* 19, 196–214 [Middle and Late Saxon occupation, p. 206]

Hughes, Mike, and Elizabeth Hughes, 'The Meon Valley Historic Landscape Project: 2nd Interim Report', *Hampshire Field Club and Archaeol. Soc. Section Newsletters*, ns 10 (Autumn), 28–9

Lane, T., and P. P. Hayes, ed., *Fenland Research 4: Fieldwork and Excavation in the Fens of Eastern England 1986–87* (Trust for Lincolnshire Archaeol., n.d.)

Medieval Settlement Research Group Annual Report 2 (1987) [national survey of year's work, including Anglo-Saxon sites]

Metcalf, D. M., see sect. 8

Milton, Brian, 'Excavations at Barrington's Farm, Orsett Cock, Thurrock, Essex, 1983', *Essex Archaeol. and Hist.* 18 (1987), 16–33 [*Grubenhäuser* and pottery]

Musty, John, 'Science Diary: a Saxon Post', *CA* 110 (July), 107 [moulded oak post from Fyfield Hall, Essex, with radiocarbon date of cal. AD 785–985 (2 sigma)]

Rackham, Oliver, 'Woods, Hedges and Forests', *Aspects of the Mediaeval Landscape of Somerset*, ed. Aston, pp. 13–30

Rahtz, Philip, 'The End of Roman Wharram Percy', *First Millennium Papers*, ed. Jones *et al.*, pp. 295–30

Unwin, Tim, 'Towards a Model of Anglo-Scandinavian Rural Settlement in England', *Anglo-Saxon Settlements*, ed. Hooke, pp. 77–98

Weddell, Peter J., 'The Excavation of Medieval and Later Houses and St Margaret's Chapel at Exmouth 1982–1984', *Proc. of the Devon Archaeol. Soc.* 44 (1986), 107–41 [includes Anglo-Saxon boundary]

Williams, Bruce, 'Excavation of a Medieval Earthwork Complex at Hillesley, Hawkesbury, Avon', *Trans. of the Bristol and Gloucestershire Archaeol. Soc.* 105 (1987), 147–63 [Saxo-Norman origins]

Williamson, Tom, see sect. 7

d. Pagan cemeteries and Sutton Hoo

Andersen, Johannes G., and Keith Manchester, 'Grooving of the Proximal Phalanx in Leprosy: a Palaeopathological and Radiological Study', *Jnl of Archaeol. Science* 14 (1987), 77–82 [Anglo-Saxon examples]

[Anon.] 'Important Saxon Discovery on Whitfield Hill, Dover', *Kent Archaeol. Rev.* 96, 121

Buckley, David, 'Springfield', *CA* 108 (Feb.), 6–11 [pagan Saxon cemetery succeeded by late Saxon village]

Carver, M. O. H., ed., *Bull. of the Sutton Hoo Research Committee* 5 (Jan.)

Draper, J., 'Excavations at Great Chesterford, Essex, 1953–5', *Proc. of the Cambridge Antiquarian Soc.* 75 (1986), 3–41 [includes Anglo-Saxon cemetery]

Evison, Vera I., *An Anglo-Saxon Cemetery at Alton, Hampshire*, Hampshire Field Club Monograph 4

Farley, Michael, 'An Anglo-Saxon Cemetery at Bourne End, Wooburn, Bucks., Reinstated', *Records of Buckinghamshire* 29 (1987), 170–4

Filmer-Sankey, W., 'The Snape Anglo-Saxon Cemetery', *Bull. of the Sutton Hoo Research Committee* 5 (Jan.), 13–17

Gallagher, D. B., 'The Anglo-Saxon Cemetery at Hob Hill, Saltburn', *Yorkshire Archaeol. Jnl* 59 (1987), 9–27

Green, Barbara, Andrew Rogerson, and Susan G. White, *The Anglo-Saxon Cemetery at Morning Thorpe, Norfolk*, East Anglian Archaeol. 36 (i) and (ii) (Gressenhall, 1987)

Grinsell, Leslie, 'Surrey Barrows 1934–1986: a Reappraisal', *Surrey Archaeol. Collections* 78 (1987), 1–41 [includes the 30–5 Anglo-Saxon barrows of Surrey]

Henderson, Julian, Robert Janaway, and Julian Richards, 'A Curious Clinker', *Jnl of Archaeol. Science* 14 (1987), 353–65 [investigation of a substance found in Anglo-Saxon cremation urns]

Kennett, D. H., 'Ritual and Rite: the Older Discoveries of Early Anglo-Saxon Cemeteries in Northamptonshire', *South Midlands Archaeol.* 18, 68–71

Perkins, D. R. J., 'The Jutish Cemetery at Half Mile Ride, Margate: a Re-appraisal', *AC* 104 (1987), 219–36

Powlesland, D., *The Heslerton Anglo-Saxon Settlement – a Guide to the Excavation of an Early Anglo-Saxon Settlement and its Cemetery* (North Yorkshire County Council, 1987)

Reynolds, Nicholas, 'The Rape of the Anglo-Saxon Women', *Antiquity* 62, 715–18

Richards, J. D., 'Style and Symbol: Explaining Variability in Anglo-Saxon Cremation Burials', *Power and Politics*, ed. Driscoll and Nieke, pp. 145–61

Smith, Paul S., and Phillip L. Armitage, 'Early Anglo-Saxon Burials from Stafford Road, Brighton, East Sussex', *Sussex Archaeol. Collections* 126, 31–51

Speake, George, *A Saxon Bed Burial on Swallowcliffe Down*, Eng. Heritage Archaeol. Report 10 (London)

Sutton Hoo Society, *Saxon. The Newsletter of the Sutton Hoo Soc.*, 7 (Spring), 8 (Summer/Autumn)

Tyler, Susan, 'The Anglo-Saxon Cemetery at Prittlewell, Essex: an Analysis of the Grave Goods', *Essex Archaeol. and Hist.* 19, 91–116

West, Stanley, *et al.*, *The Anglo-Saxon Cemetery at Westgarth Gardens, Bury St Edmunds*, East Anglian Archaeol. 38 (Gressenhall)

White, Andrew, 'Anglo-Saxon Finds from Three Sites in Lincolnshire', *Lincolnshire Hist. and Archaeol.* 23, 87–8 [Asgarby, Old Sleaford and Welbourn]

White, Roger H., *Roman and Celtic Objects from Anglo-Saxon Graves. A Catalogue and an Interpretation of their Use*, BAR, Brit. ser. 191 (Oxford)

Wilkinson, David, 'Two Anglo-Saxon Graves at Kemble', *Trans. of the Bristol and Gloucestershire Archaeol. Soc.* 106, 198–201

Willson, John, 'Saxon Burials from Priory Hall, Dover', *Kent Archaeol. Rev.* 94, 81–92

e. *Churches, monastic sites and Christian cemeteries*

Aldsworth, F. G., and R. Harris, 'The Tower and "Rhenish Helm" Spire of St Mary's Church, Sompting', *Sussex Archaeol. Collections* 126, 105–44

Anderson, Joy, 'A Dig in the Ribs', *Interim: Archaeol. in York* 13.2, 24–32 [Anglo-Saxon human bones from Ailcy Hill, Ripon]

[Anon.] 'Dover Archaeological Heritage Centre', *Kent Archaeol. Rev.* 94, 94–5 [shows location of Anglo-Saxon church beside St Martin le Grand]

Bailey, R. N., E. Cambridge, and H. Denis Briggs, *Dowsing and Church Archaeology* (Wimborne)

Bassett, Steven, *The Wootton Wawen Project: Interim Report No. 6* (Birmingham)

Bell, R. D., M. W. Beresford *et al.*, *Wharram Percy: the Church of St Martin*, Wharram: a Study of Settlement on the Yorkshire Wolds 3, Soc. for Med. Archaeol. Monograph ser. 11 (London)

Biddle, Martin, and Birthe Kjølbye-Biddle, 'The So-Called Roman Building at Much Wenlock', *JBAA* 141, 179–83

Blair, John, see sect. 7

Bond, C. J., see sect. 7

Boore, Eric J., 'Excavations at St Augustine the Less, Bristol, 1983–84', *Bristol and Avon Archaeol.* 4 (1985), 21–33 [Saxo-Norman cemetery, p. 25]

Carr, R. D., A. Tester, and P. Murphy, 'The Middle-Saxon Settlement at Staunch Meadow, Brandon', *Antiquity* 62, 371–6

Costen, Michael, 'The Church in the Landscape. Part 1. The Anglo-Saxon Period', *Aspects of the Mediaeval Landscape of Somerset*, ed. Aston, pp. 49–53

Fletcher, Eric, 'The Churches of Much Wenlock', *JBAA* 141, 178–9

Gem, Richard, 'Architecture', *The Cambridge Guide to the Arts in Britain* 1, ed. Ford, 220–45

'The English Parish Church in the 11th and Early 12th Centuries: a Great Rebuilding?', *Minsters and Parish Churches*, ed. Blair, pp. 21–30

Gilmour, B. J. J., and D. A. Stocker, *St Mark's Church and Cemetery*, Archaeol. of Lincoln 13.1 (London, 1986)

Hall, David, *The Fenland Project, Number 2: Fenland Landscapes and Settlement between Peterborough and March*, East Anglian Archaeol. 35 (Cambridge, 1987) [includes Anglo-Saxon, and Thorney]

Hall, Richard, and Mark Whyman, 'Ailcy Hill, Ripon', *Bull. of the CBA Churches Committee* 24 (1986), 17–20

Hare, Michael, *Investigations at Titchfield Church 1982–1987. An Interim Report* (privately produced, Gloucester)

Hill, Peter, 'Whithorn', *CA* 110 (July), 85–91 [major Northumbrian settlement, late 7th to early 9th century]

Hinton, David A., and C. J. Webster, 'Excavations at the Church of St. Martin, Wareham, 1985–86, and "Minsters" in South-East Dorset', *Proc. of the Dorset Nat. Hist. and Archaeol. Soc.* 109 (1987), 47–54

Holmes, John, 'A Saxon Church at West Blatchington', *Sussex Archaeol. Collections* 126, 77–91

Huggins, P. J., 'Excavations on the North Side of Sun Street, Waltham Abbey, Essex, 1974–75: Saxon Burials, Precinct Wall, and South-east Transept', *Essex Archaeology and History* 19, 117–53 [Middle Saxon cemetery, one burial with copper-alloy plate decorated in Ringerike style]

Jones, Anthea, and Jane Grenville, 'Some New Suggestions about the Pre-Conquest History of Tewkesbury and Tewkesbury Church', *Southern Hist.* 9 (1987), 9–33

Kemp, R. L., 'St. Andrew, York – Parish Church to Gilbertine Priory', *Bull. of the CBA Churches Committee* 24 (1986), 21–4

Lowe, Barbara J., *et al.*, 'Keynsham Abbey: Excavations 1961–1985', *Proc. of the Somerset Archaeol. and Nat. Hist. Soc.* 131 (1987), 81–156 [Anglo-Saxon sculpture, pp. 163–6; metalwork, pp. 138–9; cut farthing of Edward the Confessor, pp. 144–5]

Miles, Trevor J., 'The Excavation of a Saxon Cemetery and part of the Norman Castle of North Walk, Barnstable', *Proc. of the Devon Archaeol. Soc.* 44 (1986), 59–84

Milner-Gulland, Robin, 'Greatham Church: Fabric, Date, Dimensions, Implications', *Sussex Archaeol. Collections* 126, 93–103

Morris, Richard K., 'Churches in York and its Hinterland: Building Patterns and Stone Sources in the 11th and 12th Centuries', *Minsters and Parish Churches*, ed. Blair, pp. 191–9

Rady, Jonathan, 'Excavations at St. Martin's Hill, Canterbury, 1984–85', *AC* 104 (1987), 123–218 [Anglo-Saxon settlement and church]

Rahtz, Philip, and Susan M. Hirst, 'The Chapel of St Columbanus at Cheddar', *Proc. of the Somerset Archaeol. and Nat. Hist. Soc.* 131 (1987), 157–61 [the chapel of the Cheddar Anglo-Saxon palace in its later medieval phases]

Rimington, Frank, 'The Three Churches of Hackness', *Trans. of the Scarborough Archaeol. and Hist. Soc.* 26, 3–10

Rose, Edwin J., and Alan J. Davidson, '"St Catherine's Thorpe" – the Birth and Death of a Myth', *Norfolk Archaeol.* 40.2, 179–81 [Anglo-Saxon church]

Ryder, Peter, 'Aycliffe Church, a Reassessment', *Durham Archaeol. Jnl* 4, 45–51

Sherlock, D., and H. Woods, *St Augustine's Abbey – Excavations 1960–78* (Canterbury)

Tatton-Brown, Tim, see sect. 7

Tester, P. J., 'Architectural Notes on St Michael's Church, Offham', *AC* 103 (1986), 45–52

Thorpe, David A., and K. Blagrave, 'Secret Glastonbury', *Brit. Archaeol.* 7, 21–3

Bibliography for 1988

Waldron, Tony, and Gillian Waldron, 'Two Felons from Surrey', *London Archaeologist* 5.16, 443–5 [two Anglo-Saxon burials with tied hands]

Wilmott, Tony, 'Pontefract, West Yorkshire', *Bull. of the CBA Churches Committee* 24 (1986), 25–6 [church with large pre-conquest cemetery below castle]

f. Ships and seafaring

g. Sculpture on bone, stone, and wood

Bailey, Richard N., and Rosemary Cramp, *Corpus of Anglo-Saxon Stone Sculpture* II: *Cumberland, Westmorland and Lancashire North-of-the-Sands* (Oxford and New York) [includes General Introduction to the series]

Coatsworth, Elizabeth, 'Late Pre-Conquest Sculptures with the Crucifixion South of the Humber', *Bishop Æthelwold*, ed. Yorke, pp. 161–93

Düwel, Klaus, 'On the Sigurd Representations in Great Britain and Scandinavia', *Languages and Cultures: Studies in Honor of Edgar C. Polomé*, ed. Mohammad Ali Jazayery and Werner Winter, Trends in Ling., Stud. and Monographs 36 (Berlin, New York and Amsterdam), 133–56

Foster, Sally, 'A Gazetteer of the Anglo-Saxon Sculpture in Historic Somerset', *Proc. of the Somerset Archaeol. and Nat. Hist. Soc.* 131 (1987), 49–80

Harbison, Peter, 'Two Panels on the Wirksworth Slab', *Derbyshire Archaeol. Jnl* 107 (1987), 36–40

Lang, James, *Anglo-Saxon Sculpture*, Shire Archaeologies 52 (Princes Risborough)

Lowe, Barbara J., *et al.*, see sect. 10*e*

Ohlgren, Thomas H., 'The Joys of Valhalla: a Cross Fragment from Jurby, Isle of Man', *OEN* 21.2, 40–1

West, J. K., 'Architectural Sculpture in Parish Churches of the 11th- and 12th-Century West Midlands: Some Problems in Assessing the Evidence', *Minsters and Parish Churches*, ed. Blair, pp. 159–67

White, R. H., 'Viking-Period Sculpture at Neston, Cheshire', *Jnl of the Chester Archaeol. Soc.* 69 (1986), 45–58

Yapp, W. B., 'The Iconography of the Font at Toller Fratrum', *Proc. of the Dorset Nat. Hist. and Archaeol. Soc.* 109 (1987), 1–4 [font previously thought to be Anglo-Saxon now placed in the 11th century]

h. Metal-work and other minor objects

Ager, Barry, and Brian Gilmour, 'A Pattern-Welded Anglo-Saxon Sword from Acklam Wold, North Yorkshire', *Yorkshire Archaeol. Jnl* 60, 13–23

[Anon.] 'Edinburgh Castle', *CA* 112 (Dec.), 162 [bone comb of 8th- to 10th-century type, ? Anglian]

[Anon.] 'News Round-Up', *Brit. Archaeol.* 5, 27 [early 11th-century wooden knife handle]

[Anon.] 'Three Anglo-Saxon Small-Long Brooches from Leicestershire', *Trans. of the Leicestershire Archaeol. and Hist. Soc.* 62, 77–80

Fasham, P. J., 'Archaeological Investigations at Ipsley, 1968 and 1969', *Trans. of the*

Bibliography for 1988

Worcestershire Archaeol. Soc. 11, 7–22 [includes Anglo-Saxon francisca]

Graham-Campbell, James, 'Two 9th-Century Anglo-Saxon Strap-Ends from East Sussex', *Sussex Archaeol. Collections* 126, 239–41

Hawkes, Sonia Chadwick, 'Some Early Anglo-Saxon Objects from East Kent', *AC* 104 (1987), 1–7

Hood, Nancy, and George Speake, 'An Anglo-Saxon Gilt-Bronze Lozenge-Shaped Mount from Culham, Now in Abingdon Museum', *Oxoniensia* 52 (1987), 184–5

Huggins, P. J., see sect. 10e

King, David, 'Petrology, Dating and Distribution in Querns and Millstones. The Results of Research in Bedfordshire, Buckinghamshire, Hertfordshire and Middlesex', *Bull. of the Inst. of Archaeol. London* 23 (1986), 65–126

Kruse, Susan E., 'Ingots and Weight Units in Viking Age Silver Hoards', *World Archaeol.* 20.2 (Oct.), 285–301

Kruse, Susan E., Robert D. Smith, and Katharine Starling, 'Experimental Casting of Silver Ingots', *Hist. Metallurgy* 22, 87–92

Lowe, Barbara J., *et al.*, see sect. 10e

McDonnell, J. G., 'The Metallurgy of Anglo-Scandinavian Knives', *Crafts of the Blacksmith*, ed. Scott and Cleere, pp. 87–9

'The Study of Iron Smithing Residues', *Crafts of the Blacksmith*, ed. Scott and Cleere, pp. 47–52

Margeson, Sue, 'A Bird-shaped Brooch from Stoke Holy Cross', *Norfolk Archaeol.* 40.2, 199

Mortimer, Catherine, 'Anglo-Saxon Copper Alloys from Lechlade, Gloucestershire', *Oxford Jnl of Archaeol.* 7, 227–33

O'Connor, Sonia, 'The Investigation of the Coppergate Helmet', *Brit. Archaeol.* 6, 16–21

Ottaway, P., 'Anglo-Scandinavian Knives from 16–22 Coppergate, York', *Crafts of the Blacksmith*, ed. Scott and Cleere, pp. 83–6

Oxley, J., 'A Possible Saxon Smithing Site and Further Evidence from *SOU 29*, Southampton', *Proc. of the Hampshire Field Club and Archaeol. Soc.* 44, 41–7

Parker, Elizabeth C., 'Recent Acquisitions of Medieval Art by American Museums', *Gesta* 26 (1987), 79–80 [Fig. 7. Anglo-Saxon great square-headed brooch, 6th century.]

Peirce, Ian, see sect. 7

Riddler, Ian, 'Late Saxon or Late Roman? A Comb from Pudding Lane', *London Archaeologist* 5.14, 372–4

Rogers, Nicky, 'Quern Queries', *Interim: Archaeol. in York* 13.4, 35–8

Rudling, David, 'A Saxon Coin-Brooch from Alfriston', *Sussex Archaeol. Collections* 126, 241

Scott, B. G., and H. Cleere, ed., *The Crafts of the Blacksmith*, UISPP Comité pour la Sidérurgie Ancienne, 1984 Symposium, Belfast (Belfast)

Sherlock, Stephen J., 'An Anglo-Saxon Spearhead from Thornaby, Cleveland', *AAe* 5th ser. 16, 251

Stewart, J., 'An Anglo-Saxon Strap-End from Winterbourne, Bristol', *Bristol and Avon Archaeol.* 6 (1987), 62

Welch, M. G., 'A Saxon Equal-Arm Brooch from Keymer, Sussex', *AntJ* 62 (1987), 364–5

White, A. J., 'Copper-Alloy Combs from Britain and Frisia', *MA* 32, 212–13

Willson, John, 'A Bronze Horse Brooch from Dover', *Kent Archaeol. Rev.* 92, 33 [possible Anglo-Saxon date suggested]

i. Inscriptions

Foster, Sally M., 'Early Medieval Inscriptions at Holcombe, Somerset', *MA* 32, 208–11

Gosling, Kevin, 'An Anglo-Saxon Runic Inscription from Wardley, near Uppingham (SK 831002)', *Trans. of the Leicestershire Archaeol. and Hist. Soc.* 62, 80–2

j. Pottery and glass

Andrews, P., ed., see sect. 8

Arnold, C. J., 'Early Anglo-Saxon Pottery of the "Illington-Lackford" type', *Oxford Jnl of Archaeol.* 7, 343–54

Brassington, Maurice, 'Note on an Anglo-Saxon Accessory Vessel from Derby', *Derbyshire Archaeol. Jnl* 107 (1987), 35

Gilmour, Lauren Adams, *Early Medieval Pottery from Flaxengate, Lincoln*, Archaeol. of Lincoln 17.2 (London)

Leach, H. N., 'Stamford Ware Fabrics', *Med. Ceramics* 11 (1987), 69–74

McCarthy, Michael R., and Catherine M. Brooks, *Medieval Pottery in Britain AD 900–1600* (Leicester)

Mainman, Ailsa, 'The Black (and Grey) Market in Pots', *Interim: Archaeol. in York* 13.2, 33–6 [imported pottery of Anglian period]

Riddler, I. D., 'Pot Dies from Southampton: a Note', *Southampton Finds*, 1: *The Coins and Pottery from Hamwic*, ed. P. Andrews, Southampton Archaeol. Monographs 4 (Southampton), 125

Timby, J. R., 'The Middle Saxon Pottery', *Southampton Finds*, 1: *The Coins and Pottery from Hamwic*, ed. P. Andrews, Southampton Archaeol. Monographs 4 (Southampton), 73–123

Vince, Alan, 'Did They Use Pottery in the Welsh Marshes and the West Midlands between the 5th and 12th Centuries AD?', *From Roman Town to Norman Castle*, ed. Burl, pp. 40–55

k. Musical instruments

11. REVIEWS

Alcock, Leslie, *Economy, Society and Warfare among the Britons and Saxons* (Cardiff, 1987): C. J. Arnold, *Welsh Hist. Rev.* 14, 301–5; R. K. Sherk, *Albion* 20, 77–8

Anderson, James E., *Two Literary Riddles in the Exeter Book* (Norman, OK, and

Bibliography for 1988

London, 1986): M. Nelson, *Speculum* 63, 614–17; J. Stevenson, *MÆ* 57, 298–9

Andrews, P., ed., *Southampton Finds* 1: *the Coins and Pottery from Hamwic*, Southampton Archaeol. Monographs 4 (Southampton): R. Hodges, *Nature* 6 October 1988, 498–9

Arnold, C. J., *An Archaeology of the Early Anglo-Saxon Kingdoms* (London and New York): M. G. Welch, *London Archaeologist* 6, 24

Aston, Michael, and Rob Iles, ed., *The Archaeology of Avon: a Review from the Neolithic to the Middle Ages* (Bristol, 1987): J. Russell, *Trans. of the Bristol and Gloucestershire Archaeol. Soc.* 106, 234–7

Baldwin, John R., and Ian D. Whyte, ed., *The Scandinavians in Cumbria* (Edinburgh, 1985): E. Christiansen, *EHR* 103, 713–14

Bammesberger, Alfred, *English Etymology* (Heidelberg, 1984): G. Bauer, *Kratylos* 33, 204–6; P. Bierbaumer, *IF* 93, 333–7; F. Wenisch, *Anglia* 106, 146–7

Linguistic Notes on Old English Poetic Texts (Heidelberg, 1986): N. Jacobs, *MÆ* 57, 92–4; L. Melazzo, *Kratylos* 33, 202–4

A Sketch of Diachronic English Morphology (Regensburg, 1984): P. Bierbaumer, *Anglia* 106, 147–9; J. Insley, *ASNSL* 225, 365–9

ed., *Problems of Old English Lexicography* (Regensburg, 1985): R. Gleissner, *BGDSL* (Tübingen) 110, 423–8; K. R. Grinda, *IF* 93, 344–52; D. G. Scragg, *Anglia* 106, 150–3

Bang-Anderson, Arne, Basil Greenhill and Egil Harald Grude, ed., *The North Sea: A Highway of Economic and Cultural Exchange: Character – History* (Oxford, 1985): A. Fenton, *Scottish Hist. Rev.* 66 (1987), 74–5

Bately, Janet M., ed., *The Anglo-Saxon Chronicle: MS A* (Cambridge, 1986): H. R. Loyn, *JEH* 39, 295–6; T. Reuter, *DAEM* 44, 233–4; E. G. Stanley, *RES* 39, 96–7

Bates, David, *A Bibliography of Domesday Book* (Woodbridge, 1986): B. Bachrach, *Albion* 20, 450–1

Beresford, G., *Goltho: the Development of an Early Medieval Manor* c. *850–1150* (London, 1987): P. Everson, *Lincolnshire Hist. and Archaeol.* 23, 93–9; R. A. Higham, *MA* 32, 317–18

Bergner, Heinz, *Die englische Literatur in Text und Darstellung* 1: *Mittelalter* (Stuttgart, 1986): A. Crépin, *CCM* 31, 62–3

Bernstein, David J., *The Mystery of the Bayeux Tapestry* (London, 1986): B. Golding, *History* 73, 113–14

Bjork, Robert E., *The Old English Verse Saints' Lives* (Toronto, Buffalo and London, 1985): M. McC. Gatch, *JEGP* 87, 576–7; J. Harris, *Speculum* 63, 123–6

Blackburn, M. A. S., ed., *Anglo-Saxon Monetary History. Essays in Memory of Michael Dolley* (Leicester, 1986): N.U.F[ornander], *Svensk Numismatisk Tidskrift* 1988, 138–9; F. Dumas, *Revue Numismatique* 6th series 30, 285–6; H. Frère, *Revue Belge de Numismatique* 134, 214; B. Kluge, *Berliner Numismatische Forschungen* 2, 114–15; G. van der Meer, *NChron* 148, 277–80; P. H. Robinson, *AntJ* 68, 155–6

Bodden, Mary Catherine, ed. and trans., *The Old English Finding of the True Cross* (Cambridge, 1987): L. W[ankenne], *RB* 98, 232–3

Boon, George C., *Welsh Coin Hoards 1979–81* (Cardiff, 1986): H. E. Pagan, *NChron* 148, 280–1

Bridges, Margaret Enid, *Generic Contrast in Old English Hagiographical Poetry* (Copenhagen, 1984): N. F. Blake, *YES* 18, 249–50; R. D. Fulk, *PQ* 67, 270–2; D. G. Scragg, *Anglia* 106, 484–6

Brooke, C. N. L., *The Church and the Welsh Border in the Central Middle Ages* (Woodbridge, 1986): H. Pryce, *Welsh Hist. Rev.* 14, 130–1; David H. Williams, *AntJ* 67 (1987), 439–40

Brown, George Hardin, *Bede the Venerable* (Boston, 1987): W. T. Foley, *CH* 57, 222–3

Brown, Phyllis Rugg, *et al.*, ed., *Modes of Interpretation in Old English Literature* (Toronto, Buffalo and London, 1986): J. Roberts, *N&Q* 35, 202–3; D. G. Scragg, *RES* 39, 277–8

Brown, R. Allen, *The Normans and the Norman Conquest* 2nd edn (Woodbridge, 1985): G. Pon, *CCM* 31, 190–1

Butler, L. A. S., and R. K. Morris, ed., *The Anglo-Saxon Church* (London, 1986): M. McC. Gatch, *CH* 57, 81

Cameron, Angus, *et al.*, ed., *Dictionary of Old English: D* (Toronto, 1986): A. J. Frantzen, *Amer. N&Q* ns 1, 35–8; C. B. Hieatt, *Univ. of Toronto Quarterly* 58, 102–4; K. S. Kiernan, *Envoi* 1.1, 87–92; H. Sauer, *ASNSL* 225, 370–5

Campbell, James, *Essays in Anglo-Saxon History* (London, 1986): R. Abels, *Albion* 20, 293–5; S. Keynes, *JEH* 39, 296–7

Chance, Jane, *Woman as Hero in Old English Literature* (Syracuse, NY, 1986): C. Brewer, *RES* 39, 280–1; H. O'Donoghue, *MÆ* 57, 299–300; H. Weissman, *Speculum* 63, 134–6

Clemoes, Peter, *et al.*, ed., *Anglo-Saxon England* 14 (Cambridge, 1986): H. R. Loyn, *JEH* 38 (1987), 452–3

Copley, Gordon, *Archaeology and Place-Names in the Fifth and Sixth Centuries* (Oxford, 1986): B. Cox, *Nomina* 11, 166–9

Cowgill, J., M. de Neergaard and N. Griffiths, *Knives and Scabbards* (London, 1987): S. Margeson, *MA* 32, 319–21; P. Ottaway, *Antiquity* 62, 607; F. Verhaeghe, *Helinium* 28.2, 307–8

Cramp, Rosemary, *Corpus of Anglo-Saxon Stone Sculpture in England* I: *County Durham and Northumberland* (London, 1984): A. Hamlin, *Jnl of the R. Soc. of Antiquaries of Ireland* 116, 125–6; L. Ness, *Speculum* 63, 383–6

Crawford, Barbara E., *Scotland in the Early Middle Ages* 2: *Scandinavian Scotland* (Leicester, 1987): P. Bibire, *CMCS* 16, 108–9; R. Power, *Scottish Hist. Rev.* 67, 73–4

Cross, J. E., *Cambridge Pembroke College MS 25* (London, 1987): P. V[erbraken], *RB* 98, 407

Davies, Wendy, and Paul Fouracre, ed., *The Settlement of Disputes in Early Medieval Europe* (Cambridge, 1986): D. Jenkins, *CMCS* 15, 89–92; D. A. Westrup, *Michigan Law Rev.* 1988. 5, 1430–3

Drewett, Peter, David Rudling and Mark Gardiner, *The South East to AD 1000* (London and New York): D. Turner, *London Archaeologist* 6.1, 24–5

Dumville, David N., ed., *The Historia Brittonum* III: *The 'Vatican' Recension* (Cambridge, 1985): D. Corner, *EHR* 103, 172–3; D. S. Evans, *Jnl of Welsh Ecclesiastical*

Hist. 2 (1985), 94–5; L. M. Matheson, *Speculum* 63, 147–9; G. Orlandi, *CMCS* 15, 104–6; T. Reuter, *DAEM* 44, 234–5; B. K. Vollman, *Anglia* 106, 212–15

Dumville, David, and Michael Lapidge, ed., *The Annals of St Neots, with Vita Prima Sancti Neoti* (Cambridge, 1985): N. P. Brooks, *EHR* 103, 471–2; M. Griffith, *MÆ* 57, 98–9; T. Reuter, *DAEM* 44, 233; H. Vollrath, *Anglia* 106, 211–12

Elmer, Willi, *Diachronic Grammar: the History of Old and Middle English Subjectless Sentences* (Tübingen, 1981): A. Lutz, *Anglia* 106, 466–76

Evans, A. C., *The Sutton Hoo Ship Burial* (London, 1986): H. F. Hamerow, *Hist. and Archaeol. Rev.* 3, 50

Everitt, Alan, *Continuity and Colonization. The Evolution of Kentish Settlement* (Leicester, 1986): D. Hooke, *Jnl of Hist. Geography* 13 (1987), 423–4; D. Hooke, *Landscape Hist.* 9 (1987), 81–2; R. T. Rowley, *LH* 18, 31–3; J. Thirsk, *AC* 104 (1987), 392–5; K. P. Witney, *Hist. and Archaeol. Rev.* 3, 50–1

Evison, Vera I., *Dover: the Buckland Anglo-Saxon Cemetery* (London, 1987): T. M. Dickinson, *AntJ* 68, 154; S. C. Hawkes, *AC* 104 (1987), 389–92; P. T. Keller, *Kent Archaeol. Rev.* 92, 34–5

Faull, Margaret L., ed., *Studies in Late Anglo-Saxon Settlement* (Oxford, 1984): J. Blair, *EHR* 103, 96–7

Fausbøll, Else, ed., *Fifty-Six Ælfric Fragments* (Copenhagen, 1986): M. Clayton, *MÆ* 57, 297–8; M. R. Godden, *RES* 39, 529–31; David Yerkes, *Speculum* 63, 890

Fell, Christine, Cecily Clark and Elizabeth Williams, *Women in Anglo-Saxon England and the Impact of 1066* (London and Bloomington, IN, 1984): M. Budny, *AntJ* 67 (1987), 431–3; K. F. Drew, *Albion* 20, 448–50; A. Fischer, *Anglia* 106, 488–92; E. Fletcher, *MA* 32, 332

Fellows-Jensen, Gillian, *Scandinavian Settlement Names in the North-West* (Copenhagen, 1985): V. E. Watts, *Northern Hist.* 23 (1987), 229–30

Fischer, Andreas, *Engagement, Wedding, and Marriage in Old English* (Heidelberg, 1986): K. R. Grinda, *Anglia* 106, 476–84; E. G. Stanley, *N&Q* 35, 1

Frantzen, Allen J., *King Alfred* (Boston, 1986): H. Sauer, *Anglia* 106, 487–8; E. G. Stanley, *N&Q* 35, 203–4

The Literature of Penance in Anglo-Saxon England (New Brunswick, NJ, 1983): N. Bériou, *Le Moyen Age* 94, 320–3; B. Lindström, *SN* 60, 139–41; P. E. Szarmach, *Speculum* 63, 392–4

Ganz, Peter, ed., *The Role of the Book in Medieval Culture* (Turnhout, 1986): R. McKitterick, *The Library* ns 10, 347–9

Gelling, Margaret, *Place-Names in the Landscape* (London, 1984): M. Welch, *Bull. of the Inst. of Archaeol. London* 23, Review Suppl., pp. 12–13

Gilmour, B. J. J., and D. A. Stocker, *St Mark's Church and Cemetery* (London, 1986): R. E. Glasscock, *JEH* 39, 142–3; W. Rodwell, *Lincolnshire Hist. and Archaeol.* 22, 50; W. Rodwell, *MA* 32, 335

Green, Martin, ed., *The Old English Elegies: New Essays in Criticism and Research* (Rutherford, Madison and Teaneck, NJ, Toronto and London, 1983): H. Sauer, *BGDSL* (Tübingen) 110, 303–6

Greenfield, Stanley B., and Daniel G. Calder, *A New Critical History of Old English Literature* (New York and London, 1986): D. K. Fry, *Envoi* 1.1, 127–9; M. McC.

Gatch, *CH* 57, 80–1; J. C. Pope, *MLR* 83, 660–2; H. Sauer, *N&Q* 35, 506–7; E. G. Stanley, *Comparative Lit.* 40, 286–9

Grierson, Philip, and Mark Blackburn, *Medieval European Coinage* I. *The Early Middle Ages (5th–10th Centuries)* (Cambridge, 1986): S. Coupland, *History* 73, 286–7; B. Kluge, *Berliner Numismatische Forschungen* 2, 113–14; D. M. Metcalf, *MA* 32, 315–16; D. M. Metcalf, *NChron* 148, 271–2; A. M. Stahl, *Speculum* 63, 933–5; I. Stewart, *AntJ* 68, 152–3

Harris, B. E., ed., assisted by A. T. Thacker, *Victoria County History of Chester* 1: *Physique, Prehistory, Roman, Anglo-Saxon and Domesday* (London, 1987): F. H. Thompson, *AntJ* 67, 406–7; I. N. Wood, *Northern Hist.* 24, 227–31

Hawkes, Sonia Chadwick, *et al.*, ed., *Anglo-Saxon Studies in Archaeology and History* 4 (Oxford, 1985): C. Hills, *Germania* 66, 268–9

Heighway, Carolyn, *Anglo-Saxon Gloucestershire* (Gloucester, 1987): P. Rahtz, *Trans. of the Bristol and Gloucestershire Archaeol. Soc.* 106, 232–3

Herren, Michael W., *The Hisperica Famina* II: *Related Poems. A Critical Edition with English Translation and Philological Commentary* (Toronto, 1987): J. Stevenson, *CMCS* 16, 100–3

Higham, Nick, *The Northern Counties to A.D. 1000* (London, 1986): L. Butler, *Northern Hist.* 23, 245–6; G. Jobey, *AAe* 5th ser., 16, 253; H. Welfare, *Antiquity* 62, 194–5; J. H. Williams, *AntJ* 67, 405–6

Hill, David, and D. M. Metcalf, ed., *Sceattas in England and on the Continent* (Oxford, 1984): A. Dierkens, *Revue Belge de Philologie et d'Histoire* 66, 457

Hjertstedt, Ingrid, *Middle English Nicknames in the Lay Subsidy Rolls for Warwickshire* (Uppsala, 1987): G. Fellows-Jensen, *Namn och Bygd* 76, 220–3; A. D. Mills, *Studia Anthroponymica Scandinavica* 6, 171–4

Holt, J. C., ed., *Domesday Studies* (Woodbridge, 1987): B. Bachrach, *Albion* 20, 451–5

Hooke, Della, *The Anglo-Saxon Landscape: the Kingdom of the Hwicce* (Manchester, 1985): M. Beresford, *Agricultural Hist. Rev.* 36, 205–6; P. Dixon, *Jnl of Hist. Geography* 13, 424–5; D. Kenyon, *JEPNS* 18, 48–9; O. Rackham, *Southern Hist.* 9, 161–2; B. Yorke, *Midland Hist.* 12, 122–3

   The Landscape of Anglo-Saxon Staffordshire: the Charter Evidence (Keele, 1983): P. Everson, *Landscape Hist.* 9, 82–3; B. Yorke, *Midland Hist.* 12, 122–3

   ed., *Medieval Villages: a Review of Current Work* (Oxford, 1985): N. J. Higham, *Nomina* 11 (1987), 170–2

Hoover, David L., *A New Theory of Old English Meter* (New York, Bern and Frankfurt am Main, 1985): M. Griffith, *MÆ* 57, 96–7

Howe, Nicholas, *The Old English Catalogue Poems* (Copenhagen, 1985): T. D. Hill, *Papers on Lang. and Lit.* 24, 448–9; J. F. Kiteley, *MÆ* 57, 97–8; R. A. Shoaf, *Genre* 21, 117–18

Hurst, H. R., *Gloucester. The Roman and Later Defences. Excavations on the E. Defences and a Reassessment of the Defensive Sequence* (Cambridge, 1986): P. Davenport, *Hist. and Archaeol. Rev.* 3, 66; C. Heighway, *AntJ* 67, 419–20

Jones, Charles W., *et al.*, ed., *Bedae Venerabilis Opera*, VI: *Opera Didascalica, 2. De Temporum Ratione Liber* (Turnhout, 1977): A. Placanica, *SM* 3rd ser., 28 (1987), 793–8

Jones, Martin, *England Before Domesday* (London, 1986): N. D. Balaam, *JBAA* 141, 188–9

Jonsson, Kenneth, *The New Era. The Reformation of the Late Anglo-Saxon Coinage* (Stockholm, 1987): M. Blackburn, *NCirc* 1988, 118–19; N.U.F[ornander], *Svensk Numismatisk Tidskrift* 1988, 139–40; T. Talvio, *Nordisk Numismatisk Unions Medlemsblad* 1988, 152–3

Viking-Age Hoards and Late Anglo-Saxon Coins (Stockholm, 1987): B. Kluge, *Berliner Numismatische Forschungen* 2, 115–16

Ker, N. R., *Books, Collectors and Libraries*, ed. Andrew G. Watson (London and Ronceverte, WV, 1985): M. Gibson, *MÆ* 57, 91–2

Kiernan, Kevin S., *The Thorkelin Transcripts of 'Beowulf'* (Copenhagen, 1986): R. P. Creed, *ELN* 26.1, 75–7; M. Griffith, *MÆ* 57, 296–7; B. Lindström, *SN* 60, 264–7; J. Wilcox, *PQ* 67, 267–9

Klegraf, Josef, ed. and trans., *Die altenglische 'Judith'* (Stuttgart, 1987): X. Dekeyser, *Leuvense Bijdragen* 77, 485–6

Kluge, Bernd, *State Museum Berlin, Coin Cabinet, Anglo-Saxon, Anglo-Norman, and Hiberno-Norse Coins. SCBI* 36 (Oxford, 1987): N. U. F[ornander], *Svensk Numismatisk Tidskrift* 1988, 21; K. Jonsson, *Svensk Numismatisk Tidskrift* 1988, 268–9; H. E. Pagan, *BNJ* 57 (1987), 154–5

Kuhn, Sherman M., *Studies in the Language and Poetics of Anglo-Saxon England* (Ann Arbor, 1984): N. F. Blake, *Lore and Lang.* 7.1, 120

Lapidge, Michael, and David Dumville, ed., *Gildas: New Approaches* (Woodbridge, 1984): R. P. C. Hanson, *Britannia* 17, 462–3; A. P. Smyth, *EHR* 103, 162–3

Lapidge, Michael, and Helmut Gneuss, ed., *Learning and Literature in Anglo-Saxon England* (Cambridge, 1985): A. Bammesberger, *Anglia* 106, 198–200; T. Reuter, *DAEM* 44, 196–7; J. B. Trahern, Jr, *JEGP* 87, 433–7

Lapidge, Michael, and James L. Rosier, trans., *Aldhelm: the Poetic Works* (Cambridge, 1985): B. Löfstedt, *Orpheus* 9, 366–9

Lapidge, Michael, and Richard Sharpe, *A Bibliography of Celtic-Latin Literature 40–1200* (Dublin, 1986): L. Fleuriot, *Études Celtiques* 24 (1987), 347–8

Loyn, H. R., *The Governance of Anglo-Saxon England* (London, 1984): J. Beauroy, *CCM* 31, 75–7

Lutz, Angelika, ed., *Die Version G der Angelsächsischen Chronik* (Munich, 1981): E. G. Stanley, *RES* 39, 281–2

Mayr-Harting, Henry, and R. I. Moore, ed., *Studies in Medieval History Presented to R. H. C. Davis* (London and Ronceverte, 1985): H. Pryce, *Welsh Hist. Rev.* 13 (1987), 485–7

McCarthy, Michael R., and Catherine M. Brooks, *Medieval Pottery in Britain A.D. 900–1600* (Leicester): A. Vince, *Antiquity* 62, 811–12

McDonald, John, and G. D. Snooks, *Domesday Economy: a New Approach to Anglo-Norman History* (Oxford, 1986): H. B. Clarke, *Agricultural Hist. Rev.* 36, 206–7

Metcalf, D. M., ed., *Coinage in Ninth-Century Northumbria* (Oxford, 1987): M. Blackburn, *NCirc* 1988, 318

Miles, David, ed., *Archaeology at Barton Court Farm, Abingdon, Oxon: an Investigation of Late Neolithic, Iron Age, Romano-British, and Saxon Settlements* (London, 1986):

K. Branigan, *Jnl of Archaeol. Science* 14, 229–30; R. Reece, *Bull. of the Inst. of Archaeol. London* 24, Review Suppl. pp. 6–7

Mitchell, Bruce, *Old English Syntax* (Oxford and New York, 1985): F. C. Robinson, *Speculum* 63, 700–2

Mitchell, Bruce, and Fred C. Robinson, *A Guide to Old English*, 4th ed. (Oxford and New York, 1986): J. Roberts, *N&Q* 35, 349–50

Moffat, Douglas, ed., *The Soul's Address to the Body: the Worcester Fragments* (East Lansing, MI, 1987): J. Johansen, *Eng. Stud. in Canada* 14, 343–7

Moulden, Joan, and D. Tweddle, *Anglo-Scandinavian Settlement South-West of the Ouse* (London, 1986): L. Butler, *Yorkshire Archaeol. Jnl* 59, 213–14

Muir, Bernard James, ed., *A Pre-Conquest English Prayer-Book* (Woodbridge): P. V[erbraken], *RB* 98, 411–12

Neuman de Vegvar, Carol L., *The Northumbrian Renaissance: a Study in the Transmission of Style* (Selinsgrove, PA, Toronto and London, 1987): J. Henderson, *Burlington Mag.* 130, 934

Obst, Wolfgang, *Der Rhythmus des Beowulf: eine Akzent- und Takttheorie* (Heidelberg, 1987): E. G. Stanley, *N&Q* 35, 1

Ogura, Michiko, *Old English 'Impersonal' Verbs and Expressions* (Copenhagen, 1986): H. Fujiwara, *Stud. in Eng. Lit.* (Tokyo) 1988 Eng. Number, pp. 124–7

Ohlgren, Thomas H., comp., *Insular and Anglo-Saxon Illuminated Manuscripts* (New York and London, 1986): L. Nees, *Speculum* 63, 207–10; S. J. Pearman, *Visual Resources* 4, 411–13

Owen-Crocker, Gale, *Dress in Anglo-Saxon England* (Manchester, 1986): M. Budny, *AntJ* 67, 431–3; G. Clauss, *Germania* 66, 595–7; S. Lebecq, *Revue du Nord* 70, 441–2; R. Samson, *MA* 32, 327–8; K. Staniland, *Costume* 22, 118–19; E. G. Stanley, *N&Q* 35, 204–6

Pächt, Otto, *Book Illumination in the Middle Ages: An Introduction* (Oxford and New York, 1986): M. Camille, *Manuscripta* 32, 50–1

Padel, O. J., *Cornish Place-Name Elements* (Nottingham, 1985): P. Y. Lambert, *CMCS* 15, 102–3; K. H. Schmidt, *Zeitschrift für Celtische Philologie* 42 (1987), 401

Page, R. I., *Runes* (London, Berkeley and Los Angeles, 1987): E. A. Ebbinghaus, *General Ling.* 28, 149–51

Pinsker, Hans, and Waltraud Ziegler, ed. and trans., *Die altenglischen Rätsel des Exeterbuchs* (Heidelberg, 1985): J. E. Anderson, *Speculum* 63, 981–2

Pirie, E. J. E., *Post-Roman Coins from York Excavations 1971–1981* (London, 1986): L. Butler, *Yorkshire Archaeol. Jnl* 59, 213–14

Rackham, Oliver, *The History of the Countryside* (London, 1986): C. Watkins, *Jnl of Hist. Geography* 13, 427–8

Remnant, Mary, *English Bowed Instruments from Anglo-Saxon to Tudor Times* (Oxford, 1986): J. Montagu, *AntJ* 67, 433–4

Reynolds, S., *Kingdoms and Communities in Western Europe, 900–1300* (Oxford, 1984): R. Fossier, *CCM* 30, 192–3

Roberts, Gildas, trans., *Beowulf* (St John's, Nfld, 1984): C.-D. Wetzel, *Anglia* 106, 200–3

Robinson, Fred C., *'Beowulf' and the Appositive Style* (Knoxville, 1985): W. G. Busse, *Anglia* 106, 203–10

Rodwell, W. J., and K. A. Rodwell, *Rivenhall: Investigations of a Villa, Church, and Village, 1950–1977* (London, 1986): C. Hayfield, *MA* 32, 322–4

Royal Commission on the Historical Monuments of England, *Churches of South-East Wiltshire* (London, 1987): R. Morris, *Antiquity* 62, 179–81; R. Peers, *JBAA* 141, 202–3

Russom, Geoffrey, *Old English Meter and Linguistic Theory* (Cambridge, 1987): J. A. Burrow, *London Rev. of Books* 21 January, p. 19; C. B. McCully, *Lingua* 75, 379–83

Ryan, Michael, ed., *Ireland and Insular Art A.D. 500–1200* (Dublin, 1987): G. Henderson, *Antiquity* 62, 383–4; C. Hicks, *MA* 32, 328–30

Sawyer, Peter, *Domesday Book: a Reassessment* (London, 1985): R. P. Abels, *AHR* 92, 395–6; D. Hooke, *Jnl of Hist. Geography* 13, 421–3; G. A. Loud, *Northern Hist.* 23, 231–5; R. Morris, *MA* 32, 318–19

Scarfe, Norman, *Suffolk in the Middle Ages* (Woodbridge, 1986): R. Abels, *Speculum* 63, 992–3; D. MacCulloch, *AntJ* 67, 430–1

Schofield, John, and R. Leech, *Urban Archaeology in Britain* (London, 1987): D. A. Hinton, *MA* 32, 331

Schove, Justin, with Alan Fletcher, *Chronology of Eclipses and Comets AD 1–1000* (Woodbridge, 1984): A. Tihon, *L'Antiquité Classique* 56, 489–90

Shoesmith, R., *Hereford City Excavations* III: *The Finds* (London, 1985): R. A. Griffiths, *Welsh Hist. Rev.* 13 (1987), 359–60

Smith, Andrea B., ed., *The Anonymous Parts of the Old English Hexateuch* (Cambridge, 1985): J. E. Cross, *Speculum* 63, 232; T. F. Hoad, *MLR* 83, 937–9

Spitzbart, Günter, trans., *Beda der Ehrwürdige, Kirchengeschichte des englischen Volkes* (Darmstadt, 1982): G. Michiels, *Recherches de Théologie Ancienne et Médiévale* 54 (1987), 271

Spufford, Peter, *Money and its Use in Medieval Europe* (Cambridge): D. M. Metcalf, *NCirc* 1988, 286

Stafford, Pauline, *The East Midlands in the Early Middle Ages* (Leicester, 1985): M. Beresford, *Agricultural Hist. Rev.* 36, 205–6; P. Everson, *Lincolnshire Hist. and Archaeol.* 22, 66–7

Stanley, E. G., 'Unideal Principles of Editing Old English Verse', *PBA* 70 (1984), 231–73: N. F. Blake, *MLR* 83, 659–60; N. Jacobs, *MÆ* 57, 96–7

Svensson, Örjan, *Saxon Place-Names in East Cornwall* (Lund, 1987): M. Gelling, *N&Q* 35, 201–2; J. Insley, *Ortnamnssällskapets i Uppsala Årsskrift*, 55–60; M. J. Swanton, *Devon and Cornwall N&Q* 36.2, 75–8; M. Wakelin, *MÆ* 57, 101

Swanton, Michael, *English Literature before Chaucer* (London and New York, 1987): B. Millett, *Envoi* 1.1, 170–6

Szarmach, Paul E., and Virginia Darrow Oggins, ed., *Sources of Anglo-Saxon Culture* (Kalamazoo, 1986): J. Campbell, *History* 73, 111–12; J. D. Pheifer, *RES* 39, 278–80

Tanaka, Masayoshi, *The Evolution of Medieval English Towns* (Tokyo, 1987): K. Akazawa, *Jnl of Historical Stud.* (Tokyo) 585, 54–60; Y. Aoyama, *Shigaku-Zasshi*

(Tokyo) 97.1, 96–104; Y. Miyoshi, *Legal Hist. Rev.* (Tokyo) 37, 287–93; K. Ugawa, *Jnl of Agrarian Hist.* (Tokyo) 118, 61–2

Taylor, Simon, ed., *The Anglo-Saxon Chronicle: MS B* (Cambridge and Totowa, NJ, 1983): D. B. Schneider, *ASNSL* 224 (1987), 389–90

Thomas, [Anthony] Charles, *Celtic Britain* (London, 1986): A. A. M. Duncan, *Scottish Hist. Rev.* 67, 70–1

Thompson, E. A., *Saint Germanus of Auxerre and the End of Roman Britain* (Woodbridge, 1984): L. Fleuriot, *Études Celtiques* 24 (1987), 350–1; J. N. L. Myres, *Britannia* 17, 458–60

Todd, Malcolm, *The South-West to AD 1000* (London and New York, 1987): H. Welfare, *Antiquity* 62, 194–5

Tweddle, D., *Finds from Parliament Street and Other Sites in the City Centre* (London, 1986): L. Butler, *Yorkshire Archaeol. Jnl* 59, 213–14

Tylecote, R. F., and B. J. J. Gilmour, *The Metallography of Early Ferrous Edge Tools and Edged Weapons*, (Oxford, 1986): B. Scott, *Hist. Metallurgy* 22, 114

Vollrath, Hanna, *Die Synoden Englands bis 1066* (Paderborn, 1985): M. Brett, *JTS* 39, 623–8; H. Plumat, *Nouvelle Revue Théologique* 110, 132–3

Wamers, Egon, *Insularer Metallschmuck in wikingerzeitlichen Gräbern Nordeuropas* (Neumünster, 1985): C. D. Morris, *AntJ* 68, 158–9

Warner, Peter, *Greens, Commons, and Clayland Colonisation: the Origins and Development of Green-Side Settlement in East Suffolk* (Leicester, 1987): T. Williamson, *MA* 32, 321–2

Watkins, Malcolm J., *Gloucester: the Normans and Domesday – Exhibition Catalogue and Guide* (Gloucester, 1987): M. W. Ponsford, *Trans. of the Bristol and Gloucestershire Archaeol. Soc.* 105, 254–5

Watts, Lorna, and Philip Rahtz, *Mary-le-Port, Bristol. Excavations 1962–1963* (Bristol, 1985): A. Kidd, *Bristol and Avon Archaeol.* 6, 72–3

Welch, Martin G., *Early Anglo-Saxon Sussex* (Oxford, 1983): M. J. Allen, *Bull. of the Inst. of Archaeol. London* 23, Review Supp. pp. 11–12

Whittock, Martyn J., *The Origins of England 410–600* (London and Sydney, 1986): W. A. Chaney, *AHR* 93, 676

Wilson, David M., *The Bayeux Tapestry* (London, 1985): J. J. G. Alexander, *Jnl of Hist. Geography* 13, 73–5

Witney, K. P., *The Kingdom of Kent* (Chichester, 1982): G. J. Dawson, *Bull. of the Inst. of Archaeol. London* 23, Review Suppl., p. 12.

Wormald, Patrick, ed., *Ideal and Reality in Frankish and Anglo-Saxon Society* (Oxford, 1983): J.-P. Genet, *Annales* 42, 718–19